Most dissident writing in Russia and Eastern Europe has been liberal in politics – even religious in inspiration – and literary in form. Rudolf Bahro's book stands in massive contrast. *The Alternative in Eastern Europe* is a major theoretical synthesis in the best traditions of German Marxism. Bahro's aim is to explain the historical foundations of bureaucratic rule in Eastern Europe, and to advance a political programme capable of overcoming it. He focuses his account essentially on the division of labour within class societies, and in particular on the opposition between what he calls 'psychologically productive' and 'psychologically unproductive' labour – monopoly of the former being one of the hallmarks of the party and state bureaucracies in the East. Bahro also explores the consequences of the unity of production and communication in any social activity, in societies where general information is rigorously confined to the ruling officials. He then goes on to set out a concrete and comprehensive array of objectives for the transformation of the existing state system in the Communist countries into a genuinely socialist – because democratic – 'alternative'. Bahro's vision, at once far-reaching realistic, includes an international analysis of the inter-relations between revolutionary forces throughout Europe and the world.

Bahro was a member of the Communist Party in East Germany, where he worked as an organizational cadre, cultural editor and industrial engineer. *The Alternative* was initiated under the impact of the Warsaw Pact invasion of Czechoslovakia in 1968. In August 1977, soon after the publication of the book in West Germany, Bahro was arrested and charged with being a West German spy. He was sentenced to eight years' imprisonment but freed in October 1979 after an international campaign for his release.

Rudolf Bahro

Verso

The Alternative
in Eastern Europe

Translated by David Fernbach

First published by NLB 1978
© NLB 1978
NLB and Verso Editions,
15 Greek Street, London W1

Verso Edition 1981
Second impression 1984

Filmset in Monophoto Imprint by
Servis Filmsetting Ltd, Manchester

Printed in Great Britain by
The Thetford Press Ltd
Thetford, Norfolk

ISBN 0 86091 734 7

Contents

Part Three: The Strategy of a Communist Alternative

Editorial Note

The original German edition of this volume contains a limited number of quotation references, and a few other notes. All quotations have, where possible, been referenced to English editions, and further explanatory notes have been added.

Introduction

The communist movement made its appearance with the promise of solving the basic problems of modern humanity and overcoming the antagonisms of human existence. The countries that call themselves socialist still pay official allegiance to this programme. But what perspectives are people offered in the present situation, if they turn their eyes to the practice of our social life? Is there any way of telling how the new order plans to prove its superiority by a more effective organization and economy of labour? Has it attained its promised breakthrough to the humanization of collective life, or is it at least making daily progress in this field, in as much as the goal is not yet reached? What kind of better life was it that we sought to create? Was it only that mediocre well-being devoid of any further perspectives in which we try unsuccessfully to compete with late capitalism, try to overtake it on a road that, by all our traditional theory, leads straight into the abyss? We were planning to create a new and higher civilization! That new civilization is more necessary today than ever before; its image has nothing in common with the illusion of a 'perfect society' free from contradiction.

For the time being, it has turned out, we are extending the old civilization, continuing on the 'capitalist road'; compulsively, as it were, i.e. under very real compulsions, and in a most profound sense that involves our whole culture, rather than being simply a question of politics. A superstructure has emerged from our revolution which seems only good for this purpose, and for pursuing it in the most systematic and bureaucratic way possible. As all those involved are well aware, the rule of man by man has

7

lost only its topmost layer. The alienation and subalternity of the working masses persists in a new phase. Completely stuck in the old logic of international power politics and diplomacy, the new order does not even secure peace – not to be confused with the 'balance of terror' which it plays an active part in reproducing. The relationship between the two major powers of actually existing socialism even displays some quite apocalyptic features. In the Soviet Union, the liberal intellectual opposition seems to be at least at one with the government that the major strategic task facing the country is to build up Siberia, both industrially and militarily. And China is digging in, building a new great wall against the North, which this time is underground and everywhere.

The 'world socialist system' and the world communist movement are torn apart by fundamental internal contradictions, which have their main roots in the unmastered history of the Soviet Union itself, or must at least be grasped from this starting-point. Unfortunately, the ruling communist parties of Eastern Europe are today conservative forces, and among the most stubborn defenders of the status quo. As presently constituted, they have no policy at all for the period after the demise of colonialism, now experiencing its last hours in Southern Africa. In large regions of the southern half of the globe, catastrophic famine is maturing, with consequences against which all previous class conflict and war may well pale in comparison. This challenge cannot be met while the peoples of the industrially developed countries have leaders who must promise better bread and better circuses in each five-year plan in order to hold on to power. There is no need today to preach poverty, but rather to indicate the extent and – far more important – the true horizon of further human development on this planet. Who can stand up for this new direction, if not the communist movement, in the broadest sense of this term? 'Dying capitalism', if in its unchanged barbarous manner, is still proving itself a form of development of the productive forces, investing its surplus in the endless expansion of weapons of destruction bred by natural science, so as to keep down the peoples of the agricultural countries and harness the whole of the rest of the world to its will as best it can. And since it is capitalism that lays down the law of technical progress, it not only drives the less developed countries, including the Soviet Union, to spend a relatively greater share of their national product on armaments, but keeps them tied to a form of civilization based on this. Just as dying Rome poisoned the life of the provinces around the Mediterranean, so the influence of the late bourgeois way of life is still spreading, even though its continuation is irreconcilable with the existence of humanity.

The communists in the capitalist countries today are in a position to consider their task afresh in this world-historical context. They are preparing a new offensive, most visibly so in Italy, Spain and Japan, seeking to win the majority of their people for a grand consensus about the necessary transformations of the traditional civilization. In the official communism of Eastern Europe, on the other hand, there is absolutely no political theory that relates to the masses, for all the paper printed and the torrents from the rostrum. The most recent synthesis of revolutionary thought is that of Lenin, now more than half a century old. Yet the changes that have taken place since Lenin's death are more comprehensive and far-reaching than those which occurred in the time between Marx and Lenin. Should it not be self-evident from the Marxist standpoint that the practical changes in the world that Lenin's work has given rise to have overspilled the framework of his theory and in many respects burst it apart? What could have emphasized its power as a creative factor in history more than this result, a posthumous destiny so characteristic of all the world's great transformers?

The rise of the Soviet Union, in particular, was achieved in a different manner from that which Lenin foresaw, and with a different result. It took once again the path of antagonistic conflict and claimed millions of innocent victims. Today the peoples of the Soviet Union and the East European countries are recognizing more and more that the new system only corresponds in a small way to the principles it proclaims, betraying its own goals and no longer achieving anything new. The entire potential of the system has thus been demolished. As a result, we can see on all sides, and most recently in the Soviet Union itself, the same ideological bankruptcy, catastrophic for the existing power structure, that became visible in Czechoslovakia in 1968. Events in Poland from December 1970 on have only confirmed the recognition that the burgeoning crisis of our system is not due to merely temporary causes, but is rooted in deep socio-economic contradictions, essentially in the relations of production. From the political standpoint, Ulbricht, Rakosi, Novotny, Gomulka, etc. were the real organizers of counter-revolution – both with and without quotation marks.

No one could deny that the crisis has a general character. The international character of the forces that erupted in Czechoslovakia was recognized by no one more unmistakeably than the leaders of the Warsaw Pact itself, with their continuous intervention from early 1968. What the Czechoslovak transformations brought to light was simply the real structure of the society emerging from the East European revolutions and ultimately from the October revolution. And the pace of the transformations, above all the rapid restructuring of the Communist Party itself, showed how pressingly this new structure is waiting, at least in the industrially developed countries, to throw off the armour that protected it in its larval stage, but now threatens to choke it. Only with violence was the social potential released in 1968 forced back into the straitjacket it had outgrown. The potential still remains, and it will rebel again – first of all with passive resistance to the in-adequate superstructure – until one day this system will be fully rejected by history, even in the Soviet Union itself. There, too, the half-hearted reformation undertaken by Khrushchev will be followed by a more basic popular reformation, which will not just give the dominant political structures a new adaptation, but will affect their basic social substance.

This crisis, which makes necessary a re-examination of the entire course of events since 1917, is naturally a process which proceeds at different rates in the different countries involved, and does not always reach the same intensity in all spheres of social life. There are moreover advances and retreats, and there will also be periods of relative stabilization, as for example the first half of the 1970s. But it has gripped all countries of the Soviet bloc, affecting all areas of life, and it is ultimately based on the contradiction recognized by all Marxists, between the modern productive forces and relations of production that have become a hindrance to them, coming to a head. The abolition of private property in the means of production has in no way meant their immediate transformation into the property of the people. Rather, the whole society stands property-less against its state machine. The monopoly of disposal over the apparatus of production, over the lion's share of the surplus product, over the proportions of the reproduction process, over distribution and consumption, has led to a bureaucratic mechanism with the tendency to kill off or privatize any subjective initiative. The obsolete political organization of the new society, which cuts deep into the economic process itself, blunts its social driving forces.

The centre of the crisis is the Soviet Union itself; and although it has not yet reached there the same degree of maturity as for example in the GDR and Czechoslovakia, the ground is already shaking at the edges. Nothing that the Soviet leaders do to escape its consequences, on the basis of the existing conditions, can prevent its eruption. The invasion of Czechoslovakia in fact accelerated mental polarization in the other countries of the bloc. It is precisely the general, comprehensive and fundamental character of the crisis, precisely the fact that its focus lies in the Soviet Union, that enables the perspectives for a movement of renewal and the tasks of such a movement to appear in a quite different and more hopeful light. The discussions of Soviet economists and sociologists are bearing ever closer towards the decisive points, and it is not accidental that under the surface the arguments of the early 1920s are again being revived. The Soviet Union *must* reform itself, to keep pace internally with the demands of the masses, and to maintain its international position. The obsolete forces will then be prevented from putting their particular caste interests to the fore. The first requirement is to win the space for public discussion of the 'burning questions of our movement'.

For the Marxist, communist, minority in our countries' ruling parties, for all who face the coming day with a feeling of responsibility, the relatively long-run basic situation in which they find themselves means not only a test of patience, but a genuine intellectual challenge. The history of the Soviet Union, of China,

Yugoslavia and the other revolutionary countries has accumulated a tremendous and dramatic material – from the Kronstadt uprising to the uprising on the Polish seaboard, from the split in the Bolshevik vanguard after Lenin's death to the struggles over the people's communes and the 'great proletarian cultural revolution' in China, from Yugoslavia's break into 'self-management socialism' to the half-hearted turn in the Soviet Union after Stalin's death. What do these events contain in the way of more general laws of development? On what contradictions are the peoples of our countries labouring today? What is the source of the many analogies to processes in those developing countries that are taking the non-capitalist road, or tending structurally in that direction? What is the significance of the defeats of the West European revolutionary movement, from 1918 in Germany through to 1968 in France? There *must* be a connection in all this, to illuminate the present scene.

We cannot undertake to deal in detail with all these problems in one single text, even if on some of them there is already an immense amount of literature, which is still deliberately withheld from the public in our countries and hence cannot even be critically examined. What is possible, however, even without making any claims to monographic completeness, is to reach a general position on this complex of questions. We can undertake to present the preliminary result attained in an outline form of the kind given in Marx's own *Economic and Philosophical Manuscripts*. Marx later gave his preliminary work on *Capital* of 1859 the title *A Contribution to the Critique of Political Economy*. If I model my own title on this great prototype, and call my text *A Contribution to the Critique of Actually Existing Socialism,* I am well aware how far removed my critique of this actually existing socialism still is from that degree of elaboration and coherence that Marx reached only twenty years after his *Economic and Philosophical Manuscripts*. But I have set myself the same goal: the analysis of a social formation from the revolutionary standpoint. It will be remembered that by 'Critique' Marx meant a pre-eminently scientific analysis with the intention of practical change in the world. The deeper he penetrated into the essence of the relationships under investigation, the more he could renounce denunciation and invective, and let the facts and relationships he had discovered serve themselves as propaganda for his ideas. In this sense I have myself taken ever greater pains, at the various stages of work on my theme, to restrict the expression of outrage at the existing situation to its rational kernel, and always to seize in its immanent logic what to any merely idealist consciousness must immediately appear both provocative and irrational. Any mere resentment at the existing conditions is to be avoided as far as possible. The hour of theory and history must begin. The hour of politics will follow sooner or later.

The first part of the book is concerned with the phenomenon of the non-capitalist road to industrial society. Our actually existing socialism is a fundamentally different social organization from that outlined in Marx's socialist theory. This practice may be compared with the theory, but it should not be measured by it. It must be explained in terms of its own laws. All theories of deformation, however, from Khrushchev to Garaudy, lead away from this task. My own analysis leads to a general concept of the 'non-capitalist road' which includes most of the nominally socialist countries, and to the search for the origin of this non-capitalist road in the legacy of the so-called Asiatic mode of production. This is the basis for the subsequent discussion of Russia's progress from agricultural to industrial despotism, and the fate of the Bolshevik party in the process. We must try and do justice to the historical character of the Stalinist structure of domination. The political history of the Soviet Union is not one of abandonment of the 'subjective factor', but rather of its transformation, by the task that it had to undertake of industrializing Russia. It is the new tasks of today that demonstrate the anachronistic character of the old-style party, and not just certain principles of political morality.

In the second part, I deal with the systematic structure of actually existing socialism, as opposed to its historical treatment in the first part: its bureaucratic-centralist organization of labour, its character as a stratified society, the marked impotence of the immediate producers, its relatively weak impulse towards raising productivity, its political-ideological organization as a quasi-theocratic state. The essence of actually existing socialism is conceived as one of socialization in the alienated form of statification, this being based on a traditional division of labour which has not yet been driven to the critical point at which it topples over.

The final part is devoted to the alternative that is maturing in the womb of actually existing socialism, and in the industrially developed countries as a whole. This bears the character of that comprehensive cultural revolution, that transformation of the entire former division of labour, way of life and mentality that Marx and Engels predicted. Universal human emancipation is becoming ever more pressing, but the conditions for this must be studied afresh, and its contents defined appropriately to the time. The social dialectic of its first steps is characterized by the struggle to demolish the structures of domination in labour and hence also in the state, but this can only proceed at the pace that circumstances permit, as there will still be a social stratification by intellectual competence. The cultural revolution thus presupposes a truly communist party, a new League of Communists. Communists must take their distance from the state machine, and start by putting an end to the dominance of the apparatus in their own organization. They must inscribe anew on their banner the old slogan of the *Communist Manifesto,* according to which 'the free development of each is the condition for the free development of all', and be more aware than ever before that this programme cannot be confined to any merely national or continental framework. The real equality of all who bear the human countenance is becoming a question of life and death in practical politics. The world is changing at a pace that is both encouraging and disturbing – disturbing because the total process is still leading spontaneously to situations that no one intended. Peace can only be secured, and the further rise of the human species and of man as an individual can only be assured, if we can put an end to all differences in development opportunities, both within each country and in the world as a whole.

Part One

The Non-Capitalist Road to Industrial Society

The Abolition of Capitalist Private Property and the Practice of Actually Existing Socialism

For a few years, it was official party policy in the GDR that socialism was not a short-run transition period, but rather 'a relatively independent socio-economic formation in the historical epoch of the transition from capitalism to communism on a world scale'. This was not given any real theoretical foundation, even though it was propagated in a thick book.[1] Right from the start, it was formulated timidly. It was moreover quite evidently designed to serve certain apologetic purposes of the bureaucratic economic planners. It had no popular appeal, therefore, except to a few ideologists, and did not even provoke the attention of critics. Yet this was the most fruitful sociological thesis to be openly proclaimed in the Soviet sphere of influence since the silencing of theoretical discussion in the 1920s.

The initiators of this idea, people well-versed in Marxism, must have been at least approximately clear as to the scope of their innovation, and must also have understood the unavoidable half-heartedness and even confusion of its public presentation. From the Central Committee's Institute for Social Sciences, at that time, one could hear it said without beating about the bush that the conception of socialism laid down in Marx's *Critique of the Gotha Programme* must now be seen as obsolete. But if socialism

---

[1] Walter Ulbricht, *Die Bedeutung und die Lebenskraft der Lehren von Karl Marx*, Berlin 1968.

and communism are different formations, according to the new theory, what then is socialism as distinct from communism? Is it in fact still 'communism in the process of becoming'? If it is not, what direct interest is the working class supposed to have in it? Will it not lead to a new major revolution? The panic about such fearsome possibilities is conveyed by the little word 'relatively' ('*relatively* independent social formation'), which can be extended, twisted and turned at will.

Shortly before the 8th Party Congress in July 1971, this last word in socialist science was silently withdrawn from current use, for more than just one reason, and has since been expressly pronounced to be false. The *Critique of the Gotha Programme* is again correct. But this concept of a 'relatively independent social formation' concealed a certain demand, and above all a certain real experience. Sooner or later each new generation of Marxists and socialists, according to the temperament and attitude of the individual concerned, comes up against the difference, antithesis, rift, gulf, indeed abyss between the classical vision and the reality of the new society. The existence of at least a difference is so evident that even in the official documents resort is made to the defensive formula 'actually existing socialism'. This slogan, which I somewhat unwillingly echo here, is symptomatic of how our ruling parties find Marxist legitimation of their practice slipping through their fingers. It is only understandable, therefore, how the more dynamic people of the younger generation, with this new theory, were trying out a kind of *fuite en avant,* indeed even trying to escape the need for rationality. But the admission of a difference between the Marxist idea and the reality of socialism has penetrated official theory even in the conservative formula, and the question is simply whether its character is more or less fundamental.

Most Marxist critics of our orthodoxy make things too easy for themselves by taking a merely methodological approach. They stick to the confined categories of ideal and reality, so that discussion can be easily shifted to an undecidable conflict as to whether the realization of the ideal is 'inevitably still imperfect' or actually 'bad'. The 'idealists' who speak explicitly of deformations, denounce the departure from some supposed principles, and demand the introduction or restoration of various norms, while they may have temporary demagogic success, have neither theoretically nor in practical political terms reached the ground on which their opponents stand: the 'deviating' reality. Only recently, again, Svetozar Stojanović, with his *Between Ideal and Reality,* showed that from this position, even working with as little hindrance as one can in Yugoslavia, it is impossible even to get to the real terrain of struggle, that created by the revolution such as it actually was.[2] Stojanović describes the dilemma of 'étatism' versus 'anarcho-liberalism', demonstrates the socio-economic roots of the latter and in the next breath expects precisely these dominant conditions to produce more in the way of democratic socialist individuals. These are not the signs of a Marxist and materialist mode of thought. Stojanović makes things far too easy for clever defenders of the status quo. Like other theorists of deformation, he ends up with the well-known motto that, if the reality deviates from the idea, it is so much the worse for the reality.

No, the problem cannot be reduced in any way to a difference between the ideal of socialism and its reality. Contentions of this kind only repeat a reproach already made innumerable times, since the first appearance of the Bolshevik Workers' Opposition before the Kronstadt uprising of 1921, and nowhere more fundamentally than in Trotsky's now somewhat dated book on the 'betrayal' of the revolution. Somehow or other, these all come down to the thesis of the cult of personality, of the subjective factors, which were certainly present, but which explain nothing. Unfortunately a major part of the Soviet opposition is still taken up with the personal wickedness and vileness of the great dictator, instead of investigating the social structure over whose rise he presided, and which the October revolution preceded only as a gigantic spring-cleaning. It is readily understandable why Trotsky never raised the question of whether his opponent did not precisely achieve his position of leadership because he possessed the historically necessary passion to create the apparatus of power for the terroristic transformation from above that Russia

[2] *Kritik und Zukunft des Sozialismus : Zwischen Ideal und Wirklichkeit,* Munich 1970.

then needed. Snooping about Dostoyevsky-style in the moral atmosphere of the dictatorship can in no way help us to understand the objective results of the Stalin era and the political structures it has handed down, which is what we need today.

Trotsky was himself confronted by some of his supporters, shortly before his murder, with the then new idea that the Russian revolution objectively led no more to socialism than the French revolution led to a condition of general freedom, equality and fraternity. In other words the problem was not one of an inadequate realization, but rather of a new antagonistic social order the other side of capitalism. Trotsky, though troubled by this gloomy challenge to his own perspective, was courageous enough to examine the possibility, and he concluded that if this were in fact the case, then the place of communists would have to be alongside the renewedly oppressed masses. Once it is admitted with even minimal probability that a new form of domination could come about, then discussion necessarily starts to penetrate qualitatively deeper than the deformation theory can conceive of. For this theory then not only 'defames' the new order, it also embellishes it and nourishes harmful illusions. What was Marx's view of those political thinkers who criticized French capitalism, under the July monarchy and after, as a distortion of the constitution of 1793, which was never even put into force? Where did this socialism ever exist, which is said to have been deformed?

It existed in the writings of the socialists. The historian Gitermann, who has written an excellent history of Russia designed to demonstrate the preconditions of the October revolution, was therefore quite correct when he spoke in the title of a further work of the historical tragedy of the socialist *idea*.[3] This idea really did become the fate of the revolutionaries who bore it into Russia. Its perversion into a new ideology of domination, into the catechism of a modern state church, reached its logical culmination in the annihilation of the old Bolshevik vanguard by Stalin's power apparatus. The historical course of the Soviet Union was a subjective intellectual and moral tragedy for all

---

[3] Valentin Gitermann, *Geschichte Russlands*, vol. 3; *Russland in der Zeit von 1827–1917*, Freiburg 1965.

communists who can be taken seriously at the human level. In the year 1900 Lenin expected the impending people's revolution 'to sweep all bestiality from the Russian soil'. Instead of this, the tremendous progress of the Soviet Union under Stalin stands comparison, in the most terrible way, with the 'hideous pagan idol' invoked by Marx, who 'would not drink the nectar but from the skulls of the slain'.[4]

The Soviet tragedy must be grasped for what it is. Its basis is that the Russian socialist movement at the beginning of the century found a different objective task to fulfil than that to which it believed itself called. So long as there was simply the Soviet Union (with or without a Western periphery) it was possible to consider the harsh 'detour' of the socialist idea via Russia simply as a higher-order accident of European history. But since the People's Republic of China came into being, but still no proletarian revolution in the West, the indication is that the entire perspective under which we have so far seen the transition to communism stands in need of correction, and in no way just with respect to the time factor. The dissolution of private property in the means of production on the one hand, and universal human emancipation on the other, are separated by an entire epoch. History has set us the task of understanding what kind of society actually existing socialism really is.

It could of course be asked whether it still makes any sense, in the face of a task such as this, to go back yet again to what Marx understood by socialism. For from the standpoint of a materialist conception of history no demonstration that certain practices or even all practice departs from Marx's plan is in and of itself any argument against the existing conditions. The conception of politics and history expressed in the method of argument as to 'what Marx really said' is completely unfruitful; it always leads to distortions in the presentation of the 'doctrine' that are easily assailable, and thus shifts the ground of dispute to the level of scholastic battles of quotations. If in the first three chapters in particular I expressly quote Marx, Engels and Lenin on many

[4] 'The Future Results of the British Rule in India', *Surveys from Exile*, Pelican Marx Library, 1974, p. 325.

occasions, this is not for any such dogmatic purpose. The reasons are altogether different.

Firstly, Marx's theory forms part of the *objective* preconditions (objectified in a real movement) involved in the revolutions of 1917 and after. If the following quotations time and again emphasize the *historical* differences (i.e. differences to be explained and not carped at) between Marx and Lenin, and between Lenin and our present practice, the aim is *not* to deny the underlying continuity. The presentation of Marx in this first chapter is directed against the central prejudice that blocks every Marxist analysis of our conditions and sanctions permanent psychological devaluation of the socialist ideal that is *necessary* for progress: since we derive from Marx, the whole world takes our countries as socialist, even communist, although they are a fundamental step away from being so. It is not even justified to describe them as 'early socialist', by analogy with the first phase of the capitalist era. In early capitalism the fundamental features of the later fully developed capitalist formation were already present, while in our case socialization as the decisive characteristic of socialism as a formation is still completely entoiled by étatism. The most exact description is to characterize it as *proto-socialist,* i.e. we have socialism in an embryonic stage. If I mostly use, instead of this unfamiliar term, the home-grown expression 'actually existing socialism', and moreover abandon the burdensome quotation marks, this is still the sense intended. It is precisely those convinced of the reality of a genuine socialist and communist perspective in the Marxian sense who must distance themselves most strongly from the uncritical use of the concept of socialism.

Ultimately, therefore, in my conception – and this is the second reason for quoting Marx at some length – there is a question of 'deviations' of history *within* the world-historical development at whose beginning Marx stands. Here I take as my guide an idea of Antonio Gramsci's, that 'Marx initiates intellectually a historical epoch, which will last in all probability for centuries, until the disappearance of political society and the coming of a regulated society'.[5] Gramsci also recalls Rosa Luxemburg's consideration

---

[5] *Selections from the Prison Notebooks*, London 1971, p. 382.

that many ideas of Marx's appear superseded simply because the practical needs of our movement are not yet sufficient for an assessment of these ideas. Naturally, it cannot be ruled out that many particular details and specific premises of Marx's doctrine really are overtaken by events. But the overall *scope* of his theory and method is so great that it is conquering today the universities of late bourgeois society!

If, as is customary, we consult the *Critique of the Gotha Programme* to see what Marx understood by socialism, we find a very summary presentation of its particular features, without any intention of completeness. Marx indicates the *general* nature of socialism with the remark that it is the first phase of communism; so it is not a demarcated and autonomous formation with its own laws. And if only little is known of how Marx conceived communism, for all appearance to the contrary, his concept of socialism is also by no means obvious. In connection with his depiction of the principles of *distribution* under socialism and communism, Marx expresses his annoyance that the authors of the draft programme have forced him to make such a detailed reference to this, because the distribution of means of consumption is only a reflection of the *relations of appropriation* of the material means of production, which is what really interests him. In the absence of clarity as to what shape these preconditions could take under communism, 'sound commonsense' always sees Marx's formulas of distribution in terms of the presently existing relations (with technical improvements); the principle of distribution according to need is thereby transformed into a utopia, while the principle of distribution according to work, on the other hand, appears as a prophetic justification and idealizing of our present wages policy.

We can best understand Marx's scientific communism if we consider how he arrived at it. Rejecting the dogmatists on either side, those who play off the young Marx against the old and vice versa, we may assume here the continuity of Marx's theory and his character, and rest assured that he created his political economy in the service of an ideal of general human emancipation which he arrived at in his youth and which was developed ever more concretely. His categorical imperative to 'overthrow all conditions in which man is a debased, enslaved, neglected and contemptible being'[6] is both prior to and pervades any scientific founding of its realizability. This was the energizing motive that led Marx from liberal humanism via revolutionary democracy to communism, and finally enabled him to seek the theoretical foundation for the communist movement in the economic anatomy of capitalism.

Yet in this way Marx's humanism lost its previous *immediacy*. The utopians who preceded him had all proceeded more or less directly from the general species nature of man (present, moreover, in his action), had realistically shown how this was flatly con- tradicted by the existing society, and then, as it were in the second part of their theories, constructed a state of affairs that did justice to human nature. But they could never say how this 'natural' society was to arise out of the existing. This was precisely the barrier at which Marx paused for a moment at the time of his transition to communism, and where Engels came to his aid for the first time with the concrete understanding he had obtained in England of the dialectic of bourgeois society and the revolutionary role of the proletariat. The more he now penetrated into the political struggles and economic contradictions of bourgeois society, the clearer Marx came to recognize that there was no purpose in dreaming up the model of a new society, but that the proper point, as he and Engels jointly expressed it, was rather to dis- cover and promote the real movement that abolishes the existing state of things. This real movement had its champions, its 'nega- tive', revolutionary element, in the working class, but its content was the *overall* developmental process of bourgeois society, tending towards the abolition of private property. Marx and Engels never sought to provide definitions for textbooks. But when they were pressed to define their communism, then they could say nothing else than that communism was the 'Abolition of private property'.[7]

By this, however, they did not mean simply the act of its abolition, e.g. by the transformation of the state into the general capitalist, but first and foremost the socio-economic process of the

[6] 'Critique of Hegel's Philosophy of Right: Introduction', *Early Writings*, Pelican Marx Library, 1974, p. 251.
[7] 'Manifesto of the Communist Party': in *The Revolutions of 1848*, Pelican Marx Library, 1973, p. 80.

positive appropriation of the achieved social wealth by the freely associated producers. The whole strength of their scientific socialism-communism is rooted in this conception, as is (to anticipate somewhat here) the present failure not only of official Marxists, but of all orthodox Marxists, who will not understand that history had first to take up a different task than that formulated by Marx. We should perhaps stress once again here that Marx saw the preconditions for socialism and communism not in the achievements of private property as such, but rather in the specific achievements of *capitalist* private property, which embraces a tremendous complex of objective and subjective factors. The 'non-capitalist road' which has kept humanity on the move *since 1917* raises completely different problems from those analysed by Marx, and *cannot directly* have the same perspective, since it creates the *preconditions for communism* in a completely different way. The abolition of capitalist private property could only have a slight *positive* significance for Russia, since *there was little capitalist private property to abolish,* this having far from penetrated the entire national life. From the standpoint of orthodoxy, Rosa Luxemburg and even Kautsky, indeed all the Mensheviks, were right in their criticism of Lenin, who objectively placed himself in the service of a quite different, quite new, and from a world-historical standpoint extremely necessary task, which had only been prepared theoretically by Marxism in a very indirect way.

Marx's conception of communism dates from the *Economic and Philosophical Manuscripts* of 1844. Its economic aspect was given ever increasing precision in the preliminary work for *Capital,* up till the end of the 1850s, and its political aspect in the analysis of the Paris Commune of 1871. In its kernel, it remained always the same from 1844 through to the celebrated passage on the 'realm of freedom' in the third volume of *Capital,* which Engels published long after Marx's death. If Marx, who certainly stood in the Hegelian line, sought to 'abolish' (*aufheben*) capitalist private property, his *positive* attitude to the historic role of capitalism, the quite deliberately stressed acknowledgement of the bourgeoisie's revolutionary practice at the beginning of the *Communist Manifesto,* is taken for granted right from the start. As against the crude communists, as he calls them, he does not want to generalize poverty, the idyllic narrowness of natural conditions, let alone to attain this result by an egalitarian despotism, but rather to generalize wealth in its potential capacity as capital for the universal development of all members of society.

Aufheben, a basic philosophical concept of Hegel's, which recurs simply everywhere, abbreviates the concept of the 'negation of the negation', and only means to 'put an end to', to abolish or negate, in its most impoverished sense. In our present case, it means to divest the achievements of bourgeois civilization of their capitalist form. Certainly, even this demanded nothing less than political revolution, establishment of the 'dictatorship of the proletariat'. But it was not surprising that the Bolsheviks were fond of describing their October revolution, *in retrospect,* as child's play, in relation to the positive tasks of material construction that they subsequently faced, and on which the bourgeoisie in Russia had scarcely made even a beginning. In its second and far more concrete sense, *aufheben* means to preserve, but to preserve in a new and higher overall connection, so that ultimately *aufheben* means precisely to raise to a higher level. What was to be raised in this complex sense as far as capitalist private property was concerned? What had this brought about, compared with all earlier social formations? And how was this achievement to acquire, through the revolution, its new and higher determination? How is it, in fact, that we get the production of *social wealth?*

Under oriental despotism, ancient slavery and European feudalism, the surplus product was extracted from the producers for the immediate consumption of the exploiters, or for a hoard that secured their power and influence. The workers, who were not yet separated from their means and conditions of labour, could be sure of their necessities of life, apart from natural catastrophes and wars, and they produced a surplus product only in proportion to the extra-economic pressure that the rulers could exert on them without endangering their rule. Under these conditions the surplus product rose only very slowly, and the predominant tendency – as still today in many Third World countries – was to transform every rise in productivity, every increase in means of subsistence, into a rise in population. Capital, on the other hand, does not just seek more use-value, or more surplus product as such; it pursues surplus-*value*. Marx showed how the capitalist is even compelled, under threat of bankruptcy, to restrict his own consumption so as to increase his capital, in order to remain in competition. The wage-worker, for his part, can obtain his means of subsistence only by creating as much surplus-value as the 'normal' working day of the time makes possible, given a certain level of productivity. He is otherwise condemned to starve, as capital's primitive accumulation has left him without any means of production of his own. Capital thus forces from its worker, this new type of exploitee, an *unlimited* quantity of surplus labour, since productivity under this system grows much faster than do wages, which stick close to the minimum required for existence.

'The great historic quality of capital', Marx writes, 'is to *create* this *surplus labour* . . .; and its historic destiny is fulfilled as soon as, on one side, there has been such a development of needs that surplus labour above and beyond necessity has itself become a general need arising out of individual needs themselves – and, on the other side, when the severe discipline of capital, acting on succeeding generations (*Geschlechter*), has developed general industriousness as the general property of the new species (*Geschlecht*)'.[8]

In other words, labour above that immediately necessary is not something that lies in the 'nature' of man, but it needs *generations of capitalist* compulsion to create the *type of producer,* the *human* productive force, that for the first time makes possible a communism of wealth. Bourgeois society could precisely achieve its freedom and democracy, what Marx saw as its political advances that deserved to be raised to a higher level, because labour discipline was enforced by *economics*.

But there is no way, Marx implies, that a pre-capitalist country can industrialize without *either* wage-labour *or* extra-economic compulsion. One of the two is needed. The abolition of capitalist private property here means a decision in favour of terror – or for an unending torment of development, if no stable dictatorship comes into being – and the specific problem then consists in the productive function of this terror. This dictatorship has the

[8] *Grundrisse*, Pelican Marx Library, 1973, p. 325.

'moral' right that Marx allowed Ricardo against his critics, when he wrote: 'What other people reproach him for, i.e. that he is unconcerned with "human beings" and concentrates exclusively on the development of the productive forces when considering capitalist production – whatever the sacrifice in human beings and capital *values* that this costs – this is precisely the most significant thing about him. The development of the productive forces of social labour is capital's historic mission and justification'.[9]

The productivity of the revolutionary dictatorship can be measured only by the creation of the modern productive forces, and it is not technique that these productive forces presuppose above all, but rather people who are disciplined and willing to work. China, for example, has the good fortune that its population were forced in its earlier Asiatic mode of production to a labour-intensive rural economy which, however, did not involve any actual enserfment: a particularly favourable condition for its non-capitalist road to socialism, as far as the inherited *attitude to labour* is concerned.

Marx, of course, did not think of measuring the development of human productive power simply by the quantity of wealth accumulated. What he had in mind was the abolition of an entire system of production, a whole mode of production. It was in this sense that he adduced three positive and 'cardinal facts about capitalist production'.

1. In the forms of joint-stock company and monopoly Marx saw the most immediate preparation of socialism. 'The concentration of the means of production in a few hands, which means that they cease to appear as the property of direct workers, and are transformed on the contrary into social powers of production'.
2. 'The organization of labour itself as social labour: through cooperation, division of labour and the union of labour with natural science'.

'On both these counts the capitalist mode of production abolishes private property and private labour, even if in antithetical forms'.

3. 'Establishment of the world market'.[10]

---

[9] *Capital*, vol. 3, chap. 15, 3.
[10] *Capital*, vol. 3, chap. 15, 4.

All of this can be brought under the common heading of the *socialization* of the productive forces, and this on a world scale, even if not yet completed (to this extent Marx necessarily saw colonialism as part of capitalism's positive achievement). The abolition of private property, against this background, Marx saw as embracing the following systematically interconnected processes:

1. The immediate socialization of the means and conditions of production, i.e. of past, objectified labour that was formerly concentrated in capital. The expropriation of the capitalists immediately divests all this wealth of its value form, reducing it to use-value. It is therefore identical with the abolition of commodity production and money, in which the alienation of the producers from the products of their activity finds concentrated expression. (If the workers carry this out, then the disappearance of wage-labour follows of itself; labour-power loses its commodity form in the act of taking possession of the means of production. As long as the principle of payment according to work still obtains, notes may act as vouchers for the amount of labour performed, but these are not money – they do not circulate. All economy is then resolved into economy of time, but this is related to the single goal of communist production: the all-round developed, free individual, who satisfies his needs in autonomous and stimulating association with his fellows in an active, productive way, enjoying his existence.)

2. The abolition of the traditional division of labour, i.e. of the servile subjection of individuals to restricted and compartmentalized tasks. Two points have to be made here. First, the overcoming of the inherited *social* antitheses (inequalities) between man and woman, town and country, manual and mental labour, which are anchored in the entire structure of the former productive forces and relations. Secondly, the overcoming of the technical division of labour *within* the factory, within the sphere of necessary labour, by raising natural science to a higher level in production governed by scientific work. (Here the point which Marx proceeds from is that the integration of the sciences reduces their specialization even for the individual, so that application to any particular job which is naturally in itself autonomous does not exclude the universal capacity of labour, but rather presupposes

it. A reduction in the expenditure of time necessary for material reproduction is one element in this conception, as also is the idea which still enrages every well-qualified socialist philistine that *everyone* should have to take a share in the unavoidable residue of heavy, dirty, menial and repetitive work.)

3. The appropriation of the means of production by the associated producers destroys the sharpest expression of the traditional division of labour and class rule, its political expression in the state *machine*, the state *apparatus*, and raises to a higher level the necessary social functions that the state has usurped on top of its rule over men, in a non-political administration of things which devolves not on specialized officials, but on elected delegates who are at all times responsible and can be effectively dismissed.

4. The capitalist world market, finally, is abolished by the victorious proletarians of the most advanced countries in the transnational unification of mankind, which will use the globe's resources in order to bequeathe the planet to coming generations in an improved condition (initially including aid to the historically backward peoples).

This is the communism of Marx. Those who fully pursue all four of these goals, or, to be more modest, who at least maintain the conviction that they are necessary and realizable, can call themselves communists in the Marxian sense. In most countries of 'actually existing socialism' you would have great trouble finding any, and it is precisely the trained ideologists who generally have only an ironic laugh, in private, for such 'illusions' as that of an abolition of the division of labour, or an end to relations of domination and the state. We have 'quite different problems', and the most that is criticized is the poverty of the bureaucracy's recipes for 'reform'.

Marx's communism does in fact contain utopian elements. Marx overestimated, in a principled and unflinching manner, the maturity of the preconditions for communism, and overlooked certain unavoidable intermediate stages. He did not foresee that the universal emancipation of man would be blocked by a new challenge, in the form of the world-wide Gordian knot of bureaucratization and uneven development, which is of course rendered even more acute by the still unabolished residues of capitalist private property. But this is only to say that it is no longer sufficient to be a 'Marxist' in the traditional sense. We must rather raise to a higher level Marx's own legacy, the most developed theory and method of social science that we have, and transform it into the communism of the present.

The indispensable precondition for this, however, is to work out the fundamental differences between Marx's sketch and actually existing socialism. The centre of this difference bears on the material conditions for communism, the character of labour and the effects of the division of labour. In this first chapter I intend first of all to deal with the most prominent aspect of this difference, the reflection of material structures in the sphere of the state. Once the expropriation of the capitalists is accomplished, and society is secured against their attempts at restoration, the producers are faced with the positive task of disposing collectively over the entire production process and consequently also of the distribution of its proceeds. This task, for Marx, had *nothing* to do with the question of the dictatorship (that being, as it were, the 'foreign policy' of the workers against the bourgeoisie). But it is precisely this task that has since proved to be *the* great unsolved problem of the industrialized countries. Few men can imagine today how society might get rid of its state machine. And this even though it has long since been shown in practice to make a colossal difference whether the associated producers themselves control their reproduction process, or whether (supposedly? in fact?) it is conducted 'in their interest'. The colossus that under our actually existing socialism is known as Party-and-government, 'represents' the intended free association just as the state has represented society in all earlier civilizations.

There is no more striking antithesis between Marx's communism and the actually existing socialism of the Soviet bloc, even from the theoretical standpoint, than in the character of the state. While I would repeat here that I am simply recording a fact, not making any accusation, I shall show how our countries are ruled by a state machine such as Marx sought to smash in the revolution, not to let it rise again in any form or under any pretext. For Marx, the dialectician, it went without saying that the *form* of the machine with which the bourgeoisie exercizes its rule is inseparable from its *content,* so that there could never be any question of simply chasing out the old swarms of officials, renaming the positions of command and equipping it with new cadres. No, already in the *German Ideology* it was said that the proletarians 'find themselves directly opposed to the form in which, hitherto, the individuals, of which society consists, have given themselves collective expression, that is, the state; in order, therefore, to assert themselves as individuals, they must overthrow the state'.[11] For the purpose of domination and suppression penetrates the entire construction of this machine, so that it could not be made into an instrument of emancipation. For this reason, the commune had *immediately* to take its place, or the commune-state, if you prefer. Immediately, and not just when communism was achieved. Everything on the commune-state that we can read in Marx and Engels refers to the *transition to socialism,* to the first phase of communism. As Engels put it in his final remark on the subject in 1891: 'Look at the Paris Commune. That was the Dictatorship of the Proletariat'.[12] This is how the new society was to *begin,* as the following quotations, necessarily cited at some length, will show.

Marx introduced his characterization of this finally found 'political form for social emancipation', in his First Draft of *The Civil War in France,* with the description of its opposite, the centralized state machinery 'which, with its ubiquitous and complicated military, bureaucratic, clerical and judiciary organs, entwines living civil society like a boa constrictor'.[13] It began its path of development when absolutism, in the name of the newly arising bourgeois society, 'substitut[ed] for the checkered (parti-coloured) anarchy of conflicting medieval powers the regulated plan of a state power, with a systematic and hierarchic division of labour'.[14] The bourgeois revolution in France saw itself 'forced to develop what absolute monarchy had commenced, the centralization and organization of state power, and to expand the circumference and the attributes of the state power, the number of its

---

[11] *Collected Works,* vol. 5, p. 80.
[12] 'Introduction to *The Civil War in France*', in Marx and Engels, *On the Paris Commune,* Moscow, 1971, p. 34.
[13] *The First International and After,* Pelican Marx Library, 1974, p. 246.
[14] *Ibid.*

tools, its independence, and its supernaturalist sway over real society which in fact took the place of the medieval supernaturalist heaven, with its saints. Every minor solitary interest engendered by the relations of social groups was separated from society itself . . . and opposed to it in the form of state interest, administered by state priests with exactly determined hierarchical functions'.[15] Napoleon, the Restoration and the July monarchy simply continued this work, perfecting the state machine 'instead of throwing off this deadening incubus'[16] and adding 'to the direct economic exploitation a second exploitation of the people'. The Second Empire, which the Commune displaced, was the most prostitute form of an 'organized governmental power usurping to be the master instead of the servant of society'.[17]

'But this one form of class rule had only broken down to make the executive, the governmental state machinery, the great and single object of attack to the revolution'. The Commune 'begins the *emancipation of labour* – its great goal – by doing away with the unproductive and mischievous work of the state parasites, by cutting away the springs which sacrifice an immense portion of the national produce to the feeding of the state monster on the one side, by doing, on the other, the real work of administration, local and national, for workingmen's wages. It begins therefore with an immense saving, with economical reform as well as political transformation'.[18] The Commune 'was a revolution against the *state* itself, this supernaturalist abortion of society', 'a revolution to break down this horrid machinery of class domination itself'.[19] Marx indicated with an eye to Comte that the workers wanted nothing to do with those who proclaim 'hierarchy in all spheres of human action, even in the sphere of science'.[20] And he said of Mazzini: 'With him the State – which was an imaginary thing – was everything, and Society – which was a reality – was nothing. The sooner the people repudiated such men the better'.[21]

[15] *Ibid.*, pp. 246–7.
[16] P. 247.
[17] *Ibid.*, p. 250.
[18] *Ibid.*, p. 253.
[19] *Ibid.*, p. 249.
[20] P. 260.
[21] Marx and Engels, *On the Paris Commune*, *loc. cit.*, p. 241; from the Minutes of the General Council of the International, 6 June, 1871.

And the state that Mazzini had in mind was the Republic!

Marx praised the Commune for doing away with 'the delusion as if administration and political governing were mysteries, transcendent functions only to be trusted to the hands of a trained caste – state parasites, richly paid sycophants and sinecurists, in the higher posts, absorbing the intelligence of the masses and turning them against themselves in the lower places of the hierarchy'.[22] And so as not to be misunderstood, perhaps by his servile and state-worshipping Germans, Marx continued: 'Doing away with the state hierarchy altogether and replacing the haughty masters of the people by always removable servants, a mock responsibility by a real responsibility, as they act continuously under public supervision'. The working class, Engels elaborated, in view of the fact that the state organs had formerly always given vent to their own special interests, must 'safeguard itself against its own deputies and officials'. For this, 'The Commune made use of two infallible means. In the first place, it filled all posts – administrative, judicial and educational – by election on the basis of universal suffrage of all concerned, subject to the right of recall at any time by the same electors. And, in the second place, all officials, high or low, were paid only the wages received by other workers . . . In this way an effective barrier to place-hunting and careerism was set up'.[23] The Commune, therefore, could not refrain from doing what no hierarchy or bureaucracy would do: 'It published all its doings and sayings, it initiated the public into all its shortcomings'.[24]

Marx expressly declared that there would be no functionaries or 'time-servers' of the well-known type. 'Nothing could be more foreign to the spirit of the Commune than to supersede universal suffrage by hierarchic investiture'.[25] 'The general suffrage . . . adapted to its real purposes, to choose by the communes their own functionaries of administration and initiation'.[26] And so up till the national level, where representation would also be by way of an

[22] 'First Draft . . .', *loc. cit.* p. 251.
[23] 'Introduction to *The Civil War in France*', *loc. cit.*, p. 33.
[24] *The Civil War in France*, in *The First International and After*, *loc. cit.*, p. 219.
[25] *Ibid.*, p. 211.
[26] 'First Draft . . .', p. 251.

elected body, both legislative and executive at the same time. The nation was to be nothing more than the sum of the communes. 'All France organized into self-working and self-governing communes . . . the [central] state functions reduced to a few functions for general national purposes'.[27] And even the few public functions that would remain for the central government were to be 'executed by *Communal agents,* and, therefore, under the control of the Commune'.[28] In view of our own obdurate experience of the replacement of the association by its governing representatives, we must add here that 'the Commune' really is the Commune, i.e. the public community, and not just some kind of executive, an elected (or seemingly elected) council. This system implies the the radical abolition of the bureaucracy, and self-evidently also of the standing army and the centralized police. The Commune therefore really is 'the reabsorption of the state power by society as its own living forces . . ., by the popular masses themselves'.[29]

But this resembles very closely the conditions that we hear decried as anarchy. Will all this not lead to a great chaos? Marx said that 'The unity of the nation was not to be broken, but, on the contrary, to be organized by the Communal constitution and to become a reality by the destruction of the state power which claimed to be the embodiment of that unity independent of, and superior to, the nation itself, from which it was but a parasitic excrescence'.[30] Engels pointed out how the Blanquists abandoned their original conception of a dictatorial revolutionary central authority in the practice of the Commune: 'Brought up in the school of conspiracy, and held together by the strict discipline which went with it, they started out from the viewpoint that a relatively small number of resolute, well-organized men would be able, at a given favourable moment, not only to seize the helm of state, but also by a display of great, ruthless energy, to maintain power until they succeeded in sweeping the mass of the people into the revolution and ranging them round the small band of leaders.

[27] P. 252.
[28] 'Second Outline of *The Civil War in France*', Marx and Engels, *On the Paris Commune, loc. cit.*, p. 206.
[29] 'First Draft . . .', p. 250.
[30] *The Civil War in France, loc. cit.*, p. 210.

This involved, above all, the strictest, dictatorial centralization of all power in the hands of the new, revolutionary government. And what did the Commune, with its majority of these same Blanquists, actually do? In all its proclamations to the French in the provinces, it appealed to them to form a free federation of all French Communes with Paris, a national organization which for the first time was really to be created by the nation itself'.[31]

Just as the edifice of social life was to be based on the communes, so national production was to be founded on producers' co-operatives managed by workers' councils. Engels stressed that 'by far the most important decree of the Commune instituted an organization of large-scale industry and even of manufacture which was not only to be based on the association of the workers in each factory, but also to combine all these associations into one great union'.[31] 'But this is communism, "impossible" communism! . . . if united cooperative societies are to regulate national production upon a common plan'.[32]

Backed by the Commune's own programme, Engels made fun of the 'superstitious reverence for the state', which 'takes root the more readily (in Germany) since people are accustomed from childhood to imagine that the affairs and interests common to the whole of society could not be looked after otherwise than as they have been looked after in the past, that is, through the state and its lucratively positioned officials'. The state is always 'at best an evil inherited by the proletariat after its victorious struggle for class supremacy, whose worst sides the victorious proletariat, just like the Commune, cannot avoid having to lop off at once as much as possible until such time as a generation reared in new, free social conditions is able to throw the entire lumber of the state on the scrap heap'.[33] Marx and Engels thus did not have in mind any 'economic-organizational' role for Leviathan, let alone a 'cultural-educational' function. They were rather of the opinion that 'The principles of the Commune were eternal and could not be crushed; they would assert themselves again and again until the working

[31] *Loc. cit.*, pp. 31–2.
[31] *Loc. cit.*, p. 30.
[32] *The Civil War in France, loc. cit.*, p. 213.
[33] *Loc. cit.*, pp. 33–4.

classes were emancipated'.[34] Let us now turn our minds back to actually existing socialism with its cultivation of social inequalities that goes far beyond the spectrum of money incomes; with its perpetuation of wage-labour, commodity production and money; with its rationalization of the traditional division of labour; with its almost clerical family and sexual policy; with its high official dignitaries, its standing army and police, who are all responsible only to those above them; with its official corporations for the organization and tutelage of the population; with its duplication of the unwieldy state machine into a state *and* a party apparatus; with its isolation within national frontiers – and it is quite evident how incompatible this is with the conceptions of Marx and Engels.

Apologias for these conditions, I repeat, are right to refer to the whole range of historical necessities and accidents, objective and subjective factors, that are involved. They were not created by arbitrary caprice, and hence require in their totality neither justification nor excuse, but rather truthful description and analysis. The polemical tone of such a *critique*, in the strict sense of the word, is only determined by the hypocrisy with which these conditions are proclaimed as *socialism,* and hence surreptitiously implied to be eternal and natural. Our official ideologists will not say, and even cannot say, in what way a distant communism is to be different from the existing conditions we already have. They only have one single perspective, the incessantly 'increasing role' of their party and state machine. There is a singular dialectic in this argument, according to which progress towards communism consists precisely in this 'increasing role'. To block their way ideologically, it is necessary fundamentally to oppose every attempt to squeeze the existing order into Marx and Engels's categories for the *Aufhebung* of private property and the transition to communism.

If we compare it with Marx, then this actually existing socialism provokes the same outcry as that of the Catholic heretic and humanist Teilhard de Chardin, that it is 'the crystal instead of the cell; the ant-hill instead of brotherhood. Instead of the upsurge of consciousness which we expected, it is mechanization that seems

[34] 'Record of Marx's Speech on the Paris Commune of May 23rd, 1871', in Marx and Engels, *On the Paris Commune, loc. cit.,* p. 238.

to emerge inevitably from totalization'.[35] To be sure, Teilhard's perspective of human destiny is rather too general, too global in the description of concrete historical circumstances, to grasp the actual process that can give this impression. He absolutizes a tendency which is by no means the sole one at work, to arrive at a prejudice which he shares with people right across the board to Salvador de Madariaga. But Teilhard himself is anything but a professional anti-communist, and the purpose of his statement is not a crusade but an appeal. Above all, he gives voice to something that creates an instinctive rejection of our system which runs deep in the working masses of the Western industrial countries, without which anti-communist manipulation would lose much of its force. *How* unjustified then is the suspicion that our system promises them no real progress towards freedom, but simply a different dependence to that on capital? Are there not dimensions of human existence in which the new dependence would be harsher for them than the old, precisely because the achievements of the bourgeois epoch are *not raised to a higher level?* Teilhard de Chardin continues the passage we just quoted in a way which basically shows great understanding: 'Monstrous as it is, is not modern totalitarianism really the distortion of something magnificent, and thus quite near to the truth?' – Where the aim was the reabsorption of the state by society, we are faced with a desperate attempt to adapt the whole of living society into the crystalline structure of the state. Statification instead of socialization, in other words *socialization in a totally alienated form.*

This characterization, however, which is undeniably apposite to our system *in the context* of the Marx-Engels perspective, tacitly presupposes the historical reality and fertility of precisely their concept of socialization and the idea of the Commune – or else it remains dogmatic and contemplative. In France, certainly, the Commune attempt, in so far as it was applied to the specifically French economy and polity, came to grief with the victory of the Versaillais. In Russia, the revolution had to dispense with Soviet democracy in order to save its own life. (It is probable, incidentally, that Paris too, if a Blanquist or 'Bolshevik' dictatorship had been prepared on a broader basis, could have

---

[35] *The Phenomenon of Man*, London 1965, p. 282.

resisted substantially longer). Only in Yugoslavia is a system of councils on a cooperative basis a component part of actual practice. And even there, the other principle that is the objective opposite of the 'eternal principles of the Commune' was first given general sway: 'étatism', the principle of bureaucratic-centralist dictatorship. In this respect, Stojanovic is certainly correct that it is all too often 'anarcho-liberalism' rather than communism which emerges from the enterprise collectives to oppose the barriers of étatism, thus giving expression to the real internal social structure of these cooperatives. Nationalism in Yugoslavia seems to be simply the summation and integration of this tendency at a higher level.

Thus while the Yugoslav League of Communists still makes its way courageously and patiently along its narrow ridge, in both European blocs it is state monopoly that triumphs. This is precisely the direction in which they seem to run in parallel, for all their difference in origin and formation.

In the West, private property is abolished in the regulative state monopoly structure in such a way that the second wave of the organized labour movement is already setting out on a 'long march through the institutions' and meeting up in this way with the first wave. It seems to be becoming ever more impossible simply to smash the state machine, and not because of its armed strength. In the countries of actually existing socialism, furthermore, the state machine played a predominantly creative role for a whole and decisive period. The Stalin apparatus *did* perform a task of 'economic organization', and also one of 'cultural education', both of these on the greatest of scales.

For modern Marxism, then, it is of the greatest importance to understand how such a perspective can be missing from the theory of Marx and Engels, even though they were time and again confronted with it in practice, and objectively participated in it as organizers of the workers' movement. Here we come up against an impressive irony of history in the work of Marx himself. It was the very same Marx who had just generalized the principles of the Commune, and had expressly refuted the 'misunderstanding' that it might have 'found[ed] a new form of class government',[36] whom

---

[36] 'Speech on the Seventh Anniversary of the International', in *The First International and After, loc. cit.,* p. 272.

Bakunin attacked in 1873, in his book *Statism and Anarchy*, with the enormous accusation that he, Marx, was the very prophet incarnate of state socialism. Bakunin paid no attention to *The Civil War in France*. He was chiefly reflecting on his experiences of Marx in the unsuccessful attempt of the anarchists to seize power in the International, and on his impression of German Social-Democracy, which he identified, along with all its errors, with Marx and Engels. Marx took such copious extracts from Bakunin's book that the manuscript takes up more then forty pages in the Collected Works edition,[37] and this even though he had to translate it from the Russian, which he had only just taught himself. Marx could of course make short work of Bakunin's anarchist *programme,* which essentially boiled down to the idea that the revolutionary movement that was to realize the egalitarian and dominance-free ideal state of society should already function, in the present class society, as if the ideal condition were already attained, i.e. the age-old commonplace of an absolute and metaphysical identity of end and means. In 1873, however, it appeared that Bakunin had not yet finished with the anarchist *critique* of Marxism. And we can therefore read today in incredulous astonishment, in Marx's own extracts, what Bakunin claimed to have seen at the basis of Marxist theory and practice.[38]

Bakunin viewed the Marxist goal as 'a despotism of the *governing minority,* and only the more dangerously in so far as it appears as expression of the so-called people's will'. 'But this minority, say the Marxists' (Marx interrupts with 'where?') 'will consist of workers. Certainly, with your permission, of former workers, who however, as soon as they have become representatives or governors of the people, *cease to be workers* and look down on the whole common workers' world from the height of the state. They will no longer represent the people, but themselves and their pretensions to people's government'. 'This intelligent and therefore privileged minority will govern as if they understood the real interests of the people better than the people themselves'.[39]

[37] *Marx-Engels Werke*, vol. 18, Berlin 1962, pp. 597–642.
[38] 'Conspectus of Bakunin's *Statism and Anarchy*', in *The First International and After, loc. cit.*, pp. 333–8.
[39] This last sentence does not fall in the extract printed in *The First International and After*; it is in *Marx-Engels-Werke*, vol. 18, p. 603.

The concept of 'scientific socialism' is abused as the foundation of this claim to rule. Wilhelm Liebknecht's concept of a 'people's state', which Bakunin ascribes to Marx, 'will be nothing else than the very despotic guidance of the mass of the people by a new and numerically very small aristocracy of the genuine or supposedly educated. The people are not scientific, which means that they will be entirely freed from the cares of government, they will be entirely shut up in the stable of the governed'.[40] 'Since science is not accessible to very many, at least in our time, these few will manage everything', so that 'the day after the revolution a new social organization will be formed not by the free unification of the people's organizations, communes, districts and regions from bottom to top . . ., but rather by the dictatorial power of this educated minority'.[41] In Germany, 'the workers subject themselves quite blindly to their leaders, while these leaders, the organizers of the social-democratic German party, are leading them neither to freedom nor to international brotherhood, but rather under the yoke of the pan-Germanistic state',[42] which they reproduced in their own ranks. Thus what Engels did not suspect even in 1895, Bakunin imagined almost intuitively in 1873: the collapse of German Social-Democracy in 1914.

With respect to Bakunin's charge of 'government of the educated', Marx interrupts with the exclamation '*quelle rêverie!*'. And this even though it is on that very point that Bakunin's fantasies are somewhat more concrete. After the people have placed all power in their hands, the Marxists plan to establish 'a single state bank concentrating in its hands all commercial-industrial, agricultural and even scientific production, and to divide the mass of the people into two armies, an industrial and an agricultural, under the direct command of state engineers, who will form a new privileged scientific-political class'.[43] This last expression is strikingly exact. It was probably necessary to be both an anarchist *and* a Russian, to perceive behind the authority of Marx and his doctrine, in the year 1873, the shadow of Stalin.

[40] *Werke*, vol. 18, p. 636.
[41] *Werke*, loc. cit., p. 625.
[42] *Werke*, loc. cit., p. 628.
[43] *Werke*, loc. cit., p. 638.

Marx did not see this shadow, he could not and would not see it.

Now the elements which Bakunin elaborated on here are of course present in Marxism, or rather, reflected in it, since these are realities, and in no way escaped Marx's attention. The contradiction between mental and manual labour was inevitably expressed as a contradiction between science and the working class. This was already alluded to in Marx's demand for the unification of philosophy and the proletariat, at the very origin of the Marxist conception of the party, and the purpose behind it is still in no way superseded. Since the struggle for emancipation can be conducted only under the actually given conditions, and since these conditions are characterized so fundamentally by a division of labour which excludes the mass of the producers from intellectual culture, the party of emancipation must contain within it the contradiction between the revolutionary intellectuals and the working class. The systematic pains taken in our countries to present a whole host of quotations about party and class, consciousness and spontaneity, in an effort to prove a pre-established harmony, are completely irrelevant here. In reality, the most they show is that Marx and Lenin were right in their view of the *problem*. But the real purpose of this juggling is not to protect Lenin against certain misinterpretations, but rather to paper over the gulf that divides the new society into rulers and ruled. What Marx did not foresee was the notorious fact, as it has since transpired, that the unification of philosophy and the proletariat, of socialism (as science) and the workers' movement, would turn out very similar, after the revolution, to the earlier case of the third estate, from which the bourgeoisie came to power. Against the 'unscientific' understanding the people have of the character of the new order, as one of domination, no old quotations are of any use.

But what then prevented Marx from seriously discussing the possibility of such a development? Why was even the bourgeois objection that communism would simply extend the despotic system of the factory to society as a whole worth no more than ironic dismissal? (Marx and Engels both accepted moreover the technological inevitabilily of an essentially authoritarian direction in the production process of their time, and even beyond this.) I do not intend to go into psychological questions here, but rather into their Hegelian heritage, and above all the world-historical dominance of Europe in the 19th century. The Hegelian tradition, and a Europocentrism that was scarcely avoidable, may have been responsible for the way that Marx focussed his attention too one-sidedly on capitalist private property and saw the entire past and future historical process as passing through this nodal point.

As far as the problem of the modern state is concerned, Marx was in the first place burdened from the beginning by the decisive act in which he severed himself from Hegel. The break consisted precisely in reversing the Hegelian relationship of state and society, in which the state was the latter's highest, 'real' and rational existence, and showing that the state was simply the political expression of the actual life of society with its conflicting tendencies of interest. The next step was for him to reveal the real structure and dynamic of bourgeois society from the standpoint of the economy, the relations of production. If the late absolutism then prevailing in Prussia had at least the appearance of an independence of the state from society, the bourgeois state in the class struggles that followed 1789 in France was always more visibly reducible to a naked instrument of compulsion to supplement the primarily economic functioning of capitalist exploitation. It had to rise and fall with this, as I have already shown. The post-revolutionary bourgeois state never knew any function as organizer of production, in fact the very idea of this stood in complete antithesis to the essence of competitive capitalism, whose entire mode of production was based on the initiative of private capitalists. Everywhere this system broke through its limits, as a function of its own spontaneous tendencies, Marx put forward a perspective of socialist socialization. This theoretical conjuncture has shown such persistence that many Marxist observers of present state monopoly in the West are content to note that everything that has happened since the transition to monopoly simply represents the ever more perfect preparation for this socialization. In this way, it is possible to spare oneself the trouble of studying all these phenomena in their own specific importance. They *have* certainly been explained long ago, with the little blemish that the consequences that have been proven a hundred times in theory do not appear. The reproach here of course does not bear on Marx, but rather on the thinking of the post-Lenin period.

The other element in the Hegelian tradition is the methodological hypothesis of the unity of the logical and the historical; although Marx certainly adopted it in a critical manner, in many respects it still had its effects even in spite of this general distancing. It comes to the fore in the way that Marx often dispenses very cavalierly with the historical tendencies he has so genially grasped, since what appears finished from the logical point of view must immediately be historically finished too. But what creeps in here, in the way of neglect of the quantitative aspect, adds up, as the later Engels had to acknowledge, to a qualitative misjudgement, on the one hand, of the readiness of the productive forces for a victorious proletarian overthrow, and on the other hand, of the overall capacity for extension shown by capitalist relations of production. It is a disservice to Marx's economic theory of the greatest magnitude, if we do not draw 'revisionist' conclusions from the tremendous productivity of 'late capitalism' in the USA, Japan and Western Europe. Marx would have been the first to have revised himself, so as to give revolutionary practice a better basis.

A still more essential consequence, related to the methodological principle of the unity of the logical and the historical, is the *overvaluation or even absolutizing* of the role of capitalist private property, weighty as this is. What I mean here can best be seen in in the contraction that the concept of alienation experiences in the course of Marx's scientific development. In *The German Ideology* of 1845-6, alienation, 'this fixation of social activity, this consolidation of what we ourselves produce into a material power above us, growing out of our control, thwarting our expectations, bringing to naught our calculations', still appears unqualifiedly as 'one of the chief factors in historical development up till now'.[44] It would be completely absurd, for example, to exempt from the concept of alienation the pyramids, in which one of the earlier Pharaoh dynasties invested almost the entire surplus labour of several generations of the Egyptian people, in order to extend its privileges of domination into the realm of the dead. Marx and Engels write in the same section of *The German Ideology* that 'Out

---

[44] *Collected Works*, vol. 5, pp. 47-8.

of this very contradiction between the particular and the common interests, the common interest assumes an independent form as the *state,* which is divorced from the real individual and collective interests, and at the same time as an illusory community'.[45] From the historical standpoint, the state, next to religion, is the most comprehensive phenomenon of alienation, i.e. that with the greatest extension in time. The pyramids certainly did not rest on exploitation *by way of private property,* and no more do the monuments of Stalinism, which began with the mausoleum in which Lenin was mummified like a Pharaoh. If in Marx's *Capital* the concept of alienation is then used merely in connection with the relation between capital and wage-labour, this only means, as our whole discussion of the Commune showed, the exclusion of the problem of the state from the critique of political *economy.* Above all, Marx proceeded in general from the conception that capitalist private property, i.e. capitalist alienation, contained *all* earlier alienation raised to a higher level in itself. In the *Grundrisse,* he expressly refers to the capital relation as the *'most extreme form of alienation',* and interprets it as a necessary transition point which 'already contains in *itself* . . . the dissolution of all limited' (i.e. precapitalist) 'presuppositions of production'.[46]

In the celebrated section on the 'Forms which precede capitalist production',[47] Marx analyses the whole development from the dissolution of the primitive community through to the threshold of primitive accumulation precisely from the standpoint of this result, i.e. he shows the logico-historical sequence in the process of separation of the producers from all their material conditions of production. And in this connection he introduces the implicit assumption that each higher level, even if it does not always concretely appear as having proceeded from the lower, still always contains within it the results of the preceding level. In this perspective, the abolition of capitalist private property, this quintessence of all previous progress and all previous alienation, must resolve *all* the inherited historical contradictions in *one*

[45] *Ibid.,* p. 46.
[46] *Loc. cit.,* p. 515.
[47] *Grundrisse,* pp. 471ff.

unitary process. It is only this assumption that gives validity to the early thesis of the *Economic and Philosophical Manuscripts* that communism, 'the *positive* supersession of *private property* as *human self-estrangement'*, is by that token 'the complete restoration of man to himself as a *social,* i.e. human, being, a restoration which has become conscious and which takes place within the entire wealth of previous periods of development', 'it is the solution of the riddle of history'.[48]

We are only maintaining, of course, that this conception has its *formal* basis in the Hegelian tradition, since it is by no means only ex-Hegelians who get tempted into abstract absolutizing. The *content* that is absolutized here is in reality the historical role of Europe, particularly in the 19th century. Besides the maturity of the European productive forces, Marx also over-estimated the extensive spread and the intensive operation of the capitalist world market. And it was this, as well as the theoretical paradigm of the nodal line of successive relations of production, that gave rise to a capitalist perspective for the whole of the rest of the world. Indeed, this did not even need any particular emphasis, as it was going to be anticipated in any case by the proletarian revolution in the most advanced European countries.

In reality, even in Europe the oldest historical layers of oppression and social inequality were not so totally abolished by the higher formations as Marx's logical development assumed. The idea of the abolition of private property is overburdened if we extend it to include the overcoming of relations that ultimately do not rest on private property and have never completely been absorbed into it, even in Europe.

What this involves are the following three 'residues', which originally and until today are characteristic of societies in which private property has not come to develop as the *dominant relation of production :*
The exploitation and oppression of women, in the overall patriarchal family structure with which this is connected, i.e. the dominance of the man, of the head of the household (in the patriarchal society of the gens, and in other precapitalist relations, generally also over other dependents as well).

[48] *Early Writings,* Pelican Marx Library, 1974, p. 348.

– The dominance of the town (occasionally of the palace and castle) over the country, which has to provide it with food and luxuries from the surplus labour of its population.

– The exploitation and oppression of the manual worker (whoever has to perform principally physical, schematic, *executive* work) by the mental worker (whoever performs predominantly intellectual, creative, planning and managerial activity).

These three phenomena, which Marxism has always conceived as economic relations, already provide the fundamental elements of the social *division of labour* and of the *state,* and moreover an entire epoch before private property in the means or conditions of production makes its historical appearance. And abolition of private property on the one hand, overcoming the division of labour and the state on the other, can now also be separated by a whole epoch in time on the far side of capitalism. This is how it is at any rate in the countries of actually existing socialism.

For an action programme for the progressive forces, therefore, the following two questions are posed as soon as the material conditions for socialism are even approximately created:

1. What must be done in order to liquidate the common foundations of *all* patriarchal culture of domination in its material and economic basis?

2. How can societies whose industrial civilization does not rest on the abolition of capitalist private property, or does so only in part, appropriate the positive cultural and institutional achievements of the bourgeois epoch?

The first question bears primarily on the necessary changes in the social structure of the process of labour and knowledge. The second bears in particular on the unrestrained development of human subjectivity and the institutionalization of political democracy in a society freed from private property, something that will long be indispensable.

In order to answer them, however, it is not sufficient simply to make clear the inapplicability of the categories of communism to our present conditions, necessary as this negative activity is. The point is rather to understand the new field of struggle on which we find ourselves on the basis of its own becoming, its own laws. If actually existing socialism is not the abolition of capitalist private property – what then is its inner nature? We must bear in mind, however, that in investigating this epochal problem we cannot begin with countries like the GDR and Czechoslovakia, which are untypical precisely because they already had capitalist industry. The key lies in Asia, partly in a past that is far behind our own European past. And then, naturally enough, in the specific past of Russia and in the Soviet present.

2

The Origin of the Non-Capitalist Road

Since 1945 it has become apparent, though the issue was in fact decided between 1905 and 1923, that the progress of humanity in the 20th century is following different paths than Marx and Engels managed to foresee. They had analysed those social formations which the *European* section of mankind (including North America) had attained on its specific path through ancient slavery and Germanic feudalism, and drawn the conclusion that the *internal* antagonisms of capitalism they had discovered would *directly* lead to its being burst asunder by a proletarian revolution. The reactions and developments with which the peoples of Asia (which can stand here also for Africa, and with certain qualifications for Latin America too) responded to European world conquest for the capitalist market, interested Marx and Engels principally with respect to the intensification of the contradictions internal to capitalism, to the improvement of conditions of struggle for the European proletariat. It was Lenin, who, in connection with the anti-colonial movements and revolutions in Persia, Turkey, China and India which followed the Russian revolution of 1905, was the first to recognize the movement of the revolutionary storm centre to the 'East' that these proclaimed, and also began to see the next Russian revolution under this same standpoint. At the end of his life Lenin came to a generalization of this new situation which has still not been generally accepted by European Marxism, nor even by Russian.

The ultimate issue is the fact that progress in our epoch proceeds less directly from the *internal* contradictions of imperialism, but more from the *external* contradictions that are the result of these.

The October revolution, already, was not, or was at least *far more* than, the (from our confined European perspective of waiting) 'deformed' representative of the proletarian rising in the West that has not taken place. It was and is above all the first *anti-imperialist revolution* in what was still a *predominantly pre-capitalist country,* even though it had begun a capitalist development of its own, with a socio-economic structure half feudal, half 'Asiatic'. Its task was not yet that of socialism, no matter how resolutely the Bolsheviks believed in this, but rather the rapid industrial development of Russia on a non-capitalist road. Only now, when this task is by and large completed, is the struggle for socialism on the agenda in the Soviet Union. And it is of immense importance not only for us in the non-capitalist countries of Europe, but also in respect to the future of most of the world's peoples, how this transition is to take place. We need to get a clear and unprejudiced idea of the real character of relations of production in the Soviet Union, and the tendencies that are maturing in its specific social and national structure. Of equal importance is of course China. In those European countries that are tied to the Soviet Union, what is important above all – on account of its more rapid rhythm – is their *political* development as an expression of the same social contradictions that characterize the original Soviet society. But we shall deal with all this later on.

The shifting of the main line of battle from the internal to the external contradictions of imperialism, which is reflected in the slogan of the 'world countryside against the world town', perhaps dubious, but still highly significant, is of the greatest importance for a definition of all other positions in revolutionary programmes today. We must realize that this was not expected by the classical Marxist tradition. It has theoretical as well as practical implications for the Marxist conception of history. The connection and succession of economic formations, and particularly our present period of transition on a world scale, appear in a different light if we seek to understand them not only from the customary point of view of the abolition of private property, but also with respect to the fate of the traditional class societies of Asia, Africa and pre-Columbian America. In these countries, private property in the means of production, which was the basic driving force of the historical dynamic in Europe, never played the same decisive role for the social formation as in our antiquity, feudalism and capitalism. This is precisely why these are today agricultural 'developing countries', in which the abolition of private property is only the negative condition of progress, unlike the rich countries where the liberated people can positively appropriate the wealth already created, the developed productive forces.

All these non-European cultures, which are based on what Marx called the Asiatic mode of production and are in most cases far older than our own, stagnated in a motion symbolized by the wheel of Buddhist doctrine, rotating in its fixed place, when European capitalist colonialism began to burst asunder their internal framework on the basis of its industrial revolution. Under their decaying Oriental despotism, the peoples affected could not put up resolute opposition to either cotton or cannons. Even where they did oppose the cannons, this was only, as with Turkey and Russia, by active assimilation of 'European achievements' in the field of military science, which drew an ever surer capitalist penetration in its wake.

It was only realistic of Marx to conclude in 1853 that the British rule in India would objectively tackle the task of creating the material foundations for a Western, i.e. capitalist, social order. The question was not 'whether the English had a right to conquer India, but whether we are to prefer India conquered by the Turk, by the Persian, by the Russian, to India conquered by the Briton'.[1] For while 'there cannot . . . remain any doubt but that the misery inflicted by the British on Hindustan is of an essentially different and infinitely more intensive kind than all Hindustan had to suffer before', England had still brought about 'the greatest, and, to speak the truth, the only *social* revolution ever heard of in Asia'. 'The question is, can mankind fulfil its destiny without a fundamental revolution in the social state of Asia?'[2] But because the history of British rule in India scarcely displayed anything beyond the destruction of the traditional social structure, 'The Indians will not reap the fruits of the new elements of society scattered

[1] 'The Future Results of the British Rule in India', in *Surveys from Exile*, Pelican Marx Library, 1973, p. 320.
[2] 'The British Rule in India', *loc. cit.*, pp. 202, 206 and 207.

among them by the British bourgeoisie till in Great Britain itself the now ruling classes shall have been supplanted by the industrial proletariat, or till the Hindus themselves shall have grown strong enough to throw off the English yoke altogether'.[3]

This last mentioned alternative, however, is evidently un-characteristic of Marx's future perspective, and the outcome of the Indian uprising a few years later proved him right in this. It was also without any further consequences that Engels made a more favourable assessment of the chances of the Taiping movement in China, fighting as this did with more suitable methods. The two friends ultimately held firmly to the general rule with which Marx ended his concluding essay on India: 'When a great social revolution shall have mastered the results of the bourgeois epoch, the market of the world and the modern powers of production, and subjected them to the common control of the most advanced peoples *(sic)*, only then will human progress cease to resemble that hideous pagan idol, who would not drink the nectar but from the skulls of the slain'.[4] For Russia, for example, Marx held that such a revolution in the West would actually provide the possibility of a comprehensive social reorganization along the lines of the Chinese people's communes of today.[5] The traditional village communities were to join together on a regional basis, and to take over and apply the industrial achievements of a now socialist West on this broader scale.

The same basic position is repeated in Engels' final statement of 1894 on the prospects of the Russian revolution: 'However, it is not only possible but inescapable that once the proletariat wins out and the means of production pass into common ownership among the West-European nations, the countries which have just managed to make a start on capitalist production, and where tribal institutions or relics of them are still intact, will be able to use these relics of communal ownership and the corresponding popular customs as a powerful means of considerably shortening their advance to socialist society. . . . But an inevitable condition of this

[3] 'The Future Results of the British Rule in India', *loc. cit.*, p. 323.

[4] *Ibid.*, p. 325.

[5] See Marx's 'First Draft of a Letter to Vera Zasulich', in Marx and Engels, *Selected Works* in three volumes, Moscow 1969, vol. 3.

is the example and active support of the hitherto capitalist West. . . .
And this applies not only to Russia but to all countries at the
pre-capitalist stage of development. However, this will be
relatively easiest done in Russia, where a part of the native
population has already assimilated the intellectual fruits of
capitalist development . . .' The overthrow of Tsarist despotism
would 'also give a fresh impulse to the labour movement in the
West, creating for it new and better conditions for struggle and
thereby advancing the victory of the modern industrial proletariat,
a victory without which present-day Russia, whether on the basis
of the community or of capitalism, cannot achieve a socialist
transformation of society'.[6]

History has furnished a decisive corrective to this original
Marxist prognosis. While the capitalist order is already in a third
phase of its internal contradictions, and *moving* in them instead of
succumbing to them, as Marx had predicted for its first phase, and
Lenin conclusively for its second, many peoples in the pre-
capitalist countries have set out on their own road towards
socialism. The proletarian revolution in the West did not take
place; and its appearance in the form previously anticipated
has become ever more improbable. The nature and character of a
revolution are only determined up to a certain point by the
programme and the heroism of its vanguard, who can only
achieve the first steps. The Soviets of 1905 and 1917 continued the
Paris Commune, but after them this continuity was broken.
Today, adherence to the hope of a classical socialist overthrow in
the West must lead to a pessimism that is actually groundless. The
revolutions in Russia and China, in the Balkans and in Cuba, have
probably contributed not less but rather more to overall progress
than the proletarian revolutions hoped for in the West could have
done.

Marxism, in other words, set out on a different journey, via
Russia to Asia, Africa and Latin America, a route associated with
the names of Lenin, Mao Tse-tung, Nkrumah and Castro. It
represents today something incomparably greater and more
diverse then in the era of Marx, and also in regard to its significance

[6] Afterword to 'On Social Relations in Russia', Marx and Engels, *Selected Works*
in three volumes, Moscow 1969, vol. 2, pp. 403–4.

for Europe. It is not a question of its 'purity', but rather that it can simply no longer be monopolized as a tool for study and for changing social realities. (The variety of these must be stressed, so as to understand the differentiation of Marxist thought as something *positive*.) Historical materialism itself prohibits us from judging whether conditions in the Soviet Union, People's China, etc. realize 'authentic Marxism', though it can explain why the official representatives of the various tendencies struggle for sole possession of the truth. What is authentic is not the letter of theory, but the historical process. If Leninism already represents in its theory, and especially in its practice, a considerable 'revision' of the orthodox doctrine, that is the great merit of the founder of the Soviet Union.

Lenin's view of the revolutionary possibilities of the Asian peoples was rendered more acute right from the beginning by his understanding of the semi-Asiatic character of social relations in Russia. As early as 1900, when the Russian reactionary and liberal press were accompanying Tsarist participation in the imperialist police action against the so-called Boxer rebellion in China with a campaign of hatred against the barbarian Chinese, those enemies of culture and civilization, Lenin stressed, as he was repeatedly to do later, the similarity of the social problems facing the peoples of Russia and China: 'The Chinese people suffer from the same evils as those from which the Russian people suffer – they suffer from an Asiatic government that squeezes taxes from the starving peasantry and that suppresses every aspiration towards liberty by military force; they suffer from the oppression of capital, which has penetrated into the Middle Kingdom'.[7] The term 'Asiatic' here describes a specific form of relations of domination. In the same sense, Lenin was later to write: 'In very many and very essential respects, Russia is undoubtedly an Asian country and, what is more, one of the most benighted, medieval and shamefully backward of Asian countries'.[8]

Against the background of this historical affinity, he observed how the Russian revolution of 1905 was followed by very similar events in Turkey, Persia and above all in 1911 in China, while

[7] 'The War in China', *Collected Works*, vol. 4, p. 377.
[8] 'Democracy and Narodism in China', *Collected Works*, vol. 18, pp. 163–4.

India and Indonesia also began to stir. There could be no doubt, Lenin concluded in 1908, that the European policies of robbery and oppression would steel the Asian peoples for a victorious struggle against their oppressors. The Russian revolution had *two* great international allies, one in Europe (the modern proletariat) and one in Asia.[9] In 1913 he gave an article the significant title 'Backward Europe and Advanced Asia', and wrote earlier the same year: 'The awakening of Asia and the beginning of the struggle for power by the advanced proletariat of Europe are a symbol of the new phase in world history that began early this century'.[10] If the mention of Asia was initially contingent, it indicated none the less the beginning of a shift of emphasis. In considering the historical destiny of Marxism in the same year 1913, Lenin emphasized with respect to the 'new source of great world storms opened up in Asia': 'It is in this era of storms and their "repercussions" in Europe that we are now living. . . . Certain people who were inattentive to the conditions for preparing and developing the mass struggle were driven to despair and to anarchism by the lengthy delays in the decisive struggle against capitalism in Europe. . . . The fact that Asia, with its population of eight hundred million, has been drawn into the struggle for these same European ideals should inspire us with optimism and not despair. . . . After Asia, Europe has also begun to stir . . .'.[11]

Characteristic of Lenin's position is his reference to the way that the philosophical and political slogans of the anti-imperialist liberation struggle derive from the ideals of the bourgeois and the proletarian revolution in Europe. The new role of Asia in no way meant that 'light shines only from the mystic, religious East'. 'No, quite the opposite. It means that the East has definitely taken the Western path',[12] which Russia had itself embarked upon. At least at the theoretical level, Lenin continued to the last to hold the conviction that 'the social revolution in Western Europe is maturing before our eyes'.[13] But after 1917, while the Bolsheviks

[9] 'Inflammable Material in World Politics', *Collected Works*, vol. 15, pp. 187–8.
[10] 'The Awakening of Asia', *Collected Works*, vol. 19, p. 86.
[11] 'The Historical Destiny of the Doctrine of Karl Marx', *Collected Works*, vol. 18, p. 584.
[12] 'Democracy and Narodism in China', *Collected Works*, vol. 18, p. 165.
[13] *Collected Works*, vol. 31.

waited passionately for the outbreak of the revolution in the West, and in Germany in particular, which was to come to the relief of the Russian October and secure its future, a different orientation came more and more to the fore.

In November 1919 Lenin developed the following idea in addressing representatives of the Communist organizations of the East: since the imperialists would not allow the European revolutions to take their course easily and swiftly, and since the 'old socialist compromisers are enlisted on the side of the bourgeoisie', 'the socialist revolution will not be solely, or chiefly, a struggle of the revolutionary proletarians in each country against their bourgeoisie – no – it will be a struggle of all the imperialist-oppressed colonies and countries, of all dependent countries, against international imperialism'. The programme of the Russian Communist Party was based on the union of the civil war in the advanced countries with wars of national liberation. 'It is self-evident that final victory can be won only by the proletariat of all the advanced countries of the world, and we, the Russians, are beginning the work which the British, French or German proletariat will consolidate. But we see' – and this is a completely new formulation – 'that they will not be victorious without the aid of the working people of all the oppressed colonial nations, first and foremost, of Eastern nations. We must realize that the transition to communism cannot be accomplished by the vanguard alone'. The task Lenin proposes, therefore, is 'to translate the true communist doctrine, which was intended for the Communists of the more advanced countries, into the language of every people', and 'our Soviet Republic must now muster all the awakening peoples of the East and, together with them, wage a struggle against international imperialism'.[14]

In March 1923, when he wrote his final testamentary essay, 'Better Fewer, but Better', Lenin took a decisive step further. 'Shall we be able', he asked, 'to hold on with our small and very small peasant production, and in our present state of ruin, until the West-European capitalist countries consummate their development towards socialism?' After surveying the contradictions

[14] 'Address to the Second All-Russia Congress of Communist Organizations of the Peoples of the East', *Collected Works*, vol. 30, pp. 159, 161–2 and 161.

between the rich imperialist states, he reached the conclusion that 'the outcome of the struggle will be determined by the fact that Russia, India, China, etc., account for the overwhelming majority of the population of the globe', a majority being schooled and trained for the struggle by capitalism itself. He then indicated what he saw as the basic contradiction and central task of the epoch introduced by October: *'To ensure our existence until the next military conflict between the counter-revolutionary imperialist West and the revolutionary and nationalist East, between the most civilized countries of the world and the Orientally backward countries which, however, comprise the majority, this majority must become civilized.* We, too, lack enough civilization to enable us to pass straight on to socialism, although we do have the political requisites for it'.[15] Two months earlier he had written: 'If a definite level of culture is required for the building of socialism . . . why cannot we begin by first achieving the prerequisites for that definite level of culture in a revolutionary way, and *then*, with the aid of the workers' and peasants' government and the Soviet system, proceed to overtake the other nations?'.[16] In this way, therefore, Lenin derived from the enforced circumstances which the Russian revolution had arrived at by its isolation the programmatic basis of subsequent development.

For the heroes of the Second International, who charged the Bolsheviks with violating 'Marxist orthodoxy', and their imitators of today, Lenin offered the following consideration: 'Our European philistines never even dream that the subsequent revolutions in Oriental countries, which possess much vaster populations and a much vaster diversity of social conditions, will undoubtedly display even greater distinctions than the Russian revolution'.[17] What singular Leninists, then, are those who would today play schoolmaster to the Chinese revolution, the revolution of a good quarter of humanity!

Marx only touched in passing on the question as to how the non-European peoples were to appropriate the achievements of

[15] 'Better Fewer, but Better', *Collected Works*, vol. 33, pp. 499, 500 and 500–1. (Bahro's emphasis.)

[16] Our Revolution', *Collected Works*, vol. 33, pp. 478–9.

[17] *Ibid.*, p. 480.

the epoch of private property, i.e. the wealth of Europe with its industrial preconditions. It seems that he did not realize the full implications of either the tremendous material gap, or the gap at the level of the subjective factors, the historical human types, between Europe and the colonized sector of the globe. The characteristic drama of the present, which we denote with the abstract term 'development', would have been no less a problem if the hopes of the European socialists had been fulfilled – on the contrary! Both Hegel and Marx liked to refer to the unexpected, unforeseen breakthrough of a historical necessity as the 'cunning of reason'. Should we not see such a cunning of reason at work in the fact that the masses of the 'Third World' have anticipated the revolt of Europe?

The peoples of the backward countries today are involved in a race with catastrophe, a catastrophe which could claim far more victims than the molten iron of the Russian revolution – and needless victims at that. Revolutions such as the Russian and the Chinese are the precondition for victory over hunger. One of the earliest ideas of Marxism, that the 'overthrowing' class, or the formerly oppressed classes, needs the revolution as its own action, in order to 'rid itself of all the muck of ages and become fitted to found society anew',[18] is nowhere more valid than for those doubly oppressed peoples whom capitalism found at a lower stage of social development. What they need is not bread from Canada, but rather bread from Asia, from Africa, and for this they need a new form of life, similarly non-capitalist to that in the Soviet Union and in China. How else are the colonized peoples to overcome their inferiority complex, to find on a massive scale the new consciousness and self-consciousness required for their ascent, except through a revolutionary liberation of their own? The external conditions for this may be favoured by the existence of other socialist powers, but the popular masses of the Southern hemisphere can in no case be freed from outside.

What they initially require most of all for their material reconstruction is a strong state, often one that is in many respects despotic, in order really to overcome the inherited inertia. And such a state power can only draw its legitimation and authority

[18] *The German Ideology*, in Marx and Engels, *Collected Works*, vol. 5, p. 53.

from a revolution, and thus put a stop to the decay and corruption characteristic of the old 'Asiatic mode of production'. This state power *must* be in charge of any 'development aid' that comes from outside with technical knowledge, and is therefore always inclined to fall into the old colonial manner. There are very few people like Norman Bethune. That is why state power resulting from liberation must be established before any European advisers proclaim a '*Communauté*'. It must take the same attitude towards advisers of this kind as the young Soviet power did to bourgeois specialists. And if such advisers are now coming from the Soviet Union itself, as well as from the other countries tied to it, the same arrangements must apply to them too, until they have given proof of their internationalist solidarity and fraternity. For the history of the liberation movement since the Second World War has proved irrefutably that the pace and the effect of emancipation for the masses depend on the achievement of precisely this state of affairs.

Let us try and imagine what the peoples still under pre-capitalist conditions and colonial exploitation would have obtained if the West European proletariat at the turn of the century had anticipated the liberating revolutions outside of Europe. Can we assume that a spirit of human solidarity, the practice of equality towards all who bear the human countenance, would have immediately and unreservedly been achieved? The working classes of Europe are objective participants in colonialism, and this was never without its ideological effects. At the Stuttgart Congress of the Socialist International in 1907, a clause in the draft resolution that the Congress did not condemn all colonial policy on principle, since under socialism this could have a civilizing effect, was rejected by only a narrow majority. Lenin also reported how the attempt was made in the Congress's commission on the colonial question 'to ban the immigration of workers from backward countries (coolies – from China, etc.)'. 'This is the same spirit of aristocratism', Lenin observed, 'that one finds among workers in some of the "civilized" countries, who derive certain advantages from their privileged position, and are, therefore, inclined to forget the need for international class solidarity'.[19]

[19] 'The International Socialist Congress in Stuttgart', *Collected Works*, vol. 13, p. 79.

The immediate, trade-union interests of the Western working classes, who would themselves have developed a considerable need to catch up, both materially and culturally, and would not have been as driven to solidarity from the foreign policy standpoint as was the poor Soviet republic, could have been kept on reins only by the most extreme revolutionary consciousness and selflessness. The bureaucracies of the social-democratic parties and trade unions, however, tended rather to cultivate colonialist prejudices. For the sharpened awareness of the present-day reader, even Frederick Engels' position is not completely free from a certain 'expert' European arrogance, as can be seen for example in many of his articles on the Indian insurrection of 1857-9. More than a few authorities of the Western labour movement would have had a good try at teaching the 'savage' and 'half-civilized' peoples how to behave, and after the first unsuccessful attempts to spread a Protestant work ethic in Asia and Africa, withdrawn angrily like the righteous guardian from his ungrateful ward. The labour bureaucracies were all inclined, at the very least, to an educational colonialism. And nothing is more likely than that the peoples affected would have been forced to turn against such hypothetical socialist governments – even if under somewhat more favourable conditions than before, and with a European left-socialist minority on their side.

Above all, we must repeat once more that these peoples have an unconditional *need to rebel for themselves,* if they are to reshape their society. They must begin by taking a cultural distance from Europe, even while assimilating its technical achievements. For the export of European civilization is colonialist to the roots, even if pursued by a workers' government. Neither Russia nor China would have managed to attack their own problems of development at such a pace, with such an unleashing of the human productive forces, if they had not been forced to solve them in revolutionary self-preservation against a hostile environment.

If a socialist or communist order, as we have since had to realize, cannot be based on material preconditions that are merely provincial in character, then the task of overcoming the lack of civilization which Lenin referred to must be fulfilled by the revolutionary peoples themselves, by creating the labour discipline they need in the course of their struggle, this being the major world-historical task in preparing for socialism. *With the revolutions in Russia and China, with the revolutionary process in Latin America, in Africa and in India, humanity is taking the shortest route to socialism.* There, in the 'East', the real wretched of this earth have awakened. The role of the working class, who gave the decisive impulse to the Russian revolution and who obviously have a task in Europe, must be seen afresh in this context. Moreover, even their revolution in Europe would not have led directly to the socialism for which Marx hoped, but far more probably to the phenomenal form so familiar to us, which Bakunin already feared from the look of the Prusso-German Social-Democrats and the style of leadership in the International. Time and again, our bureaucratic centralism is explained in terms of Russian backwardness, though in fact this is only responsible for certain excesses. In so far as the hierarchical apparatus of function-aries of the workers' organizations is the potential state machine, what this is preparing is not a new Paris Commune, but rather a state monopoly freed from capitalism.

We can envisage the state monopoly tendency better, a tendency which is coming to form the object of the liberation struggle the world over, if we compare this modern transition period towards classless society with the ancient economic despotism which was the predominant form of entry into class society. This is a further reason why the history and present developmental tendencies in the East are of particular interest to us. We shall see that the character of this epoch, as it develops into the 'conflict between the counter-revolutionary imperialist West and the revolutionary and nationalist East', is the present consequence of all former world history. On the essential points, it needs only the further develop-ment of the premises already provided by Marx and Engels in their materialist overview of historical evolution.

In the little catechism that our propagandists distribute for basic study and so on, the richness of this historical picture is reduced to the idea of a regular succession of five formations: primitive communism, slavery, feudalism, capitalism, socialism-communism, with perhaps a concept of the overall process thrown in in the shape of the dialectical principle of *aufheben,* the 'negation of the negation'. In particular, a kind of dogmatism is quite falsely imputed to the classics, according to which every society must essentially go through all these formations. As a kind of exception, therefore, the completely anti-historical metaphor of 'leaping over' whole social formations must be applied to various peoples. It is not even theoretically enlightening when applied to the peoples of Soviet Asia, for whom one might expect it to be most illuminating. (A historian familiar with the facts must be completely lacking in any real understanding for the historical process if he can bring himself to declare that the Germans, by 'immediately' reaching feudalism, had 'leapt over' slavery, which is not indicated by anything in their formative period. – The patriarchal domestic slavery which we find among the Germans, in common with all other ancient peoples, nowhere proved in the ancient East to be the preliminary stage to a use of slaves in the major productive function, like that of classical antiquity).

Up until a short while ago, it was not even permissible in our countries to seek a genuine concept of that social order which the European colonialists who swarmed out across the globe from the end of the middle ages found in existence in almost all non-European countries (in so far as these were not still tribal), whether in Mexico, Central America and Peru, in India and China, in Africa and the Near East. Whereas these were in reality various stages of stagnation and decay, even in America and Africa, of that most ancient formation of class society which Marx described economically as the Asiatic mode of production, and politically as Oriental despotism, a great number were however discovered to be cases of slavery or feudalism, endowed with certain 'peculiarities', since Stalin had banned the concept of the Asiatic mode of production. While Marx saw the *only social* revolution in Asia as that carried out by the British, our present textbooks have to ascribe to India and China, for example, some time in the first or second half of the first millenium A.D., a transformation from 'patriarchal slave-owning society' (an expression all the more meaningless in as much as its users admit that slavery was never a characteristic relation of production in it) to feudalism. What serves as evidence are certain similar features with European feudalism that are established purely descriptively, and which actually attest simply to the inner logic of the Asiatic formation. For Marx, who accepted the biological model of the organism in his conception of the development of historical societies,[20] and had derived his concept of feudalism from the development of Germanic Europe, what gives feudalism its *decisive* characteristic is that it produces *immanently* from itself the preconditions for its revolutionary dissolution by capitalism. What kind of 'feudal relations of production', then, are those which 'reproduce[d] themselves with the immutability of natural conditions',[21] not only in East Asia, but even in Turkey, and did so right down to Marx's own time?

What is at issue in all this is *how general* is the validity of Marx's thesis in the *Preface to the Critique of Political Economy* according to which each social formation gives rise to the next higher by way of social revolution. In this list of 'progressive epochs of the economic social formation', Marx puts the Asiatic mode in first place. He had precisely shown in the *Grundrisse* why nowhere and never has this led of itself to a higher mode of production. Even in ancient slavery, the deadly antagonism between forces and relations of production was observable only in its destructive aspect. The decline of the Western Roman Empire did not see any revolutionary class. Reading backwards from feudalism, to be sure, the *coloni* and various other ties of dependence appear in the wake of a latifundium slavery that had become untenable, as the germs of a new order. But was it not Engels' opinion that it took the external impulse of the Germans to give the Roman agony a positive outcome, even if they were driven under the influence of Rome to accelerate their own formation of a class society? 'It was not . . . their specific national qualities which rejuvenated Europe, but simply – their barbarism, their gentile constitution. . . . Only barbarians are able to rejuvenate a world in the throes of collapsing civilization. And precisely the highest stage of barbarism . . . was the most favorable for this process. That explains everything'.[22]

---

[20] See the Postface to the Second Edition of *Capital*, vol. 1, Pelican Marx Library edition, 1976, pp. 100ff.

[21] *Ibid.*, p. 239.

[22] *The Origin of the Family, Private Property and the State*, London 1972, pp. 215–6.

The masses of the Third World are in their overwhelming majority no longer raw barbarians (in any case, the Morgan-Engels designation is outdated), but since they no longer live under their obsolete civilizations, which capitalism has decomposed, indeed can no longer go on living in this way, and are in fact pressed down even below their traditional conditions of existence, they are driven to militant revolt. And they can free themselves from their old chains and their new ones alike, through their ability to found an autonomous new civilization.

In his concern to universalize the laws of historical development that characterize modern Europe since the beginning of the emancipation of the towns in the high middle ages, Marx was evidently less mindful of a different point of view which his acquaintance with Darwin might have suggested. In the development of the human species, the historical laws that Marx discovered replace the biological laws of evolution, or more precisely, being higher, they raise the latter to a higher level. But the founders of Marxism themselves shared the general conviction that this was a protracted process and in any case still not concluded in capitalism. As is shown by the tremendous increase in material on ancient history and ethnography in the course of the last century, the early class societies are still marked – if in a modified form – by the same method of succession that is characteristic of the development of species. In the evolution of species we find that the most advanced form at time t never originates from the form furthest developed at time $t-1$. It is always a branch that is not yet too highly specialized, and with too restricted a structure, a still 'unformed' branch, that reaches the next highest level. We do *not* stem from Neanderthal man, even though he is a link in the chain leading towards us. Succession, here, does not mean a unilinear development. The same is also true for the first three formations of class society, Asiatic, ancient and feudal.

Marx confirms this himself in his concrete depictions in the *Grundrisse*. He investigates the relations of landed property in the ancient East, among the Greeks and Romans, and among the Germans, as respective predispositions towards the 'Asiatic mode of production', ancient slavery and feudalism, and assumes that they *succeed* one another historically as well as logically. But nowhere does he maintain that the Germans, for example, had actually to go through the earlier forms. Perhaps there is a common starting-point, a more primitive state of society which is differentiated into these various configurations according to the environmental conditions that the various communities have to face. But each of the three 'indigenous' formations proceeds *immediately* from the primitive society, even if slavery does not predate the Asiatic mode of production, or feudalism slavery. Marx wrote in 1853 for example that the Scottish clan system, which belonged to the final patriarchal phase of primitive society, stood 'a full degree' below feudalism, i.e. not two or three degrees.[23] The more developed formations depend on the one hand on the production techniques and organization accumulated by earlier ones, as well as on several institutional advances, while on the other hand they presuppose that the earlier forms have already passed their peak, being now in the stage of stagnation or decline.

By far the greater part of those peoples who broke out of primitive society before the middle ages, and in Africa even up to recent times, 'chose' some variant or other of the Asiatic mode of production, since it could bring them the greatest progress objectively possible, as a rule perhaps the only progress possible. Before I go on to deal in more detail with this mode of production, which at today's level of knowledge we can best describe as economic despotism, it is necessary to remember first of all that in the case of the original founders of the ancient civilizations the new mode of production emerged directly from the struggle with nature for a richer agriculture product, which the land in question could only yield by cooperation on an overall social scale, i.e. via the state. Tribes who arrived on the scene later, and overran civilized peoples such as these, were primarily assimilated precisely by the mode of production they came across, which drew them into the established despotic tradition via their need for large-scale cooperation in the collective military suppression of the numerically greater original population. Slavery and feudalism

[23] 'The Duchess of Sutherland and Slavery', in Marx and Engels, *Articles on Britain*, Moscow, 1971, p. 144.

first arose only in natural conditions where agriculture did not demand large-scale cooperation, because it was based on sufficient natural rainfall instead of on irrigation. Secondly, the Greeks and Romans, and still more so the Germans, developed on territories that had not been decisively stamped by earlier civilizations. The Spartans were led not to ancient slavery, but only to a variant of the Asiatic mode of production, precisely because they specialized in the collective suppression of a foreign population. The ancient economic despotisms are generally characterized by the way that they do not dissolve the gentile structure and raise it to a higher level, but rather conserve and overlay it.

We can sum up the situation as follows. Original slavery existed only where there was no previous economic despotism. Original feudalism existed only where neither slavery nor economic despotism had taken firm hold. Naturally, with the progress from formation to formation the historical context becomes denser, and the much slower development in America and in sub-Saharan Africa shows how decisive was the geographical concentration of population around the Near Eastern centre of the ancient world.

Only with European feudalism (and not quite so clearly, also with Japanese), did humanity hit upon that particular 'indigenous' form which does not suffer from the fundamental internal barriers of the two previous ones, whose crisis does not portend an endless stagnation, a chain of fruitless internal breakdowns and repetitions. Original capitalism, however, has only existed where this feudalism developed beforehand, with its immanent tendency of transformation. Feudalism-capitalism is essentially a single development, the dialectical unfolding and extension of one (or if Japan is included two) of the many human civilizations.

Now while this so-called Western civilization drew in more or less all the core territories of ancient slavery, at the peak of its capitalist phase it faced the entire legacy of the oldest civilized mode of production as foreign booty to be exploited. The peoples of these countries are still affected today by the fact that their distant ancestors were the first to create a high culture and had therefore to subject themselves to a social structure which did not contain any immanent explosive dynamic. Yet it is evident that without the work of the ancient Sumerians, Egyptians, Indians, Cretans, etc., we could not have had Greece and Rome, nor our own feudalism and the English industrial revolution. Spontaneous solidarity of those far removed does not lie in human nature. It presupposes a knowledge of the historically arising dependency and commonality of our future fate. In the countries of the Soviet bloc, too, the history books are completely out of proportion in the way that they blow up the last few hundred years of European history. The progressive movements in Europe and North America must make a special effort to understand the specific forms and problems of emancipation that arise from the 'Asiatic' inheritance of the rest of humanity.

This task will be that much easier, the more deeply they grasp the fact that the further emancipation of their own societies beyond the bounds of capitalism comes up against the barrier of *state monopoly* structures. For in its classically high form as economic despotism in ancient Egypt, Mesopotamia, India, China, and Peru, the Asiatic mode of production, the formation of transition to early class society, exhibits an instructive structural affinity to our own epoch of decline of class society. In 1881 Marx finally expressed the view once again that the road to communism can be understood as a dialectical process of return to relations equivalent, but at a higher level,[24] to archaic ones.

The transition stage between communism and developed class society, which was initially crossed 'forwards', and is now to be crossed 'backwards', is characterized in both cases by a specific function of the state which arises directly from the social division of labour and cooperation. Productive forces which belong to the state, which are either no longer social or are not yet so, are what provide the specific characteristic of both epochs. We will understand better the real contradictions that lay in wait for us beyond capitalism, if we take a somewhat closer look at the old 'Asiatic mode of production', the old economic despotism.

It would obviously be pointless to try and *explain* the present epoch and its perspectives from a structural analogy of this kind. The modern state monopoly structure is not only moving in the

---

[24] See 'First Draft of a Letter to Vera Zasulich', *loc. cit.*

opposite direction, it is moving above all with a dynamic that presses it irresistibly forward. The comparison is only intended to give us a sharper view of its problems, as well as to reinforce the impression that a society subjected in this way to the pyramid of state direction of labour, such as our own, can in no way be thereby seen as socialist, as free from the exploitation and oppression of man by man.

Taken more exactly, the expression 'Asiatic mode of production' does not describe a finished formation, but rather the *connecting link* between the final patriarchal phase of primitive society and the class societies of Asia, a link which consists of a specific type of archaic agricultural community. Where Marx discusses the 'Forms that precede capitalist production' in the *Grundrisse,* he speaks in the same sense of the 'ancient' and 'Germanic' forms, as well as of the 'Slav and Rumanian'. What he is concerned with here are not those formations whose character is already well developed, but rather the various indigenous forms of appropriation of the land that then provide the basis for the difference between the three pre-capitalist formations *in the transition* to class society. Later Marx apparently still counted Asiatic society as the primary, archaic formation, *in as much as* in this form the original common property of the village community was not dissolved into private property, but was in practice *statified,* so that the mass of producers there remained directly united with their conditions of labour. But in all the ancient high cultures that arose in the millenia before classical antiquity on the Euphrates and the Tigris, on the Nile, the Indus, and the Huang Ho, in Asia Minor, in Crete, in South Arabia, and on the Ganges, men unmistakeably confronted one another as exploiter and exploited, ruler and oppressed.

What are the origins of this indigenous class society without private property?

When the retreat of the last Ice Age brought the Afro-Asian desert band into being, this gradual deterioration of living conditions found the scattered human groups in the areas affected at the most different stages of development of the primitive community. Around the 'fertile crescent' of the Middle East, in particular, many populations had been involved in the Neolithic agricultural revolution and had made the transition to agriculture.

The growing productivity of their labour led to the increasing relative concentration of their population. The decimation of vegetation by both men and herds acted in the same direction as the unfavourable climatic tendency. The struggle for existence became more intense. The exceedingly fertile loess corridors of the great rivers had previously remained unsettled, even though they made possible three harvests a year. The Biblical tale of the Flood illustrates the risk the first communities took in the 6th millenium B.C., when, at first sporadically and on a seasonal basis, they occupied the flood-plains of the rivers.

By the 4th millenium B.C., there was already a settled population in what is now southern Iraq, at the confluence of the two rivers. This was only possible because they drained the marshes and managed to control flooding. A task of such magnitude could not have been undertaken by the later Greeks, Romans or Germans at the beginnings of their respective civilizations. These rivers could not be managed by individual kinship units and families producing in isolation, nor even by village communities. The task itself forced the periodic coming together of several communities, a mass of simple labour-power in the form of *large-scale co-operation*, which meant more than the mere summation of individual efforts and whose proceeds could not be seized by a particular section of society; i.e. they could only be appropriated by the society as a whole. The land thus remained common property almost everywhere that this formation arose, on account of these decisive 'preconditions of production', whether it was cultivated collectively or by the family within the village community. To put it more exactly, private property could not develop, and that is something different.

Gordon Childe established that the conditions of human life under these circumstances placed an extraordinary means of power in the hands of the society, which could be used to discipline its members. 'Rain falleth upon the just and unjust alike, but irrigating waters reach the fields by channels that the community has constructed'.[25] Even with agriculture in the regions of adequate rainfall, the tribal magician exerts a central supervision

---

[25] *Man Makes Himself*, London 1965, p. 109.

over the annual course of life and labour. Here, however, society's office-bearers necessarily soon obtained an incomparably greater authority. Formerly only the illusory mediators of productive activity (as this mediation necessarily was and remained), they now became the real organizers of production. The tribal deity no longer just demanded the regulative activity of the priests, but revealed to them plans for canals, dams, and very soon also for temples, which functioned also as grain stores. All these public works had to be prepared and organized, labour-power had to be divided up, managed, and – since man is not hard-working 'by nature' – also compelled. Correct plans presuppose a study of river flow, its behaviour in the various seasons, i.e. a step forward from intuitive magic to systematic observation. The sacrificial tribute that the deity received grew with production, and this was also necessary in order to employ one section of the people for a protracted time in the central functions. A stock was also needed as insurance against the natural disasters that the river could produce. A storage economy such as this required book-keeping, the art of reckoning, and writing, and these were indeed all invented.

For millenia, there had been *one* magician, medicine man or shaman for whom a surplus product was produced. But now the scope of intellectual tasks created a *corporation of priests,* organized hierarchially in the temple, who elaborated the plans of the deity for his people and managed his wealth. The division of labour between agriculture and handicrafts had already preceded this new division. It had introduced exchange into the community, yet did not directly break up its primitive communist structure. The first ruling exploiter class in history grew directly from the needs of the production and reproduction process itself, in the shape of the priestly caste, this process being mediated not by commodity production and private property, but rather by large-scale cooperation and its direction. This caste appropriated, in the name of the deity, the surplus product created by the manual workers it directed. With its power of disposal over the wealth available, and over the available portion of living labour, it brought expanded reproduction and thus the further destiny of the majority also under its determination and control. This is precisely one of the two roads to *class* formation which Engels mentions in *Anti-Dühring*.[26] With respect to Egypt, Marx refers to 'the domination of the priests as the directors of agriculture'.[27] 'Division of labour', according to *The German Ideology*, 'only becomes truly such from the moment when a division of material and mental labour appears'.[28] Yes indeed! For this is identical with the earliest class antithesis, which found its very first pure and unadulterated expression in the form of the theocracy, and not only in Mesopotamia and Egypt.

But to the extent that the towns arising around the temples and their cultural activity successively advanced, so that their growing wealth provoked the envy of neighbouring rulers or barbarian tribes, the significance of the war leader and military organization increased. The internal affairs of the temple also gave rise to an ever more differentiated expenditure. A separation came about between ideological and administrative tasks, even if the management of those lands that belonged directly to the deity generally remained in the hands of the priests. The kingdom arose. First in Egypt, then also in Mesopotamia, the need was felt to control the river system as a whole, for a territorial state. It was now that the great king appeared, the emperor, the 'Oriental despot' in the full sense of the term. He often took over the function of the high priest, and appointed himself representative of the deity, even the deity's incarnation or son. In his person, and – by clever government – in the ideal case in his person *alone,* the two branches composing the ruling class coincided: the hierarchy of priests and the hierarchy of officials, i.e. the ideologists and the civilian or military bureaucrats.

Engels maintains that this 'political supremacy has existed for any length of time only when it discharged its social functions'. 'However great the number of despotisms which rose and fell in Persia and India, each was fully aware that above all it was the entrepreneur responsible for the collective maintenance of irrigation throughout the river valleys, without which no

[26] Part Two, chap. IV.
[27] *Capital*, vol. 1, *loc. cit.*, p. 649, note 3.
[28] *Loc. cit.*, pp. 44–5.

agriculture was possible there'.[29] Bad government under such conditions meant bad harvests and rapid impoverishment of the population. But of course this Oriental despotism, like any other system of class rule, did not pursue the well-being of the people as its ultimate purpose. 'An Oriental government never had more than three departments: finance (plunder at home), war (plunder at home and abroad), and public works (provision for reproduction)'.[30] It is not for nothing that Engels places public works last, even though in all the ancient despotisms, particularly at their beginnings, there were emperors who appeared as progressive 'transformers of the world', and kept their Great House (this is how the name Pharaoh translates) in some kind of order.

If the original road to Oriental despotism was theocracy, the road proceeding from the inner structure of the original community itself in its ascent to civilization, this was never the only road. For those tribes who experienced its formative period not as settled tillers of the soil, but rather via the adventure of war-like migration, their mode of life led to a warrior king rather than a priesthood as its summit, this warrior king then also forming the sacred summit when conditions were favourable. When such tribes took possession of land by conquest and the subjection of an alien population, the gentile aristocracy grew into a state bureaucracy, with the new ruling class naturally being replenished almost always from other groups.

It was in this way, for example, that the realm of the Hittites arose in Asia Minor, in the second millenium B.C. This society in its first phase showed certain early feudal tendencies, just as, conversely, many Germanic states that were formed around the Mediterranean, e.g. by the Vandals under Genseric, displayed certain features of despotism. The organization of the ruling summit of the Hittite empire, the court, in particular, exhibits striking similarities with Merovingian and Carolingian France. The decisive difference was not at the top but rather at the bottom. As opposed to the Hittites, who in their later great empire based themselves on the exploitation of the northern Mesopotamian

---

[29] *Anti-Dühring*, Part Two, chap. IV.
[30] Engels to Marx, 6 June 1853; *Selected Correspondence*, Moscow 1965, p. 82.

and Syrian region, where the population reproduced itself in the Asiatic mode, the Franks had a population which derived partly from the dissolution of slavery, and partly from the Germanic tradition of familial production. The Hittite empire also shows that the basis of despotism need not be irrigation, but can be any form of large-scale cooperation, such as for example the co-operation in a systematic war of conquest practised by the Mongols, or cooperation in the subjugation of a conquered population. Despotism was more durable, however, when it was directly based on economic necessity.

One case particularly suitable as an example, on account of its classical clarity and transparency, is the economic despotism of the Incas, which began with the subjugation of an already civilized people in the Peruvian highlands by a foreign gentile aristocracy, and ended with a great empire that embraced almost the entire central and northern Andean region, together with stretches of the coast. This great empire was far more real than the Carolingian empire in its heyday. Control was secured by strategic highways across all parts of the country, which provided for surprisingly rapid communication. In the newly conquered areas, units of population were exchanged for others from the core regions of the empire. The language of the royal clan, which had grown to be a fairly numerous nobility owing to its privilege of polygamy, was established as the idiom of general intercourse. 'Presents' formed the basis of the luxury of the gilded capital, and an echo of this could be seen also in the provincial centres.

These tributes by themselves, even if they might once have been the basis of imperial rule, and later still represented the first returns from any new subjugation, were merely the outward sign of power, not its inner foundation. This foundation was the unlimited disposal of the Inca over the *total surplus labour of the population*, more than two-thirds of the total labour performed; this, too, was a realm where church and state hierarchies coincided. The economic base, whose extremely significant extension is what gives Inca rule its historical justification, was a highly developed maize cultivation on terraces, irrigated with great difficulty from glacial streams, maize being the queen of Indian food plants, as well as the focal point of the state magic that guaranteed the annual agricultural cycle. The 'son of the sun' and his highest dignitaries took part once a year in agricultural labour, symbolically wielding their golden hoes. (The Pharaohs, too, used to 'turn the first sod' for their edifices of state). For the country's more than ten million peasants, every working day was regulated and sanctioned by religion. How then did this vast exploitation function?

As in almost all economic despotisms, the ruler had the entire land at his disposal. Marx emphasized this 'royal property' in the soil as that kind of negation of the original common property in the East which was specific to this social formation. The original 'Asiatic form' of appropriation by the village community generally remained in existence for the immediate production process. But the actual reversal of power relations, of the power of disposal, can be recognized in all cases by the head of the village community, even when he is still elected from below, coming to assume the lowest rank in the official bureaucracy and being primarily answerable to those above, answerable according to regulation for tax collection and/or for the periodic recruitment of corvée workers, military forces, etc. The free members of the old village community (which had long had within it a suppression of women, of young people, and domestic slaves), including the elders, became *Gemeinfreien*, 'freemen' who may just as well be regarded as slaves of the state. Marx wrote in any case of the 'general slavery of the Orient'.[31] How is this general feature expressed in the case of the Incas, who moreover also had at the very bottom of their society a caste of domestic slaves for the most menial tasks?

In the Andean empire the state land was divided three ways. The first portion belonged directly to the Inca, i.e. it was directly government land. The second portion was dedicated to the temple, to the deity, and so was also immediately subject to the ruling power. The final and smallest portion remained with the *ayllus*, the village communities, for providing themselves with means of subsistence. In the villages, the elders still met together, and in their turn were in contact with the ordinary members, so that everyone might have the feeling of being heard and having agreed.

[31] *Grundrisse, loc. cit.*, p. 495.

Even the former village leaders had not disappeared. But they now formed a kind of minor nobility. By their function of raising labour-power for the state and temple fields, as well as for the numerous public works, and of regulating the simple reproduction of their units, they too escaped manual labour, and so formed the lowest stratum of the ruling class. Represented by the Inca, this class appropriated the surplus product in the form of labour-rent, a manner in which exploitation, domination and disposal over almost the entire reproduction process directly coincided.

The knowledge of domination was monopolized too, ensuring that information of functional importance remained secret. In ancient Mesopotamia, there was already an 'initiation' for bureaucratic apprentices, budding scribes. The priesthood, as the pinnacle of this system, successfully prevented any simplification of the complicated hieroglyphic writing that would make access to it any easier. The Indian Brahmans prosecuted the distribution of the Veda, the 'knowledge', among those not entitled to it, as one of the most heinous of sins. It was an Inca who gave this attitude its classical formulation: 'Little people must not be taught that which only the great may know'.

The Inca regime, then, which at the time of the Spanish invasion was still evidently just passing the zenith of its economic and cultural capacity, was more than simply a system of exploiting surplus labour. Evident as the privileges of the ruling system were, its direct and indirect parasitism, only a fraction of the surplus product went into these, even if this should not be underestimated. Still committed to the traditional role of the clan father, the Inca, Great Patriarch as he now was, remained aware that care for his subjects was the most important interest of his rule. He governed wisely and justly, not 'tyrannically', in other words: 'There was nothing that the will of the Inca could not alter – but this will did not give one person what was due to another'. And from the traditional village community he had inherited the responsibility not to let any individual suffer material want. The goods that were concentrated in the public storehouses were distributed among the population according to fixed principles, recognizing the equal claims of all 'freemen'. There were 'fields for widows and orphans'. Labour service was organized in such a way that the portion of the *ayllus* could be looked after properly. There was hardly any other system of domination that came so close to its possible optimum.

Even the highest dignitaries could approach the Inca only with a burden on their head. A Frenchman wrote: 'Apart from him and his family there are no other men; for all others have become parts of the economic machine and numbers in the administrative statistics'. Families and urban populations were registered in groups of tens, hundreds, and thousands, each of which had their chief. The duty of obedience and subordination was so total that violent punishment for deviant behaviour was an ever present possibility. Any action that went against the rules and laws of the statified social life was at the same time both a crime against the state and a sin against the deity, and was treated almost as rebellion, being generally punished with death. Nobles, for their part, were punished with dismissal from office. The worst that could befall them was thus the withdrawal of their share of power. There was also a system of internal spying.

The overall result was the historical 'de-skilling' of the immediate producers, who sank in a few generations to a position of apathetic dependence and loss of initiative, a condition which was never that of the free member of the archaic village community. Once deprived of their leadership, they stood almost as helpless before the Spanish conquistadores as the peasants of India before their various conquerors.

It is particularly worthwhile to examine economic despotism in somewhat greater detail (drawing on a survey by Eva Lips) in as much as this system is repeatedly characterized as socialist or communist, e.g. as 'religious state communism'. This is not completely senseless, as the Inca state really was superimposed on archaic relations, as well as providing the model for so much utopian writing. This characterization, moreover, should not be contradicted even by those who see the task of socialism as lying principally in establishing a more perfect welfare state than capitalism, and who for readily apparent reasons seek to obscure the question of the political structure of the *power of disposal* over our social wealth. The genuine parallels to our own social structure, which would be hard to deny, stretch as far as they do because our structure, though the other side of capitalism, is still not socialist.

It was a modern Peruvian, Carlos Delgado, a functionary of the then new and progressive military regime, who formulated the general conclusion a few years ago that all historical experience shows 'that enlightened minorities have always created repressive bureaucracies. In the name of one myth or another, this or that ideal, such bureaucracies – on account of their absolutism, their fantical intolerance and their insatiable hunger for power – are ultimately no longer different from any kind of ruling oligarchy of the past'.[32] Here Delgado was specifically summing up the experience of so many Latin American revolutions. Frantz Fanon has described the decay of African liberation movements after their victory in very similar terms, as a process of oligarchic bureaucratization. But the phenomenon is not new, but an old one, stretching back further then those ruling oligarchies of the past that were based on *private property*. If the classes bound up with private property are destroyed or rendered impotent, then the earlier element of the division of mental and manual labour emerges once again as an autonomous factor of class formation, and does so as long as this division of labour is at all reproduced. As in the early era, power comes from 'knowledge', not only of nature, but also of society itself. Why this 'knowledge', where it rules, is always organized as a bureaucratic hierarchy with the tendency to have a despotic summit, is something that requires later explanation. First of all we intend to make absolutely clear the *fact* that the rule of intellectual workers is one of the oldest historical realities, and one that is far from being superseded.

Gordon Childe quotes from one of a whole number of related Egyptian documents dating from the New Kingdom, i.e. more than 3000 years ago, the following admonition from a father to his son:

'Put writing in your heart that you may protect yourself from hard labour of any kind and be a magistrate of high repute. The scribe is released from manual tasks; it is he who commands. . . . Do you not hold the scribe's palette? That is what makes the difference between you and the man who handles an oar'.[33]

[32] *International Politics*, Belgrade, 4 April 1972, p. 22.
[33] *Loc. cit.*, p. 187.

Writing is the basis for social advance and membership of the ruling class of kings, priests and officials, which of course perpetuates itself ever more as it develops by recruitment from its own ranks. In Egypt and China, in particular, officials and scholars were one and the same. The class of Chinese state bureaucrats, the imperial officials, could very accurately be described as *literati*. Plato's 'rule by philosophers' was in fact no more than the idealized reception of the ancient Egyptian political superstructure, with simply a Spartan oligarchy of 'guardians' at the summit instead of the Pharaoh.

The fact that the overall social interest from which this leadership developed stood right from the start in irresolvable conflict with its own particular interests, found expression in the birth of the first reflective ideology, an ethics of the honest official, who remains aware of his responsibility and is moderate in the use of his privileges. In the 25th century B.C., the Egyptian Pta-Hotep compiled for his son, whom he wanted to bring up as a high official of the kingdom such as he was himself, a doctrine that represents perhaps the first list of the desirable 'qualities of leadership', the first catalogue of bureaucratic virtues. Pta-Hotep portrayed man's first duty as that of fitting into society, which must thus have been something of a problem. This enlightened man then recommended the following principles, not from any religious motive, but with regard to their usefulness here on earth: modesty above all, mixed with generosity, honour and love of truth, respect and obedience to parents, self-control, moderation in all things, propriety in dealings with superiors and inferiors alike. Finally he exhorted his son: 'Do not be proud of being a scholar – take council from the uneducated as well as from the educated'.[34] The final maxim is decisive for the stability of bureaucratic rule. When contact with those below is broken, the hour of rebellion is not far off.

The extent to which this ethic presupposes and affirms the new relations of domination as a given fact becomes exceedingly clear when we recognize its good council through the respect that was shown it by the Chinese Taoists. When the earlier and indigenous

[34] *Synchronoptische Weltgeschichte.*

form of economic despotism in China broke down in a struggle that lasted centuries, the intellectuals took cognisance of its contradictions in the form of a complex philosophical movement. While most of these thinkers were concerned to elaborate a *better system of rule*, the Taoists oriented themselves towards the disinherited of the former archaic community. From their position, they saw with extreme acuity the essence of the reversal that had taken place since the disappearance of the primitive community. In the *Tao Te Ching* by Lao Tzu, the book of the right way to let social life develop in harmony with nature, we can read:

'When the great way falls into disuse
There are benevolence and rectitude;
When cleverness emerges
There is great hypocrisy;
When the six relations are at variance
There are filial children;
When the state is benighted
There are loyal ministers'.
'Favour and disgrace are things that startle; . . .
Favour when it is bestowed on a subject serves to startle
as much as when it is withdrawn'.[35]

Lao Tzu saw the roots of the great confusion that had overtaken China in the period of the Warring States as lying in the new wisdom with its piety, cleverness, rectitude, skill and desire for profit. He counterposed to it the idealized traditional wisdom of the tribe, which 'lets things happen' instead of 'making things happen', is 'wise' instead of 'learned', and still remains close to the female, maternal element. His sage embodies the virtue that

' . . .gives them [the myriad creatures] life yet claims no
possession;
It benefits them yet exacts no gratitude;
It is the steward yet exercises no authority.
Such is called the mysterious virtue'.

---

[35] Penguin edition, 1963, chapters XVIII and XIII. The 'six relations' are those of father and son, elder and younger brother, husband and wife.

'Therefore the sage benefits them yet exacts no gratitude,
Accomplishes his task yet lays claim to no merit'.

'Therefore the sage takes the left-hand tally, but exacts no
payment from the people.
The man of virtue takes charge of the tally;
The man of no virtue takes charge of exaction'.[36]

'Ever generous in all things, not confined in any dealings',
this was the sage as defined to the Taoist Chuang Tzu. He is the
opposite of the scholarly bureaucrat and reveals the latter as a
figure of domination even in his enlightened idealization.

But if the whole discussion over the character of the 'sage', the
right and proper behaviour of the educated, is a discussion by
those experts who are called upon to govern the social life of men
in the state, this is characteristic of the origin of the Chinese ruling
class, its provenance from the division of labour and cooperation
itself, unmediated by private property. Naturally, private property
came in time to play a growing role in most economic despotisms,
and in China this meant private property in land as well. Yet it
never subjected the state to itself, or remodelled it according to its
own basic interests. The Chinese empire could expropriate the
great landowners every few hundred years in an agrarian reform
(even the Russian reform of 1861 would have been impossible in a
truly feudal state). The privileges and abuses of the officials were
the most solid road to well-being, and to property, in the ancient
economic despotisms. In the African countries, too, those that are
today taking the non-capitalist road, 'the energetic measures to
educate and reeducate the officials' meet with 'serious resistance,
conditioned by the widespread view of state service as a source of
personal enrichment'.[37] The very same problem is involved when
Frantz Fanon describes the transformation of the local African
intelligentsia which took place after the revolution of national
liberation, even of those elements who were still national and
revolutionary, into a 'bureaucratic bourgeoisie'.

[36] *Ibid.*, chapters LI, LXXVII, LXXIX. The 'left-hand tally' was the half
held by the creditor.
[37] *World Marxist Review*, 1972, no. 7.

Furthermore, the career of official in ancient China was open to every citizen who had the intellectual and economic capacity to prepare himself for the regular state examinations in official ideology and administrative doctrine, and so become a 'scholar'. In this way, a significant percentage of officials was newly arisen, particularly at some periods in Chinese history. This meant a gain in stability for the ruling power. 'The way that the Catholic church of the middle ages built its hierarchy out of the best brains in the nation, without regard to status, birth, or wealth, was likewise a major means of reinforcing the rule of the priests and suppressing the laity. The more a dominant class is able to absorb the best people from the dominated classes, the more solid and dangerous its rule'.[38]

Marx, however, though this is his own observation, did not concern himself more closely with a question that is not answered by the reproduction of the Christian church hierarchy, i.e. whether 'philosophers' (as in Plato's *Republic*), 'scholars' or bureaucrats can rule the state *independently,* even if he recognized this as a fact in the case of the Egyptian priesthood.[39] From the standpoint of a bourgeois society completely stamped by private property, he saw this archaic situation as having no relevance to modern problems. He had also studied the Asiatic mode of production predominantly from the standpoint that it does not lead to private property, and only touched in passing on the political structure that arises under such conditions in the shape of the institution of the despot as the *de facto* proprietor of the land. But the despot is in fact only the representative and administrative summit of a ruling class, which stretches down through the church and state bureaucracy to the tax collectors and village elders as well as to the heads of the official corporations of merchants and craftsmen. What is involved here is a *ruling class* organized as an ideological and administrative state apparatus. In that era, the division of society into rulers and ruled was in no way simply a division into rich and poor. Rich people who were nothing more than rich were to be found almost only in a similarly ambiguous position to that of the Jewish financiers in

[38] *Capital*, vol. 3, chap. 36.
[39] See above, p. 71.

early capitalist Europe. But if they served as high officials, in order to have influence, then they faced the characteristic danger of being suddenly cast into exile, prison, or put to death. In any case, we have already seen that Marx considered the rule of mental labour over manual as always a fundamental aspect of class society, even though in his controversy with Bakunin he rejected the possibility that this could acquire a significance of its own, at least for the epoch beyond capitalism.

We shall now see how this whole problem developed concretely in the practice of the victorious Russian revolution, and go into Lenin's own train of thought in his final years. For already *before* Stalin, in the first years after the civil war, the new social structure could already be seen in its basic outlines, such as it exists right through to today. Stalinism in the narrower sense, as a period of massive application of physical terror, tends rather to conceal this structure than to reveal it; it is the same as with Cromwell or Napoleon. If we therefore focus on Lenin's struggle with the new conditions, we are not turning away from certain 'bad things', but seeking rather to get to the very centre of Soviet social relations.

3

From Agricultural to Industrial Despotism

Capitalism is cosmopolitan, and tends therefore in the long run to effect a decline in national tradition. An anti-imperialist people's revolution, on the other hand, can only be national in the highest degree, even and precisely when the working class that takes part in it is internationalist in spirit. When the Bolsheviks seized power, they were clear that they were more than just the representatives of the working-class interest, that they had in fact undertaken the task of *solving the problems of the Russian people as a whole, creating a new Russia out of the old*. They had therefore to go 'through' the old Russia, to remould it step by step using the material that they found to hand. The whole history of a people, the structure of domination under which it first became a state, the mode of production that determined its labour process – all this is expressed in its national character. Just as the communist movement in the West can only raise to a higher level something which is already there, in this case capitalist private property, so the revolutionary movement in Russia equally had to take up its own inheritance. '*Aufhebung*' is not an abstract demand. The more backward the country that sets out on the non-capitalist road, the more the character of this '*Aufhebung*' emerges as an inescapable destiny. It is not primarily the will of the vanguard that decides what will disappear and how fast, what will be preserved and what will be raised to a higher level.

The Bolsheviks had scarcely any choice. It is not at all their fault, therefore, if today we can see that the social life of Russia, and the entire Soviet Union, will have to be revolutionized even more than it has been so far, before life there assumes even an approximately socialist character. The course of the Russian revolution has not basically refuted Lenin's optimism, and not at all if one thinks how far the countries of the late capitalist West still are from a harmonious form of life. But the Soviet Union may be overtaken by the attempt begun only later to create a new China from the old. The mobilization that was forced on Soviet society in the first three decades of its existence already began very early on to resemble that medieval instrument of torture, the iron maiden. Not only does it inhibit the normal growth of the powerful social body, but it wounds it incessantly with scarcely blunted barbs.

Yet there can be no meaningful and conscious solution to the Soviet problem, which concerns socialists the world over, without a deep understanding for the new Russia's process of development, for the courage and will-power of Lenin's Bolshevism, for its positive and creative achievements. For this, however, as we can only just indicate here, at least a minimal acquaintance with Russian history is needed; this history has never stood under a lucky star since the decline of the once brilliant Kievian state of Rus, but has been a history of constant princely wars, the rule of the Mongols, and the despotism of the Moscow Tsars, who began their career as tax collectors for the Golden Horde. The most basic impulse of Lenin and his colleagues, as of the three generations of Russian revolutionaries who preceded them, arose from their feeling of a moral responsibility to put the talents of their people to better use. The naive poster from the revolutionary period in which a half-peasant, half-proletarian Lenin is sweeping the vermin of monarchs, landlords and capitalists from the globe with a broom, truly expresses the deepest level of political motivation by which the leading Bolsheviks were inspired. There is a lot that can be said about the objective contradictions that did not let them get as close to their goal as they hoped, both emotionally and theoretically. But one can see from their biographies and faces, from Lenin through to Stalin (unfortunately too many of us have never seen a portrait of most of them), that Russia gave in them many of its best people, and it is difficult to imagine any elite who could have fulfilled their chosen task better.

Before we pursue, in the present chapter, how Lenin wrestled with the socialist perspective of the revolution in the compromises that prove necessary for its survival, we must recall once again the, at first sight, astonishing fact, that the leaders of the Russian revolution originally had no very precise idea of the character of the powerful pre-capitalist character of Russian society. If a subjectively tragic shadow lies over Lenin's last years, this is because, on top of having his illness weighing on him, he saw himself having become the plaything of *symptoms* which he did not comprehend in their 'second order essence' – to use a category from his own philosophical writings. This partial helplessness did not just affect Lenin. After his death a large portion of the old guard accompanied the rise of Stalin with endless discussions about an impending 'Thermidor', a threat of *bourgeois* counter-revolution on Stalin's part. Even in Bukharin's belated rage over the 'new Ghenghis Khan', the Bolsheviks had only an inkling of the true nature of Stalinism. What shocked them was not merely the specific irrationality of the despotic terror, but rather the irrationality of the phenomenon as a whole, that it could possibly have arisen out of the proletarian revolution for which they had spent their lives. They no longer understood the process they were taking part in. And yet their dilemma was rooted in the Leninist tradition, to which Stalin was rarely completely unjustified in appealing.

It would require a special monograph, if one that is highly necessary, to present afresh the specific framework of Lenin's theory of the Russian revolution, i.e. the specific synthesis of Russian history, economic and class structure this involved, from the standpoint of the post-revolutionary experience. It would appear that Lenin overestimated the *degree* of capitalist develop-ment in Russia at the beginning of the 20th century in a way similar to that in which Marx and Engels did for Western Europe in the mid-19th century. It would be particularly necessary to investigate whether he was not premature in concluding from the penetration of commodity production and wage-labour into the Russian village the existence of a *capitalist class* within the peasantry, i.e. one producing for the sake of surplus-*value*. In any case, by focussing on the new, capitalist formation of Russian society, Lenin failed to recognize the full specificity of its old, pre-capitalist character. In *The Development of Capitalism in Russia,* he paid detailed attention to the germs of the new formation in pre-capitalist relations, but he treated these from the basic assumption that Russia had embarked on the West European road 'from the middle ages into modern times' that Marx had analysed, simply with a certain delay. On this assumption he certainly saw peculiarities of detail, but not *the* basic peculiarity of Russia.

I have already quoted one of Lenin's numerous assertions about the Asiatic features of Russian relations. Yet since he assumed one and the same social formation for the middle ages from Western Europe through to Asia, explicitly so in his 1919 lecture on the state, a formation that he designated as serfdom, he could not apply the expression 'Asiatic', as Marx and Engels had done, to the basic socio-economic *structure,* but only to certain superstructural phenomena in the state and mode of life of Russian society. The fundamental anchorage of these therefore escaped him. The best proof that this was indeed the situation is the genuine surprise Lenin and many other communists experienced when faced with the rebirth of the old bureaucracy within the post-revolutionary Soviet institutions.

As opposed to Marx and Engels, Lenin had no general theoretical concept of the traditional 'Asiatic mode of production' as a socio-economic formation. Given his unbounded respect for Marx and Engels, it is highly improbable that he was familiar with this conception but had tacitly rejected it. He simply never discusses it. In the lecture on the state which I just mentioned,[1] Lenin expressly bases himself only on Engels' *Origin of the Family,* where Engels does not touch on the problem of the Asiatic mode. Lenin was of course familiar with the passage in the *Preface to The Critique of Political Economy* where Marx classes this without comment as the first of four formations of class society, but he could not have been familiar with the theory pertaining to this, which was developed in the then inaccessible *Grundrisse,* only surfacing in *Capital* in a few isolated remarks. Similarly, Lenin could not have known the detailed drafts Marx made for his ultimately very short letter to Vera Zasulich of 1881, where Marx saw the fundamental

[1] *Collected Works*, vol. 29, pp. 470–88.

character of the traditional Russian mode of production as analogous to the Indian, and stressed the typical complementary relationship between the fragmented patriarchal peasantry, still redistributing the land in their village communities, i.e. possessing it collectively, and the central despotism. In Lenin's first major text against the Narodniks, he went so far as to reduce the ramified system of Tsarist bureaucratic despotism simply to the agency, if if not already of the bourgeoisie, then at least of the compromise between landlords and capitalists, as if this despotism was simply a case of Western European absolutism.

The Tsarist state machine had always been *more* in pre-capitalist times than the executive organ of the nobility, *more* than a 'serf state'. And beside its modern function, which Lenin of course did see correctly, it maintained till the end of its days an *independent socio-economic relationship* to its historic peasant base, this persisting *alongside* the serf relationship (which presupposed the Tsars). This was precisely the sense in which Marx and Engels called the old Russia 'semi-Asiatic'. Firstly, the feudal estates with peasant serfs comprised only one section of the peasantry. There were always state peasants as well, and their relationship to the Tsar was not a feudal one. Both categories, moreover, were exploited by the state in a poll tax of typically 'Oriental' character, via the bureaucratic pyramid that stretched right down to the village elders. Secondly, the natural economy of the landed estate no more gave rise to any organic overall social interconnection than did the limited peasant economy confined to local micro-markets, since the towns were almost completely mere adminstrative and garrison stations, bureaucratic bases without a burgher class.

The great Tsars, such as Ivan and Peter, were the most effective of despots. Whether it was his capital that Peter was having built, or – as is vividly described by the Soviet proletarian writer Andrei Platonov – the Yepifan locks, he always recruited labour-power by the arbitrary summoning of the peasants, just like all other enterprising despots since the Pharaohs.[2] He could not proceed

---

[2] *The Yepifan Locks* is the title of one of Platonov's best-known novels, published in the 1930s. Peter the Great's construction feats are seen very much through the perspective of the Stalinist Five-Year Plans.

otherwise. And whenever one of the Tsars really did make use of the possibilities that his objective function offered him, the nobles, even those 'of Rurik's race', proved themselves at once his most unwilling slaves and his most prominent ones. It was the general rule to whip them paternally. Since Ivan the Terrible, who to a large extent bankrupted the higher nobility that had already been broken by his father, the Tsars several times created new strata of bureaucratic nobles from the cliques of their *parvenus,* and made them into landed proprietors. Only gradually, as also in India, did they acquire their simultaneously feudal quality, and they never cut the despotic umbilical cord. Any noble who was not content to stagnate among his peasants, had always to give the latent foundation of his landlord role practical effect and enter the Tsar's service.

At the beginning of this century, therefore, Russian society had three formations superimposed on one another:

(a) at the bottom, the Asiatic formation: the Tsarist bureaucracy together with the Orthodox state church and the peasantry.

(b) on top of this, since the abolition of serfdom, an only half liquidated feudal formation, which had however never fully extricated itself from the earlier first formation: ex-landlords and ex-serfs in conflict over the land.

(c) finally, uppermost, and concentrated in a few towns, the modern capitalist formation: industrial bourgeoisie and wage-labourers. (In the village, the antithesis between capital and wage-labour was still not dominant, and had only in rare cases shed its patriarchal shell).

It is the relation between the two pre-capitalist formations that led Engels to call Russia 'semi-Asiatic in her condition, manners, traditions, and institutions'.[3] Naturally, by the beginning of the 20th century this was all mortally undermined and glossed over with a European veneer, particularly as far as the Tsarist side of the basic 'Asiatic' relationship was concerned. But what necessarily survived, when the capitalists were chased out together with these landed proprietors who were yesterday still semi-bureaucratic,

[3] 'The Turkish Question' (1853), in Karl Marx, *The Eastern Question*, London 1897 and 1969, p. 21.

semi-feudal, and had scarcely yet transformed themselves even into Junkers? What survived (later to be socially ruined, but by no means remoulded) was the peasant basis of Tsarist despotism, along with its 'petty bourgeois' periphery in the non-industrial towns of the provinces (the traditional Russian *meshanin* – petty-bourgeois – was no potential bourgeois), as well as the 'countless army of officials, which swarms over Russia and plunders it and here constitutes a real social estate'.[4] *This* is all part of the 'petty-bourgeois elemental force' which the Bolsheviks confronted after their victory: 100 million peasants and 15 million petty bourgeois against their proletarian basis of 5 or 6 million. What Lenin wrote about peasant Russia in 1921 bore a different accent from *The Development of Capitalism in Russia.*

'Look at the map of the R.S.F.S.R. There is room for dozens of large civilized states in those vast areas which lie to the north of Vologda, the south-east of Rostov-on-Don and Saratov, the south of Orenburg and Omsk, and the north of Tomsk. They are a realm of patriarchalism, and semi- and downright barbarism. And what about the peasant backwoods of the rest of Russia, where scores of versts of country track, or rather of trackless country, lie between the villages and the railways, i.e., the material link with the big cities, large-scale industry, capitalism and culture? Isn't that also an area of wholesale patriarchalism, Oblomovism and semi-barbarism'?[5] Over these same conditions Engels had written in 1875: 'Such a complete isolation of the individual communities from one another, which creates throughout the country similar, but the very opposite of common, interests, is the natural basis for *Oriental despotism,* and from India to Russia this form of society, wherever it prevailed, has always produced it and always found its complement in it. Not only the Russian state in general, but even its specific form, Tsarist despotism . . . is the necessary and logical product of Russian social conditions'.[6]

Was it not inevitable that this tremendous bloc, the most ancient Russian economy only in its earliest capitalist ferment,

[4] Engels, 'On Social Relations in Russia', in Marx and Engels, *Selected Works* in three volumes, Moscow 1969, vol. 2, p. 390.

[5] 'The Tax in Kind', *Collected Works*, vol. 32, pp. 349–50.

[6] *Loc. cit.*, p. 394.

should also levy an institutional tribute on the Bolsheviks? Did it not force them, at least in a transitional stage, to replace the Tsarist bureaucracy with a new one, which Lenin was later to describe as only 'lightly anointed with Soviet oil', in order to keep the gigantic empire alive under the new power, after it had been devastated by war and civil war, starved and disorganized? Against the arising Soviet bureaucracy, which he himself had necessarily helped to found, Lenin was to lead his last great struggle, and the only completely unsuccessful one of his life, since he was himself standing on the very ground that he sought to turn upside down. The Bolshevik seizure of power in Russia could lead to no other *social structure* than that now existing, and the more one tries to think through the stations of Soviet history, which would lead us too far afield for our present purpose, the harder it becomes to draw a limit short of even the most fearsome excesses, and to say that what falls on the other side was absolutely avoidable.

With regard to the basic situation which, owing to the productivity of 'late capitalism', persists *through to today*, let us proceed once again, from the conception of Marx and Engels of the preconditions for socialism, not forgetting here that behind whatever technique is characteristic of a given point in time, which can of course be destroyed, it is the historically developed productive powers of man that are the sole decisive quantity. The Narodnik Tkachov maintained against Engels that the social revolution in Russia would be far more easy than in the West; in Russia the power of capital existed only in embryo, so that the working people had only to struggle with the political power, i.e. Tsarist despotism. Engels replied that to annihilate all class distinctions 'requires not only a proletariat that carries out this revolution, but also a bourgeoisie in whose hands the productive forces of society have developed so far that they allow of the final destruction of class distinctions. . . . Only at a certain level of development of the productive forces of society, an even very high level for our modern conditions, does it become possible to raise production to such an extent that the abolition of class distinctions can be a real progress, can be lasting without bringing about stagnation or even decline in the mode of social production'.[7]

[7] *Loc. cit.*, p. 387.

It had been the constant theme of the Mensheviks since the 1905 revolution that in this sense Russia was not ripe for socialism. Not only Plekhanov, but Gorky himself, in the 'semi-Mensheik' *Novaya Zhizn,* reproached Lenin for staking the promising political future of the Russian working class on an ambitious but premature adventure which could only end in social catastrophe, i.e. in the destruction of the proletariat by a task beyond its strength. It would be entoiled by peasant Russia. As was shown by the attitude of Zinoviev and Kamenev before the October insurrection, this fear reached right into the Bolshevik party itself. Zinoviev had been Lenin's most trusted companion, right to the very end of the emigration years. Lenin was of course familiar with the 'incontrovertible proposition', as he called it,[8] that the development of the productive forces in Russia had not yet reached the level required for socialism, as much so as any of his opponents. Before we come to his counter-*arguments,* we must just emphasize that aspect of his position that stood at the beginning and end of all arguments, and which all opportunists, most recently again in France in 1968, must reject as 'voluntarist' if they are not to blush with shame.

It was precisely with respect to the decisive strategic question of the seizure of power in Russia, where the new state power would first of all be just the down-payment on a *distant* socialist future, that Lenin pronounced that 'Anyone who fears defeat on the eve of a great struggle can call himself a socialist only out of sheer mockery of the workers'.[9] And as if to block the final escape route for those 'responsible politicians' afraid to look danger in the eye, he commented a year before his death on the *Recollections* of the Left Menshevik Sukhanov:

'Napoleon, I think, wrote: *"On s'engage et puis . . . on voit"*. Rendered freely this means: "First engage in a serious battle and then see what happens". Well, we did first engage in a serious battle in October 1917, and then saw such details of development (from the standpoint of world history they were certainly details) as the Brest peace, the New Economic Policy, and so forth. And

[8] 'Our Revolution', *Collected Works*, vol. 33, p. 478.
[9] 'New Times and Old Mistakes in a New Guise', *Collected Works*, vol. 33, p. 24.

now there can be no doubt that in the main we have been victorious'.[10] 'Now', in 1923 – but in 1917?

'Our Sukhanovs', Lenin continued, 'not to mention Social-Democrats still farther to the right, never even dream that revolutions could [not] be made otherwise'.

It is true that the Bolsheviks came to power *with* the will of the masses. And in his final year Lenin justified their action in remarkably reserved terms, indeed almost defensively, and thereby so much the more impressively. He referred to Europe, to its eruption into the barbarism of the World War that lay so shortly behind, and asked: 'What about a people that found itself in a revolutionary situation such as that created during the first imperialist war? Might it not, influenced by the hopelessness of its situation, fling itself into a struggle that would offer it at least some chance of securing conditions for the further development of civilization that were somewhat unusual? . . . the opportunity to create the fundamental requisites of civilization in a different way from that of the West-European countries'?[11] And Lenin immediately went on to indicate that constellation from which the Bolsheviks could draw their most comprehensive justification, the circumstance that Russia lay between Europe and 'the revolutions maturing or partly already begun in the East', 'in a position which enabled us to achieve precisely that combination of a "peasant war" with the working-class movement suggested in 1856 by no less a Marxist than Marx himself as a possible prospect for Prussia'.[12] Lenin, moreover, confirmed several times after October, as if in paraphrase of Engels' polemic against Tkachov, that it would be easier to seize power in Russia than in the West, but far harder to maintain it, and almost infinitely harder to create the economic base for it that was ultimately necessary. *How* he saw the solution of this task, and *what consequences were unavoidable* if the Bolsheviks did not want to turn back half way, if they wanted to stick to the *other, non-capitalist* road to civilize Russia – all this is a question of very topical interest for that

[10] 'Our Revolution', *Collected Works*, vol. 33, p. 480.
[11] *Ibid.*, p. 478.
[12] *Ibid.*

'mastery of the past' which is indispensable for the communist movement today.

The most important aspect of this issue is as follows. Given the balance of class forces in Russia, and its entire economy, Lenin *had* right from the start to take a *different attitude towards the role of the state in the transition period* than that of Marx. In the developed capitalist society that Marx assumed, the dictatorship of the proletariat was supposed simply to break the political and military resistance of the bourgeoisie, a bourgeoisie which was necessarily isolated as a class, since it was already economically superfluous. In reality, however, even in France, the workers' power, if it had won its battle for survival in Paris, would have confronted the necessity for a centrally organized struggle for the economic transformation of the rural and urban petty production sector. And the mere ideological influence of the workers concentrated in the provincial centres on a parcellized peasant property that was far more strongly anchored in French tradition than in the Russian, would similarly have needed to be supplemented by a systematic pressure of re-education. The old relations of production could not yet have been dissolved simply by example, or even by industry providing a technique that encouraged amalgamation.

In Russia the restructuring of the predominantly patriarchal and petty-bourgeois economy and culture, and first of all its 'external' subjection to proletarian hegemony, was the condition of survival for the workers' state, and had therefore to become the decisive function of the dictatorship. This was a gigantic task of political *organization*, the task of 'organizing the unity of the nation' as Marx had formulated it with regard to the Commune, at that time however on the assumption that all that was required was to find the adequate form for an economic connection that was in essentials already provided by the comprehensive national market. Here we can offer no opinion as to how far that union of existing manufacturing enterprises (still extremely scattered geographically!) and communes from the bottom up could have served in France as the means to achieve a unified socialist economy. In Russia, however, the national market, both in its volume and its commodity structure, was still very far from providing a basis for national unity. In particular, economic alliance with urban large-scale industry was not an indispensable condition of reproduction for the overwhelming part of the rural population. If we leave aside the textile industry, they got by principally with provincial and village handicrafts. In conditions such as these, a system of workers' councils, functioning from the bottom up, in a large-scale industry concentrated in a few localities, would inevitably have led to a particular corporative alliance *against* the majority of the nation. It was not fortuitious that Lenin later used the expression 'alliance between the peasants and the workers led by proletarian rule',[13] a leadership *which had necessarily to stand also above the particular interests of the workers.* (Though this did not necessarily exclude a system of councils *within* the factories. If in the immediate aftermath of October these showed a tendency to consume the productive equipment, i.e. the industrial substance, given the economic and cultural situation of the working masses and in view of sabotage from the managerial, economic and technical specialists, that was simply a specific aspect of what is unfortunately a very far-reaching characteristic. The Yugoslav case proves that a combination of central state power and factory councils, even if not the optimal solution, is at any rate *possible*).

In the meantime, the construction of a new state machine has proved unavoidable, everywhere that a new social order has arisen based on the workers and peasants. Lenin, who recognized this early on in Russia, gave Marxism a new twist that had not been foreseen from the orthodox standpoint, and he could not have done otherwise. His decision had already been made in the entire work he carried out to create the Bolshevik party of a new type. It was not understood in the West, even by Left Socialists such as Rosa Luxemburg, precisely because it already represented the new type of state *in nuce,* the type Russia needed for its renovation under the 'hegemony of the proletariat'. Behind Lenin's conception (formally but wrongly derived from Marx and Engels) of the relationship between state and economy, state and organization of labour, state and distribution under socialism, there stood in the

[13] 'New Times and Old Mistakes in a New Guise', *Collected Works*, vol. 33, p. 23.

last analysis that minimum condition for the hegemony of the proletariat that he summed up after the revolution in the phrase that the Bolsheviks had to 'learn to run the country'.[14]

Lenin's *State and Revolution,* representing his immediate theoretical preparation for the capture of power, was fondly quoted against later developments by those illusionists who held in their polemic to the traditional elements of the position it developed. But on the decisive question it conceives Soviet power in just the way that this was then being created. This decisive question Lenin saw in summer 1917 as being 'whether the old state machine . . . shall remain, or be *destroyed* and replaced by a *new* one', with the revolutionary class 'commanding, governing with the aid of a *new* machine'.[15] In as much as he was still convinced that it would be possible to do without bureaucracy, this new state machine certainly appeared simply as 'an organization of the armed workers, after the type of the Commune'. But Lenin also speaks already of an 'apparatus' of armed workers, and of ministries being 'replaced . . . by committees of specialists working under the sovereign, all-powerful Soviets of Workers' and Soldiers' Deputies'.[16] Yet how could these committees, the later People's Commissariats, persist in this subordinate position vis-à-vis the Soviets, if Lenin attributed to the state of the transition period the following function that would inevitably bring it into conflict with many of the *immediate* popular interests that were represented in the Soviets? 'Until the "higher" phase of communism arrives, the socialists demand the *strictest* control by society *and by the state* over the measure of labour and the measure of consumption'. 'Of course, bourgeois right in regard to the distribution of *consumer* goods inevitably presupposes the existence of the *bourgeois state,* for right is nothing without an apparatus capable of *enforcing* the observance of standards of right. It follows that under communism there remains for a time not only bourgeois right, but even the bourgeois state, without the bourgeoisie!'[17] Here there is the unmistakable voice of compulsion, a compulsion

---

[14] 'Integrated Economic Plan', *Collected Works,* vol. 32, p. 145.
[15] *Collected Works,* vol. 25, p. 486.
[16] *Op. cit.,* pp. 84–6.
[17] *Ibid.,* pp. 470 and 471.

directed not against the former ruling classes, but one that can only be addressed to the 'backward elements' of the working class and the people itself. Here Lenin takes over those functions of the state which for Marx were to be carried out by 'free association'. This 'free association' for Lenin is something that does not enter at all into at least the first phase of communism, for he speaks expressly of 'the conversion of *all* citizens into workers and other employees of *one* huge "syndicate" – the whole state – and the complete subordination of the entire work of this syndicate to a genuinely democratic state, *the state of the Soviets of Workers' and Soldiers' Deputies'*.[18] 'All that is required is that they should work equally, do their proper share of work, and get equal pay.[19] And as if Lenin expressly wanted to vindicate the bourgeoisie dispatched by Marx, he adds, indicating that this is of course not the final goal: 'The whole of society will have become a single office and a single factory, with equality of labour and pay.'[20] Finally we have the generalization Lenin formulated already just before writing *State and Revolution*: 'Socialism is merely state-capitalist monopoly *which is made to serve the interests of the whole people* and has to that extent *ceased* to be capitalist monopoly'.[21]

These are the foundations on which our system still rests today. We have no need to keep the stress on state *capitalism*. There was a special sense in which Lenin applied this category to genuine capitalist elements who were linked in various ways to the proletarian state as concessionaries. Related to socialism as a whole, however, as he conceived it here, this 'state capitalism' meant nothing more than state disposal over all social funds and products, which had been divested by the revolution of their capital character. Despite occasional experiments, there has never been any question in the countries of actually existing socialism of production being for any kind of *profit* on the state's part. What is at stake has never been primarily surplus-value, but simply surplus product. The state plan primarily prescribes quantities of use-

[18] p. 470.
[19] p. 473.
[20] p. 474.
[21] 'The Impending Catastrophe and How to Combat It', *Collected Works*, vol. 25, p. 358.

values, and the competition of economic functionaries for bureaucratic ascendancy passes by way of production figures and tons. Only secondarily is our state the collective *bourgeois,* in its capacity as society's *employer.* When Trotsky assumed that at some point the functionaries in charge would seek to appropriate the factories *privately,* he only provided proof of the anachronistic character of the model with which he sought to grasp the Stalin period.

Unusual therefore as it might seem at first sight, exploitation in our system is a *political* phenomenon, a phenomenon of distribution of political power. In his *State and Revolution,* of course, Lenin neither could nor would recognize this, any more than Marx in his earlier dispute with Bakunin. The new functions of the state, Lenin insisted, would in no way allow any rights or accoutrements of superiority, not a shimmer of privilege. Social control would not be conducted by a state of officials.[22] These were no mere pretexts. After the revolution Lenin struggled against 'commissarized' communists, against 'communist dignitaries'. It was just that he conceived the bureaucratic outcrops of the workers' state, which he looked straight in the eye, as an unavoidable tribute to the old society, somewhat in the sense depicted by Platonov, the writer we have already mentioned, in his satire *Gradov City.* Lenin insisted time and again, above all, that the new Soviet bureaucracy was the superstructure of the *old* peasant fragmentation, which in fact represented only one of its roots, the negative one. It compelled the state to build up within a few years central institutions with tens of thousands of officials, who in their majority could only be recruited from the traditional bureaucratic estate.

But was Lenin wrong in refusing to derive the bureaucracy also from the character of the new state power? In April 1918 he wrote: 'The more resolutely we now have to stand for a ruthlessly firm government, for the dictatorship of individuals *in definite processes of work,* in definite aspects of *purely executive* functions, the more varied must be the forms and methods of control from below in order to counteract every shadow of a possibility of distorting the

[22] *The State and Revolution, loc. cit.,* pp. 420-1 and 470.

principles of Soviet government, in order repeatedly and tirelessly to weed out bureaucracy'.[23] But if, as Marx had shown, the labour process was governed despotically within the factory, and if Engels and Lenin accepted this as an objective *datum* that would persist beyond capitalism, then if this factory system was applied to the labour process of society as a whole, no balance between 'above' and 'below' would at all be possible. Even the very use of the term 'below' indicates relations of domination. Lenin's depiction of socialism as a state monopoly at the service of the whole people is certainly a reaction to Russian society, but *even without* the specific Russian backwardness it could only lead to a socialism characterized by obedient subordination of the producers to a *political* managerial pyramid erected to manage social labour. In place of a control from below by the masses, there appeared early on the study of mass *opinion* from above. The apparatus had to have its ears tuned to the masses, or else it could be corrected only by their insurrection, as most recently in Poland in 1970.

This *general* problem of state monopoly we shall still postpone for a while. It concerns all present-day socialist movements. Just as the real essence of capitalism only appeared in 'pure' form in the bourgeois republic, so the essence of 'socialist' state monopoly, its hard kernel, only came to light on the basis of the attempted democratic revolution in Czechoslovakia in 1968, as a reality that is still not dissoluble. It was not by chance that the leading economic theorist of the reform movement, Ota Sik, did *not* want genuine workers' councils, but rather a regime of directors, merely with councils attached to them. But since we are at the moment still living under the form of absolutism that was displayed immediately after the October revolution under the influence of Russian conditions, and was consolidated after the civil war, we must still pursue further what is universal in the Russian peculiarities.

What Lenin founded and Stalin built up was not the superstructure of any developed industry, in the way that there is now a political struggle between 'conservatives' and 'progressives', but rather the superstructure of *industrialization*, the tool for creating

---

[23] 'The Immediate Tasks of the Soviet Government', *Collected Works*, vol. 27, p. 275.

the economic foundations of socialism which were lacking, however this socialism was itself to be understood. *The decisive objective fact, reflected in Lenin's revision of Marx's concept of socialism and his conception of the state, was the absence of a bourgeois development of the productive forces,* the absence of capitalist work habits, discipline and skill in the broadest sense. In May 1918, when the comparatively little large-scale industry that Russia possessed was *not yet* at a standstill, as it was after the civil war, Lenin developed the following line of thought against the 'Left Communists': 'Socialism is inconceivable without large-scale capitalist engineering based on the latest discoveries of modern science. It is inconceivable without planned state organization, which keeps tens of millions of people to the strictest observance of a unified standard in production and distribution' – as represented at that time by Germany, and in the Stalin era by America. 'At the same time socialism is inconceivable unless the proletariat is the ruler of the state. . . . And history . . . has taken such a peculiar course that it *has given birth* in 1918 to two unconnected halves of socialism existing side by side like two future chickens in the single shell of international imperialism. In 1918 Germany and Russia have become the most striking embodiment of the material realization of the economic, the productive and the socio-economic conditions for socialism, on the one hand, and the political conditions, on the other.'[24]

At that time, none of the Bolsheviks had accepted that their one 'half' would remain alone, a view that from the standpoint of historical materialism one could hardly then go on regarding as a 'condition for socialism'. But in the period of daily 'waiting' for the revolution in the West, Lenin already formulated that programme which was to prove Stalin's contribution to world history: 'While the revolution in Germany is still slow in "coming forth", our task is to study the state capitalism of the Germans, to spare *no effort* in copying it and not shrink from adopting *dictatorial* methods to hasten the copying of it. Our task is to hasten this copying even more than Peter (*sic*) hastened the copying of Western culture by barbarian Russia, and we must not hesitate to use barbarous

[24] '"Left-Wing" Childishness and the Petty-Bourgeois Mentality', *Collected Works*, vol. 27, pp. 239–40.

methods in fighting barbarism'. In 1921 Lenin added: 'So long as there is no revolution in other countries, it would take us decades' to extricate ourselves . . .'.[25]

At least for the overwhelming majority of the Russian population of the time, the peasantry, this meant the prospect of decades of revolution from above, in the 'interest' of an unborn third or fourth generation. It meant that they could not be spared the pains of primitive accumulation of capital. In the 'second revolution' of collectivization, the peasant masses were the object of progress. Even the poverty of the village was torn apart only by a machine of violence which would have made Peter the Great turn green with envy. Forced collectivization so oppressed the Russian village that the gigantic Soviet Union still cannot do without American wheat. When Lenin died, Gorky anticipated in his great obituary the ambiguous drama between the peasants and the Bolsheviks. 'Everything unusual prevents people from living the way they would wish. Their aspirations, when they have such, are never for fundamental change in their social habits, but always simply for more of the same. The basic theme of all their moans and complaints is: "Don't stop us living the way we're accustomed!" Vladimir Ilyich Lenin was a man who knew like no one before him how to stop people living their accustomed life.'[26] Individual unhappiness grows, when the course of history is accelerated.

The Bolsheviks did not wish for this fearsome collision with the peasant majority. Precisely because they sought at all costs to avoid it, the Bukharinist 'Right' first sided against the Trotskyist 'Left', who wanted almost immediately the civil war was over to force industrial accumulation at the cost of the better-off peasants. Since the peasantry had to pay for the 'five lost years' by far greater rigour later on – and at a tremendous material and political cost for the entire society – it is easy to conclude in retrospect that the Left Opposition were correct. But why then were they unable to convince the party, at a time when the formation of political opinion, while certainly deformed already by the weight of the

[25] 'Speech no. 6 at the Tenth Congress of the R.C.P.(B.)', *Collected Works*, vol. 32, p. 224.
[26] *Lenin und Gorki*, Berlin and Weimar, 1964, pp. 53ff.

apparatus, was as yet in no way dominated by the secret police? Why did even Lenin himself, who had inspired the GOELRO plan,[27] first oppose the demand for a comprehensive industrial plan, and then oppose correspondingly greater power for Gosplan? Once the NEP had created the *formal* conditions for the minimum satisfaction of the peasantry, the first task in reconstructing pre-war industry, and above all of course *manufacturing* industry (tools, agricultural machines, textiles, etc.), was to cover *materially* the resources procured from the peasants. This was the first point to concentrate on, since the relative stability of the internal political scene depended on it. This is why Stalin could explain to the Central Committee in 1926 that the projected Dnieprostroi dam would be of as much use to the USSR as a gramophone to a peasant without a cow.

By the end of the 1920s, however, it became clear that the dynamic of peasant commodity production that had been unleashed by the revolution had outstripped industrial development. Discontented with rising prices for scarce industrial goods, the kulaks proceeded to blackmail the Soviet power by holding back grain for the towns. The unprepared turn that now followed, towards collectivization of the rural economy without industry having prepared the ground, and hence also to the violently excessive rate of accumulation of the first five-year plans, was a *response* to the question of survival of the non-capitalist order raised by the kulaks at the head of the peasantry. In view of this development, to which the Bolsheviks were *driven,* the criticism that is possible on 'purely economic' grounds, i.e. that the overall process of industrialization was far from achieving its potential optimum, can have only an academic character. Without the apparatus of force that the Bolsheviks set in motion, Russia today would still be a peasant country, most probably on the capitalist road. And it should not be forgotten that the political weakness of the opposition and thus of the hypothetical alternative it represented was itself part of the secondary phenomena of the given situation. Historians, particularly Soviet ones, may establish how far modifications might have been possible, which could have

---

[27] GOELRO, State Commission for the Electrification of Russia.

reduced both the extent of the sacrifices and losses, and the depth of the subsequent depression in the rural economy. But the collision itself was unavoidable, all the more so as history has since shown that even a sufficient supply of modern agricultural machinery in no way moves peasants automatically to accept collectivization. In Soviet Russia the peasants were the strongest class in the population, and up till 1928 the sole class to reap the benefit of the social revolution. They had to be the object of a second revolution.

How then did things stand with the Russian working class, the proletarian base of the dictatorship? This question became acute even earlier, in the passionate trade-union debate of 1920–21, shortly before the Kronstadt insurrection. Factory work and factory discipline had only changed their alienated character in a spiritual sense since the workers' party had come to power: a political revolution cannot produce a new life for the worker as a person. In a backward country, the generation that takes possession of the factories is still a whole epoch removed from even the material rewards of its action. Hence it was only that stratum of the working class that managed to rise above its purely corporate interests and achieve political consciousness that had changed more than just temporarily its attitude to work. Yet it was precisely this element that escaped further factory work, being needed for a different and more satisfying role in the new social and state edifice. The hour of the revolution showed that the old society had left only a minority of the oppressed class with the mental energy for an active leap forward. Most workers certainly summoned the strength for the collective action of conquering power under proven leaders, and very many sacrificed themselves in the civil war. The function of leadership, however, a position of command, demands a degree of self-consciousness and capacity for articulation that among the exploited is only an individual accident. This is precisely the basic reason why the working class, as against the bourgeoisie, cannot achieve victory without an intellectual vanguard, without an *organized* 'brain' which takes the most suitable proletarians out of their average milieu, both mentally and emotionally. What then happens to the working class, and within it, after victory is achieved?

Every revolution always kindles in the hearts of its participants a boundless hope for a great and happy change in all their conditions of life. Hölderlin says in his *Hyperion* something that not everyone manages to express, but which almost all feel, when the movement they belong to succeeds: 'Our people of the future are not to be recognized by their banner alone; everything must be made new, everything basically changed, pleasure becoming serious and work a joy'. This is a psychological fact. And there follows massive disappointment and disillusion with how little has changed in everyday life, above all for those at the base, who are unequipped to translate the compromised perspective into an active role in the long-run transformation of society. For those many people whom the revolution has not led to free activity (in a certain subjective sense), life has not fundamentally altered. Only external circumstances change more quickly, the scenery and props, too quickly indeed for many people.

Many workers met the new Communist leadership – which was, moreover, not always free from that 'Communist conceit' of the more advanced which Lenin counted among the main enemies of the revolution – with reserve, soon with mistrust or even rebellion under the influence of the Menshevik, Social-Revolutionary and anarchist tendencies whom the Bolsheviks had suppressed. The Bolsheviks had to enlist the trade unions to organize disciplinary tribunals against slackness and theft, and tried to install a system of bonuses against the strongly egalitarian tendency.

Since the civil war had given rise to a vicious circle in the supply of foodstuffs, fuel and transport, large-scale industry practically collapsed. The factory workers and their families went hungry. They could often only produce small-scale items like the famous fireworks, and were compelled to exchange a portion of them in kind on the black market in order to keep alive.

With the NEP in 1921, designed as this was to secure the economic linkage with the refractory countryside, ideological tension in the working class was further intensified, since although alleged to rule politically, it had still to play second fiddle in consumption. All the early party oppositions, from the 'Left Communists' through the 'Workers' Opposition' to the 'Democratic Centralists', expressed in some way or other the disillusion of those strata of workers who saw themselves robbed of their birthright, a disillusion which was by no means focussed simply on the particular problem of supply, but was ultimately related to the renewed subaltern role that the majority of workers had in society.

This is misconstrued by Ernest Mandel, for example, when he attributes the growing alienation between the working class and the party primarily to the policy of enforced renunciation of consumption, i.e. to the inadequate resolution of a 'basic contradiction between the non-capitalist' (this word conceals Mandel's profound imprecision in seeing Soviet relations as post-capitalist) 'mode of production and the bourgeois relations of distribution'.[28] As early as the immediate post-civil war situation, when there could be no question of too high a rate of accumulation, the Bolsheviks did not have the political preconditions for a democratic discussion with the majority of workers as to the necessary extent of the sacrifice to be made. The swamping of the 'old' working class, from the end of the 1920s, with the millions thrown into industry by the transformation of agriculture, showed how illusory was the idea of a mass determination of the distribution of the surplus product in the concrete Soviet case. The Yugoslav practice, on the other hand, which was possible after the Second World War under the indirect protection of the Soviet Union, has not completely proved that socialist democracy 'in and of itself' is economically more effective in Mandel's sense. For the Soviet Union in the 1920 and 1930s, the opposite would unfortunately seem to have been true.

When the United Left Opposition of 1926 girded its loins against the Stalin-Bukharin majority in the party leadership, the Politburo of the Italian Communist Party sent an admonishing letter to the Central Committee of the Russian Communist Party, addressed principally to Trotsky, Zinoviev and Kamenev, in which it summed up the problem of the working class in the Soviet Union in the following terms: 'Comrades, history has never seen a dominant class, in its entirety, experiencing conditions of living inferior to those of certain elements and strata of the dominated

[28] *Marxist Economic Theory*, London 1968, p. 565.

and subjected class. This unprecedented contradiction has been reserved by history as the destiny of the proletariat. In this contradiction lie the greatest dangers for the dictatorship of the proletariat, especially in those countries where capitalism has not had any great development or succeeded in unifying the productive forces. It is from this contradiction, which moreover already appears in certain forms in those capitalist countries where the proletariat has objectively reached a high social function, that reformism and syndicalism, the corporate spirit and the stratifications of the labour aristocracy are born.

'Yet the proletariat cannot become the dominant class if it does not overcome this contradiction through the sacrifice of its corporate interests. It cannot maintain its hegemony and its dictatorship if, even when it has become dominant, it does not sacrifice these immediate interests for the general and permanent interests of the class. Certainly, it is easy to be demagogic in this sphere. It is easy to insist on the negative sides of the contradiction: "Are you the ruler, o badly dressed and badly fed workers? Or is the Nepman in his furs, with all the goods of the earth at his disposal, the real ruler?" Similarly the reformists, after a revolutionary strike which has increased the cohesion and discipline of the masses, but which as a result of its long duration has yet further impoverished the individual workers involved, say: "What was the point of struggling? You are ruined and impoverished!" It is easy to be demagogic in this sphere, and it is hard not to be when the question has been posed in terms of corporate spirit and not in those of Leninism, the doctrine of the hegemony of the proletariat, which historically finds itself in one particular position and not in another'.[29]

This is a striking argument, and irrefutable in strictly Leninist terms. But what, then, if the working class shows itself 'lacking in understanding', if the contest of leaders only reflects the fact that the link between vanguard and class is already stretched to breaking point? What then, if the working class as a whole is not this 'holy congregation', if it cannot be kept to a life devoted to

[29] Antonio Gramsci, *Selections from Political Writings 1921–1926*, London 1978, p. 431.

earthly transcendence? According to the Italians, its dictatorship could not then exist. Or else the attempt must be made to *force* it to rise above its corporate interests, and to this end reproduce the dictatorship of the proletariat within the proletariat itself. To remain on the ground of concrete reality, it is necessary to bear in mind that the industrialization that Russia faced had necessarily to multiply the *number* of workers, with millions of unenlightened country folk entering its ranks, who would have to be forced to rapidly acquire an unaccustomed industrial discipline. How could the corporate spirit be restrained in such conditions, if not by the political atomization of the new masses of workers? What form was the relationship between vanguard and proletariat to take?

In theory, the mechanism of proletarian dictatorship is completely clear, as Lenin described it for example in April-May 1920, addressing the West European communists. In '*Left-Wing*' *Communism,* Lenin speaks of a transmission mechanism between the party and the masses. It is fashionable today to get somewhat worked up about the 'mechanical' character of Lenin's conception. On closer examination, however, this proves unnecessary, even if in a further passage the trade unions actually figure as a 'cogwheel'. For Lenin's conception of the role of the trade unions included a second 'cogwheel' turning in the opposite direction, i.e. the protection of the workers against their state as an apparatus. In this function, space is provided for the corporate interests of the proletariat. In the trade-union decision of the 11th Congress in 1922, reference was specifically made to 'a certain conflict of interests in matters concerning labour conditions between the masses of workers and the directors and managers of state enterprises'.[30]

This conflict of interests was attributed to the commercialization of the reproduction process and the introduction of economic accounting, and to 'all authority in the factories [being] concentrated in the hands of the management'.[31] The trade unions were to combine carefully the struggle to increase the productive

[30] 'The Role and Function of the Trade Unions', *Collected Works*, vol. 33, p. 186.
[31] p. 189.

forces with the defence of the interests of the workers against bureaucratic encroachments. In 1920 Lenin explained the functioning of the proletarian dictatorship in the following manner, as profound as it is enlightening: 'Actually, all the directing bodies of the vast majority of the unions, and primarily, of course, of the all-Russia general trade union centre or bureau . . . are made up of Communists and carry out all the directives of the Party. Thus, on the whole, we have a formally non-communist, flexible and relatively wide and very powerful proletarian apparatus, by means of which the Party is closely linked up with the *class* and the *masses,* and by means of which, under the leadership of the Party, the *class dictatorship* is exercized'.[32] Since the working class cannot be homogeneous, and since it cannot govern as a 'sack of potatoes', the need for such an *organization* of its political life as ruling class is self-evident. The old German Social-Democrats, moreover, had not organized their influence in any essentially different way. The Leninist *conception* has not the slightest flaw, on condition that the rule of the working class is a genuine reality.

But when our *present* state machine is defended by appeal to this conception, this is no more than a conjuring trick. It is suggested as something self-evident that *our* system functions according to this conception of Lenin's, as a way of concealing its fundamental nakedness. To the extent that the apparatus *links* the party with the class and with the masses *politically*, and not in a mere mechanical and administrative contact, to this extent one can speak of a 'dictatorship of the class'. To the extent that this is not the case, we have a 'dictatorship *over* the people and *over* the working class'. And what is it that decides this proportion, which of course always gives rise to a qualitatively determined relationship, not just to a transient quantitative one? To take the bull by the horns, how is it decided *negatively?* By the withdrawal or retreat of the majority of workers from the 'apparatus', which is precisely the way it becomes an apparatus in the customary sense. All that remains of Lenin's living mechanism is then the bureaucratic skeleton. The proletarian element vanishes even from the style of the milieu. The career official, even if from proletarian

[32] '"Left-Wing" Communism – An Infantile Disorder', *Collected Works*, vol. 31, p. 48.

millions of proletarians, who may not be class conscious, are often ignorant, backward and illiterate, but who, being proletarians, follow their own Party'.[36] Their place is in the trade unions as a *school* of communism and administration. 'When they have attended this school for a number of years they will have learned to administer, but the going is slow. We have not even abolished illiteracy.'[37] 'To govern you need an army of steeled revolutionary Communists', precisely the Bolsheviks, who have had twenty years of Party training'.[38] If the entire class is *later* to be able to take direct charge of the state and economic management, 'this calls for education'.[39]

The real difficulty, however, lay less with the specialist experts than with the political experts, at least in the connection we are concerned with here. If the spectrum of political attitudes in the working class is ruptured at a certain point, then the chain of continuous influence is replaced by a confrontation. If this rupture is to be overcome without changing the fundamental course (which would in no way have been possible), then the *political* control, the *political* feedback from bottom to top can no longer be an *active* function, at least in practice. Then the dictatorship of the proletariat, though still formally described as such, as it was in May 1920, is realized as a graded relationship between educators and educated, with the trade unions functioning as a transmission belt to the working class, while the workers in turn give instruction to the peasantry, the absolute 'laity'. It is very quickly forgotten that 'the educator must himself be educated'. 'This doctrine must, therefore, divide society into two parts, one of which is superior to society', as Marx wrote in the third thesis on Feuerbach.

There certainly remains room for the workers to control *individual* subordinate functionaries, but not their corporation, the party. The party could only educate and control itself. And in this polemic Lenin described the party in similar terms, yet with a positive accent, to those Bakunin had used in a negative sense in his attack on Marx, as a modern order of 'those who know'. 'We

[36] 'Speech no. 1 . . .', *loc. cit.*, p. 58.
[37] *Loc. cit.*, p. 61.
[38] p. 62.
[39] 'Speech no. 2 . . .', *loc. cit.*, p. 65.

have been fighting in the Party for over twenty years, and we have given the workers visual proof that the Party is a special kind of thing which needs forward-looking men prepared for sacrifice; that it does make mistakes, but corrects them; that it guides and selects men who know the way and the obstacles before us.'[40] This is unambiguously reminiscent of the self-portrayal of the authenticated priesthood of ancient times, and the fount of all later party metaphysics and mysticism. Yet it is no fantasy, as Marx dismissed Bakunin's attack, but simply the expression of the new social formation *in statu nascendi*.

Lenin was particularly decisive in rejecting all attacks on the policy of nomination, the installation of important party, state and trade-union functionaries from above. Abandoning this would be to give up the leading role of the party, he said, and that in turn would spell the defeat of Soviet power. If this is correct, and everything speaks for its being so, then we have exactly that same hierarchical investiture that Marx considered incompatible with the spirit of the Commune. In such conditions, all could not even be equal within the party, which, now ruling alone, was always the natural target for careerist elements, for all its constant struggle to clear these out.

Above all, the Old Guard itself came to be hierarchically graded according to level of function in the apparatus, and as time progressed this came to be correlated more with obedience not to doctrine, but rather to the line of the dominant fraction. For it was far more important that the state machine should function as a single and united command post, and appear closed from outside and below, than to question *whose* command post it was. Since representation of the petty-bourgeois strata was necessarily excluded in favour of the balancing of interests from above by the proletarian dictatorship, in the long run no indirect representation of other tendencies by fractions of the party could be permitted either. Isaac Deutscher, in his works on Stalin and Trotsky, and in his *The Unfinished Revolution*, showed convincingly how the ban on fractions reduced the party's powers of self-control, and gradually killed off its internal life. From now on oppositions were wrong by

[40] 'Speech no. 1 . . .', *loc. cit.*, p. 62.

their very emergence. Anyone who wanted to change something had to go the whole way and seek to win power over the party. A mechanism of power struggles necessarily arose, as was also the case in Oriental despotism.

It became clear after the civil war that the 6 million trade unionists, a figure still quoted, in no way meant the existence of a working class capable of action and rule. Lenin chose such acute formulations in depicting the loss of this 'cogwheel', so decisive for the transmission belt to the peasants, that his opponents charged him with practising, in his own words, the dictatorship of a non-existing class. Lenin in fact portrayed a situation in which the party had become a substitute or place-keeper for the working class. In the period when the power apparatus for the positive task of the revolution was being formed, when it took the shape that would remain basically the same for decades, the great majority of workers could not be permitted any say, since they had been declassed by the collapse of large-scale industry; the proletariat was 'dislodged from its class groove'.[41] 'The factories and mills are idle – the proletariat is weak, scattered, enfeebled.' Even more strongly: 'Since large-scale industry has been destroyed, since the factories are at a standstill, the proletariat has disappeared'.[42] 'Very often the word "workers" is taken to mean the factory proletariat. But it does not mean that at all. During the war people who were by no means proletarians went into the factories; they went into the factories to dodge the war. Are the social and economic conditions in our country today' (1922) 'such as to induce real proletarians to go into the factories? No.'[43] On top of this, ever since October one levy of conscious elements after the other had been raised for key military and political tasks and drawn into the new apparatus. The bourgeoisie was therefore quite correct to 'take into consideration the fact that the *real* "forces of the working class" now consist of the mighty vanguard of that class (the Russian Communist

---

[41] 'New Times and Old Mistakes in a New Guise', *Collected Works*, vol. 33, pp. 23–4.
[42] 'The New Economic Policy and the Tasks of the Political Education Departments', *Collected Works*, vol. 33, p. 65.
[43] 'Eleventh Congress of the R.C.P.(B.); Speech no. 2', *Collected Works*, vol. 33, p. 299.

Party . . .) plus the elements which have been most weakened by being declassed, and which are most susceptible to Menshevik and anarchist vacillations'.[44]

Soviet power, in other words, the dictatorship of the proletariat, already rested on the rule of the Communist Party alone. As Lenin continued: 'The slogan "more faith in the forces of the working class" is now being used, *in fact,* to increase the influence of the Mensheviks and anarchists, as was vividly proved and demonstrated by Kronstadt in the spring of 1921'.[45] The vanguard was still propelled by the 'historical', future interests of the working class, but no longer by its immediate interests. From now on it was no longer a question of whether the working class trusted the party and its leaders, but rather whether the party could trust the working class. From time to time this is affirmed. It is not the workers who thank their leaders, but rather the leaders who thank the workers for their achievements, and this seems to have its rationale. Paternalism becomes the basic feature of the relations between the party apparatus and the working class. In this situation, which has remained stable for a long period, that room for manoeuvre which is important in certain circumstances for the further development of the subjective productive forces as well as for the restriction of unproductive consumption, could only depend on the amount of 'pedagogical' expertise and enlightenment of the 'educator', i.e. on an essentially *inner*-party development. This is where the paralysis and decimation of the most conscious elements by the Stalin apparatus had its most devastating effect, in as much as it made exploitation of this room for manoeuvre impossible, and gave free rein to the most stupid bureaucrats, those most uncultured both politically and morally.

The dilemma of Leninism, which destroyed the unity of the old party centre after Lenin's death, is expressed most clearly in the way that Lenin's remedy *against* bureaucracy, the recruitment of new and unspoiled cadres from the working class, meant their *recruitment for an apparatus which had long been in confrontation with the masses.* Whenever the opposition spoke of bureaucracy,

---

[44] 'New Times and Old Mistakes in a New Guise', *loc. cit.,* p. 27.
[45] *Ibid.*

always aiming more or less consciously at the role of the party apparatus itself, not primarily at the bureaucratic excrescences of the Soviet apparatus, Lenin threw back the question: where are the reliable and educated worker cadres you have trained, so that we can put *our* people in the positions which we now have to entrust to alien elements? Lenin could not argue in any other way, even if he had already recognized that the struggle against bureaucracy, i.e. its presence, would last as long as it took to create the material basis of socialism. He certainly did not foresee that the work of education among the masses would only have the continual effect of drawing off their most energetic elements, those most enlightened in the sense intended, for work higher up, so reproducing on a massive scale their incompetence and incapacity for government.

We can see from the experience we have today that in seeking the causes of bureaucracy Lenin proceeded from a false position. At the 11th Party Congress he described a case in which the purchase of French canned meat for Soviet paper money which had little value, i.e. an extremely favourable deal, could not be concluded without Kamenev's agreement, Kamenev standing in for Lenin during his illness as Chairman of the Council of People's Commissars. 'Of course, how could a Russian citizen decide such a question without the consent of the Political Bureau of the Central Committee of the Russian Communist Party! This would be something supernatural. . . .' 'From the report I have before me I gather that . . . one responsible Communist said to another responsible Communist: "From now on I shall not talk to you except in the presence of a lawyer".' 'It turned out that no one could say who the culprits were . . . and from what I have told you it is evident that the culprits will never be discovered. It is simply the usual inability of the Russian intellectuals to get things done – inefficiency and slovenliness.' 'There are saboteurs today, of course, . . . but can we fight them when the position is as I have just described it? This is worse than any sabotage.'[46] And what did Lenin see as the causes? 'All the necessary institutions were

---

[46] 'Eleventh Congress of the R.C.P.(B.); Speech no. 2', *loc. cit.*, pp. 293, 295, 296 and 297.

available. What was lacking, then? Culture. Ninety-nine out of every hundred officials of the M[oscow] C[onsumers'] C[ooperative] S[ociety] . . . lack culture. They were unable to approach the matter in a cultured manner.' 'Any salesman trained in a large capitalist enterprise knows how to settle a matter like this.' 'We need a cultured approach to the simplest affairs of state.'[47]

We have since come to understand, most recently in the GDR and Czechoslovakia, how under our present system any salesman can in fact unlearn this skill and behave in exactly the same way. What Lenin wrongly attributed at that time to the specifically Russian lack of culture, was the beginning of what Andras Hegedüs, a former Hungarian Prime Minister, described a few years ago as a 'system of organized irresponsibility'. The Hungarians have a long history of this. In the days of Maria Theresa, the Hapsburg army had a saying: 'Better do nothing, than do something wrong'. This mentality prevails in any bureaucracy and hierarchy where the members are responsible to and dependent on only those above, and have absolutely no powers of horizontal cooperation.

Lenin of course became aware very soon that even the new cadres tended to become bureaucratized, so that this evidently had some connection with the nature of the institutions themselves. Why else did he want to exclude from the apparatus at least those who were to concern themselves directly with political and cultural enlightenment among the masses? 'When you are appointed to some office you become bureaucrats. . . .'[48] On ticklish questions, our propagandists of today pay more attention to saving the faces of their superiors than to the reactions of the audience they are supposed to convince.

Yet in the given circumstances, even Lenin himself was driven to bureaucratic remedies. His battle against bureaucracy, and against such derivative phenomena as corruption, etc., culminated in concern for an institution which was itself merely part of the apparatus: the Workers' and Peasants' Inspection as an *official body*. Even though he was disappointed with its performance, he

---

[47] *Ibid.*, pp. 295, 297 and 298.
[48] 'The New Economic Policy and the Tasks of the Political Education Departments', *Collected Works*, vol. 33, p. 76.

devoted his last major essay to reorganizing its function and operation. Since it had two major tasks, to winkle out bad elements among the ranks of officials, and to rationalize the work of administration after the Western model, he wanted to concentrate here 'our best Party forces'.[49] And he sketched out a prototype for these functionaries, who were to combine both revolutionary incorruptibility and expertise.

Yet in this proposal he already encountered the disdainful mockery of the party and Soviet bureaucracy, who in this case were to prove victorious. At the head of the People's Commissariat for Workers' and Peasants' Inspection, incidentally, had stood Stalin until April 1922; it was Stalin's apparatus which Lenin wanted to take in hand and organize afresh. But the Workers' and Peasants' Inspection was and remained a fiasco not because in this case the devil would have had to be driven out by Beelzebub, but rather because an apparatus *cannot* be rectified by another apparatus. Lenin was not the first to hit upon such an institution. In 1722, three years before his death, Peter the Great set up a 'procuracy' to supervise the functioning of the entire administrative apparatus. Even the most humanitarian and enlightened despot in Indian history, the great Maurya emperor Ashoka, set up a 'workers' and peasants' inspection', in the middle of the third century B.C., in the form of a 'plenipotentiary for justice', with the task of controlling the morality and reliability of his extensive officialdom and protecting the people against their abuses. An official workers' and peasants' inspection is the admission of the absence of that popular control which the Commune was designed to establish, the proof of a state machine isolated from the working people.

In pursuing the *political* development that took place within Lenin's party after its seizure of power, the real sense of the events does not sufficiently emerge. The historical function of the Bolshevik 'party of a new type' consisted in preparing the apparatus for the productive overthrow of the Russian social structure it inherited, for forced industrialization, and producing

[49] 'How Should We Reorganize the Workers' and Peasants' Inspection?', *Collected Works*, vol. 33, p. 481.

this out of its own ranks. Stalin's 'transformation of nature', or the colonization of the North and Siberia, would have been as impossible as the construction of the Great Wall of China without forced labour on a most major scale. That was why Ivan Denisovitch was recruited. All the party struggles of the 1920s between 'Left and 'Right' were nothing but the birthpangs of the new despotism. The combatants recognized too late that what was at stake was nothing to do with 'Left' and 'Right', and that they had only one unmistakeable result: the strengthening of the apparatus. What appeared negative in the destruction of inner-party democracy was the reverse side of the process in which the unambiguously hierarchical relations of subordination for the real economic revolution from above were created and made secure. When the obedient and handy tool was finished, there was no longer a Communist Party, nor even a Leninist Party. There was a political administration flanked by organs of terror. The only elements of communism that still remained were the individual conflicts of conscience of the comrades scattered in its organization.

As Plato already discovered, the existence of *homo politicus* is tragic when 'he has not found the state that suits him'. This was the experience of Trotsky, Zinoviev, Bukharin and many other former revolutionaries, who had *subjectively* anticipated a different state than that which was the actual result of their efforts. They were remarkably incapable, particularly Trotsky, of finding a place in their alienated product. They lost power because *they* did not fit into the state that was in the process of developing. Stalin won power because he did fit it. It was not only on account of the constant threats to it, but rather because of the positive task of driving the masses into an industrialization which they could not immediately desire, that the Soviet Union had to have a single, iron, 'Petrine' leadership. If a more gifted man than Stalin had managed to adapt himself to this aim, then the *ideological* resources that the old party tradition already possessed would have stretched somewhat further, and the most extreme expressions of the terror would have been avoided. Russia would have been spared the Caesarian madness, but hardly more. The yawning gulf between material progress and socio-political emancipation was unavoidable, as Dostoyevsky's tale of the Grand Inquisitor had anticipated. Only a great leap in the technical and cultural level of the masses could create the preconditions for socialist relations of production.

We should not fail to recognize, however, that this is a jusification of the same kind that Marx accorded the revolutionary activity of the bourgeoisie. It pertains to an antagonistic reality, in which 'the higher development of individuality is ... only achieved by a historical process during which individuals are sacrificed'.[50] In no way does it force us to echo the sovereign cynicism of Goethe's *Westöstlicher Diwan*:[51]

'Should this torture then torment us
Since it brings us greater pleasure?
Were not through the rule of Timur
Souls devoured without measure?'

All the less so, in as much as the concrete form of industrial development can of course in no way be interpreted fatalistically. We may particularly measure the possible modifications that a few more years of life for Lenin might have meant, by the tremendous results that the survival of Mao Tse-tung had for China – however these are to be judged.

The Stalin period robbed Leninism of its humanist perspective. In a radically pragmatic manner, it used only those elements that were necessary for its actual practice, and made a universal virtue out of every Soviet necessity. Lenin's measures, taken in a mortal struggle for survival in a besieged fortress, were not designed as irreversible limitations on the life and developmental capacity of the party in new and altered situations. *By holding to everything that Lenin had once done* (such as the ban on fractions, which made the formation even of mere *tendencies* impossible), the party under *Stalin solidified the first early structural form of adaptation to an extraordinary situation.* In historical evolution as in biological, acts of violence of this kind can also lead the organism in question up a blind alley.

Not wanting to leave the idea of a possible better path to

---

[50] *Theories of Surplus-Value*, Part Two, London 1969, p. 118.
[51] Marx also quoted this in his article on 'The British Rule in India'.

complete contingency, I would suggest one point for further reflection. Can we conceive of a different procedure from that of Stalin, given that the aim was to carry through that consensus in the party that was absolutely necessary for a unique but more favourable practice of proto-socialist industrialization? Lenin had predicted the collapse of Soviet power if the Politbureau were to be split by the clash between Stalin and Trotsky. Since this split did come about, the logic of Lenin's prophecy was that the annihilation of one of the two fractions was the condition of survival. Would it have been possible under Lenin's continued authority – *i.e. given a higher level of theoretical work!* – to have secured the unity of the party, i.e. above all of party leadership in the practice of political administration, in a context of genuine discussion of the alternatives at issue? For only on this condition could the party centre remain sufficiently alive, under the ban laid on it at the 10th Congress, so as later to remove this same ban when the time was ripe, in full consciousness of the situation. In Lenin's conception the way ahead was a means towards the socialist goal, however distant this lay. *This consciousness* was designed to survive in the party nucleus and be handed on to the next generation. When Stalin prematurely proclaimed his socialist constitution, while having the Old Guard shot, he both affirmed and simultaneously completed the destruction of this consciousness. From now on the immediate movement was everything, the goal nothing, at least in the everyday practice of the party and state machine. If the communist ideal still survived in some cryptic way, as was shown particularly during the War, so that in the 1950s it could break out in the shape of an almost religious yearning for Lenin, this was above all an intersubjective reality, a social fact without social form, without any organized manifestation.

The question of a past possibility is always speculative and inherently unanswerable. Yet in this case it is at least worth *asking*, since today the question is what form of party life and development is possible once Stalinist rigidity is left behind. The post-Stalinist party has adapted to the new situation only in externals. Lenin saw three phases of communism: the dictatorship of the proletariat (until the foundations of socialism were established), socialism, and then communism. Criticism of the present condition of the Soviet state system can be summed up in the simple fact that it has still not advanced one single step beyond the structures that were created in the very specific conditions of the 1920s for the first of these three phases. In this rigid continuity, the Soviet Union finds it difficult to complete even the foundations of socialism, precisely because this is not simply a technical task. Soviet society needs a renovated communist party, under whose leadership it can use the productive forces that were developed in the decades of industralizing despotism to break out to new shores, towards genuine socialism. If ironically a hypothetical alternative to Stalin might have been a different personality cult around a surviving Lenin, then an alternative to the present party policy can be based on a powerful bloc of progressive forces and interests in industrialized proto-socialist society. Both the objective basis for a new policy and the subjective factor are present on a *massive* scale. And the adequate intellectual and political organization of these subjective forces is the task for which the party must be renewed.

1972–1973

Part Two

The Anatomy of Actually Existing Socialism

4

A Résumé of Premises

Before embarking on a systematic presentation, it is necessary to summarize the major ideas of the discussion so far, so as to keep the premises clearly in mind.

Marx and Engels were convinced, as is well known, that capitalism in its stage of free competition had essentially already brought about, or would bring about, the productive forces that provided the material conditions for universal emancipation, for the free development of all individuals. Once the exploiters were expropriated, they reckoned, the driving forces unleashed for a society now liberated from all former antagonisms would in a short time see to it that the sources of social wealth would flow abundantly enough for communist organization to prevail in the relations of distribution, making any state regulation superfluous. The extent to which they overestimated the maturity of the productive forces is shown by the simple fact that a further one hundred years of rapid industrial progress has been made on the basis of this antagonistic formation, while in recent decades a second industrial revolution, this time a scientific one, has been carried through.

Disarmament would probably put the *richest* capitalist countries in a position to guarantee *today* the elementary requirements of free individuality for all, on the basis of the productivity now attained, but *only within their own frontiers*. And here we see the other and still more momentous aspect that forces us to speak of the immaturity of the productive forces in the 19th century: industrial progress has by-passed the overwhelming majority of the world's population. At the present time the problem might well consist in industrialism, taken from a global standpoint, having developed so disproportionately. Has it not in some regions already overstepped its useful limits and intensified a parasitism that is typical of capitalism to bring about an acute crisis in our metabolism with nature? And is it not working, in a manner determined by its inner antagonistic mechanism of reproduction, to make the poverty of the rest of the world ever greater? This catastrophic drop in productivity and standard of living actually guarantees that the historically privileged nations will not disarm, so that in this way too emancipation is hindered. (At least globally, not necessarily an emancipation within certain local limits, which cannot be genuine emancipation.)

But the resources set free by disarmament would initially yield simply a sum of dead capital, as long as society did not reorganize them in a structurally different way. Let us assume that we have the necessary quantity of produced goods at our disposal. Let us further assume that the capitalist mode of production is abolished. It would then be finally clear that equal opportunity in the relations of *distribution* of material goods and possibilities of education is not a sufficient lever to produce free individuals on a mass level. *For social inequality is anchored in the division of labour, in the structures of technology and cooperation themselves.* In the whole of former world history only the agents of general labour were free, i.e. the privileged planners and politicians, thinkers, scientists and artists – in so far as the reflected self-consciousness that is subjectively decisive for freedom is only attained in relation to the totality of human objects.

The domination of past, objectified labour over living labour pervades the entire tremendous apparatus of production, the infrastructures, the bureaucratic superstructure and the production of ideology. There is even a certain hope to be gained from the fact that ever fewer of those who possess power of disposal can have the feeling of having any effect on the universe. Our leading economists are all trained in Marxism, but if they quote for example the law of economy of time, they scarcely ever take man's all-round development as their criterion as Marx did, but for the most part simply the costs of labour-power and machinery, of productivity as measured by the law of value. The bureaucratic informational superstructure of the modern apparatus of production gives the separation of mental and manual labour deeper roots than ever before, or more precisely, the separation between planning or command and execution. The same separation that the Chinese philosopher Meng-tse described nearly two and a half thousand years ago in the following terms: 'Some work with the mind and some with the bodily powers. Those who work with the mind rule others, and those who work with their powers are ruled by others. Those who are ruled carry others, and those who rule are carried by others'. This universal principle is certainly undermined by the fact that the 'carrying work' now involves a large number of compartmentalized intellectual operations as well, but this is by no means sufficient to break it down.

Even the richest peoples, therefore, if they could throw off the capitalist shell tomorrow, would still face a long struggle to take control of their technical and social apparatus from within, i.e. to divest the functions of regulation and administration bit by bit of their immanent character of domination. (The momentous anticipation of this goal was one of the essential inspirations of the French May revolt of 1968. It goes without saying, moreover, that Marxism would not have played as great a role as it did in this movement's motivation, if Marx had not himself been aware of this problem of restructuring.)

In any case, communism presupposes mature industrialism, although the question of what precisely constitutes maturity is, naturally, settled not just by technical criteria but rather by social movements. To this extent, even criticism of Marx and Engels' overestimation of the productive forces must be toned down. Given the present structure of industrial societies in both formations, the productive forces will never become mature, despite and precisely on account of their technical dynamic. Yet even today those countries that first set out on the industrial capitalist road are those materially closest to socialism. Nowhere is the *beginning* of the transformation more pressing than it is there. But it is also nowhere more hard. And neither the less developed nor the underdeveloped peoples can afford to wait for them.

Lenin was the first Marxist to recognize in the awakening of Asia, as a response to the destruction of its traditional social structure by modern imperialism, the perspective that the popular masses of the colonial and semi-colonial countries would not remain in the role of passive objects of super-exploitation and absolute poverty. The Russian revolution showed that these peoples could not escape their pariah role simply by political and military liberation struggles and revolutions. The specific task of these revolutions is the restructuring of the pre-capitalist countries for their own road to industrialization, the non-capitalist one that involves a different *social formation* from that of the European road. While Lenin did not have sufficient time to generalize all the consequences of this development, he did assert very clearly that the industrialization of the Soviet Union to the point of catching up with the developed capitalist countries would only create the *preconditions* of socialism. He could only hope, more as revolutionary than as historical materialist, that the political structure of the country, the character of the relations of domination, could be kept at the level of anticipation of 1917, if not without temporary compromises and retreats.

While the socialist illusion of the Russian revolution is historically explicable, and was in the highest sense necessary, it still does not tally with the Marxist conception that manifest socialist relations should be possible on the basis of a fundamentally weaker productivity than was already displayed by competitive capitalism. I do not maintain that the process of industrialization must in all circumstances bear an antagonistic character. But if its pace is a question of survival in the better equipped imperialist environment, and if the non-capitalist country, unlike China today, has to struggle for its autonomy without any rear cover, then there is hardly even the chance of escaping this. While the history of the Soviet Union or People's China, in fact of our whole social structure, with the crises and collisions that are typical of it, cannot be explained as long as it is investigated on the assumption of socialism – whether apologetically or in order to denounce it – the riddle is solved when we consider the consequences of industrialization on the non-capitalist road, empty as this term may at first seem. Countries such as the GDR and Czechoslovakia must therefore be left aside for the time being, since here political forms that developed on a different basis were applied on a markedly foreign terrain, even if they are superficially reminiscent of Prussian (more than Hapsburg) tradition.

The term 'non-capitalist' covers developments that display very different phenomenal forms according to the traditional milieu that is to be transformed. The singularity of the concept, on the other hand, indicates the common basic tendency that all these developments are dictated by the demand that produces them. In its very negativity it expresses the fact that it is still European and American *capitalist* industrialism, now joined also by the Japanese, that sets the rest of the world its problems, even if the balance of forces is gradually tilting against it. The state repression in the countries of actually existing socialism is in the last analysis a function of their industrial underdevelopment, or more exactly, of the task of actively overcoming this underdevelopment by an 'inorganic' restructuring, so as to preserve their national identity. ('Inorganic' in the sense that the Russian peasantry, for example, had simply no organic socio-economic inclination towards collectivization.) The pressure of a materially superior civilization can not be met by a minority regime that gives itself such a task without erecting a defensive 'iron curtain' both internally and against the outside world, and without comprehensive regimentation against any 'spontaneity'.

The industrial civilization that has changed European life beyond recognition in the last two centuries leaves other nations no alternative; whether they had already reached the threshold of capitalism and industrialization in their own evolution, or whether it encountered them epochs removed from it – they must go through this crucible. If those too brusquely ejected from an earlier age have always turned time and again to the past, in search of the lost paradise, similar illusions today are assured of a rapid and bitter end. The 'guarantees of harmony and freedom', if they exist, can only be attained the other side of industrialism, which means by the social mastery of the material basis industrialism has created. And only those nations whose history, and the immensity of their demand, gives them the capacity to organize themselves for the forced march into the modern era, have a prospect of maintaining their identity and bringing the treasures of their cultural tradition into that global human culture that is already in the process of arising. Their traditional life is not mercilessly shattered only by the direct aggression of the rich countries, but even more so by the overall effect of their technical and scientific civilization. Even the genuine 'blessings of western civilization', for example its achievements in hygiene and medicine, act initially in the agricultural countries to increase the spread of poverty, prolong the torment of the path of development, and deepen the feeling of despair, given their particular law of population.

In order to understand what has been happening in the most vital countries since 1917, not those of the 'Third' world, but more specifically those of a precapitalist 'Second' world, we must in the first place understand the civilizing role of the state that has been confirmed throughout world history. Marx and Engels in no way denied it, yet their concentration on bourgeois conditions gave the European labour movement too specific a concept of the state, one which sees only its function of domination, its relationship to the special interests of the economically ruling classes. When we look at history tectonically, this function is only the secondary one. Primarily, the state was *the* institution of civilization, of the original formation of the different social bodies. It arises with the earliest class antitheses, but it is not simply their derivative or product. Of course, the objective general interest whose instrument it formed was diverted straight away by the special interest of the minority who bore it. But this antagonism only became acute when the rulers forsook their general functions in pursuit of their own particular interests, and so provoked the rebellion of the oppressed. How far the overall relationship was justified, however, can be precisely measured by the historical gulf that today lies between the exploited industrial workers and engineers of the rich countries, and – let us say – the 'freemen' in the Indian tribes of Latin America.

The anti-state and anti-authoritarian ideology of many intellectuals in the West, though it is generally too unenlightened, does have its historical justification in countries that have already industrialized, where the material conditions for the demise of the state are maturing. But those people who are just in the process of organizing themselves for industrialization cannot abandon this instrument, and their state can be nothing other than bureaucratic.

The state as taskmaster of society in its technical and social modernization – this fundamental model can be found time and again since 1917, wherever precapitalist countries or their decisive minorities have organized themselves for active entry into the 20th century. If from this standpoint the Soviet Union is identical not only with China, but also with Burma, Algeria or Guinea, and not only with Guinea, but recently also with Peru or Zaire, and not only Zaire, but even Iran, where a Shah stemming from an era before classical antiquity is conducting his own 'white revolution' – this only underlines the fundamental value of the state in this context. And we can conclude that the cause that has produced such a common feature in the most varied of historical milieus, while it certainly had to find a more or less favourable national soil, is in the last analysis not of an internal nature but rather an external one. In a way similar to how the advanced civilizations of the ancient world – the Babylonians, Egyptians, Chinese or Romans – started a ferment in the barbarian tribes on their borders, drew them into their own crises and forced them to form a state of their own, so modern capitalism and imperialism has borne the germs of dissolution into the stagnant hearths of earlier civilizations, destroyed their social balance and provoked their reorganization. It was international imperialism that shook the ground beneath the thrones of the Romanovs and Manchus, and which brought Asia, Africa and Latin America to rise against it.

Russia had the good fortune – which was at the same time the reason for the prolonged self-deception as to the character of its revolution – that one class in the post-revolutionary society already stood on the ground of modern industrialism, even if this was for the most part that of the 19th century: textile factories, munitions, railways, mining and metallurgy. The small working class was the motor of the revolution and the pledge of its industrial possibilities. In completely pre-capitalist countries the traditional social structure, the traditional constellation of economic interests, does not enable a single class or group to assume the hegemony in such a reorganization. Tribal, caste and kinship relations, together with the political inheritance, provide an overwhelming tendency for any progressive orientation to be corrupted. Authorities rooted in the old relations are completely unsuited for initiatives that would inevitably lead to the destruction of these roots. The only alternative here is a bureaucracy, civilian or military, whose members are corruptible chiefly through their power over the process of transformation itself. The discipline of obedience to instructions, which can only be made effective with a despotism of some kind or other, is the surest guarantee that the progressive interests will carry the day, in the actions of individual officials who are personally rooted in the old structures by a thousand threads. Party centres such as Lenin and Mao Tse-tung were able to forge for their future bureaucracies, are up till now still unparalleled prototypes of a discipline not rooted only in terror, and which therefore proves extraordinarily fruitful.

It was also the influence of industrial capitalism that fostered a social basis of recruitment for this necessary state apparatus, or gave groupings that were already present their modern significance. As a rule, the combination of imperialism with local commercial and money-lending capitalists who become comprador elements holds back the development of a national industrial bourgeoisie for so long that, when the time comes for the political reorganization that introduces economic transformation, they are not sufficiently consolidated to become representative hegemonial classes. Where the bourgeoisie can still make its influence decisively felt, as for example in India, the nation pays with the slowing down of industrialization and of the necessary reorganization in general. In the typical case it is generally a quite different social grouping which separates itself from the upper and middle strata of the old society, gets its education in the industrialized countries, undertakes agitation for liberation and national renewal, appears politically, ideologically and militarily at the head of the liberation struggle and finally, in a changed and expanded connection, creates the state machine for 'development' and forms its cadre: a national intelligentsia, and, when the crisis in their conditions of life comes to a head in such a way as to sufficiently mobilize the masses, a social-revolutionary intelligentsia.

The basis of this intelligentsia is not a specific socio-economic position of power – it grows into this only in the process of the post-revolutionary transformations – but rather the consensus of the popular masses, who can no longer go on living as before and are therefore waiting for a leadership. Precisely in the ideal case of a revolution of national liberation – i.e. if this succeeds in effectively out-manoeuvreing the traditional powers and mastering the necessities of development of the productive forces – the basic structure of society on the non-capitalist road is anticipated in the relationship between the agitated masses and the intelligentsia as a grouping organized for political and military leadership. The intelligentsia as a bureaucratic officialdom will become the (hopefully effective) guardian and goad of the working masses, who have little to hope for in their own lifetimes on the long, hard road of renunciation that leads to an indigenous industrial base, and who will soon come to understand this. The antagonisms or 'contradictions among the people' at which the remoulded society toils are then perfected.

If everything that has been said so far on this theme is brought together, we can then give the following as historical roots for the subjection of Soviet society to a bureaucratic state machine:

1. The pressure of the technological superiority of the imperialist countries, enforced by their policy of military intervention and encirclement. This factor has in fact exerted a *deforming* effect from outside on the development of the political superstructure, and represents the deepest reason for the *excesses* of the Stalin terror. The constant external threat reinforced the pressure that already burdened the process of political self-management within the ruling party and created the specific fortress neurosis in which friend and foe could no longer be distinguished.

2. The semi-Asiatic past of Russia,
   — with the inherited fragmentation of its agricultural base,
   — with the extremely heterogenous national composition of its colonialist multi-national state,
   — with the political traditions of Tsarist autocracy going back to the despotism of Baty Khan, and
   — with the psychology of the masses still trapped to a large extent in primary patriarchy.

Antonio Gramsci coined the concept of revolution-restoration to express the way that the political leap must always be followed by a settlement with the past, because the new social forces never immediately embrace the totality of economic relations and the productive forces that bear these, and are therefore constrained to compromise precisely for the sake of their own hegemony. The averting of political restoration and the defence of the state had to be paid for with important concessions to the old way of life and ideology. The people, including a working class for the most part newly recruited, were waiting for their *nachalniki* (bureaucrats).

3. The revolutionary situation itself. Even those formations renowned for their pluralist economic power structure stood at their beginning and end under the sign of an overwhelming state power. Periclean Athens fell between Solon, Pisistratos and his sons and Cleisthenes on the one hand, and Alexander on the other, republican Rome between the Tarquins and the Caesars, feudal particularism between Charlemagne and Louis XIV, capitalism of free competition between the military dictatorships of Cromwell and Bonaparte, and the state monopoly regime of the present. On the methods of primitive accumulation of capital (of *capital*, mark you!), Marx wrote: 'But they all employ the power of the state, the concentrated and organized force of society, to hasten, as in a hothouse, the process of transformation of the feudal mode of production into the capitalist mode, and to shorten the transition. Force is the midwife of every old society which is pregnant with a new one'. (This sentence is customarily quoted in connection with the political revolution.) 'It is itself an economic power.'[1] In the first years of Soviet power, the Bolsheviks, in particular Preobrazhensky, openly discussed the implication of the 'primitive accumulation' of modern productive forces in Russia. And here we come on to the fourth decisive root of the preceptor role of the state power in the Soviet Union, a correct understanding of which is of extreme importance for a realistic perspective of further transformations.

4. The productive forces that had to be accumulated under the pressure of the capitalist environment, in order to create the

---

[1] *Capital*, vol. 1, *loc. cit.*, pp. 915–6.

preconditions of socialism, themselves bear an antagonistic character. If, as Marx maintains, the means of labour 'indicate the social relations within which men work' ('It is not what is made but how, and by what instruments of labour, that distinguishes different economic epochs'),[2] how then can we base communism on the Taylorism we have today, on a kind of machinery that is for the most part that depicted in Marx's *Capital?* Even such a writer as Rostow is correct in rebutting this pretence, which has long been more hypocrisy than genuine illusion. Whether the role played by the level of the productive forces is made into something absolute or not, these certainly cannot be overrated. The slogan that labour is a cause for renown and honour is no better than the work ethic of Protestantism at covering up the underlying fact that industrial work, in the form so far prevailing, bears a compulsive character. This is precisely the reality that this slogan presupposes. Via a principle of reward according to work that is in no way taken from Marx, the Soviet state has fulfilled the most important double function of achieving labour discipline and combatting the egalitarian tendencies of the masses. This was the precondition for economic advance in the conditions inherited from the Russian past.

The kernel of the state economic policy was positive, in its rigorous centralization of the entire surplus product of the workers, and later and above all also of the peasants; yet the purpose was to accumulate more on this narrower basis than the capitalists whom it was seeking to overtake. From the standpoint of the working masses, this meant wage-labour in its most naked form, labour for the simple reproduction of their physical existence as producers. Under the given conditions, competition and the Stakhanov movement could be geared only to the intensification of labour, to a quicker turnover of the means of subsistence, to a greater differentiation among the immediate producers. At the same time, however – and this subjective side of industrialization is the greatest achievement of that epoch of blood and iron, as far as its significance for the future goes – the state power had not only to see to the quantity of the collective worker, but also to its quality;

[2] *Ibid.*, p. 286.

it had to create a technical and educational intelligentsia in vast numbers. All in all, the Soviet state, with the party as its core, was not the substitute for a working class too weak to exercize power, but rather the special substitute for an exploiting class.

But what explains the fact that *now,* when the hardest work in the Soviet Union is already over, when the material preconditions of socialism are at least achieved far above that minimum that Lenin once took to be necessary, the Stalinist superstructure still so obstinately persists?

Above all, that the measure of accumulation needed for socialism is not determined within the system itself, but rather in so-called economic competition with capitalism. Both the quantity of needs produced and satisfied by Western industry, and their quality, which is highly questionable when taken as a whole, directly effect Soviet planning to a greater or lesser extent, more or less refracted, as 'indicative figures'.

The dilemma of Soviet economic policy is reminiscent of the children's tale of the hare and the tortoise, where the tortoise bends the rules of the game. Each time the Soviet economy pauses for breath after a bout of exertion it hears a voice from the end of the course shout: 'I'm already here!' The tremendous burden of military expenditure, which is kept on a par with that of NATO only at the cost of a far greater share of national income, might well be the decisive handicap. The arms race is the real issue at stake in 'economic competition'.

The decisive question is how the Soviet Union is to organize its economy and society in order to stand up to Western state monopoly. For a country that creates them belatedly, it is hard to copy the techniques of the modern productive forces without having the form of social organization in which these originally appeared. The theorists of the workers' movement, moreover, from Engels via Plekhanov and Kautsky to Lenin and Bukharin, were of the express opinion that monopoly capitalism in its then stage of development had already brought about the forms of management and organization needed for socialization. These had only to be liberated from the old relations of production in order to give them a completely new social function. In the economic sphere, Soviet state monopoly displays in many ways this linear extrapolation of state-monopoly tendencies envisaged by the coryphées of the Second International, particularly in the German war economy.

At that time, the cybernetic tendency of the productive forces was as yet still little apparent, even in monopoly capitalism. Since actually existing socialism under the sign of primitive accumulation is not the *Aufhebung* of developed capitalism, it has not managed to fulfil the demand that points beyond capitalism of finding forms of 'organic' self-regulation for the overall economic process. Under these conditions, it has rather had to begin the construction of the general framework at the lower level of mechanical regulation, and only then begin to work at improving this inorganic mechanism by the insertion of a more advanced form. One part of the present problem is that a form of regulation that figured in the West only as transient and somewhat abnormal could play a decisive role given the unformed character of the developing Soviet economy, which moreover was forced throughout its life to be a kind of permanent war economy. The military-industrial complex in the USA finds its involuntary pendant in the military-bureaucratic complex in the Soviet Union, which together with its security organs proves to be a tremendous brake on internal political progress.

Originally, following Marx, the socialist revolution was expected not only greatly to simplify and clean up administration, but also and especially to bring a radical reduction in expenditure on the circulation sphere. Commodity production was to disappear, and money along with it. The first discovery of post-revolutionary political economy in the Soviet Union in this respect was that money would be needed at least in its informational sense, as *money of account,* in order to plan, guide and control the overall economic process. Eventually the entire 'socialist' economy had necessarily to be recognized as one of commodity production, and the law of value had again to be given sway, from above as it were. The final phase of this process, which is taking place at the present time (while in Yugoslavia even corporate capitalist competition has been reintroduced, at least in form), brings the recognition of the market as regulator of the satisfaction of needs by production. Even those countries which, unlike the GDR and Czechoslovakia, actually were industrializing on the non-capitalist road, had to make use of categories expressing the capitalist reproduction process. The informational super-structure of the industrial reproduction process in general was vested with the specific form of these categories. This 'in general' must naturally be understood in a historical sense, not a metaphysical one. Money circulation, cost accounting in terms of the law of value, etc., represent in their general nature the *historically necessary, because most developed* secondary materialization of exchange of information as to society's economic needs.

But it proves tremendously difficult to escape, by way of such partial 'capitalist restorations', from the premises of economic despotism, from the far-reaching determination of *form* specific to Soviet economy and society as a function of its 'Asiatic restoration'. Up till the Second World War, and probably even through the period of reconstruction, the rigid centralism in which a cumbersome administrative system was combined, rather in-inadequately, with bold economic initiatives from the party and state leadership, was evidently still appropriate to the productive forces, as shown by results. What was required was extensive development, and here the balance between linkage downwards and feedback upwards played the decisive role, not yet those horizontal linkages that become decisive in intensive national economies geared to the specialized satisfaction of needs. By now, however, falling rates of growth are already impending, not to speak of the restriction of the qualitative factors and particularly of labour productivity.

The relationship between people and leadership is institution-ally the same as in the 1930s, where it functioned despite the terror in the direction of progress. But today this relationship proves increasingly ineffective. Here the inertia of the institutions plays a particularly ominous role, as it is anchored in the immediate vital interest of several million peoples, those who created the Stalin apparatus or were at least moulded by it, representing it right down to the tiniest kholkoz village. Every time contradictions come to a head, they tend spontaneously to regress to the same 'measures', campaigns and 'structural changes', in variations that are no longer even resourceful in their senile mechanism. In its present form, the Soviet system of government is locked in a vicious circle, consisting on the one hand of the dilemma of economic competition, on the other of the social and mental regression of the party, state and economic bureaucracy. This vicious circle must of course be broken starting with this second element. The party and the Soviet state can refer to their forceful economic achievements – but these belong to history. The party will lose its birthright if it is not in a position to renovate both itself and the state in a fundamental way, i.e. socially instead of just bureaucratically.

Does the solution lie simply in an immediate demolition of the state machine? Does the gigantic Soviet economy not need any state plan, any central disposal of the most important investments for new factories, new technology, and for the ever more pressing infrastructure? Has the state principle played out its civilizing role? Here we should not make things too simple. Late capitalism sees the formation of a *state* superstructure over the economic process precisely on the basis of its highly developed productive forces. The monopolies become *particular,* without this forcing them to change in their internal aspect, because they give rise to an economic connection for which they are not in themselves sufficient. The state in these conditions is far *more* than the executive of the capitalist class. Why else do even the *communist* parties, where they possess such major influence as in France and Italy, set themselves the task of conquering the state machine rather than destroying it? Conquering it together with the social-democrats, moreover, who already set about this task some eighty years ago? Although the state still functions as the instrument of class suppression as well, society can no longer afford the destruction of its *apparatus* without this disorganizing its process of reproduction. For this machine acts as the organizer of productive forces that have outgrown capitalism. And the state cannot disappear as domination over men, it cannot be reduced to the administration of things, without the traditional division of labour being overcome. The abstract centralist form of the state, by which the administration of things is entoiled, will only become positively superfluous to the extent that a system of social self-organization grows up from below into this inorganic scaffolding. The state too must be *raised to a higher level.* But this implies that instead of working under the bureaucratic control of an ossified party *apparatus,* it works under the ideological supremacy of an organized communist movement, which decisively prevents it from holding back the construction of this social self-management.

At present, the state apparatus which is quite decisive for the performance of Soviet society in its given constitution is the playground for a sociologically obsolete stratum, under whose influence no alternative can be opposed to the far more flexible international management of capitalist state monopoly. Given the existing situation, the much vaunted coexistence and practical cooperation with the West will only lead the Soviet Union repeatedly to play the role of second fiddle. And then Soviet society will never get rid of the terror that fetters its productive forces. How long still, to take only one example, will it be necessary to demean tens of thousands of highly skilled people by employing them as state parasites in the censorship bureau? No pains that are taken to refurbish the traditional legitimacy can conceal the fact that the country needs a leading authority with a basically new legitimation, one which will fix its course in a guaranteed democratic communication with the working people, and is again inspired by the idea of a new civilization. The concrete elaboration of this alternative, however, depends on a more exact analysis of our existing conditions. Even Marx and Engels gave us no prognosis for these new relations of domination. It is up to us to get to their root, in the full spirit of the young Marx's proclaimed intent, to make social conditions dance by singing them their own tune.[3]

In order to grasp the general nature of actually existing socialism, we shall go on to ask the following questions:

— What consequences did planning and management on an overall social scale have under the conditions of a non-capitalist industrialization?

— What social structure had to emerge, given the corresponding conditions of reproduction?

— What did this mean for the immediate producers?

[3] 'Critique of Hegel's Philosophy of Right: Introduction', *Early Writings*, Pelican Marx Library, 1974, p. 247.

— How can a society develop its economic capacity when capitalist mechanisms of incentive and discipline are absent, while industrial work maintains its individually unsatisfying character?

— And finally: What form did the political superstructure, the party and state machine, have to take on the basis of all these circumstances?

In its critical realism, this analysis may at first present the appearance of an apology. All those characteristic forms of domination over which, as naive communists, we were first disillusioned and then, enraged, will show themselves to be practically unavoidable consequences of a definite historical progress. We must remember that Marx proceeded similarly with the rule of the bourgeoisie, rejecting any romantic and sentimental criticism of capitalism. Theories of deformation are all rooted in a Romantic manipulation of history. If only people, especially those in the Bolshevik party, had willed more intensely and acted more wisely, if instead of actually existing socialism we had genuine socialism, or at least a different and better road! There is no need to be fatalistic to distrust conclusions of this kind. They do not provide any key to history or to the present, and neither therefore to the future of our system.

5

The Overall Organization of Society on the Basis of the Traditional Division of Labour

As long as labour takes up all or almost all the time of the great majority, society is necessarily divided into classes. For in this condition, the advance of the productive forces, the spread of commerce, the development of the state and law and the foundation of art and science were possible only by way of an increased division of labour, which necessarily had at its root the major division of labour between the masses concerned with simply manual labour and the small number of privileged people who pursued the management of labour, trade and state affairs, later on concerning themselves also with art and science. There had to be a particular class freed from labour proper, free to take charge of these common social affairs, whereupon they never failed to burden the working masses with more and more labour to their own advantage. All political force originally depends on an economic social function. The law of the division of labour lies therefore at the root of class division. But this does not prevent the ruling class, once it is in the saddle, from never failing to transform its social leadership into exploitation of the masses.

The above paragraph, the ideas of which can all be found in Engels' *Anti-Dühring*,[1] evidently refers to the foundation of class domination in general, and not to any one particular kind. Already in *The German Ideology* Marx and Engels had described how 'the *division of labour* implies the possibility, nay the fact, that

---

[1] Part Two, Chapter IV and Part Three, Chapter II.

intellectual and material activity, that enjoyment and labour, production and consumption, devolve on different individuals, and that the only possibility of their not coming into contradiction lies in *negating in its turn the division of labour*'.[2]

Has the servile subjection of individuals to the division of labour been overcome in the Soviet Union and the other countries of actually existing socialism? Has this process at least begun? Or is there not a gigantic *special* apparatus that takes on the functions of economic and political management? Do the state and law, science and art, not have an institutionalized *special* existence? Have the labouring masses ever had time for philosophy and state affairs? Have these working masses improved their social status (instead of simply having improved their living standard in a modest way), or do we not have a new concentration of privileges of the most diverse kinds at the opposite pole of society? It is enough simply to pose these questions, to establish that our peoples have not crossed the limits of class society. And yet the class boundaries, as we shall go on to see, run along quite different lines to those maintained by official theory.

Class domination, however, has already been reduced to its most basic starting-point, and this is where it is now so obstinately defending itself. I have shown how the Bolsheviks came to establish their party and state apparatus as a substitute for an exploiting class, as the *labour lord* of Soviet society. *Overall social organization on the basis of the traditional division of labour can only be overall state organization, it can only be socialization in this alienated form,* especially in the modern mass societies with their hyper-complex process of reproduction. Among Marxists it should really go without saying that genuine societal property cannot exist under the sway of the traditional division of labour. If the opposite is publicly broadcast, this is with the intention of putting across to the 'little man' (the Russians say 'man in the ranks') something that he does not really believe, i.e. that he is master and owner of the general social wealth. Undoubtedly, if our formation is seen in the perspective of world history, it has shown an objective tendency to overcome the antagonistic structure. Our

---

[2] *Loc. cit.*, p. 45. (Second emphasis Bahro's.)

relations *could* be a *process* in which the functions of management were losing their class character. But in that case the leading elements of society would be the first to uncover the latest forms of the oldest contradictions. By concealing them, they confirm and reinforce themselves in their role as the dominant stratum.

The reduction process that Marx rightly undertook in order to extract the *particular* historical character of capitalist commodity production can be twisted to conceal the universal contradictions of *all* antagonistic production that lie behind the specific dialectic of the capitalist mode of production. It is then sufficient to chase out the bourgeoisie today, and tomorrow we can be free from all domination, exploitation and alienation in the factories left behind, or in those newly built with what under the rule of capital was the 'most advanced technology', pursuing work that promotes the individuality of the producers. If this does not seem immediately to lead to complete contentment, then the blame falls above all on the 'ideological residues of capitalism in the consciousness of our people'. This masquerade has succeeded to such an extent that even Marxist critics of our system ascribe the evident unreality of emancipation to mere 'deformations', which proceed from the new political superstructure – no matter with how suspect a regularity – but do not lie in the economic nature of social relationships.

As against this I must stress once again that this alienation is rooted in the division of labour itself. To trace it merely to commodity fetishism is also false in a genuine historical sense. The abstract labour that *appears* in commodity value first attained epoch-making importance in world history not so much in exchanges conducted on the margin of the primitive communities, but rather in the ancient economic despotism. Its taxes and forced labour already embodied 'labour as such' for the state, despite their natural form, even if the proportions of this labour were not a matter of indifference to the bureaucracy. In the last analysis it would always take cattle instead of corn, cloth instead of boots. A thousand peasants levied today for road building could be used tomorrow for something completely different, in a dispensation that is quite unforeseeable for those affected. The first consistent commodity system in history, which supplied the Mediterranean and Near Eastern market at least a thousand years before the

Greeks, was constituted essentially from the surpluses of these despots, not just from the products of private petty producers. Everywhere that the division of labour and large-scale cooperation develop, the organizing agency relates to labour in an increasingly abstract manner; it is guided more or less by the commensurability of products and activities, recognizes 'labour as such', and demands it *quantitatively* as the basis of its autonomous social power.

Precisely from this time on, it is also true that 'as long as a cleavage exists between the particular and the common interest, as long, therefore, as activity is not voluntarily, but naturally, divided, man's own deed becomes an alien power opposed to him, which enslaves him instead of being controlled by him'.[3] This foundation of class society in the division of labour lies at the root of all its later formations, in the sense that even after its modern overlays are removed it can still appear in a 'pure' form, though of course no longer the old, archaic form. The Russian revolution precisely serves to demonstrate to us how the era of the division of labour is also the era of rule by man over man, as expressed in a basic patriarchal structuring of all decisive social relations, from the ancient Eastern despotism through to that crude despotic communism of the poor which the young Marx indicated as a possibility that was basically already dispensed with.

We have to make clear that the root of the problem of government is the question as to what constitutes the human and historical substance of the ability to regulate the overall social framework. In what way did the wise men of the clan in the closing phase of primitive society, or the early priests and prophets, attain power over their people? They gradually monopolized the manipulation, formulation and rationalizing of the rites and myths that governed the annual cycle of labour and life in harmony with natural requirements. They successively appropriated the common interest, which according to Marx 'does not exist merely in the imagination, as the "general interest", but first of all in reality, as the mutual dependence of the individuals among whom labour is divided',[4] though of course this 'general interest' needs formu-

[3] *The German Ideology, loc. cit.*, p. 47.
[4] *Ibid.*, p. 46.

lating. The developed division of labour, along with a society's relationship to its natural environment and to other communities, forms the objective basis for a 'general interest' which, under the conditions listed at the start of this chapter, could only become the special business of certain particular individuals and groups. Thus far the state is still not just an illusory commonality. It is the corporation in which society sees itself reflected; it shows that the society has a real existence as such, and is more than the sum of its parts. It reproduces it ideally as a complex system, one which is not yet permeated with consciousness at the lower levels. The self-knowledge of society as a producing subject must find expression in a special state entity as long as individuals are unable to gain an overall view of the totality into which they are integrated. In short, the common higher interest becomes the particular interest of those at the top. Their particular economic interests then make their first appearance, with this factor as their major source.

Our popular textbooks often give the bland Enlightenment-type idea that these priests first appropriated the power of disposal over the common wealth and only then discovered the religion of domination, linking this up with naive popular mythology and adding it on as a kind of justifying ideology. In reality it was the other way round. The power of disposal grew out of the priestly magic as a task of consciousness that, while privileged, was expressly *necessary* for the progress of the community. To use an anachronistic expression taken from our present situation: in order to expropriate these priests, it would first be necessary to socialize the *magic,* and only then – or rather, *in this way!* – the wealth. And what is involved in magic is nothing more than the ability to understand the whole community in its internal functioning and hence represent its needs vis-à-vis the natural and social environment.

The object of this original appropriation and exercize of power is therefore the actual process of the community's life and labour in its conceptual and practical totality, a process to which the rule of the priests lends, or originally lent, a perspective of cultural advance. From the subjective mastery of this creative task flow wisdom and vocation, the mysterious 'charisma' of spiritual (but not necessarily 'rational') leadership. The personal authority of the 'sage' then appears as an individual prerequisite for the priestly office. But the *appropriation* of this 'knowledge' already objectively presupposes precisely the hierarchical management of labour in the broadest sense. The Hebrews and Hindus have bequeathed particularly precise testimony of this constellation that was so decisive for their cultures. The Mosaic law, for example, was precisely a knowledge of this kind.

As the geneticist Theodsius Dobzhansky wrote: 'We do not know whether it is a by-product of the aesthetic faculty or of the more fundamental faculty of self-awareness which confers upon some persons a quality of wisdom which seems curiously unrelated to their mastery of cumulative knowledge'.[5] The aesthetic faculty and the faculty of self awareness are certainly closely related, as Christopher Caudwell particularly demonstrated in *Illusion and Reality*. And what Dobzhansky means here by the constant growth of knowledge is evidently first and foremost the fruits of modern specialism, in which the traditional division of labour has reached its final pinnacle. Modern 'wisdom' is very clearly related to this bad infinity of knowledge, and this in a negative sense. But most clearly among the ancient peoples, where it is not divided and is therefore no more than just this, 'wisdom' appears as the individual form that proceeds from privileged intercourse with the 'gods', with the 'higher' objective powers, i.e. from manipulation of the general connection of a complex community, a connection that transcends any mere particularity.

The first acquisition of reflected consciousness of the social totality had a tremendous progressive significance. Men had set out on the road towards class society with a consciousness given as a fact of nature. Then a minority began to make history with their *self*-consciousness. This achievement was the beginning of an entirely new level of human evolution, a new level of genuine 'phenomenology of spirit': the stage of the human spirit 'existing for itself', i.e. of the personality recognizing the world and at the same time aware of its own individuality. Marxism, as the most mature product up till now of social man's self-knowledge, began with the demand to realize historical self-consciousness in *all individuals*. That is precisely what is meant by Marx's early demand that philosophy should be 'raised to a higher level' in the action of the proletarians.

Self-consciousness, fully developed, universal individuality and personal authority are only possible, according to all our psychological knowledge, as a function of active access to the totality of the community, through something that Spinoza indicated fairly exactly, even if in a spiritual and contemplative fashion, when he praised the 'intellectual love of God' as the greatest happiness for man. Universality and totality are of course concepts of quality and not quantity. The point is that the real possibility of participating in the *synthesis* of the historical process is the only way to escape from a subaltern existence.

On the social average, individual capacity for participation in the social synthesis has two preconditions, particularly at the level where what is involved is 'governing the state':

1. A degree of expertise which up till now has only been acquired by special intensive training, bestowed so far almost exclusively on those individuals who met some kind of candidature requirement for synthetic, 'general' work. Up till now the prevailing principle has been that of 'qualification for the job', and if someone needs only to use his hands in this and not his head, then he learns coordination of movements rather than coordination of concepts. The training of a cook includes philosophy and politics only at an extremely catechismic level, though even this can be in principle a great step forward, and justifies Lenin's celebrated demand *as a slogan*.

2. The effective opportunity to perform a series of ever higher synthetic functions, to stand at the head of hierarchies of social information or at least to participate in some form or other in the generalization process.

The process of knowledge which the transition to civilization promoted could not be effected all at once – neither subjectively nor objectively. Above all, however, the community as a whole could not possibly achieve it all together. And if we nowadays divide society into the 'sages' and the 'subalterns', at the level of its subjects, into 'those up there' and the 'little people', this goes back originally to this advance in evolution.

What those at the bottom have since devoted the greater part of their waking time towards, and above all of their psychological time, is not simply manual or schematic work, but rather life and labour in a *particular* context. Because they formerly produced and reproduced the traditional local community in one small place, they had also to know it collectively. True, this local community generally continued in being, and reproduced itself as before. But its members no longer performed what Marx called 'directly social' labour, activity involving a relationship to the generality. For the most essential connection that their surplus product now created and helped to bear was straight away withdrawn from their view together with this surplus product itself. The 'general labour' was performed elsewhere, in the distant centre, now in an abstract, separated, semi-religious and semi-intellectual form. Only there, and only for those concerned with it, could the wider connection that was produced in the region of the state, and 'internationally', become the object of knowledge.

To put it more exactly, it is very imprecise to characterize the progress of social differentiation and class formation which turns on the antithesis between intellectual and physical labour by saying that those who first come off badly, and are then oppressed, incur the loss of their 'old right' to participate in the formation of the general will. In their village settlements, even the conquered populations often maintained their communal traditions. But now these entire communities, which were previously sufficient to themselves in their character as a complete social universe, became incompetent parts of a superimposed whole, and moreover parts that did not echo this new and greater connection on a microcosmic scale, but were ascribed only subaltern functions in it. What were monopolized were essentially not traditional functions, but rather functions that had newly arisen and had previously not existed. The first leader of a league of clans or tribe, for example, based his power on an interest that had previously found no institutional expression, indeed that he had perhaps articulated for the first time. The simple tribe members, the 'freemen' of the new era of class domination that was coming into being, initially lost social power not absolutely but only relatively. They needed only to stay where they were to become subaltern. Naturally, the original functions of these units contracted in consequence, along with the autonomy of their kinship or village communities, but this contraction was compensated for by their new relationship to the centre, which was never a completely passive one. In general, an oppressed population of a higher social formation is superior for precisely this reason to those of their former companions who shrank back before a civilization that spelled servitude.

Progress never consists principally in negating favourable conditions of development simply because these are privileges, but rather in generalizing them. The most developed industrial civilizations of the present are faced with the mighty task of generalizing the privilege of 'general labour', of overcoming conditions of existence anchored in the traditional division of labour, in life-long subjection to particular activities. The present situation, in which the objectified productive forces press irresistibly towards the re-establishment of an overall social cooperation, while the traditional division of labour is still dominant, must continue to create conditions of individual and collective impotence from which the modern priesthood alone are apparently excluded. They know relatively less than the old official Ammon Rés about the overall social context which they have to govern.

But it follows from the very nature of this social context that the solution does not lie simply with the subalterns. The immediate needs of subaltern strata and classes are always conservative, and never positively anticipate a new form of life. The peasant uprisings under Oriental despotism necessarily ended up by installing a new despot. The slaves of antiquity, when they rose up, sought to take the place of the slaveholders, if they did not try and make their way back to their various homelands. The peasants of the feudal epoch struggled for their *old* freedoms. And the proletariat's spontaneous aim is to share the mode of life of the bourgeoisie, at least the petty bourgeoisie that stands closest to them; the despair of the early proletariat was based on the fact that, being pressed down below its minimum subsistence needs, it could not develop any hope of such a perspective. New perspectives only arise if, in a more general social crisis, a fraction of the upper strata or classes, or more effectively, a new 'middle class', organizes the mass of the oppressed for a reformation or revolution. It is necessary to go back to the origin of inequality, domination and exploitation if we are to understand this mechanism of progress, which proceeds from the *totality* of a social system full of contradictions and is not produced just by *one* of its poles. The dialectic of progress has been rather distorted in Marxist literature since Plekhanov's mechanical and dualistic treatment of it in the altogether unfortunate categories of 'popular masses' and 'individual'. New and higher cultures are never created without the masses, without an essential change in their condition of life, nor without their initiative, at a definite stage of maturity of the ongoing crisis. But in no known historical case did the first creative impulse in ideas and organization proceed from the masses; the trade unions do not anticipate any new civilization. The political workers' movement was itself founded by declassed bourgeois intellectuals, which in no way means that the most active proletarian elements did not soon come to play a role of their own in the socialist parties and tend themselves to become intellectuals. It can also not be denied (and in fact has not been sufficiently stressed) that the modern working class is in many important respects different from former exploited classes. Yet it is generally true that in history the working masses perform principally the task of quantitative accumulation.

The formation of the new historical power bloc is therefore always the formation of a *structured* organism, in which several elements of the old society combine into a new quality. This is how it was in our revolution. What was decisive was not the 'alliance' of elements, the decisive thing was the leadership that stood above these. It is markedly improbable that an oppressed class from the old society, formerly excluded to a large extent from the synthesis mentioned above in its actual process of life, could constitute the new type of society *by itself*. This in fact happens nowhere. If it did manage this, it would have had all the more surely to differentiate itself internally in a very fundamental way, i.e. create a new stratification from its own ranks. What we are dealing with today is precisely a highly complex technology and organization of the reproduction process, which is not seriously disturbed simply by political changes, but which materially incorporates relations of super- and sub-ordination of the most far-reaching kind, as well as extreme differences in psycho-physical requirement. This is the way that our society is stratified; of course, it goes far beyond the simple dichotomy between manual and mental labour.

Since that early time when the conscious stratum of social life began to separate itself off institutionally in the first shamanistic priesthood, there has thus been a manifold differentiation within it so that a very large part of the population in modern industrial societies is at least formally engaged in activities that involve and develop man not just as a physical force of nature, but rather directly in the specific organ that gives him a privileged place in nature by its particular organization. The greater part of the mental labour performed in our society results from the *technical* division of labour within production and the processing of information. The average activity of the engineer and economist does not *appear* as a subordinate function of the ruling class, in as much as all it involves is the mediation of the production process itself – little as the two tasks can be separated in practice!

In its origin, the mental labour that we find today so minutely subdivided is the activity of social management. Yet in more developed civilizations, the conceptual pair of mental and manual labour actually hinders analysis rather than helping it, at the present time more than ever. Even in earlier eras, the bulk of mental labour was already not the concern of the real upper stratum or class itself. The lower scribes and book-keepers of the Oriental priests and despots were certainly maintained out of the surplus product, but their revenue amounted only to a fraction of that which those at the top of the pyramid consumed. (Though they did have the bureaucratic career open to them.) In classical antiquity, mental labour stretched down into the ranks of the slave class itself. The work of supervision, too, was left by the Greek slaveholders to their (slave) managers, as they deemed it unfitting to concern themselves with it directly. What they kept for themselves, besides sensual enjoyment, was above all, according to Aristotle, affairs of state and philosophy, precisely the tasks of social synthesis.

What we have here, therefore, is an elementary and early relationship, even if I am going to formulate it in a 'modernistic' way. The organizational mastery of cooperation on the basis of the division of labour is *from the very beginning a problem of information, the problem of a structure of consciousness* which appears as a relationship between people. The hierarchical management of labour is the institutional expression of informational linkages, and this whole apparatus ultimately reflects the articulation of the process of material reproduction according to the stages of elaboration, forms and degrees of combination, and the necessary internal division of labour in the process of information processing. All individuals who take part in cooperation also dispose of consciousness as a natural force, but not all participate in this as their principal activity.

Domination, exploitation and alienation are concepts whose real content, against this general background, is precisely one and the same, at least at its core. It is always a question of greater or lesser portions of the concrete labour that is divided up and singularized, to be performed by the mass of the producers, being combined in the name of a particular common interest, and hence one embodied in a particular class subject, so that now this concentrated objectified labour becomes the means of commanding the living labour – for the overall purpose of increasing this alienated wealth both quantitatively and qualitatively. Independent both of its concrete form and of the degree of parasitism at the pole of social power (which may even approach zero at certain historic moments), the exploitation and oppression consists in the producers being robbed of the power of decision and disposal over the conditions of their material life, so that their social and, not uncommonly, even their biological existence as individuals is placed in the hands of a paternalist destiny that is by its very nature incomprehensible.

Do the working masses of the 'socialist' countries have even the least positive influence on the decisions that bear on their material fate, and ultimately therefore on their overall fate? On decisions as to the proportions between accumulation and consumption, between production for war and for peace, between building of homes and building of monuments, between expenditure on education and expenditure on the propagandist self-portrayal of the power structure, between the costs of liberating women from domestic slavery and the costs of security for those 'in charge of society'? Of course not. Are the peoples affected asked whether war should be waged over an uninhabited island in the Ussuri, or whether there should be military intervention against the socialist renovation of Czechoslovakia? In no way. There is only the indirect negative control through the danger of spontaneous mass upheavals, which, when they occur, signal the total refusal of the power structure *in terms of its own standards*. In the last analysis they show that the political superstructure has *got stuck* in the vicious circle of the traditional division of labour, the concentrated expression of which it represents.

Undoubtedly the criticism of actually existing socialism receives its strongest impulse from the provocation of a state power which has entrenched itself in the existing division of labour *in order to conserve this*. But to be constructive, it can in no way confine itself to mere denunciation, on this decisive point. Merely political changes would by themselves in no way improve the realities that created the existing order and have now raised the task of demolishing it. We must know how the social division of labour that today prevails is represented at the level of modern industrialism, i.e. what is its nature and how is it reproduced? Otherwise we shall ultimately restrict ourselves to repeating the inherently illusory demand that every cook should learn to govern the state, which she simply cannot learn in the normal case if she is to remain a cook.

For what does governing the state mean, if the state represents first (in its archaic provenance) and last (beyond private property in the means of production) the active superstructure of the division of labour, the form of its overall social organization, its secondary model, in substance an *intellectual and informational* one? Itself operated according to a division of labour, it reflects in its various different levels and branches the structure of the entire process of social reproduction. Later on, even the technical division of labour according to branches of the economy and tasks within the factory will also become a problem (i.e. the relationship between specialists, their mutual horizontal replaceability, etc.). *What is at issue at present is the decisive vertical division of labour,* the tendency for the collective social worker to be polarized through the bifurcation of the process of material reproduction into a process of matter and energy on the one hand, and a superior process of information that guides and directs it on the other.

The structure of information systems for the governing of complex systems, as disclosed by cybernetics, is a hierarchy of regulative levels. A process regulated at several different levels – and social cooperation has been a many-levelled enterprise ever since the beginning of civilization – is conceived as a whole only at the apex of the informational hierarchy; only here can there be a formal integral consciousness of the procedure in question. (Informally, of course, many people can get such an orientation in certain circumstances.) For this reason, the communist association of the future, as I want to establish here in advance of the discussion in Part Three, must constitute itself not only outside or above immediate production, it must constitute itself *as a totality* at the peak of the pyramid that informationally mediates the metabolism with nature and the social process. The members of a communist society will move matter and process information at whatever level is needed, if one takes any particular point in time. What matters, however, is that socially they are *subsumed* neither by the metabolism with nature *nor by the processing of information.* To the extent that the intervention of living labour is concentrated more and more on the informational process, this second subsumption is brought into the focal point of debate.

The decisive function of management is planning, which with the increasing complexity of the reproduction process becomes more and more the central element in all these levels of regulation, and above all in the national economy as a whole. If the plan directs the national economy, or to start with at least its so-called commanding heights, then in this role it gives the new relations a positive index as non-capitalist, even proto-socialist if no traditional exploiter interests have a decisive share in control. The plan is absolutely necessary once the direction of development, the pace of growth and the proportionality of production can no longer be arrived at empirically by the market mechanism, in so far as the overall social level is concerned. The needs of society, which under capitalism are indicated by effective demand, must be translated into a planned requirement, and in this connection, of course, the limited means for their satisfaction must also be taken into account.

The specific task of planning as such seems at first sight to be the calculation of matrices designed to ensure correct proportionality within the total quantity of use-values to be produced (including services in the widest sense), and in fact this work and its preconditions in the establishment (or research) of primary data does claim the lion's share of planning time at all levels of the hierarchy. It is a tremendous task of calculation to reckon the structure of production and output two or three times a year (draft plan, plan itself, more precise plan, plan corrections) for the innumerable positions into which it is articulated and divided among the various branches of the economy and its units, 'materially' (i.e. according to quantity, e.g. number of items), financially and in terms of time, as well as balancing the expenditures of labour-time, machinery and material that are needed. Scientifically, as it lays claim, our planning is accurate at least in principle with respect to its methodological procedure for ensuring proportionality. We can assume that accounting is 'faithful', i.e. mathematically correct, down to the second decimal place, in that book-keeping spirit that makes our economy so accurate in detail. With modern computers, national economic accounting is soluble in principle also with respect to the expenditure of energy it requires, once the phase of adaptation to electronic data processing is completed. To this extent, nothing seems to stand in the way of approximation to the Weberian ideal type of unbiassed and effective bureaucratic managerial organization, which was the tacit purpose of that 'Marxist-Leninist science of organization' of blessed memory.

But where does the scientific character of planning cease? With its premises, i.e. before it begins. These premises, by which I mean the priorities and preferences that go into the elaboration of the plan, can in no way be determined in an objective scientific manner as long as there are still antagonistic interests in society, such as are given with the unequal distribution of scarce resources for subsistence and enjoyment, and above all with the unequal distribution of education and that labour which serves as a means of self-development and appropriation of culture. The bureaucratic balancing of interests *from above,* of which planning is the major instrument, while it may well dampen the excesses of certain particular interests, and temporarily distort the parallelogram of forces, still recognizes none the less the real differences.

Above all, however, it is in the nature of the hierarchical state organization of labour to create an all-pervading new and vertical edifice of conflicting interests with the levels of its own apparatus. This is not only expressed in the way that administrative competence at each lower level is more strictly circumscribed than is good for its vital functioning, but it has also far-reaching economic consequences. Each higher level draws resources for its own 'priority projects' and other special requirements before the balancing of accounts even begins, and thus programmes into the system a kind of 'red shift' for those below; one example is the representation of the GDR capital at the expense of all other districts. The ordinary basic units, which have to fulfil their routinely upgraded plans each year irrespective of this, have trouble in simply maintaining the value of their output. A large number of municipalities and factories are economically unable to satisfy the elementary reproduction requirements of their population or employees at the normal standard. Waste and shortage of material resources for the plan go hand in hand. In the service and welfare sector even the civilizing substance is partly sacrificed or rationalized away. Since the plan as a whole is always stretched to the limits of capacity, and proportionality only secured with difficulty, the 'priority projects' prove a sure means of disturbing the economic balance of the overall process and so permanently burdening the working conditions of the mass of working people (e.g. with the overtime and special shifts that have long been indispensable for plan fulfillment). The conditions for plan fulfillment are allotted to the base far more than they are influenced by the base itself, not to speak of the counterpart of the base's manoeuvring with undisclosed reserves, which also does not contribute to an economical use of resources. The engineer, in particular, has scarcely any influence in his capacity as technician and technologist, and is hence guided more by the bureaucratic channels of decision than by the impetus for practical change.

Engels directly ascribed the emergence of special interests, manifesting themselves in the vertical dimension, to the problems of organization and management under the traditional division of labour. 'Society gives rise to certain common functions which it cannot dispense with', he wrote to Conrad Schmidt on October 27th, 1890. 'The persons appointed for this purpose form a new branch of the division of labour. . . .This gives them particular interests, distinct, too, from the interests of those who empowered them'[6] – even under primitive conditions. How much more must this be the result, then, when what is involved is the gigantic corporate association for information processing that is built around today's national planning? In actually existing socialism the subject of the plan is not society, but the state bureaucracy.

What kind of 'interests distinct from the interests of those who empowered them' does the planning state and economic bureaucracy have, and *must* it have by necessity – even when we abstract from the rivalry between its various levels and branches, as well as from the improper appropriation of particular advantages by individual functionaries? These particular *overall* interests of the bureaucracy, represented at the top of the apparatus, are not easy to ascertain, since they represent as of now the reverse side of the objective requirements that justify the existence of the bureaucracy as the planning subject. They are inseparably connected with these requirements, since it is precisely the particular task of planning to perceive the general interests. These are the interests of the *state* in their aspect of distinction and antithesis from those of society. They are the *fundamental* determinants of the form and manner in which social interests appear in the plan, and can therefore only be seen in the individual decisions if the unspoken *premises* of these decisions are investigated; it is *not* generally in the details that the devil lurks.

It is particularly at the overall economic level, then, that the formulae of bureaucratic interest sail so easily unrecognized under the flag of the general interest. Let us examine these formulae somewhat more closely.

Doesn't the raising of living standards require for a long period as *high a rate of accumulation* as possible, as *great an increase* as

---

[6] *Selected Correspondence, loc. cit.*, p. 421.

possible in the national income? Accumulation of the surplus product has been up till now *the* progressive economic function. But at the same time, this growth has been the specific domain of the central power of disposal, the instrument and expression of its economic *policy,* in which what is involved is not only the maintenance of balanced proportionality, but rather the enjoyment, extension and ensuring of its own power both at home and abroad. It is always particularly easy to squander extra growth for the greater convenience of the government and the governors. The policy of maximal increase in output, which is pursued so continuously under ever changing names, acts furthermore as a source of irrational overall expenditures of living and objectified labour.

Is the *concentration of investment* on 'priority projects' not genuinely better than fragmenting it on many smaller objectives? Even this question cannot be answered without further explanation, since here, too, what is involved is not least the question of *which* objectives are concentrated on and *which* areas are neglected. Private car production, for example, may be developed both for private and for bureaucratic need, but it is also possible to reconstruct the transport system and the infrastructure in general. Yet everywhere that the return on investment is too slow, not sufficiently visible or not at all so in the form of commodity production, serious investment is only undertaken if the disproportions have already become striking. Much concentration of resources is only necessary at all because too many priority projects always draw after them many new priority projects in their wake. In the course of their realization, which is generally more costly than originally estimated, whereas the effect generally falls short of what was anticipated, investments frequently cut even deeper into the ongoing reproduction process than was already planned, particularly since additional capacities have almost always to be withdrawn from elsewhere in order to meet the completion date.

Who could be against a frictionless, disturbance-free functioning of the overall reproduction process, and the precondition for this, *absolute fidelity to the plan* on the part of the economic partners? The problem is that the plan simply does not provide any reserves to cope with disturbances. While it would often be well worthwhile to 'disturb' the course of the plan in the interest of rationalization, it is rather rationalization that is disturbed in order to save the production plan. It is not even always economic necessity, but often simply bureaucratic formalism, which demands the fulfillment of the plan in value at any price, irrespective of the composition of production, i.e. the use-value structure, or costs. The discipline of the plan becomes an end in itself, as a way of subjecting people to the hierarchical rank order.

Is it possible to have real planning, guidance and control without reliable and complete *reporting* from bottom to top, particularly reporting that is accurate with regard to dates? The apparatus always takes pains to establish an ethic of information delivery. Yet given the conflict of interest over the relationship between plan injunctions and actual reserves, and over investments, the central need for *control* information from the base is constantly growing. How much labour is wasted because society still functions antagonistically? The flow of information set in train by a central institution, with the overall matrix of its structural elements, immediately bypasses the individual manager subordinate to it, generally along with all his subordinate functionaries into the bargain. The functional organs at the base have long known their task from the higher organs of economic management by the time they learn it from the management of their own unit. Over the years this procedure acquires a posterior rationality, since the formally responsible managers no longer need to feel responsible for the proportionality of their own outlays. The overdetermination of the base, the guidance of the lower functionaries by bureaucratic discipline instead of by industrial and economic success, naturally has the opposite effect to that of intensification.

Is it not quite apparent, finally, that the *apparatus* on which everything is somehow or other dependent stands in indispensable need of greater expertise, refinement, *perfection*, in view of its palpable deficiencies? But this attempt expresses not least the interest of the bureaucracy in its own existence, preservation and expansion, and leads to the incessant growth of the apparatus, which consumes a very major portion of the growth in productivity. The internal laws of social life in the apparatus acquire ever greater influence on the definition of social interests; the so-called basic economic law of socialism is here a further cloak beneath which much can be concealed. The 'role of the state' is evidently growing: there is no field in which actually existing socialism has made greater progress than in the breadth, depth and diversity of the bureaucratization process.

As can be seen from all this, subjectivism is the inevitable accompaniment of a planning that is scientific in form, but rests on the dictated *balancing of interests from above.* A centre that prevents any authentic expression of the various particular interests that cut across one another in society, can only carry through the integration in a substitute way, in an act that is external to the interest groups and is not their own action. And it can only do this on the basis of its own particular interests. There are therefore two sources of subjectivism which overlap one another in economic decision-making: the real particular interests from which the centre proceeds, and the inadequate knowledge of social needs which its very structure prevents from representing in an adequate form. (The last mentioned inadequacy has found its expression in an institution that is supposed to compensate for the long march of knowledge up through the ponderous hierarchy while sparing the short route via a genuine arbitration of interests in public life. Party and government want to find out, via the same market research sociology that has proved a means of reinforcing the ruling ideology in the West, what society desires, where the inevitable 'little man' is finding things difficult. An institute for studying public opinion has been founded within the Central Committee apparatus itself. There could scarcely be a more palpable way of showing that this is in fact not a party at all, but simply an apparatus over an administered membership. The most modest minimum of genuine communist activity and democratic social life would make these troublesome investigations super-fluous, not to mention the steel vaults into which their results disappear.)

Every proto-socialist society has seen numerous examples of how economic decisions, often even without rational cover, have been made 'subjectively' (the official expression, since the palace revolution against Khrushchev, for the subordination of society's economic needs to the particular interests of rival bureaucratic cliques). Down to the level of individual branches of industry, and even particular enterprises, we get situations time and time again in which 'money no longer plays a role', in other words no expense is spared, in order to iron out a mistake or to obstruct its revelation until responsibility can no longer be pinned down, or else to keep to the planned completion date for some modern Potemkin village. In this respect society has every reason to suspect that the bureaucratic 'system of organized irresponsibility' (an excellent conceptual coinage of Andras Hegedüs) is as expensive as capitalist anarchy. The apparatus plays around with the surplus product created by the working masses in a manner which, in the light of visible waste of the national income at various levels, gives rise to the cynical justification, to be heard time and again, that cases are known in which even greater sums have simply disappeared. The covering up sometimes goes so far that pride is even taken that the socialist economy doesn't break down despite all the abuse it gets.

But only in sensational cases is it the 'subjectivist' extravagances, the evident abuses of bureaucratic authority, that cause the losses. A rejection of the bureaucracy such as that seen in Poland in December 1970 is a *constant* danger inscribed in the system. This is why the official struggle against 'subjectivism' is a permanent necessity, nothing more than a matter of keeping in power, and is really taken seriously. If it is used too often, then the scapegoat procedure gets worn out, and is no longer any use, and one day even the long-suffering Soviet people might come round to the idea that the reason harvests rise or fall does not lie with the ministers of agriculture and their rank in the Politbureau. It is not a question of bad intentions at the top, but rather of the uselessness of the bureaucratic principle, when accumulation exhibits a tendency to stagnate as production grows in extent and increases in differentiation.

Referring to Hegel's concern for 'the security of the state and its subjects against the *misuse* of power by ministers and their officials', against which Hegel sees the hierarchical organization itself as a partial corrective, Marx noted: 'He could hardly be unaware that the hierarchical organization is itself the *principal abuse* and that the few personal sins of the officials are as nothing when compared to their *necessary* hierarchical sins. The hierarchy punishes the official when he sins against the hierarchy or commits a sin which is superfluous from the hierarchy's point of view, but it will come to his defence as soon as the hierarchy sins through him; moreover, it is hard to convince the hierarchy of the sinfulness of its members. . . . But what protection is there against the "hierarchy"? The lesser evil is certainly eliminated by the greater in the sense that its impact is minimal by comparison'.[7] The struggle for an honest management does of course have its importance none the less, and is all the more urgent, the more Asiatic a country's tradition is prior to its revolution. But in the advanced industrial countries, where there generally is already an inherited ethos against official corruption, the more general view must shift from the petty sins of the members to the big sins that are bound up with the *existence* of a bureaucracy lacking all control from outside itself.

The overall conclusion which we reach here is that the institutional superstructure in our countries, in its competition with the opposing state monopoly establishment in the West, pursues insufficiently specific socio-economic goals because it *confronts the proto-socialist society in a corporative manner*. In our system, too, the key question is 'economic growth', i.e. the increase of the disposable surplus product as an indication and social guarantee of this system of domination's capacity to rule. Naturally, the masses get something out of it, at the present level of industrial development, so that their prolonged subalternity can be *quantitatively compensated*. The consumption of material goods on both sides makes for a relatively short time shift, in historical terms. The ruling parties in actually existing socialism, as a result of the original underdevelopment of most of the countries in question, are certainly still 'most socialist' where they at least advance the productive forces quantitatively, and in the most favourable cases structurally as well. But this no longer has any long-run perspective, and human emancipation remains far

[7] 'Critique of Hegel's Doctrine of the State', in *Early Writings*, Pelican Marx Library, 1974, pp. 114–5.

6

Social Stratification under Actually Existing Socialism

Classes are both actually and conceptually the product of those social formations in which the overall social connection came together in the hands of the typical private proprietors of the time, who monopolized the conditions of labour under their management. Today this class society in the strict sense is in the throes of complete dissolution, on a world scale, and not least in the classical capitalist countries themselves. Naturally, there still exist in these countries the classes characteristic of capitalism, similarly to how, let us say, the classes and estates of feudal society still existed in Germany in the 1830s. Those interpretations of the late-capitalist social structure that one-sidedly orient themselves simply to a stratification model of the social structure are therefore deceptive, in as much as they make too light of the continued existence of the capital relation. But the description of the present reality there in terms of the traditional criteria of class structure is also no longer sufficient.

Those (new) features of the social structure in the late capitalist industrial societies, however, which can be more or less conclusively described in terms of stratification models, all find their very closely related counterparts in the countries of actually existing socialism, and this is simply because they express the state of the productive forces *more directly* than do the traditional characteristics. Our social structure – and this is why stratification models are a far more appropriate description *in our own case* – is precisely the subjective mode of existence of the modern productive forces. It is the social structure of the social collective worker, i.e. already beyond the capitalist structure. If we

163

TABLE 1

Level of function in overall social labour:	in the metabolism with nature (technical aspect of the reproduction process)	in the organization of human cooperation (social aspect of the reproduction process)
5. Analysis and synthesis of the natural and social totality	Choice of goals and paths of development, selection of corresponding activities on the basis of value judgements as to human needs in the given social ensemble	
4. Creative specialist work in science	Study of natural processes in order to expand technical control over nature	Study of social processes in order to draft changes in structure for the guidance and governing of social cooperation
3. Reproductive specialist work in science	Guidance and regulation of technologically mastered natural powers and processes	Guidance and regulation of social cooperation; education and training of human capacities
2. Complex specialist empirical work	Transformation of natural materials; supervision of natural processes	Transformation and transmission of information
	with understanding of their laws and/or responsible (joint) guidance of the particular labour processes they require	
1. Simple and schematic compartmentalized and ancillary work	Intervention of physical or psycho-physical human energy as an 'applied force of nature':	
	in production, transport and material services	in administration, accounting, data preparation, communications

↑

A Hierarchy of labour functions

B and corresponding structures of consciousness

↓

1. Particularized experiential knowledge for elementary tasks which were formerly the basis for the integral life activity of simple communities (containing within them in undifferentiated form all the higher functions), but which have now been reduced to isolated ancillary functions in the various different spheres of the general reproduction process.

2. Systematic and vocationally specific generalized experiential knowledge in production and administration.

3. Applied science in technology, economics, medicine, education, management, etc.

4. Particular sciences of nature and society as active structures of abstract and systematized knowledge of laws.

5. Motivation elaborated into finished ideologies and mentalities in the shape of philosophy, art, political strategy.

represent the character of the various work functions into which people have still to be divided, in one way or another, from the standpoint of the *hierarchy of knowledge* needed for their accomplishment, then we get something like the opposite table.

This is the hierarchy of work functions and corresponding levels of consciousness that is *inscribed* in proto-socialist industrial society *at a particular historic level of the social division of labour*. It is not just the mere differentiation of work functions and their requirements, but rather the subjection of individuals to these, that creates social stratification and the bureaucratic phenomenon. In this connection, while the relationship between social structure and productive forces in our case is certainly more direct (comparatively) than in late capitalism, it is still not immediate. And this is precisely connected with the fundamental residue of all relations of domination which we dealt with in the previous chapter, with the autonomization of 'general' work, with the still not overcome existence of a *particular* agency of general progress. The demarcation of the various spheres that is institutionalized and constantly reproduced by way of technical-economic and educational policy, the dominating tendency towards the confinement and restriction of individuals to particular levels of function, is what produces the pyramidic organization of the social collective worker in the process of production and management organized according to the division of labour.

It is sufficient here to assume an extremely simplified model, and ignore for the time being the diversity of the total reproduction process. The following diagram gives a sketch of the social structure of proto-socialist industrial society in its differentiation according to degree of education, level of management, functions of the reproduction process and branches of the division of labour, in the particular sphere of the economy.

With the exception of two factors which we have not taken into account here, i.e. the superior level of technological development in late capitalism and the relative surplus of expertise in our own countries, this structure completely coincides with that produced by capitalism, leaving out of consideration here of course the special political superstructure in our own case and the continued existence of the capital relation in the other. To object to the

TABLE 2

Productive functions:	Scale and jurisdiction:	Qualification:
Planning and Management	Economy as a whole	
	Branch of economy	
	Branch of industry	
	Combine	
	Factory	University level
	Department	
	Section	Technical college
	Shift	
Preparation of production*		Specialist
Ancillary productive processes**		Skilled worker
Basic productive processes		Semi-skilled worker
Ancillary workers		Unskilled worker

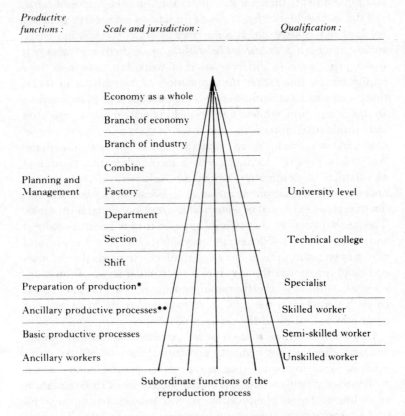

Subordinate functions of the
reproduction process

* Research and development, construction, project engineering, technological and technical control, etc.

** In particular installation, supply, servicing and maintenance.

abstraction, for a *particular* process of knowledge, of the contrary aspects of the two relations of production, would in fact mean pleading that the structure outlined here has a 'natural necessity' and an 'eternal' character, whereas in reality it *depicts the common historical basis of the two industrial societies and the pledge of their ultimate convergence in socialism.*

Let us turn first of all to the relationship of management and execution. The following well-known passage from *Capital* is much beloved of our apologists since it argues that the specific role of capital rests on a more general necessity which would still make itself felt in a form different from the capitalist. Marx writes: 'All directly social or communal labour on a large scale requires, to a greater or lesser degree, a directing authority, in order to secure the harmonious cooperation of the activities of individuals, and to perform the general functions that have their origin in the motion of the total productive organism, as distinguished from the motion of its separate organs. A single violin player is his own conductor: an orchestra requires a separate one'.[1]

Marx goes on to speak of the dual character of this direction as on the one hand a necessary management of labour, on the other hand an agency of capital valorization. In a further passage dealing with the same problem, he expressly adds: 'In despotic states, too, the work of supervision and all-round intervention of the government involves both the performance of those common tasks that arise from the nature of all communities, and the specific functions that arise from the opposition between the government and the mass of the people'.[2] I shall come on to analyze further that special interest which devolves in our own case specifically on the management of labour, but will assume already here that from it (though not from it alone) there necessarily result certain effects that are to a large extent analogous as far as the relationship between managers and managed is concerned. What is fundamental here is firstly the 'greatest possible self-valorization of capital', i.e. of the funds that appear

[1] *Capital*, vol. 1, Pelican Marx Library edition, 1975, pp. 448–9.
[2] *Capital*, vol. 3, chap. 23.

in our case in the form of state capital, and above all the investment fund, i.e. buildings and equipment. This is why shift work, which is admittedly unhealthy, is promoted precisely for those people who do *not* have to perform any general and managerial work!

In our case, too, this gives rise to a relationship of reciprocal pressure between management and operatives, particularly bringing the lower organs of management, especially foremen, but also the technological control personnel, into a permanently precarious situation between these two basic interests. As a result of the fact that technique and technology, together with the requirements for economic handling of material, machinery and labour-time, confront the workers in the capacity or function of state capital, the *entire* technical-economic staff, *including* the specialists and even the most minor managerial employees, are viewed with mistrust and latent hostility. 'The office staff don't work'. At first sight, this reaction has a certain irrational character, but it correctly generalizes the fact that the whole of this staff (placed with a frame around it in Table 2) represent the power of objectified labour against the living labour that is subordinated to it. Since the role of fixed capital, as Marx describes it for example in the *Grundrisse*,[3] has changed in our case only in name, we can particularly explain why in our society the real line of division within the factory runs between scientist and engineer on the one hand and the machine operator on the other – a line sharper than that between foreman and worker. As Marx says in *Capital*, 'as the means of production extend, the necessity increases for some effective control over the proper application of them, because they confront the wage-labourer as the property of another',[4] and from the all too evident need for such a control in our factories we can draw a conclusion as to the real relations of property: our workers do not treat the material means of production any differently, in essentials, to how capitalist wage-workers treat objectified capital. One need only read 'state' for 'capital' in the following passage: 'Their unification into one single productive body, and the establishment of a connection between their

[3] pp. 690 ff.
[4] *Capital*, vol. 1, *loc. cit.*, p. 449.

individual functions, lies outside their competence. These things are not their own act, but the act of the capital that brings them together and maintains them in that situation. Hence the interconnection between their various labours confronts them, in the realm of ideas, as a plan drawn up by the capitalist, and, in practice, as his authority, as the powerful will of a being outside them, who subjects their activity to his purpose'.[5]

This substitution is not intended to deny or reduce the distinction between capitalist and state (which is ultimately something more and something different from the 'collective capitalist'). It is intended simply to emphasize a common *basic* structure underlying the differentiation, a structure which is all the more consistent and clear on the far side of capitalism. I have taken Marx's description, originally intended as specific to capitalism, as a paradigm for this general model.

I would now like to quote another passage from *Capital*, which is again very pertinent to this point. 'If capitalist direction is thus twofold in content, owing to the twofold nature of the process of production which has to be directed – on the one hand a social labour process for the creation of a product, and on the other hand capital's process of valorization – in form it is purely despotic. As cooperation extends its scale, this despotism develops the forms that are peculiar to it. Just as at first the capitalist is relieved from actual labour [*Handarbeit*] . . ., so now he hands over the work of direct and constant supervision of the individual workers and groups of workers to a special kind of wage-labourer' (I would add that this special wage-labourer remains in his function even if the capitalist historically disappears! – R.B.). 'An industrial army of workers under the command of a single capitalist' (and more than ever under the command of a single state! – R.B.) 'requires, like a real army, officers (managers) and N.C.O.s (foremen, overseers), who command during the labour process in the name of capital. The work of supervision becomes their established and exclusive function'.[6] In Volume 3 of *Capital*, in the chapter already quoted above, Marx went on to give a

[5] *Ibid.*, pp. 449–50.
[6] *Capital*, vol. 1, *loc. cit.*, p. 450. Translation slightly amended.

positive assessment of this division of labour, which originally develops within the figure of the capitalist, but then separates off from him as a particular form of wage-labour. This makes the capitalist superfluous as far as production is concerned, and the traditional relationship can be dissolved by the associated workers themselves appointing and paying a manager, instead of the capitalist.

Who would deny that under our present system it is rather the managers who employ the workers? Who would deny that the combined managers, united hierarchically in the state, confront the workers as individuals? This image of the 'officers of capital' proves a useful means for defining the actual position of the ordinary workers and cooperative peasants under our social system. They are still 'organized like soldiers', as Marx and Engels already wrote in the *Manifesto*.[7] It is not just a metaphor to compare their position with that of rank-and-file soldiers in various divisions, who are equally subordinated to the impenetrable functioning of the pyramid of rank, towering above them from the corporal up to the general and commander-in-chief. As far as the *sum* of individuals subjected are concerned, the pyramid gets ever narrower at each higher level. To the *single* atomized individual, however, it appears in the inverted form of a funnel, broadening ever wider from sphere to sphere. Each higher level is a greater heaven. For the higher the level, the greater the staff. The individual can in no way think of having direct dealings with the state. The furthest he can reach is merely 'the humblest gate-keeper of the law', as Kafka expressed it. The small-man mentality is essentially the reflection of this state of affairs.

As with mutiny in the army, so in our ostensibly socialist society massive rebellion is the only means for the immediate producers to exert a significant influence on the general line of march. Otherwise their *initiative* is confined to the execution of commands or decisions. It is social relations that are to blame if they are forced into unproductive and regressive forms of protest. If proof of this overall argument were required, it need not be sought

[7] *The Revolutions of 1848, loc. cit.*, p. 74.

primarily in theory. In December 1970 the workers in the Polish coastal cities provided the most stubborn proof, and the recent repetition of this confrontation, this time with a more flexible leadership, has doubly emphasized that the fundamental situation can only be overcome with a genuine change in the system.

As far as the division of labour within the function of industrial management and planning is concerned, I must recall once again that while under capitalism this was produced completely from scratch – the early industrial bourgeois were in many cases their own foremen, book-keepers and sales agents – hierarchies of managerial functions comparable with the modern economic bureaucracy existed also in other modes of production, and particularly that of economic despotism, with an equally express purpose of labour organization. And yet the pyramid of supervision never had so many levels as it does today; the managerial superstructure of actual-socialist state economies, in particular, has no quantitative equal in the past, and in the last analysis no qualitative equal either.

The systematic character of the hierarchy and its number of levels follow essentially from the articulation of the production process itself – the closer to the base, the more independent of the relations of production and especially from the caprice of the managing subjects. From the shift up to the combine, it is generally the genuine combination of actual processes of production which is reflected with greater or lesser accuracy in the structures of management. The question as to how many immediate producers a manager can optimally direct is decided by the character of the labour process to be conducted. Viewed cybernetically, i.e. from the aspect of control and regulation, which separates off with the beginning of civilization, producing units from the factory to the economy as a whole are analogous to biological organisms, which also adapt and reproduce themselves via a hierarchical regulation. The hierarchy of levels of management exists objectively as the articulation of the information process which mediates the inter-connection of the separate work performances.

Given overall social, or rather overall state planning and management, the so-called partial or sub-systems can only have 'autonomy' in a narrowly circumscribed sense, one qualitatively different from that contained in the demand for autonomy for the individual. The autonomy of the industrial sub-system is a space in which human judgement can be exercized, but only in a conditional sense is it a space of freedom for human self-consciousness. I shall leave open here whether the humanist demand for individual autonomy is utopian in its aim – which has been based ever since the ancient Gnostics on the hypothesis that the human individual can *immediately* correspond with 'god', i.e. with the totality, know it and participate in it. This never excluded in any absolute way – except at its mystical summit – his fitting in as a member or 'sub-system' of a more confined connection. It is simply the essential distinction between a 'realm of freedom' and the realm of necessity such as obtains particularly in production.

The question of emancipation should not be posed in such a way as if the management structure of production could be simply dissolved. What is possible, however, is to lead people out of their subordination to the modern machine system, and thus free the '*administration* of things', the *regulation* of production processes, from *domination* over men. (For the time being, I am considering the management apparatus only in its role vis-à-vis the directly productive functions of the production process, not with respect to its internal contradictions, which determine the detailed profile of the bureaucratic management.)

Originally, then, the still undifferentiated managerial function of early capitalism, as in the production of sewing needles by manufacture, which Marx took as an example, confronted a worker who was essentially just as undifferentiated, i.e. unskilled, who was supposed to be able to learn his work from scratch in a few weeks; a pronounced non-specialist, in other words, and in a concrete historical sense particularly the negation of the earlier handicraftsman. Today this type forms only the lowest rung of the collective worker, containing not only a shockingly high percentage of women, but also a relatively high proportion of people who have been damaged either genetically or by their milieu.

In the meantime, however, a new occupational ladder has developed within the operative function, with its own stratification and a spread previously unknown, a scale which I would see as having four levels and culminating on the side of the subjective factor in that *stratum of technical specialists* (see Table 2, p. 166) who in our present social formation still confront the rest of the production personnel as an agent of alienated technique and technology. Next to it stand those groups of specialist workers who operate outside the basic processes of production. The Romantic critique of civilization which cannot free itself from the yearning for handicraft, even though this is inherently stultifying, often fails to realize that in modern industry, where countless patterns of one kind or another are always needed, a far greater number of people than ever before may be employed simply in the specialized handicraft of tool and die making, which can be highly satisfying as a form of concrete labour. The same is true in specialist engineering and in research departments. Even the more talented skilled workers in the machine shop that every factory contains find the opportunity for occasional creative work by hand and machine. These workers are at least in control of the machinery that falls within their sphere of work, i.e. they have at least a certain technical overview and enjoy on top of this the extended room for manoeuvre that comes from the difficulty to be had in replacing them.

Monotony prevails above all in basic production proper, in the manufacture, assembly, checking, packing and storage of mass-produced articles, where the tasks to be performed often do not require any skilled workers and where the lowest wage groups are also always to be found. This situation precisely results from the fact that the activities in question are ripe for automation, or are at least becoming so.

But while all this involves a differentiation and specialization that has been taking place qualitatively since the revolution from the Neolithic era to Bronze Age civilization, even if at an incomparably higher level, modern industrialism creates in the *scientific* technical specialists (using this term here in the broadest sense) a completely new type of producer. Certainly, this type too has his predecessor in the Oriental, ancient or medieval master-builder and mechanic, but never in the sense of a relatively autonomous social stratum rooted firmly in the general division of labour. Civilization, which is based on the divorce between intellectual competence and the immediate labour process, has led via industrial capitalism to an intellectualizing of the immediate process of production, and the gradual withdrawing from it of manual labour. The 'transformation of science into an immediate productive force' is not exhausted in the natural-scientific foundation of technology, as achieved in the wake of the first industrial revolution by way of the formerly indirect collaboration between research scientists and mechanics. The modern engineer, in particular the engineer with university-level training who combines these two aspects, is the exemplary key figure of mature industrialism. His object is provided by the complex machine systems that we interpose between ourselves and our objects of labour in the process of metabolism with nature. Engineering creates the material preconditions for turning basic production 'on its *head*', negatively in Taylorism, and positively with automation and electronic data processing.

'Engineering' is of course only a generalized metaphor for the whole complex of production preparation, which extends from basic research via development, construction and project engineering through to installation and the reproductive maintenance of the new technique. On top of this, the type of specialist who is concerned with ancillary functions in the management staff, e.g. with organization and data processing, is ever less distinguishable, sociologically and socio-psychologically, from the technician in the narrower sense. Those numerous economists who do not participate in key economic policy decisions for their productive unit also approximate to this type. I am assuming no more here than that the key role in the present stage of development of the productive forces falls on the engineer.

If the concept of the working class can still be used – and in late capitalism it is still correct to use it – then the engineer, along with the technical or the economic specialist, is its privileged representative. He can transfer into management with relative ease, as well as withdrawing from the 'establishment' in the opposite direction. What is new, and has been developing in the course of the last hundred years or so, is firstly that the lower managerial functions are deeply embedded in the material production process itself, since administrative and technical directions and interventions are combined. Secondly, by way of the specialists, the immediate functions of labour spill over from the preparation and organization of production into the administrative sphere, and dictate decisions to the managing subject. The specialists – and despite their difference from the traditional strata of the production staff, this must be unconditionally maintained – represent, in their capacity as living mental labour, a new fraction of the division of labour not within *managerial activity,* but rather within *production activity.* And these specialists show a tendency to subsume the managerial functions, or at least subject them to their own control.

They pay for it, however, with an insidious bureaucratization, at least with being subsumed under the control mechanisms internal to the bureaucracy. For this reason, they often put up a passive resistance to the management, and show a readily apparent unwillingness to take on managerial functions. Yet the official indoctrination and political obligation of the 'management cadres' naturally rubs off on them too, tempting suitable candidates not only with the scent of careerism, but into unprincipled behaviour as well. Management functions almost inevitably require party membership, and it is only too evident that very few people today, mostly young ones, are attracted to the party from honest motives. This phenomenon, however, can be got rid of immediately by a political change, whereas the general tendency to bureaucratization is more deeply rooted.

Engineering – let there be no illusion on this point – is still not in itself universal labour, it is subsumed under the extreme division of labour in science and technique. And the specialist is as a rule in no way an intellectual in the traditional sense. Not infrequently, he is as far from being a 'philosopher', from capacity for government, as the celebrated cook. But his subjection to scientific and technical specialism has given him a *capacity for abstraction* which, even if originally applied to a non-human, 'purely objective' and not socially conceived object of nature and technique, and for all its confinement by mechanism, positivism and scientism, can subsequently be deployed as a tool for subjective reflection, and thereby also for historical reflection. Hence the engineer potentially stands far closer to 'philosophy' than does the cook, and the social antithesis between the specialists and the established general political and economic management could provide the progressive dynamic for the most immediate phase of the transition process.

If I stress here how the specialists come to the fore in the collective worker, this is not of course to deny that the immediate producers at the bottom of the pyramid also undertake activities which already overstep their special role in the labour process. Thanks to the universal natural endowment of the human brain, to a fundamental biological development that preceded its possibilities of social realization, even the systems of caste, slave and racial oppression that we have discussed above never managed to reduce human subjectivity to its principal labour function alone. Today, more than ever, there exists at all levels, in part already actual, in part still potential, a *surplus of human expertise,* which under the existing relations of production is neither required nor made use of, but experiences rather a permanent pressure for its reduction. 'Plan together, work together, govern together!' echoes the slogan from the loudspeakers, meaning that everyone is to show more system-conforming activity in his due place. But as soon as anyone ventures to overstep the limits of the prevailing regulations and institutions, he invariably hears the real message of the government: 'Cobbler, stick to your last'. And this at all levels, not simply in political life. We must thank Edward Gierek for the forthright way in which he summed up the problem of our societies after the Polish December crisis, with the slogan: 'You work well, and we will govern well!' The division of labour inherited from previous class society still means that the over-whelming majority of individuals are decisively limited by their subjection to a particular single trade that is programmed into them at an early age, so that in other spheres they can at most participate in a passive way. But it all comes down to whether a realism of this kind is presented fatalistically and apologetically, or alternatively in a critical and hence revolutionary way. This realism can only be critical and revolutionary if it neither sees the dominion of the traditional division of labour as an unalterable fact, nor leaves the task of overcoming it to future generations. We must recall once again here what Marx understood by the abolition of the traditional division of labour.

Uncomprehending critics of this 'Marxist utopia' like to counter it by bringing up the increasing number of highly specialized tasks in the very diverse levels and fields of human activity. But apart from the tendency towards integration in science, which also promotes a *horizontal disposability* that is completely to the advantage of the individuals concerned, it is essentially not a question of giving this specialist or that access to so and so many further special disciplines at his own functional level. Alienation is not a problem between the fitter and the laboratory assistant, or between the geologist and the physicist. People who have learned the dialectical structures of philosophy, cybernetics, mathematics and art are capable in principle of understanding any problem, no matter how complex, and moreover, understanding it more profoundly than would be necessary for egalitarian social communication; but this need in no way make them incapable of pushing a heavy hand-truck without tipping it over. Yet this *vertical universality* is precisely what is prevented by the prevailing division of labour! It prevents it so much that we can observe how people whose early training and work experience has made them into skilled workers, say, cannot genuinely rise above the original structural level of their given consiousness in middle age, even by successfully completing a tortuous course of further study.

Our society erects in capital letters the motto: 'From each according to his abilities, to each according to his work', while at the same time operating a plan that governs the proportions in which the members of society, as they grow up, will attain the various levels of ability and consumer satisfaction, in fact of human realization in general. In Orwell's *Animal Farm,* the slogan on the barn wall according to which 'All animals are equal' is later extended to say 'but some are more equal than others'. To understand the real kernel of this incisive correction we must translate it into a language closer to that of economics. It would then run: Society (i.e. human civilization and culture) belongs to all individuals, but some are more social than others. The appropriation of culture is a question of *active, conscious participation* in its various functional levels and realms of expression.

And if someone has to concentrate his energy eight hours a day on activities that demand a relatively low level of coordination of consciousness, in some particular isolated field, he will in all probability be excluded automatically from a share in decision-making on a broader scale and at a higher level, since he is not in a position to acquire the capacities of differentiation and abstraction that are required for this. He then belongs fundamentally to the oppressed of the society in question.

The excuse that the distribution of individuals to various spheres under actually existing socialism simply reflects the natural distribution of aptitudes and talents must be decisively rejected, because differences in capacity for education are for the most part produced in the course of childhood socialization, and this is dictated by the prevailing division of labour and its planned reproduction. Individually, it is certainly possible to raise oneself above the limits of a subordinate compartmentalized task, which will then generally lead sooner or later to pursuing work of a more general kind: some kind of managerial function in economics or politics, a scientific or artistic activity. This is very similar to saying that any shoe-shine boy in capitalist society can become a Rockefeller – even if quantitatively there is now a somewhat greater chance of advance. In bourgeois society, too, at least when compared with the past, there are no longer any absolute restrictions on access to synthetic functions and the prerequisites of education. And even in traditional China, from the Han dynasty on, juridical equality theoretically permitted quite broad strata of the population social advance through a bureaucratic career. Peasants could compete with gentry in the examinations. The problem is not a completely new one. What is involved is the subjective aspect of 'economy of time' – time for the development of the essential human powers.

There are two closely related mechanisms that prevent manual workers, or more precisely all those who have to spend their normal working-day in abstract and compartmentalized work, from access to the social synthesis.

The first mechanism is underdevelopment of the motivation to learn, which affects the disadvantaged strata already in childhood. In complex societies, where knowledge of the overall connection (not simply acquisition of a manipulated picture) is a process of many stages from appearance to essence, training and exercize of the capacity for abstraction and reflection are needed if the decisive relationships are to be grasped. In this respect, individual opportunity in our society is on the whole *just* as unequally distributed as in late capitalist society, irrespective of certain minor differences. For further details, I shall quote here a work from the Mitscherlich school of educational psychology:

'Whether or not those modes of behaviour that count as "intelligence" in the current definition and are immediately significant for the development of *reflection* are developed already in childhood, depends on the *time perspective* that the child internalizes in the domestic environment.'

What the authors mean by this is the time perspective of the adults around them, whether they live their lives with a qualitative horizon of expectation, with the hope of change (improvement) and advance (in some more or less far-reaching sense), or whether they have come to terms with a monotonous lapse of time which only brings repetition of the same tasks and enjoyments, and where time is measured only in minutes, hours and days devoid of meaning. In a time framework such as this, 'neither revolution nor hope are *conceivable* for the individual, hardly even curiosity; there is no "exploratory drive", no strategic thinking, i.e. no development, and in this way the chances of intelligent problem-solving behaviour and reflection being formed are reduced. In these contrasting "time perspectives" . . . what is reproduced above all is the form of labour: either monotonous and with a very sparse degree of freedom in the choice of organization of one's own pattern of labour, without the motivating hope of advance, development or change, dependent and disposed of by others, the object of strategic plans; or alternatively changing, mobilizing, disposing, with (partial) strategies of organization or problems. The very degree of fragmentation of labour can be influential. As observation shows, society honours workers and junior employees for stability (the celebrated "long service bonus") and gives even more senior employees scarcely any rewards for curious inquiry. The sharpness with which the functions of intelligence develop seems to be itself dependent on the kind of activity and the pattern of work. The reason working-class children are then less "intelligent" than children from the middle class is because they grow up shadowed by the latent depression of their fathers (mothers), whose own development is already inhibited by the time adulthood is reached. Some people are accustomed to the "protracted adolescence" of the school pupil and student (not to speak of the "repeated adolescence" of gifted people who enjoy very privileged positions); others become still more stultified as they grow older. They know very well that they are to remain workers – a knowledge that is internalized, needing no further articulation. They remain for ever "at the bottom". . . . If this is correct, then the lesser degree of intelligence and reflective capacity of the lower social strata is to be explained from the social *impotence* of the wage-earners, which forces them more or less to acceptance, to a consumer attitude, to oppression, to lack of perspective, and hence implies renunciation of intellectuality'.[8]

If this first mechanism helps to explain how the prevailing division of labour already makes sure of subaltern individuals for the next generation, then the second mechanism involves the continuous blocking of a breakthrough to participation in the social synthesis. Here we can introduce some considerations of the French Marxist Lucien Sève, under the heading 'time schedule of the personality'.[9] What Sève means by this is that the proportions in which the individual spends his time on abstract wage-labour (that lost to mental growth) and passive reproduction of his energy and needs on the one hand, and on productive and consumptional educational processes, i.e. the acquisition of new abilities, on the other, is expressed in specific proportions of mental application and expenditure of energy for different classes of behaviour, which gradually become fixed and reinforced. From this point of view, *every* modern industrial society exhibits a continuous scale between the extremes of those people who (leaving out parasites) can perform all their necessary labour in

[8] Brückner, Leithäuser, Kriesel, *Psychoanalyse*, Frankfurt a.M., 1968, pp. 38ff.
[9] Lucien Sève, *Man in Marxist Theory and the Psychology of Personality*, Hassocks 1978.

the form of productive consumption, i.e. as creative activity, and those others whose necessary labour is simply lost for their own development.

By the mere fact that certain sections, groups and strata claim for themselves, as their major occupation, a life-long universal and creative activity in politics, science and art, thus monopolizing that work which inherently leads to the development of the individual's essential powers – by this fact they condemn other groups and strata to occupational limitation, if not to the stultification of their brains. And naturally enough, they project this condition materially into the future, through their decisive influence on the planning of investments, educational institutions and mass communications. Just as the bourgeoisie cannot imagine any future in which its own privileged position is not reproduced, so most of our politicans and functionaries, and our scientists and artists too, cannot imagine any perspective in which they no longer figure as privileged.

If we take the structure of our society as a whole, a structure that corresponds to that of the collective worker, we can establish at a glance the relatively continuous 'vertical' transition from one stratum to another, one level of material and cultural life to the next. With exceptions that are not statistically important, though they could easily be avoided and in critical situations sometimes even are avoided, there is a relatively smooth distribution of individuals along the various continua. It is also significant that the differentiation of incomes, though sometimes sharpened for certain better-off circles by a cumulative effect, is not as acute as the more decisive gradation according to level of education and position in the process of social reproduction, not even when the privileges of the *arriviste* dignitaries are included. On this score – as a residual gesture to traditional Marxist concepts – there are still certain restraining limits and a more or less deliberate resistance to the uninhibited exploitation of positions for the base purpose of enrichment. The real privileges are of a political kind, the rest more or less simply accoutrements.

Viewed as a whole, therefore, the problems of our social structure do not rest on socially 'unjust' relations of *distribution* being immanent to the system (in as much as such injustice is not rooted in the very principle of distribution according to work). Yet the pyramid of division of labour and management exhibits a bipolarity that goes far beyond the political phenomenon of a radically unequal distribution of power. In the Soviet sociological literature of recent years, the 'cultural' components of social stratification have been more strongly emphasized, components of cultural expertise in the broadest sense. The cultural continuum is broken by readily comprehensible factors deriving from degree of urbanization, level of education and the sexual duality. As against the urban, highly skilled and male element (in countries that were yesterday still agricultural, the difference between industrial workers and peasants is of course still considerable), which statistically tends towards the top of the pyramid, the rural, unskilled and female element tends towards the bottom. Here, particularly in the perpetuation of the oldest historical residues of the class division, we have what in countries on the far side of capitalism, even the highly industrialized Western ones, is the decisive task of the progressive forces. Political revolution or reformation only has any meaning if it improves the conditions for the technical and at the same time cultural revolution that liberates people step by step from the chains of the traditional division of labour and the state, and ensures them the preconditions for the free development of all, right down to the primary cells of society.

7

The Working Class as an Inapplicable Concept in Proto-Socialist Society

For all its quantitative overlap, the concept of the collective worker, which was my point of departure in the previous chapter, has nothing in common with the concept of the working class. Left-wing criticism of our conditions, which I fully sympathize with emotionally, often pursues a dogmatic logic when it erroneously, and indeed in an objectively reactionary way, erects as its aim a repetition of the cycle we have already undergone. The concept of the working class is simply inapposite for defining the essential structural characteristics of our society and discussing the problem of its future perspectives. In 1969-70 it was commonly stated in the GDR that the working class meant all those who were physically or mentally productive; this was the leading class which held political power. Even if invented for purposes which were for the most part apologetic, aiming to veil social contradictions, this still meant that all 'workers and employees', including the 'large sections of the intelligentsia' who are indistinguishable from the former in our population statistics, together of course with the whole party, state, trade-union and economic bureaucracy, should be theoretically kept in a single watertight compartment. Now, no definition of the 'working class' is given any longer, since – though this is of course not admitted – it is objectively impossible to give one. The concept of the working class no longer has any definable object in our social system, and, what is far more important, it has no object that can appear as a unity in practical action.

Those 'workers and employees' then already made up over 80 per cent of the total population. With the progress of agricultural cooperation beyond the original small-scale units, the collective worker here too has had its sociological structure brought directly into line with the industrial, proceeding from relations of production which are evidently no longer determined by the rudimentary right of property. As far as the basic problems of our social structure are concerned, 'workers' and 'cooperative peasants' can already be taken as identical, which of course does not make attention to their specific differences superfluous. The reason for simply identifying them here is that our society is no longer characterized by a 'horizontal' class division, but rather by a 'vertical' stratification, even if one which still has sharp transition points. The basic relationship is not that between a working class and all other elements of the social structure, but rather in their common equality vis-à-vis a third factor. Between an industrial worker and a manual working cooperative peasant there is scarcely more than a distinction in form as far as their position in the production and reproduction process is concerned.

The most that the categories of class structure can do for our non-capitalist order is to interpret it *in terms of its past*. From this point of view it presents itself as a result of subtraction: the sum of the classes and strata of bourgeois society minus the bourgeoisie and the junkers. Even taking into account that after this subtraction the valencies and relative weights of the remaining elements are decisively changed, this does not give us anything more than a merely morphological description, whose criteria of demarcation stem from the old society. Beyond capitalism, the concept of the working class not only loses its operative sense, it now becomes available for decking up this or that new special interest, particularly for the pseudo-legitimation of the substitute bureaucratic power. In the countries of actual socialism, moreover, there is scarcely one theorist who would undertake to give a serious definition of the working class.

Individuals only form a class in so far as they stand in a common antithesis to another class with respect to their position vis-à-vis the conditions of production and existence. Classes are fundamentally correlative categories, and fit together with all other elements of the social formation, in particular, of course, with its dominant elements. They can only be defined in terms of the overall disposition of a society. The proletariat loses its specific socio-economic identity together with the bourgeoisie, so that in the post-revolutionary situation it is necessarily completely different criteria, in fact criteria of internal structuring, that become relevant. (The discovery of these criteria is of course delayed by the way that the new ruling elements seek to salvage and reinforce the old identity in the confrontation with the external enemy, in the shape of the remaining bourgeois states, and there is certainly an objective basis for this.)

As a form of indirect proof, let us start by considering the facts from the standpoint of the traditional concepts, and in particular the customary concept of the proletariat, meaning the industrial workers with the exclusion of the technical intelligentsia.

In the late capitalist countries the reformist tendency has long been dominant in the workers' movement. It became so with the differentiation of a 'labour aristocracy', i.e. with one major portion of manual labour becoming skilled in the course of capitalist industrialization, and with the growth of the stratum of employees based on the differentiation of the function of management. But the division of the workers' movement into different parties, instead of simply wings, can only be understood in terms of the success of the Russian revolution, i.e. it has never been a purely internal phenomenon of the highly industrialized capitalist countries. The German workers movement, in particular, came to grief in the 1920s as a result of this split and the subsequent 'Bolshevization' of the KPD, its most active element. Rosa Luxemburg's hesitations against the Left wing becoming a separate party, which she never entirely abandoned, had a genuine rational kernel. There was not a single Western country in which the independent communist party, though its ideological purpose was entirely pertinent, managed to fulfil the expectations placed on it. Even in recent years, the inherited anachronism of the old Comintern strategy decisively worsened the prospects of the Portuguese revolution, as the PCP was responsible for the country's political spectrum being broken left of centre instead of right, and moreover for the left wing of the military being split and its best forces eroded. It can only be hoped that the Portuguese experience finally puts the seal on this whole unfortunate type of communist strategy. Today, when the impulse of the Russian revolution is exhausted, while the old basis persists in the West at a new level, the 're-social-democratization' of the strongest communist parties, in Italy, France, Spain, Finland, etc. is proceeding apace, with a consequent tendency towards reunion (though by no means on the positions of the *present* social-democratic leaders). But be this as it may, the traditional workers' movement in the late capitalist countries has not come to power. Revolutionary activities such as those in France in 1968 arose from social forces who were formerly not counted as part of the working class. It is clear that the historically older strata of workers maintain their presence, and need to continue their representation in the communist party, but it is no longer possible to base the general strategy on their interests.

With the transition to state monopoly, the social-democratic movement also reaches a new phase of development, reflecting the latest shift of forces within the 'wage-earning' collective worker, a shift towards the specialist stratum. How can the social-democrats be the dominant party of government? In the classical American case in particular, as W.H. Whyte demonstrated after the euphoria of the 'managerial revolution', management has proved to be a socially and politically conservative element.[1] Yet in America we have a late capitalism which has still not completely left behind its former pioneering days, and which despite its 'Pentagonization' still lacks the extreme unction of state monopoly. Whyte focussed precisely on the management of corporations, where universal labour is still performed for particular purposes – in relation to the framework of the existing society. The advance of *state* management, in its results and its social perspectives, is designed to cope with the adaptations that are needed at an ever faster rhythm, as a result of the rapid spontaneous development of the overall social process, in a reforming manner, i.e. in agreement with the fundamental class interests of a financial oligarchy which is itself in the course of transformation. This intention was Kennedy's secret and his brilliance, seeking as he did to use his inherited family wealth as the springboard for a higher type of national

---

[1] W.H. Whyte, *Organisation Man*, Harmondsworth 1961.

leadership than that of the industrial bourgeoisie. Kennedy sought to give the American state a social role that it had never played domestically in previous American history. (Kennedy's murder signalled, as much as did the murder of Walter Rathenau in 1922, the danger of a conservative and fascist counter-revolution, a backward rather than a forward flight from the permanent crisis of transition to a new and higher civilization.)

In Western Europe the bloc of forces required for the fascist solution seems already to have been dissolved by history; its hour has past. The demise of the conservative-reactionary bloc in post-war West Germany is a very significant symptom for our whole continent. If the signs are not misleading, Western Europe is being social-democratized, perhaps even France, although there the traditional ruling forces followed an étatist course even in the past. Brandt was analogous to Kennedy, but he rose into the state machine 'from below', with a quite different mass base, and in particular not just a temporary psychological one. Because of its whole history, the German bourgeoisie was in no position to put a figure like Kennedy at the head of the nation, a figure such as Rathenau. All it could produce were petty lawyers such as Stresemann and Adenauer. Nothing therefore remained for the neo-liberals but to support the social-democrats – who should of course not be taken at their name. Social-democracy of the Wehner-Brandt-Schmidt style, and this is the essential point, can no longer be qualified as a 'bourgeois workers' party', simply because at the helm of the economically powerful state apparatus it becomes an independent variable, without thereby regenerating itself in some 'neo-proletarian' manner. This process is of course not yet completed, the position not yet decisively consolidated. Much will depend on whether the EEC gives rise to a supranational *state* superstructure.

What is West European social-democracy today, and West German social-democracy in particular? And this irrespective of whether its political course veers more to the right, as with Brandt, or more to the left, as with Palme? It is neither a bourgeois party nor a workers' party, let alone a 'people's party'. By the qualitative core of its mass base it is above all the party of the 'new working class', the broad stratum of specialists which we have already discussed, and which naturally enough produces also its kindred ideologists.

The student unrest in the West is the rebellion of future specialists with their demand not to become specialists, not to get trapped in the subaltern position prepared for them in the beehive of late industrialism. This stratum, with its students in the lead, is both anti-capitalist and anti-managerial (against the 'establishment'). Immature and recently dogmatic as they are in their views (because their self-awareness is still new), they still give expression, at least potentially, to the interests of the working class as a whole, and particularly of the young workers, since while there is of course a difference between specialists in the disciplines of natural science, technology and economics on the one hand, and skilled manual workers on the other, there is in no way an antagonism. In research divisions, for example, they work together in a comradely way, without paternalistic tutelage of one group over the other, and exchange advice from their respective specialisms. At least tendentially, we have here that 'communication without domination' which is so greatly praised.

Now to the extent that the capitalist element in a society is suppressed, this stratum can appear as the true counterpart of the étatist management, irrespective of whether it presents itself as social-democratic or communist, and can stand at the head of the great majority charged with the executive functions of the collective worker. Against private capitalism and the particularism of the monopolies, their interests coincide to a certain extent with the étatist management, which in its striving for rational regulation from above sees itself obstructed by the traditional 'pluralism' of the bourgeoisie and the corporations, and damaged thereby in its social perspectives. (How often do ideologists and journalists of this colour express their envy of the *dirigiste* power of our top bureaucrats!)

Social-democracy in power is the party of a compromise of interests between the 'system-transcending' specialist stratum of the electorate and the 'system-reforming' oriented portion of the management, especially the state portion, which naturally enough continues to respect as its limit the long-run interests of monopoly capital. Strictly speaking, the two wings find a common language only in confrontation with the conservative fraction of the bourgeoisie. Yet particularly when the non-establishment wing is strong and makes itself into the *de facto* representative of all working people outside of the management, thus championing a superior version of the general interest, a rivalry can prove relatively fruitful for a longer evolutionary period, and dialectically prepare the way for a more fundamental anti-capitalist line for the masses. The Young Socialist wing of the SPD today groups around it the most progressive elements of West German society, which does not mean that they should get entirely absorbed in the SPD and compromise with its party discipline. But today it is sectarianism that is the greatest sin. In the long run the day of a great Marxist party is bound to dawn, a union of all genuine socialists in West Germany. But this will articulate politically a qualitatively different subject than that of 'the working class'.

What is the position of the working class, then, in the countries of actually existing socialism? From the very beginning, the Bolshevik dictatorship was no more identical with the rule of the working class than the Jacobin dictatorship was with the rule of the sans-culottes. None of the earlier social conflicts, nor any of the more recent either, allow us to establish anything which could be even approximately interpreted as a tendency to the constitution of an authentic workers' power.

The introduction of self-management in Yugoslavia led in the first instance primarily to a division of social power between the state and a decentralized management, one which can be made formally responsible to the immediate producers in general, but cannot be effectively controlled by them. None the less, the League of Communists there can still maintain the abstract principle of workers' power, because it has capitulated neither to the state machine nor to the management.

The 'Great Proletarian Cultural Revolution' in China affected the working class in that country rather as an object – though this was not its essential aspect.

In Czechoslovakia in 1968 it was unambiguously the 'intelligentsia' that dominated, being above all their 'glorious revolution' (by analogy with the 1688 revolution in England, in which the real beneficiaries of the bourgeois revolution adapted the political system to their needs).

In Poland in December 1970 the working class was provoked to rebellion by the stupidity of the party-state apparatus, but was then immediately and completely led to an acceptable alternative *within* the apparatus: the uprising gave the impulse for what one could call a 'small proletarian cultural revolution' from above, i.e. the purging from the apparatus of some of the most reactionary, inconsiderate and unteachable bureaucrats. This should be seen as an outcome *adequate* to the socio-economic and political preconditions.

The essence of our internal situation is precisely expressed in the way that the working class has no other cadres and no other organization than that by which it is dominated. In so far as the workers confront the new state as the general capitalist, i.e. in the very respect in which they still maintain their old identity as wage-workers, they stand in this confrontation without any other leaders than a few spokesmen who arise spontaneously and are quite untested. The unions, the original fighting organizations for their particular class interests, appear almost exclusively in a supporting function for the state machine (even if this function of care and control may in itself be very pleasant). Deprived of these associations which are adapted to their immediate interests, the workers are automatically atomized vis-à-vis the regime. They are in any case no longer a 'class for itself', and not at all so in a political sense.

If the Czechoslovak reform movement had had any success at all, then whatever the outcome, the workers would have got back their trade unions, which would have improved their social and political condition. Yet on the other hand, with this very restoration, their subaltern role as wage-workers of a state managed by a bureaucracy would have been acknowledged. It must remain an open question to what extent the non-sovereign workers' councils that were already envisaged would have gone beyond this situation, since the social policy of the new communist party had yet to appear in practice. But it can still not be fortuitous that the principle of workers' councils has never yet led to the results that were anticipated. Precisely under actually existing socialism, it has been shown quite clearly that the industrial proletariat as such has not attained the perspectives predicted of it. What Marx compressed in the concept of a world-historical mission of the proletariat is dissolved in the *history* of non- or post-capitalist industrial societies. But if general emancipation is a process of generations, it cannot be a movement led by an already harmonized subject which remains the same throughout this change. To deny the still antagonistic character of this movement is to see its result as theoretically present already at the beginning. The immense majority of proletarian individuals necessarily find their condition changed only in name, and in certain circumstances they must even pay for a modest gain that consists principally in 'social security' with a slower growth in their living standard.

Today, the official theory and propaganda that maintains the 'leading role of the working class' serves the sole purpose of justifying the domination of the apparatus. The idea of working-class power is used to conceal a reality that is diametrically opposed to it. The working class as a whole, and the worker members of the party in particular, are allocated the political role of ballast when this is needed to reinforce the weight of the party-state machine against any attempt of effective correction. It was not by chance that Novotny tried to appeal to the workers before his overthrow, even if to no avail! Nor that the organizational apparatus of the party is careful to reinforce the 'workers' quota', the only section of the membership needing such artificial stimulation! For the workers are in no hurry to take on the kind of 'leading role' that the system ascribes to them. It has rather been shown, in Czechoslovakia as in Poland, that they play a progressive role in society precisely when they emancipate themselves from the tutelage of the party apparatus.

Now those people who prefer not to see the real relationship between working class and party-state apparatus, and would rather stick to dogmatic reiteration of orthodox doctrine, will naturally object that Marx's concept of the proletariat, while it is focussed on the industrial workers in its economic analysis, is in no way restricted to them. On this point I shall confine myself for the time being to the contention that the historical bloc that crystallized around the 'proletarian' interest, and found its most advanced expression in the socialist parties, was characterized from the very start by an internal contradiction that inevitably split open after the seizure of political power. Marx's conception of the party, and still more so that of Lenin, had precisely this contradiction as its inner theme. Theirs was the programme of a revolutionary elite which drew towards it the intellectual element of the working class, uniting with it so as to use the material of the actual workers' movement, which because it pursues its *particular* class interests does not and cannot have this tendency, to undertake tasks such as the general emancipation of man or the renovation of Russia.

It is one thing to lead the workers to full awareness of their economic class opposition to the bourgeoisie, but something else entirely to seek to make them conscious of their 'universal' interests. This is to simultaneously both assert and deny the specific alienation of the working class as a concrete reality, and to equate the possibility of emancipation for the proletarian individual with the possibility of emancipation for the entire class. We can study how this substitution of one problem for the other functions in the following text of the young Gramsci; I quote Gramsci here because as early as September 1920, writing in *Ordine Nuovo,* he already had an understanding of the problem that is in advance of the present average level: 'What a force of expansion the worker's sentiments will acquire, bent as he is for eight hours every day over his machine repeating the ritual gestures of his craft, as monotonous as the clicking of a circle of rosary beads, when he becomes the "master" – the measure of all social values? Surely the very fact that the worker still manages to think, even when he is reduced to operating in complete ignorance of the how or why of his practical activity, is a miracle? This miracle of the worker who takes charge each day of his own intellectual autonomy and his own freedom to handle ideas, by struggling against fatigue, against boredom and against the monotony of a job that strives to mechanize and so kill his inner life – this miracle is organized in the Communist Party, in the will to struggle and the revolutionary creativity that are expressed in the Communist Party.

'The worker in the factory fulfils merely an executive function. He does not follow the general process of labour and production.

He is not a point that moves and so creates a line; he is a pin stuck in a particular place, and the line is made up of a succession of pins that an alien will has arranged in accordance with its own ends. The worker tends to carry this mode of being of his into every aspect of his life. At all times he adjusts easily to the role of material executor, of a "mass" guided by a will that is alien to his own. He is intellectually lazy; he cannot and does not wish to look beyond his immediate horizon, so he lacks criteria in his choice of leaders and allows himself to be easily taken in by promises. He likes to believe he can get what he wants without making a great effort himself or thinking too much. The Communist Party is the instrument and historical form of the process of inner liberation through which the worker is transformed from *executor* to *initiator*, from *mass* to *leader* and *guide,* from brawn to brain and purpose. . . . The Russian revolution was a revolution carried out by men organized in the Communist Party: in the Party they fashioned for themselves a new personality, acquired new sentiments and brought into being a morality whose goal is to become a universal consciousness striven after by all mankind'.[2]

The Marxist intellectuals have always had an idealized picture of 'the worker', one that referred to no one other than themselves. Because of this fixation on *the* worker, who becomes party member, communist intellectual and organizer, so much Marxist discussion in Europe since 1914 ends up by declaring that the interests that the workers really do display are not their real interests. In actual fact, the Marxian concept of the proletariat expresses the utopia that communism will follow on from capitalism in its stage of free competition after a brief transition period. Marx and his successors, therefore, were themselves not properly aware of the real significance of the contradiction contained from the very beginning in this conception of the party, even though in the organized Marxist-socialist movement the solidarity of 'workers by hand or brain' has necessarily been sworn time and again. We have even seen above how Marx refused to face the possibility of a new economic despotism.

And yet this possibility is present already in the earliest germ of

---

[2] *Selections from Political Writings 1910-1920*, London 1977, pp. 333-4.

the party idea, in the demand for the unification of philosophy and proletariat, for the 'lightning of thought' to 'strike deeply into this virgin soil of the people",[3] or to put it more concretely, for the unification of the revolutionary intellectuals with the working class. The spirit was always preceptory and remained so, especially in Leninism, even if the concepts became ever more concrete and mature with the deeper understanding of the economy. Only 'philosophy', only the intelligentsia permeated with the last word of social science (Heine called Marx and his friends 'doctors of revolution'), could make the proletariat aware of its true nature, its present situation and its future interests. Who else would launch the lightning strike so greatly desired?

Right from the beginning, the socialist parties had a double face, and by no means just in Russia: both parties *of* the proletariat, and parties *for* the proletariat. Their founders and their pre-revolutionary leaders were understandably, with few exceptions, intellectuals from the intermediate strata. It was not the working class who gave itself them as its leadership, but they who gave themselves to the working class. And workers, if they were to take a place among them, had to become intellectuals themselves, with the facts of the division of labour and class structure of bourgeois society, which were reflected even within the workers' organizations, having the permanent result that these workers' intellectuals cease to be workers, to live as workers, and transfer to a different milieu, to a different particular existence as ideologists and organizers, as the movement's 'officers'. After victory, they confront their class comrades as functionaries in the ruling apparatus. The immediate problem today does not lie in this reality itself, but rather in its neglect and ignoring by theory, a neglect which is most closely connected with the immediate special interests of these workers' officers. Even Marx and Engels reflected less critically and more emotionally on their own role in the workers' movement than on almost any other object of their attention, though they were certainly much aware of it and very often distanced themselves from the movement's immediate

[3] 'Critique of Hegel's Philosophy of Right. Introduction', in *Early Writings*, *loc. cit.*, p. 257.

leaders. Even with them, therefore, we find a residue of the characteristic blindness of the subject towards itself.

It seems to me that their entire concept of the proletariat was never completely free from the Hegelian antithesis between (rational, essential) reality and (merely empirical, accidental) existence, and this for reason of their own subjective needs. The actual empirical proletariat, even though summoned by them to represent the whole of humanity in its progress, is a class that, left to its own devices, only attains trade-union expression of its interests. As the result of an overwhelming structure of historical reality, the same as formerly affected church organizations concerned with the saving of souls, consciousness of its 'true', 'world-historical' goals had to be brought into the workers' movement from outside. Yet it was still simply a question of interests and goals in the sweet by and by, in as much as their realization in *time* was postponed to the same indefinite future as that of the goals of religious subjectivity, i.e. beyond the lifetime of the individuals concerned. The working class had therefore to be educated to raise itself individual by individual above its empirical, immediate interests, to overcome the dead weight of what according to Marx's own theory was the decisive situation of work and life, and this could only be achieved, as a general rule, by a minority. Already in the relationship between 'philosophy' and 'proletariat', therefore, as well as in the whole later discussion about bringing revolutionary consciousness into the working masses from outside, the unification of socialism (as a science) with the workers' movement, the problem of 'spontaneity and consciousness', etc., we have a society foreshadowed which, in the words of the *Theses on Feuerbach*, must be 'divide[d] . . . into two parts, one of which is superior to society'.[4] For 'philosophy' can only be the 'philosophers' with their intellectual-educational and administrative retinue! And the Hellenized form in which the philosophers were to rule by way of a transmission belt of 'guardians' was precisely that in which Plato recaptured the essence of the ancient Egyptian economic despotism.

A perspective of this kind – only now looking not backward but

[4] *Collected Works*, vol. 3, p. 4.

forward – corresponded completely to the requirements of that intelligentsia dissatisfied with capitalism, which had abandoned the historical phase of Romantic negation, and now sought an alternative in progress forward, increasingly opting for revolution. The programme of general emancipation gives preferential expression to the striving of such an elite for totality, for universalization and completion of their mode of life and subjectivity. It is only for them that the contradiction between immediate and world-historical interests disappears in practice. The demand directed at the workers, that they should sacrifice their immediate corporate interests for the sake of a goal that is not necessarily attainable in this particular life, but is none the less a necessary human goal, or at least an overall national goal, provides for a genuine enjoyment of life for those people concerned with training and organizing the army for such a purpose. Later these come to constitute the core of the ruling party, state and economic bureaucracy. The intellectual vanguard already pioneers this role in the leadership of the political workers' movement. The riddle of their pre-revolutionary sacrifice is disclosed by Hegel's observation that martyrs generally find due reward in their action (at least psychologically). Through their political and organizational work, in which both themselves and their authority are confirmed, the general historical interest comes to be their own particular interest.

Gramsci's idea, therefore, formulated with Russia and Italy particularly in mind, according to which the proletariat can only remain the ruling class by giving up its present vital interests in favour of its hegemony, and placing itself in the service of a scientifically proven interest of humanity, simply boils down to the fact that has since become quite evident enough, that the proletariat *cannot* be a ruling class. This was admitted in all essentials by Lenin himself in his celebrated essay 'Better Fewer, but Better', when instead of appealing to the working class as a whole, he appealed to the most enlightened elements in Russia, meaning the most advanced (most cultivated, most intellectualized) workers and to the minority of intellectuals and specialists inspired by the revolution.[5]

[5] *Collected Works*, vol. 33, p. 489.

It goes without saying that neither Marx nor Lenin, in their conception of the party, committed anything that could in any meaningful sense be called a 'mistake'. On the contrary. They sought and found a solution that corresponded to the real conditions of the emancipation struggle of the working class. Up till the seizure of power, the 'philosophers' are genuine representatives of the specific general interest that they formulate, just as previously were the bourgeoisie and its Enlightenment *avant-garde*; they led the way to a new social formation. It was simply that Marx and Lenin, like other ideologists before them, were deceived as to the objective contradictions that were necessarily involved in their conceptions and activities. This is something quite different from the disingenuous deceit of those 'Marxists' of today who are professionally employed to concern themselves with concealing the contradictions of the new social structure that are already fully disclosed. Today the dilemma of the Marxist-Leninist conception of the party is evident from logic alone. Every class previously called upon to rule was naturally also in a position to formulate and represent its overall social role for itself. The conception of 'bringing' consciousness into the supposed hegemonic force from outside, which in its time was completely adequate politically, anticipates the break-up of the theory to which it pertains.

The workers – individual exceptions apart – were never Marxist in the strict sense. Marxism is a theory based on the *existence* of the working class, but it is not the theory *of* the working class. It was always Left intellectuals who found themselves in a position to understand Marxism as a whole. And this was all the easier for them in so far as it appointed them, under the banner of the future proletarian interest – this being simply a further expression for the 'general' or 'universal' interest of a post-capitalist humanity – to be its historically privileged advocates. Politically, these represent the 'bourgeoisie of the fourth estate', i.e. they lay claim to future domination of the historical bloc which they lead to power. Their rise to political power corresponds with the process of differentiation of the industrial collective worker, increasingly registered already by Marx, this signifying the social advance of a new stratum of intellectual specialists and 'managers'.

The form of the workers' movement and its actual destiny proclaim a society whose central conflict rests directly on the character and complexity of industrialized labour. For the time being I shall only say that Marx, as a result of his concentration on the problems of the capitalist formation, failed to recognize the so-to-speak *class-like* character of the functional differentiation within the industrial collective worker in its independent significance.

But even apart from this, there is nothing in the framework of Marxist theory that proves a *world-historical* mission for the proletariat. Marx and Engels postulated this *before* they had analysed in detail the laws of the capitalist mode of production. All that emerges from *Capital,* and forcibly so, is the role of the proletariat as antagonist of the bourgeoisie *within* the relationship of wage-labour and capital, and the intensification of the class struggle that is derived from this is linked with the phenomena of competitive capitalism and its reproduction in the competition between the monopolies. That the proletariat is to be something beyond this, i.e. the actual collective subject of universal emancipation, remained a philosophical hypothesis, in which the utopian component of Marxism was concentrated. Discussions of the falling rate of profit can in no case close this gap.

Marx introduces two arguments as to why the proletariat can found a new society – and this in a movement that is no longer dialectical, i.e. without a new contradiction developing out of it. The first of these, which is negative, is that the proletariat is the focus of all former alienation, impoverishment and debasement. It was a mental structure of Marx's from very early on to describe the society he faced in such a way that no solution appeared possible other than total revolution. After 1848 this relic of utopianism faded into the background, we might even say the underground. But the impulse from which it proceeded still remained. The most general core of this idea, i.e. to direct the revolutionary interest to the conditions for releasing the under-developed and underprivileged of every society and of humanity as a whole, still remains an absolutely necessary component of every ideology of liberation. Marx's conclusion presented in the *Communist Manifesto,* that only an association that ensures the free development of each is the condition for the free development of all, i.e. that only in this way can we have a society without violence, without terror either from above or below, continues to form the decisive rational motive for the revolutionary committment of the most advanced strata to general emancipation. It is and remains the firm ground on which to base an ethic of Promethean solidarity towards the so far less developed members of the social totality. There has never been an oppression or even a prejudice that did not react back on its author in a transmuted form. And the more despotically an elite has to rule, the more wretched and unhappy is its own life too. The formulation of the *Manifesto* reiterates the old dream of the Enlightenment for a republic of kings.

The idea of equality has always been raised for discussion by an ideologically defined fraction of the ruling class, a fraction which need only have begun to inquire more profoundly into the preconditions for harmonizing their own conditions of existence. Only in times of sharp social crisis could the oppressed immediate producers reject the ideas of their servile nature and put forward universal demands. They could never realize them on a large scale, because their situation restricted their possibilities of cultural appropriation from childhood on. The political emancipation of an oppressed class, taken on the mass scale, can only lead to the satisfaction of a few of its pent-up compensatory needs. After the revolution, there begins the struggle for a new distribution of the material goods which the society can produce for consumption, and it needs several new generations (*at least* two generations on the basis of evidence that has to a certain extent been corroborated by social psychology) to establish a new subjectivity as an average type. In Marx's time, particularly because this predated the work of Freud and his school, psychology had not yet reached the level of development that today enables it to declare it as simply impossible that an oppressed and alienated class of immediate producers, subjected to the division of labour, could 'itself' become the ruling class and in this role exercize hegemony over the entire cultural process of its society.

In reality, therefore, Marx's vision, the structure of which is closely related to the New Testament doctrine that 'the last shall be first', can be realized only in a process of post-revolutionary transformation that proceeds over generations, assuming that industrialization is essentially completed. The actual process thus proceeds by way of the differentiation of the social collective worker, which in tendency is still antagonistic, by way of hierarchical organization and division of labour. And it is at this point that Marx's second and positive argument for the world-historical mission of the proletariat is introduced, an argument which from an *abstract* standpoint is still completely valid today. Only the proletariat is linked from its very beginnings with modern production, and in so far as the entire society tends to become polarized between the proletariat and the bourgeoisie, and the latter becomes parasitic, losing its functions in the reproduction process, there remains no other bearer of the future society than the proletariat – the productive collective worker. In as much as the new society is seen only through the spectacles of the old, and we can establish the decline of the intermediate strata, the proletarianization of the collectivized peasantry and the rise of a new intelligentsia from working-class origin, in short, in as much as the tendency is for the entire society to be transformed into workers and employees of the socialist state, it is only logical to define the 'working class', as was done at the end of the Ulbricht era, so that it embraces all members of the overall process of reproduction, from the cleaning lady up to the highest politbureaucrat. It is significant that this play on the concept served to conceal a wave of most far-reaching official pandering to the technocratic managers, who ventured to put forward quite brazenly their claim to trace a 'structure-determining path' for our society. The more recent confused discussions as to the relationship between the 'working class' and the 'intelligentsia' cannot lead to a logically respectable conclusion, since it is impossible to separate '*the* intelligentsia' from the productive collective worker. The whole confusion just shows once again how the traditional concept of class has been overtaken by the structural development of the productive forces, and especially so in a society in which the functions of intellectual management and mediation in the reproduction process are no longer in the service of private capitalist valorization, so that their particular position is no longer subsumed under *traditional* class antitheses. Intellectual labour marches today at the head of the subjective productive forces.

Lenin, incidentally, avoided the concept of the 'intelligentsia' immediately after the revolution, once it was a question of designating the very diverse kinds of experts. He spoke almost always of 'specialists', and was inclined to extend this term to reach far into the former 'educated strata'. It could even apply to merchants, in as much as they were culturally superior to shopkeepers. A particular stratum of ideologists, such as continues to appear in every modern society, did not figure in Lenin's perspective for the simple reason that the traditional elements of this stratum had to be oppressed, while the progressive, 'genuinely enlightened' elements were concentrated in the party or its periphery. It was certainly possible to speak of the old intelligentsia, but not in relation to the new social structure. In any case, Lenin's terminology immediately stressed the articulation of the intellectual professions as subordinate functions in the collective worker, in which the specialists would form a particular stratum until fully developed communism was achieved.

This needs all the more to be stressed in so far as the specific intelligentsia of non-capitalist industrial society could at that time still not appear as a sociological phenomenon. The 'socialist intelligentsia' of today is recruited in its overwhelming majority not from the traditional educated strata of the middle class, but rather from the working classes, so that – particularly in the Soviet Union itself – there is sociologically only a thin thread of continuity between 'old' and 'new' intelligentsia. The new intelligentsia at first bade fair to becoming a fairly homogeneous stratum closely linked to the party. In its first generation, the characteristic dichotomy between specialists and ideologists (the latter only too soon as officials for the political-administrative and ideological apparatus) did not yet appear so sharply, since the educational goal of an identity of 'expert and socialist' started off by having some substance to it. The dominant ideologists were those who identified themselves subjectively with the goal of the party. This was a period in which many specialists really did become communists, and in which young people, at least, did not join the party for the sake of a career.

The 'socialist intelligentsia' of today, however, if we simplify the concept to embrace everyone with a level of skill superior to normal secondary education, is a conglomerate of groups and strata that are extremely heterogenous both socio-economically and politically, and occupy very different social functions and positions, marked moreover by all those contradictions that are generally typical of the social structure of non-capitalist industrial society. When we look more closely, it rather seems as if there might be a decisive conflict between two different fractions of this 'intelligentsia', even though their summits are both organized in the single party. In reality, however, one of these fractions, the opposition one, whenever it can form and develop, confronts the other, that grouped around the party and state apparatus, as the representative of a new *general* interest – in unfavourable cases merely an egoistic representative. In Czechoslovakia this fraction clearly stood at the head of the entire productive social body, which demanded a new superstructural form.

In the light of this situation, programmatic and strategic debates that conceive the organized post-revolutionary party and state apparatus in the conventional sense of a 'workers' party', or misguidedly conceive the alternative intellectually dominant League of Communists in this same way, overlook right from the start the basic reality of non-capitalist industrial society. Their exponents operate at the tail end of the historical process, as has always been the fate of sectarian rearguard groups. This is in no way to ignore the major theme of a political representation of interests for the underprivileged, or, more correctly, the underdeveloped strata of the collective worker, or to place this in charge of the pedagogic discretion of 'knowing' intellectuals. It is not a question of replacing the alleged 'leading role of the working class' by a factual 'leading role of the intelligentsia'. The interests of the managerial, scientific and ideological intelligentsia, who are competent in their own eyes, bear as little a universal character as those of the immediate producers. The whole problem of general emancipation must be placed on a new basis, as far as its practical political form is concerned.

8

The Driving Forces of Non-Capitalist Industrial Society and their Inhibition

Just think of the picture the old socialists painted: the great dynamic of social and economic development, and the effort of all in solidarity for the common good! That same 'great beginning' which Lenin so enthusiastically described when the workers on the Moscow-Kazan railway started their first revolutionary subbotnik.[1] This was precisely the ultimate foundation for our confidence in the superiority of the socialist mode of production, our obstinate persistence in the conviction that we would 'catch up with and overtake' capitalism in a relatively short period. We did not doubt the basic coincidence between individual and social interest, and saw in this the incomparable driving force of our harmonic progress.

Unfortunately, little of this proved true, the reason, we believed, being certain survivals of the past in people's consciousness. In this respect, it seemed that the whole tremendous superstructure would take rather longer to transform. And we went over to the troublesome institution of emulation from above, preparing its 'initiators' by deliberate preselection. Today the universal appeal for emulation is always held ready by those cadres of the party and trade unions responsible for economic policy. This is a tragi-comedy with ritual touches, painful for all taking part in it. The very word 'emulation' should already be sufficient to reduce the illusion of socialism to absurdity.

[1] Subbotnik, voluntary weekend work.

We are suffering from what Rosa Luxemburg predicted to Lenin as early as 1918, without Lenin having had any alternative to the course he chose. Lenin would find, she held, that the bureaucracy would be the only active element in Soviet state and society. Rosa Luxemburg, however, with her socialist perspective, naturally failed to see that the bureaucracy, irrespective of the inevitable negative results that she anticipated, would also and above all play a positive role as an initiating apparatus of economic and social transformation. I have already discussed this fully enough. In any case, it is wrong to *ascribe* the absence of mass initiative simply to the activity of the bureaucracy (if this is undoubtedly a *secondary* effect) without previously recognizing that the role of the bureaucracy as the 'sole initiator' was *primarily a substitute for the mass initiative that was lacking.* Who is going to take the initiative in a post-capitalist society, if the masses keep to Pushkin's stage direction from *Boris Gudonov*: 'The people remain silent'? The apparatus did not originally challenge any rights or activities of the working masses that were positively exercized. All that it can be reproached for is that it further reproduced their traditional passivity. Active interdiction took place first and foremost within the party, principally affecting the intelligentsia (then beyond this the intellectual elements in general), and this was a consequence of the compulsion inherent in the situation of having to organize society along bureaucratic lines before it was socially and ideologically reorganized.

In the first period after the political overthrow, the weakness of the forward impulse was concealed on the one hand by the revolutionary enthusiasm of a minority, particularly young people, on the other hand and above all by the mobilization of the masses made necessary for survival in view of the damage wreaked on the national economy by war and revolution. Our own case was somewhat similar in the years after 1945. The grey romanticism of the 'rubble women' and the stubborn patching up of damaged machinery is still remembered, not without a certain nostalgia. But in 1953, the confrontation over norms showed clearly enough that this phase was already long since past. The new contradictions already appeared as an established fact, even though the picture was obscured, as in Hungary in 1956, by the attempted comeback of nationalist and other reactionary elements.

The basic attitude of the immediate producers to 'their' state is not essentially different, even today, from that of the workers in capitalist society to 'their' corporations. Given the perpetuation of the division of labour, commodity production and money, nothing has altered in the principles of how work performance is assessed. Wages are simply the price that the appropriator state pays for the commodity labour-power. It is a *salto mortale* of pure ideology to recognize the commodity nature of material products under actually existing socialism, and at the same time to deny the commodity nature of labour-power which is the other side of the same coin.

The idea of socialist emulation, identical with the hope for the mass initiative of the immediate producers, necessarily proved utopian. Conditions which first had to be produced were counted on from the start. The immediate creation of *use*-values for 'distant kith and kin', for society, presupposes a state of affairs in which no special ethic or altruistic motive is needed any longer, no idealization of self-sacrifice, since labour has already become a 'vital want', or, perhaps more comprehensibly, a natural expression of life, for the individuals involved, their decisive means of enjoyment and development, as the *social* activity in which they can confirm one another and develop in mutual communication. But as long as emulation between individuals still proceeds in a context of fundamental social inequalities, it cannot directly involve the qualitative comparison of productive expressions of life.

Why, then, if the new motivations are lacking, do not the old motivations at least work as well under our system as they do under capitalism? There they also remain tied to the relation of wage-labour, even when the capitalist *state* appears as entrepreneur. One section of bourgeois propagandists make the mistake, not just out of hostility, but simply from stupidity, of believing that our propaganda for a better qualitative use of labour-time, and even more so a better quantitative use, indicates a high pressure of work in our factories. In reality, both intensity of labour and labour discipline are lower than under capitalism. For although labour law and social policy bestow a social insurance somewhat comparable to the 'state socialism' of the Incas, in that earlier formation this always went together with a form of extra-economic compulsion. Fourier had already realized that 'the people would give themselves over to leisure if they had at their disposal an adequate *minimal existence*, an ensured supply of food and a decent livelihood, since the civilized mode of production is too repugnant'. And with '*grisette*-like naïveté', as Marx summed up this conception,[2] without however completely rejecting the underlying idea, Fourier concluded: 'In the socialist order, therefore, labour must offer as much stimulation as our festivals and entertainments do today'. 'The remedy against idleness and other burdens that might destroy the association lies in the research and discovery of an attractive system of production that transforms labour into an enjoyment, guaranteeing that the people persist in labour and hence achieve the *minimal existence* aimed at'.[3] This attractive system of production, moreover, was for Fourier a question of the *social organization and division of labour*, in no way one of its technical level (and the error lies, I believe, in this complete neglect of technique).

The concern shown by individuals, which need in no way be necessarily antagonistic, not only for the conditions of mere existence, but rather for those historically determined conditions of development that subsequently determine the measure and the manner of their enjoyment of life in society, is the most universal basic feature of history in general. As long as the sphere of labour only consumes an individual's energies, without being able to offer productive consumption of a mental kind, then the individual's goal must be to give out as little as possible and take in as much as possible, which latter can then be transformed outside this sphere into self-maintenance, and in the favourable case into self-development and enjoyment of life. It is certainly true in the abstract, and is moreover rationally understood even by the apparently most uncomprehending people involved, that the general average of the individual share depends on the overall amount of products available for distribution. But it remains

[2] *Grundrisse, loc. cit.*, p. 611.
[3] *Le Nouveau Monde industriel et sociétaire*, in *Oeuvres complets*, Paris 1848, vol. VI, pp. 245–52.

incontestable that the level of the individual share does not correspond to the degree of effort, that the distribution is unjust and its real principles uncontrollable. It is scarcely possible to influence the relative level of income under our system (less so in fact than under capitalism, since if the proportions are adjusted in favour of a particular group, this is not due to its own trade-union struggle, but rather to the party and government), and above all, the absolute level of what is available for distribution is determined by uncontrollable influences and interests (the world market, the deductions from the total product; investigations independent of the apparatus into macroeconomic proportions and the deployment of resources these require are badly needed). Individuals are thus thrown back on their own egoism. And there is no genuine moral authority, no genuinely respected agency, that could make any demands to the contrary, since the bureaucracy, by manipulating the budget and the principle of reward according to work, is never in the right in the eyes of the masses, so that in general they in no way consistently identify with its demands.

Our state – and despite its draconian and martial forms of law, the same applies also to the Soviet – is essentially, i.e. from the standpoint of its place in history, in no position to *enforce* the same intensity of labour as capitalism can. It forms part of the assumptions of its existence, the elementary conditions of its constitution in the play of both domestic and international forces, that the contradiction between it and the immediate producers does not become too marked. From the standpoint of political economy, under actually existing socialism the workers have a far greater opportunity to blackmail the 'entire society' than do the trade unions under capitalism, and they do actually use this, against all surface appearance, even if they can do so only in an unfruitful way, i.e. by holding back on their output. This is less true for the lowest stratum of workers, least of all for women, who perform the lion's share of piecework in our industry. But the majority of skilled workers determine the rhythm of labour by their own consensus, and the specialists in particular, even when they perform lower managerial functions, are not exposed to the same pressure of work as they would be 'over there'. Most of them know this very well, especially the older ones.

Differentiation organized by the principle of reward according to work, as practised in our economic system, tends to function in the opposite sense from how Marx and Engels foresaw it. According to the *Critique of the Gotha Programme*, the motto 'to each according to his work' precisely does *not* apply to gradation according to skill, which is how the principle has most generally been practised in our case. In *Anti-Dühring*, Engels writes quite unmistakably: 'How then are we to solve the whole important question of the higher wages paid for compound labour? In a society of private producers, private individuals or their families pay the costs of training the qualified worker; hence the higher price paid for qualified labour-power accrues first of all to private individuals: the skilful slave is sold for a higher price, and the skilful wage-earner is paid higher wages. In a socialistically organized society, these costs are borne by society, and to it therefore belong the fruits, the greater values produced by compound labour. The worker himself has no claim to extra pay'. For 'production is most encouraged by a mode of distribution which allows *all* members of society to develop, maintain and exercize their capacities with maximum universality'.

In our system, on the contrary, we have precisely the customary 'mode of thought of the educated classes', according to which 'it must seem monstrous that in time to come there will no longer be any professional porters or architects, and that the man who for half an hour gives instructions as an architect will also act as a porter for a period, until his activity as an architect is once again required. A fine sort of socialism that would be – perpetuating professional porters!'[4] As far as the specific functions of economic management are concerned, Marx and Engels assumed they would be rigorously simplified, instead of becoming ever more complex, both objectively, and additionally so for reasons of subjectivism. Lenin, too, in the period immediately after the revolution, proceeded from the idea that these functions should be performed for workers' wages – and this not so much from economic considerations as from temporary political ones.

[4] Part Two, Chapter VI.

With Marx and Engels, the principle of reward according to work bears simply on the average labour-time expended. In *Capital* Marx writes with explicit reference to the socialist economy, in which the money form would disappear: 'There is no reason why the producers should not receive paper tokens permitting them to withdraw an amount corresponding to their labour-time from the social consumption stocks. But these tokens are not money; they do not circulate'.[5]

The inequality and injustice that is involved here is based on the difference in physical attributes, these being taken as the basis for various different activities, including of course also intellectual activities, of definite duration and intensity, as well as on the different conditions of individual existence. If someone performs fewer units of labour in his particular occupation than another person does in a different occupation, then he should receive less than the other. In our system, however, work performance – in this sense of productive expenditure of average labour-time – rather declines in the higher functions. Not only in the field of administration, but also in research, construction and planning establishments, and many other similar positions too, far more labour-time is wasted than in immediate production. We are not of course referring here to the special case of the high party, state or economic functionary, surrounded in many cases by his own apparatus, or of the scientist and engineer devoted to their work, who are naturally not representative of the stratum of employees and specialists in general.

Within the various occupations – and here again particularly strikingly so among the specialists, whereas among the workers (particularly women workers) in mass production the norm is frequently still determinant – the principle of payment according to work has a very attenuated application. Once the plan targets and salaries are fixed and settled, the sun shines equally on the righteous and the unrighteous, the clever and the stupid. At most, a certain rivalry can still be provoked between different collectives. Taken as a whole, however, in industry the principle of reward according to work is no longer any general use as a stimulus for

[5] Volume 2, Pelican Marx Library, 1978, p.434.

particular efforts for the common good, nor are the various movements of socialist emulation. There is only bureaucratic competition, which I shall come on to speak of later. People do not spoil each other's norms. Bonusses are simply parcelled out. If the management really could carry through the differentiation it seeks to promote, output would not be significantly improved, but the normal working atmosphere would certainly be worsened. It is only the special bonusses for overtime in the eternal bottle-neck areas, which is questionable both economically and socially, that achieve something of their immediate purpose. The workers are partially successful in seeing to it that the surplus costs that accrue in this way do not come out of the general bonus fund, i.e. that there genuinely is an extra income. In this way, limits are imposed which our economic system in its present form cannot overcome, even though the managerial staff, a portion of the specialists and the top level of skilled workers complain in somewhat resigned tones about the lack of labour discipline, as expressed in the wastage of material, too high a level of rejects, disorder in the workshops, etc.

Industrialism, as a result of its world-historical role in preparing the way for a new civilization, creates among the oppressed and exploited masses of the entire globe a striving that can be expressed in the formula: 'Equality now!' The socialist movement assumed on its first appearance that the maturity of the productive forces would make possible the socio-economic equalization of all individuals. But under the given circumstances, 'equality-mongering' (as the demand for equality was already termed in the immediate post-revolutionary period), i.e. the attempt to equalize starting from the relations of *distribution*, meant *a weakening of those stimuli that alienated labour required*, as long as the social inequality of individuals showed itself as having long-term roots in the *material productive forces*. And the less the compulsion of labour had been internalized by the previous generation in the particular country in question, the more devastatingly was this result evident. The struggle against the egalitarian aspirations of the masses and for carrying through the principle of reward according to work in the relations of distribution, is therefore a major function of the proto-socialist state. In practice, of course, the end result is inevitably a compromise, which necessarily varies also from one country in our system to another.

We might say, in psychological terms, that exploitation, which was the original lever of a remarkable level of expanded repro-duction, is 'ashamed' of itself under actually existing socialism. It must make use of a complicated and inhibiting facade. The powers that be no longer feel free to admit their own role. What makes them blush is precisely the best part of our ideological and moral tradition. In this way the working masses can bring it about that the relations of distribution are more egalitarian in practice than the level of development of the division of labour would justify, in purely economic terms. Distribution and hence 'material' incentive is in no way the major source of social differen-tiation in our society, and this in a situation where the character and organization of labour itself still does not generate any pro-nounced impulse to better performance. As far as the immediate producers are concerned, the dynamic of the productive forces suffers from a twilight between a 'not yet' and a 'no longer'.

But this is still to confine our discussion to Fourier's conception of the 'minimal existence'. In reality, however, 'production soon brings it about that the so-called struggle for existence no longer turns on pure means of existence, but on means of enjoyment and development',[6] even if in the first instance this is so only for the privileged classes. From this point of view, what we must investi-gate above all today is the natural function of labour itself as the fundamental means of development for the essential human powers. From our discussion of the traditional division of labour as the deepest source of social inequality, expressing itself in the various levels and structures of development of the personality, it follows that the focal point of the conflict of interests in society must move successively further from the distribution of compen-sation for labour towards the distribution of labour itself, once the means of subsistence are by and large secured. According to sociological investigations in various countries with our social system, the content and character of labour, together with the opportunities for advance and development that are bound up

[6] Engels, *Dialectics of Nature*, Moscow 1972, p. 308.

with the job, have already overtaken salary as a motivational factor, and the more highly skilled people are, the more pronounced this tendency is.

In this way, competition for the appropriation of activities favourable to self-development, for appropriate positions in the multi-dimensional system of social division of labour, becomes the specific driving force of economic life characteristic of actually existing socialism. It is not by chance that competitive behaviour between individuals in our system is so strongly focussed on the phase of education, in which access and admission to favourable positions in the system of overall social labour is determined, with those strata who have already acquired education and influence holding the centre of the stage. This struggle has a marked political character, summed up in the question whether social advance is to be won in a 'pure' competitive struggle, or whether this should be half-heartedly and superficially corrected by the application of social and political discrimination in favour of those strata who are disadvantaged in the division of labour, not to mention also by extensive bureaucratic and unofficial corruption. In any case, care is taken that sons and daughters of cadres never do too badly; they 'belong to the working class' because daddy or mummy works in some ministry or other.

The same political content is at issue in the ensuing debate over occupation of privileged jobs and management positions in factories and other institutions; is the decision to be made on grounds of technical competence or bureaucratic virtue? Particularly in the productive economy and in the municipal sector, the overbloated apparatus of management is a heavy burden on the productive or operative base, consuming the cadres' time, energy and power of concentration for its own need to control information. But there is another aspect involved as well. The social structure within the apparatus, which is not held in check by any independent social power, systematically subordinates productive cooperation for the appropriation of 'good work' and 'lucrative positions' – which on the premise of the continuing traditional division of labour is normal and definitely to be promoted – to a different model of incentive of its own: *bureaucratic rivalry*. Subservience to those above, severe discipline towards those below, and only in the third place competence – this is the prevailing order of selection criteria. The result is that the productive and creative elements suffer from an increase of mediocrity, indeed incompetence, dishonourable behaviour and insecurity in official positions, not to speak here of the political standardization that is required.

The problem is that all the conditions for the development of creative initiative in the economy are provided by bureaucratic structures, so that even for the sake of beneficial productive activity it is necessary to enter into the struggle for a career, for rank and influence, and to adapt to a large extent to the corresponding models of behaviour. Naturally, in a society that is still generally antagonistic, creative activity cannot remain outside the fundamental conflicts of interest; it is itself intrinsically privileged. In the last analysis, the most active elements strive to escape from work for simple reproduction, for mere functioning. As we have already said, they obtain their subsistence from work that fosters the personality. But not only this! Creative work is scarce, it is necessary to struggle with other individuals for access to it, since its objects will be bestowed, in a manner determined by the social formation, on the particular functional unit that is programmed for it in advance, irrespective of all other interests (actual or potential). And this scarcity of creative work is in turn attributable, by and large, to the restriction of the fund for expanded reproduction, in terms of both material and time. Either the enterprise in question receives new investment in the current five-year plan, or it does not, and this immediately provides different premises for the individuals involved. Objective contradictions are involved here, which are then resolved by the hierarchy, in a way that very often gives rise to major losses in creative energy and economic rationality.

The bureaucratic centralist form of planning, in which what those at the top receive from below is principally only passive factual information and 'questions', while what they hand down are active imperatives, stamps the mechanism by which tasks are allotted to individuals. It is a point of principle that people do not have to seek tasks for themselves, recognize and deal with problems, but they are rather assigned to tasks as duties. The means to deal with these tasks are accordingly also allotted on the basis of a balance sheet, and the longer this is, the more even the most necessary resources are rationed.

It has been said that class society treats the mass of its members like a miserly stepmother, as far as the means of subsistence are concerned. But actually existing socialism also acts the step-mother to privileged individuals, in allocating them the material resources for the productive tasks it ordains for them. Under capitalism, capital in the money form was scarce, while under our system, what is lacking are labour-power and materials, one day this kind, the next day another, as well as investment goods and construction capacity. All these things are hopelessly rationed, since there is in fact no economic mechanism to bring supply and demand into agreement. Here the plan is itself a permanent source of trouble, since, as I have already indicated, it forcibly seeks, according to its ideal essence as representative of social needs, always to extract more from production than society can ordinarily produce.

Ultimately, the centralized power of disposal – and it is on this that the bureaucratic rivalry of the active elements in the hierarchy and among the specialists is focussed – must be distributed among the various collective and individual subjects of economic life, i.e. legally delegated to them, and above all assigned to them through material and financial planning and accounting. But since the determination of the planned quantities presupposes on the one hand a *knowledge* of social needs and requirements, and on the other hand of local capacities and consumption quantities, here again it is the bureaucratic information process to whose specific characteristics the combatants must orient themselves. The bureaucratic universe is curved back on itself just like the cosmic universe in relativity theory; there is no straight line leading out of it.

In his polemic with Proudhon, who took it as self-evident that 'industrial emulation [is] necessarily emulation with a view to profit', Marx stressed the historical character of competition as a form of emulation. The immediate object of *industrial* emulation would necessarily be the *product*, and not profit. And for this reason competition 'is not industrial emulation, it is commercial emulation. In our time industrial emulation exists only in view of commerce. There are even phases in the economic life of modern nations when everybody is seized with a sort of craze for making profit without producing. This speculation craze, which occurs periodically, lays bare the true character of competition, which seeks to escape the need for industrial emulation'.[7] As under capitalism commercial emulation appears as the alienated form of industrial emulation, so in our system it is bureaucratic emulation that plays this role, a bureaucratic rivalry which has its own laws. It goes without saying here that, just as under capitalism commercial emulation takes hold of more or less all areas of social activity, so in our case bureaucratic rivalry, once it has assumed this universal character, is also not simply confined to the industrial sphere, even though it is ultimately anchored in this.

It is also understandable that it is above all the intelligentsia whom our system presses most strongly into the behavioural model of bureaucratic rivalry. The objective tendency of state organization and management of labour leads to bureaucratizing the entire intelligentsia, or at least reliably controlling it by way of bureaucratic mechanisms that today affect the material conditions of intellectual production even in the artistic sphere. Not to speak of course of those cadres involved in the economy. (It is a constant complaint, incidentally, and one based on hard facts, that the broad mass of specialists are always reluctant to take on any kind of managerial functions. Even when they feel capable of it, they do not want to. In science, too, it is not genuine scientists who get to the top, but rather the bureaucrats among them, as the Soviet writer Granin has described in many of his works.) In any case, the transformation of the intelligentsia into a bureaucracy is the predominant tendency. University and technical education, particularly the former, is precisely the entrance ticket to a bureaucratic career, in no matter which branch.

Before we now go on to establish what the bureaucratic management of the industrial process that has replaced commercial management necessarily involves, or must have as its result, it is worth looking back again at how Marx conceived the general

---

[7] *The Poverty of Philosophy*, Chapter 2, 3; *Collected Works*, vol. 6, p. 191.

nature of the bureaucracy. As far as the terms 'bureaucracy' and 'bureaucrat' are concerned, it is unavoidable that they often degenerate into mere invectives of political debate, just as does the term 'bourgeois'. Yet in both cases the terms have an objective content. The source in Marx is his early settling of accounts with Hegel's doctrine of the state, in which the bureaucrats, the 'executive civil servants', figure very pertinently as *'representatives of the executive power'* as against the representatives of the social classes, and above all against 'the many', i.e. the people.[8] (In the interest of accommodation to our particular conditions, we could of course say 'vis-à-vis' [*gegenüber*] here instead of 'against' [*gegen*]; it makes not the least bit of difference, particularly where the executive has the kind of overbearing position vis-à-vis the already bureaucratized instance of popular representation as it does in our case.) It is equally pertinent that Hegel opposes these government representatives, as the *'universal* class', to the particular classes of 'civil society'. For Hegel, so Marx maintains, the executive is nothing but 'administration, which he treats in terms of *bureaucracy'*.[9] It goes without saying that Hegel conceives the 'middle class' from which the bureaucracy stems as the 'educated' class.

Let us bear in mind throughout Marx's subsequent argument the implications that his observations of a traditional state bureaucracy have when the state immediately appears as the organizer and regulator of all economic life, indeed of all social life in general, while the social organizations have only the same kind of servile independence towards it that the estates or 'corporations' had in Prussia before the March revolution of 1848.

Marx stresses first of all that it is the *formal* regulation of real social affairs that gives bureaucratic activity its specific content, so that it must always find itself in a defensive position against changes that would disturb its repose. 'Accordingly, the real purpose of the state' – i.e. the regulation of society's general business – 'appears to the bureaucracy as a purpose *opposed* to the state . . . The bureaucracy appears to itself as the ultimate

---

[8] 'Critique of Hegel's Doctrine of the State', in *Early Writings, loc. cit.*, pp. 100ff.
[9] p. 105.

purpose of the state. As the bureaucracy converts its "formal" purposes into its content, it comes into conflict with "real" purposes at every point. It is therefore compelled to pass off form as content and content as form. The purposes of the state are transformed into purposes of offices and vice versa.'[10]

In and of itself, already, the more or less well-founded conviction of the need for administration and thus for its institutional consistency suffices to champion both its principle and its existence in every critical case. The 'real purposes' must come to grief against the institutions that have arisen to regulate them. The conflict between formal and real purposes (the formal purposes in their turn being of the utmost reality as far as the political foundations of society are concerned) is nowhere more serious in our society than in the process of industrial reproduction, and this even though bureaucracy naturally cuts with a far more directly painful effect in the spheres of mental and cultural life. But it chains the productive forces at their very roots, and the bureaucratic organization of the economy is the well-spring of the general bureaucratization.

'The bureaucracy', Marx continues, 'holds the state, the spiritual essence of society, in thrall, as its *private property*'.[11] Though the characteristic spirit of bureaucracy, according to Hegel himself, is one of 'mere business routine' and 'the horizon of a restricted sphere',[12] it sees itself as a 'hierarchy of knowledge'.[13] 'The apex entrusts insights into particulars to the lower echelons while the lower echelons credit the apex with insight into the universal, and so each deceives the other.' Where state activities are *not* transformed into particular offices, on the other hand, so that the state is not separated from society, then 'what is crucial . . . is not the fact that every citizen has the chance to devote himself to the universal interest in the shape of a particular class, but the capacity of the universal class to be really universal, i.e. to be the class of every citizen'. The examination system, however, 'is nothing but a Masonic initiation, the legal recognition

[10] p. 107.
[11] p. 108.
[12] p. 116.
[13] p. 108.

of the knowledge of citizenship, the acknowledgement of a privilege . . . [it is] nothing but the *bureaucratic baptism of knowledge*, the official recognition of the transubstantiation of profane knowledge into sacred knowledge (it is plain that in every examination the examiner is omniscient). It is not recorded that Greek and Roman statesmen ever took examinations. But then what is a Roman statesman compared to a Prussian civil servant!'[14]

In practice, the bureaucratic pyramid that concerns itself with the regulation of all social affairs necessarily lays claim to absolute knowledge, i.e. its plans assume that the real social needs are indeed synthesized by the knowledge process of the specialized apparatus. In practice, however, they are at best simply brought under a system of classifications, for the bureaucratic methodology can only lead from the concrete to the abstract, and not back again from there to the concrete-in-thought, which would in this case be the social process as a model; it can only lead to a mechanical aggregate. What is living in the totality escapes the bureaucracy's procedures of generalization, but the details that the bureaucracy overlooks are not anyone else's concern either. The individual bureaucrat may even be a philosopher, but it is impossible for the bureaucratic apparatus to be a collective philosopher. This does not say anything against the historical necessity of such apparatuses, but they must be kept dependent on society, rather than making society dependent on themselves, and this is only possible if the bureaucratic apparatuses either remain confined to particular spheres, not being charged with their social connection, or else if at all levels disruptive interventions of social forces are at any time possible, and able to tear apart the network of bureaucratic necessities.

But 'the universal spirit of bureaucracy is *secrecy*, it is mystery preserved within itself by means of the hierarchical structure and appearing to the outside world as a self-contained corporation. Openly avowed political spirit, even patriotic sentiment, appears to the bureaucracy as a *betrayal* of its mystery. The principle of its knowledge is therefore *authority*, and its *patriotism* is the adulation of authority'. 'The state thus exists only as a series of fixed

[14] pp. 112-3.

bureaucratic minds held together by passive obedience and their subordinate position in a hierarchy'.[15] In as much as the less stupid people in the bureaucratic number among whom the state is divided attain an awareness of their conditions and see through them subjectively, there arises that specific state Jesuitism that is the characteristic spirit of our own social science. 'The bureaucrats are the Jesuits and theologians of the state',[16] says Marx. In our case they have been redivided between practical and theoretical bureaucrats. The bureaucracy is a republic of priests.

Within the bureaucracy, however, '*spiritualism* degenerates into *crass materialism*, the materialism of passive obedience, the worship of authority, the *mechanism* of fixed, formal action, of rigid principles, views and traditions. As for the individual bureaucrat, the purpose of the state becomes his private purpose, *a hunt for promotion, careerism*'. And the interesting question for us here is how far this bureaucratic rivalry can play a driving role in the considerably changed environment of overall state economic and social planning. For at first glance it seems relatively harmless in comparison with competition for maximum profits. It does not offer a proper parallel to the criminal brazenness of capital, by which Marx, for all his criticism, was so impressed. The basic problem, in fact, is precisely that as a substitute for commercial competition it is too harmless an impulse for the productive forces. (It should not of course be thought that there is a second arrangement that could *permanently establish* the same kind of expansive economic growth as that based on the pursuit of surplus-value. This would not even be desirable.)

For the individual bureaucrat, social need appears as mediated not by the market, but by the plan. This makes the difference that where the bourgeois, if he reads the market right, has the promise of wealth, when the bureaucrat fulfils the plan all he gets is avoidance of anger, and at most a share in the inflationary flood of orders and decorations. His career is in no way directly bound up with plan fulfilment. For successful carrying out of the plan, or otherwise, is seldom the individual merit or failure of a single

[15] p. 108.
[16] p. 107.

manager, but depends rather on *conditions* in which his subjective behaviour is only one. The 'crass materialism' of *economic-bureaucratic* rivalry certainly involves passive obedience, worship of authority, the hunt for promotion, etc., but it is not this that provides its focus. For a start, the economic functionary is always faced with the plan and its conditions of realization. The decisive point for him is *how high the plan is in relation to its conditions of realization*, and it is this that determines his situation, the whole year through.

The 'material interest' of the economic functionaries, considered as a dynamic element in their economic behaviour, depends only little on money, i.e. their salary, the level of this being more or less fixed with their position (of course, this could be higher at times than it is). It turns rather on good positions; but this already means those that among other things also stand in a favourable position vis-à-vis the subjective problem of plan fulfilment, whether because better conditions for this are to be found, because one is further removed from the immediate pressure of the plan, or whatever. In everyday behaviour, for which we can take the salary and position of the broad mass of functionaries as temporarily constant, material interest is directed towards the *conditions of plan fulfilment*, and basically to the work situation as a whole, which with increasing age is not least a question of health.

People accordingly strive precisely to arrange their fields of activity to the best advantage with respect to the degree of freedom of their own behaviour. The essential cause of their inactivity, their retreat into behaviour which is also even subjectively bureaucratic, is that the economic functionaries are so persistently disappointed. Once there is no longer any more labour to be found, the individual bureaucrat has the problem of keeping the plan figures below the limit of his unit's performance, and bolstering the funds of material and capacity from a reserve. Both these things lead in particular to the partial concealment of capacity, and to anchoring the customary measure of disorder and disorganization that is predetermined by the overall domestic political situation in the norms of use of material and labour-time, loading of machines, etc. So if capacity appears limited in relation to a national economic need, it is always more expedient to call for more extensive investment, than to attempt any kind of reconstruction while the plan is already in progress.

We can see from this that the interest of the bureaucratized economic functionary is not necessarily bound up with the *development* (extension and specialization) of use-value production, and therefore tends not only periodically (as with bourgeois commercial emulation) but quite generally to a competition 'which seeks to escape the need for industrial emulation'. This holds precisely for the economic functionaries taken *en masse*, who, for whatever motives, do not go after promotion on the basis of performance. Capitalist competition would immediately get rid of these characters with no spirit of enterprise, whereas in actually existing socialism there is evidently no mechanism to expel people who show such a lack of initiative from the positions they have occupied. The problem also appears, naturally enough, in the lower reaches of the bureaucracies of capitalist corporations, but it ceases at the top of these economic units, whereas in our case there is a bureaucratic continuum that stretches from the most insignificant charge-hand up to the very summit of party and state. On the average, therefore, every level of economic management is characterized by a predominance of inertial forces, who struggle for stability under the status quo and invest the developmental functions they occupy with this same spirit.

It is only logical that this type should get caught up in the struggle for positions of political and administrative power instead of in emulation for economic results for society. He never shows greater energy than when it is a question of getting rid of 'trouble-makers'. Certainly the bureaucrat as economist must also subordinate himself to economic laws, but the development of production is not his own purpose, as it is under capitalism with respect to the quantity of value, not even a social purpose, but first and foremost simply a means to stabilize the bureaucratic situation. This purpose comes into its own in the hectic and uneconomic activity that precedes party congresses and other similar festivities, these preferred goalposts of bureaucratic emulation, which are typically purely artificial notches on the economic process. Ever since its first great historical appearance in economic despotism, bureaucracy has proved itself a tool of *simple* reproduction without qualitative development, as much as of unproductive consumption of possible surpluses. This is where it is in its proper element.

Thus the essential obstacle to economic dynamism consists in the fact that right down to the factory director and head of department, the laws of bureaucratic behaviour time and again take precedence over economic rationality, which in *this* connection, at least, would be the higher criterion. The economic functionary is simply too often forced to gear his own desire for self-maintenance to extra-economic criteria. The capitalist entrepreneur is quite unambiguously primarily an economic person, at least in the era now drawing to a close, in which he was the epoch-making figure. The 'socialist' industrial director, on the other hand, is necessarily first and foremost a bureaucratic person. How he stands in the eyes of the managing director of his industrial branch, or even simply of his enterprise, how he stands with his party district leadership, or even with the local leadership, etc. is not only just as important as the economic success that he achieves together with his collective, and cannot only in many conditions make up for failure, it can even predetermine the 'economic' success that our system is sometimes ascribed. Apart from the fact that the industrial director is generally dependent on the superior rungs of the hierarchy in a thousand ways, as it is these who have appointed him and confirmed him in his position, etc., the economic reform in our country, even when it was at its height,[17] never went so far as to establish, at least formally, the autonomy of industrial enterprises, or even let them simply provide the state exchequer with an obligatory and calculable tax. The delivery of profit to the state, i.e. the rate of profit, remained subject to periodic manipulations which followed from incalculable conjunctures of economic policy. The time, direction and relative magnitudes of expanded reproduction depend on so many influences and decisions over and outside the enterprise that there is often not a single person in a factory, after an investment has been undertaken, who could say that these are his own

[17] Bahro is referring here to the New Economic System of Planning and Management (NÖSPL), in force from 1963 to 1967.

decisions (apart of course from technical details). This is true in particular for the larger factories and combines. The factory manager functions like the head of an office, and his situation also brings with it the psychological tendency to compensate for his inadequate satisfaction as an economist in his disciplinary measures.

The result of this general state of affairs, in which the factory manager is simply an excellent example, is that the celebrated virtues of the German postal service – though even this has come down in the world – have been extended to cover the entire economy. Whereas industrial bureaucracy remained until well into the monopoly capitalist phase simply a subordinate function of the capital in command, and has still not emancipated itself from this completely, despite all theories of the 'managerial revolution' and 'organization man', in our system it has full charge of the entire reproduction process. The economic apparatus of the party is itself too much of a superior bureaucracy to be able to correct this in any fundamental way, amending only the course of execution, not the basic principles; in particular, it is not the kind of agency that could interpret the requirements of the productive forces. It acts, however, under the assumption that its own structure and functioning must be time and again proved correct in the course of the overall process.

On top of this, we are distinct from late capitalism in having *one single* bureaucracy, whose functional organs only have rudimentary possibilities of material competition, or interests in this. The demarcation of competence that is necessary in bureaucracies regularly excludes the formulation of alternatives when decisions are to be made. The very number of levels and networks, which can ultimately be coordinated under bureaucratic centralism only via the overburdened summits of the pyramids in question, is responsible for the tremendous clumsiness of the overall mechanism, which even those at the top are not really masters of. Whereas the productive forces have for a long while depended on innumerable horizontal linkages, this being in fact simply the expression of an advanced state of socialization, we are still trying to manage the economy of the entire country according to the command system legitimized by the 'Marxist-Leninist science of organization' (a modern cameralistics, or state property management system, which has recently faded away again), a system that was the organizational achievement of bourgeois industrial management in the era before computerization. But the cybernetics of state and economy, which up till a short while ago was preached as the latest managerial science, was nothing more than a new guise for the old bureaucratic centralism, which was to be assisted somewhat by improved information.

All this should help to explain the relatively unproductive character of bureaucratic rivalry for rank and influence, for range and level of power of disposal, as a behavioural impulse. Initiative within the bureaucracy is always restricted and discouraged (if it does not by chance have a positive effect on a 'higher interest'), not so much by getting the initiator into trouble, which today only seldom affects our courageous bureaucrats, but rather by experience of the fruitlessness of personal investment in any affair that oversteps one's own realm of competence. As far as careers are concerned, in any case, a progressive image is far more useful than genuine activity, which disturbs 'normal functioning' and may always be inconvenient, for whatever reason. The purpose of rivalry, for employees with the desire to get ahead, can only ever be to present a 'positive' appearance to those above. The pressure to conform is thus built into the initiative mechanism right from the start, in fundamentals at least. There is certainly space for instrumental understanding, but hardly for 'negative', 'system-transcending', dialectical reason.

Only at the very summit are there exceptional possibilities of initiative – so at least it seems, and formally this is indeed the case. In particular, however, there is the possibility of putting through inadequate solutions. For every real attempt at reform that is undertaken within the bureaucratic rules of the game is necessarily still-born, even if it proceeds from the highest authority. Bureaucracy as the dominant form of management and work organization produces a specific human type of conservative mediocrity, people who can outshine through 'creative' conformity (in the favourable case), correct accomplishment of any orders they are given (on the average), or unfruitful officiousness (at the negative end of the scale).

Given bureaucratic centralism, it is in this generally unfavourable context that the outcome is decided, i.e. how far the summit manages, using the opinions of its specialists, to make productivity, achievement and relevant functioning into the *precondition* for promotion and recognition. The technocrat with his economic orientation, oriented that is to the economy of objectified labour, is a progressive figure compared with the conservative polit-bureaucrat, who is principally concerned simply with the conditions of reproduction of his position of administrative power. The technocrat is objectively working at the liquidation of his role, in as much as he sets progressive productive forces in motion, whereas the bureaucrat daily sanctifies the status quo.

In the GDR, given its relatively developed civilization, and the fairly high social and cultural skills of the masses, bureaucracy appears in a basically unprovocative form. Particularly since the Polish events of December 1970, the pose of absolute knowledge has been abandoned, and the spirit of tutelage, though essentially unaltered, is practised with a certain mildness. In the Soviet Union, where gradations of rank have been re-established in a real spirit of restoration, and are bolstered in addition with both official and unofficial privileges, so that the social continuum there shows a clean break where the bureaucracy, the *nachalstvo*, begins, the situation is far more acute. As against the position in the GDR and Czechoslovakia, it would need more than a few months of political spring to bring this glacier to melting point, though even in the Soviet Union visible rifts are appearing. In any case, the princely arrogance of the top cadres there will be far more difficult to restrain, as can simply be seen from the absolutely blatant inequalities of social custom. There is a real class division in common morality, however incredible this may sound. It is possible to be addressed by a superior in the familiar form, without being able to answer back similarly. Marxist Bolshevism has nowhere been more completely laid to rest than in the realm of social communication between social strata with unequal powers of co-determination.

This cannot be altered simply by reforms from above. The enlightened elements who are gradually gathering in the party centre, the younger staff officers, meet time and again with the

resistance of the whole conservative hierarchy of party functionaries, which cannot be overcome. In the provinces, the party
secretaries have greater personal power, a far wider radius of
action and more comprehensive means of discipline than the
Tsarist governors did in the past.

What the Soviet Union is suffering from today is the old
' "bossing" of state officials',[18] the excesses of the *apparatchik*
and *nachalnik* in which the old patriarchy of this peasant country
and the new patriarchy of industrial despotism have amalgamated
with a party discipline congealed into rigid orders of obedience.
The basic relationship in which the people of this gigantic land
find themselves, and which extends far into the private sphere,
is that of boss and underling, and this has not been in the least
disturbed by Khrushchev's half-baked political reform. Even
though today it is increasingly anachronistic, and is being very
gradually undermined from below, by the younger workers and
engineers, teachers and scientists, it still remains the real kernel
of the 'leading role' of party and state. It cripples in the most
consequential way the entire life and labour of Soviet society.

Unfortunately the evil does not consist simply in the Soviet
nachalstvo being just a bureaucracy or 'management'. I have
already pointed out that we have to see bureaucracy as a fact
that has objective roots in the present stage of development of the
productive forces. As we can see, Yugoslavia too, despite its
pursuit of the anti-bureaucratic road, has in no way transcended
the antithesis between self-management and étatism. The Soviet
Union has a dogmatically encrusted, *unenlightened* bureaucracy,
whose members are on the whole not distanced at all from their
roles, and with striking naïvety offer their mentality of adaptation
to the requirements of their career as a philosophy. In particular,
those unenlightened elements who are politically and morally
linked to the traditions of the Stalin period are still predominant
at the top of the pyramid. If no more profound social upheaval
ensues, so many people will take their cue from them that the
overall course of progress can only come about in a desperately
slow fashion. The best elements of Soviet society lie in chains,

---

[18] Lenin, *The State and Revolution*, Chapter 3; *Collected Works*, vol. 25, p. 426.

unaccustomed to initiative and embittered.

The *spiritual wretchedness* of the bureaucracy is conditioned by the vicious circle that traps the entire ideological self-consciousness of Soviet society that it censors. In view of the unbridgeable gulf between the socialist programme and Soviet reality, the oligarchy sees the legitimacy of its claim to power linked to the perpetuation of a false picture of the world. It can therefore not allow any competent reflection of its dilemma in political theory, or of social relations in general. Soviet social scientists have to take tremendous pains to bring their insights into the true nature of these relations into formal agreement with the traditional dogmas. There are of course people in the party leadership who are privately aware of their situation. But since they are constantly compelled to reproduce the traditional phraseology for public purposes (and moreover even for the Politbureau itself), and are moreover mentally absorbed by their characteristic style of work, this private reflection cannot go beyond the cynical establishment of the realities. All they produce then are pitiful self-justifications for the good of their own souls. Their whole position, their interests and mentality, forces them to block out objective analysis and understanding. They need only the instrumental knowledge required for simple reproduction of the established system. Everything beyond this is superfluous and harmful.

But there is *one* source from which the present-day Soviet Union can be viewed without too much concealment, as far as its character as an authoritarian society is concerned. This is its literature, which is not compelled to give its generalizations an unambiguous conceptual expression, and in certain circumstances can in fact express more truth in the form of mere naturalistic description than entire reports to the Party Congress could cover up again. In present-day Soviet literature there are two stars of first magnitude, with very different positions, though ones that are not altogether without points of contact: the Kirghiz writer Aitmatov and the Russian Solzhenitsyn. And there are a whole constellation of major writers such as Nekrasov, Antonov, Belov, Kasakov, and many others,[19] who set to work with the honesty of the true

[19] Since this was written I must add the names of Trifonov, Tendriakov, Shukshin, Abramov, Rasputin, Salygin, Gelman and Vampilov.

artist. In Soviet literature, just as in traditional Russian literature, criteria of morality are placed far above those of aesthetics, since the writers (and today also film directors) are the only public conscience with a comprehensive view of the country. But the depth and profundity of their reflection in the last decade has again brought their aesthetic mastery of the actual material to the front rank of world literature formerly represented by Gorky and the young Sholokov.

Since Stalin's death, the type of *nachalnik* that represents the central problem of Soviet society has been critically portrayed by several authors, for example Ovechkin, Granin and Nikolayeva.[20] Their books centred on the alternative between the 'good' and the 'bad' boss. They posed the Hegelian question as to how state and society can be protected from unworthy members of the bureaucracy, and also gave the Hegelian answer. Behind this stood the honest illusion that the abuses of the autocrats both great and small could be reduced to the mysteries of the 'personality cult', that ultimate ideological product of Khrushchev's. Solzhenitsyn has up till now been the only writer to investigate the protection of society from *hierarchy as such*. The functionaries whom he depicts with tried and true psychological realism in his *Cancer Ward*, and particularly in his towering novel *The First Circle*, do not so much denounce the bureaucracy as individuals, but rather disclose without compromise and in full detail how it is the hierarchy as such that sins in these members, whom it has robbed above all of their human substance. It is also very clear in Solzhenitsyn's work that the 'administrators of things', and in particular the 'managers of the productive process', experience this demoralization far less than the tools of the political and police apparatus, and that these latter groups are recruited right from the start from quite different types of people. For all his backward-looking perspective, Solzhenitsyn has given us the most pronounced alternative in Soviet literature up till now to the bureaucratic functionary, in the figure of the politically and socially committed natural scientist Niershin; and it says a great deal for

[20] Valentin Ovechkins, Daniel Granin, Galina Nikdayeva; an earlier novel of Granin's was translated as *Those Who Seek*, Moscow 1957.

the writer's objectivity that the most impressive figure in *The First Circle* is the one who still adheres to the Leninist tradition.

Solzhenitsyn is naturally an exceptional phenomenon. It is basically the party apparatus itself that is to blame for having laid the mantle of the great Russian literary tradition, its continuing ethical legacy, on the shoulders of this one man. Those who continue to write in such a way that their books are printed and distributed in the Soviet Union itself are right in their own way. But the role of Solzhenitsyn has the advantage for Soviet literary life that he fully matches other writers and even sets them standards, even the most important representatives of the written word, whom the powers that be would not like to force into the same position as Solzhenitsyn; for it is not easy to refute or correct his art.[21]

Chinghiz Aitmatov in particular can undoubtedly be compared with Solzhenitsyn in his powers of characterization, and he also comes close in the honesty and courage of his work, even though he has chosen a different course of struggle. The radical questions he poses are systematically trivialized by sympathetic criticism, in an attempt to conceal them. Precisely the fact that he is chosen to represent the alternative to Solzhenitsyn widens his room for critical manoeuvre. Already in his *Farewell, Gulsary* Aitmatov went as far as to call one of the Stalinist leather-coated idols a new *manaper* (as the old Oriental oppressors of the Kirghiz people were known), and pronounced judgement on a once ardent revolutionary who had resigned himself to passive obedience by saying: 'At some point you ceased to be a communist'. In a later work, *The Story Goes* ('The White Steamer'), he denounced at a

---

[21] After *Gulag Archipelago* and Solzhenitsyn's expulsion from the Soviet Union, I would add that the whole problem of Solzhenitsyn would not exist if the party had presented the Soviet people and the whole world with even the documentary reports of its very own investigations of 20 or 15 years ago, when the time was ripe for this. If the *Gulag* report has been greeted with such a mountain of calumny, this is a sign that it contains all too many elements of truth, and in the court of history the CPSU will lose the case for libel. Since the party has not given a report, and does not plan to do so, we now have this one. Its major role in the present ideological struggle is that it denounces the political and moral collapse of the CPSU *after* Stalin!

deeper level than Solzhenitsyn, as far as his philosophy of history goes, and without the latter's populist romanticism, the patriarchal foundation of class society as a living reality. And his parable ended by opting for a utopian commitment, for a new break out towards freedom and against all opportunist adaptation to circumstances.

Another outstanding writer, Antonov, in his story *The Torn Rouble*, laid bare the mechanism of destruction of initiative and individuality that is characteristic of our societies. The story presents a paradigm of that inhibition on productivity that hinders Soviet society in overcoming its final phase of industrial underdevelopment. It shows at the same time the misfortune of that growing number of individuals who are unable to realize the capacities they have been given by the material and cultural progress of their country. A similar background marks the still sharper story by the writer Belov, titled *We're Certainly Used To It*.[22] Taking an example from North Russia, Belov vents his anger at the hopeless existence, deprived of all rights, of the kolkhoz peasants in all too many Soviet villages. As in Hemingway's novel *The Old Man and The Sea*, it is only in the struggle with nature that man appears in his rights as the highest being. For Belov's hero, the forest is his sea. These conditions are not pregnant with revolution; the most they can produce are local and impotent rebellions. The old village is more impotent today than at any time in Russian history. And it is as true as in the 19th century that a new revolution would be needed to give its servile souls their one conceivable opportunity to win back their dignity as free citizens: the opportunity for political self-determination in the struggle against the 'bosses', against the whole boss system, even though of course only the urban element could achieve victory in this struggle. From Solzhenitsyn through to Aitmatov we have artistic proof that the life of the Soviet people must be revolutionized anew from the bottom up.

These genuine artists, who are nowadays finding their successors, are generally already aware that they must look for their heroes among the non-privileged masses. They have made their choice in favour of the so-called 'simple people'. Those in charge of the functions that these 'simple people' carry out are stylized as more or less 'positive heroes' by second-rank writers, with little if any aesthetic effect. Yet it can still be informative to take a look at these self-portrayals of the Soviet ruling stratum written from the manager's eye, which are sometimes partially critical, if on the whole affirmative.

The typical differentiation which we get within the hierarchies of functionaries – and moreover at first a psychological one, which becomes political only at a very advanced stage – is that between 'progressives' and 'conservatives'. The works of the Khrushchev era, which I have already referred to, could even take up a political position (if only in a superficial sense) in favour of the 'progressive' party, at least as long as the semi-reformation was in power. At that time even such a notorious and artistically inept reactionary as Kotshevov, who had specialized in 'workers' dynasties' – one of the ideological disgraces of Stalinism – saw himself called upon to deal with the theme of the good and the bad party secretary. More recent literature of this orientation avoids the political edge, which is not to the detriment of the books involved, as this has previously always led to illusory solutions. It simply shows characters who come into psychological conflict over the solution of tasks of some kind. The more realistically the milieu of the workplace and the apparatus is depicted in this connection, the better for the reader – and for the foreign sociologist, who in this way acquires authentic fragments of Soviet reality. The boss relationship is self-evident in all books of this genre, it is the uncritically accepted reality. All that is at issue is a more productive functioning of the hierarchy, and, as the author sees it, a more humane one, the portrait of the clever, courageous and expert manager. These novels must be judged principally according to their author's intent, since as works of art they are completely mediocre, if some are less clumsy than others – and also, as already said, by the sociological testimony of their details. To indicate this we can take two recent novels, Popov's novel of the steelworks[23] *Gained In Struggle*, in the

[23] *Soviet Literature* 6–7, 1971.

tradition of *Battle Under Way*, and Lipatov's *The Story of Director Pronchatov*.

Popov's fable depicts the promotion of a young specialist, the engineer Rudayev, to be manager of the most important department in the works. His opponents are his predecessor, stuck in a tyrannical style of management and in technological conservatism, and the protagonists of an extension who have already started construction on technologically obsolete lines. Rudayev wins through with the aid of a new factory director: in a fairly improbable manner the foundations of the extension are torn up to make room for the more advanced project. The book pleads for the informal involvement of engineers, and of at least an interested minority of workers, in the process of preparing technical and economic change. Thus it makes certain claims on behalf of the specialists, but in a manner that is at root undramatic and completely conformist. This tendency is concealed by the official party policy. Nothing is more characteristic of the harmlessness of the author than the way that, quite certainly without any 'bad intent', he has a party functionary of whom it is said that one must keep on the right side of him, since he is in charge of the whole region's resources, appear on the scene as a 'building contractor'. This is one of these give-away details, and by no means the only one in that book.

Lipatov is basically bolder than Popov, one could say that his conception does not *completely* follow party lines. He demands unrestrained power of disposal over men and machines for those technocrats who get things done, never mind how. The Siberian timber transporting station where his novel takes place is threatened by the appointment from outside of a colourless functionary as director. The outspoken chief engineer Pronchatov was nominated the legitimate heir to the job by the deceased former director. The old man even bequeathed him, for use in the coming battle for power, a major timber reserve which he had kept silent about. Pronchatov's careerism, which is as shameless as it is deliberate, is celebrated and justified in the name of progress, as he pulls out all the stops, including his position as the son of a cadre, to achieve a 'useful goal for society'. His motto is: You (the workers) sent me off to study, in order that I should do your thinking for you; and the director of the station must be the man who promises to send down the most wood. He takes no step vis-à-vis the party and state bosses that is not calculated with a view to becoming director. Here again, the reward lies in the details, such scenes as those between Pronchatov and the party's regional committee, in which we can gauge from the behaviour of the functionaries, and Pronchatov's own tactics, the internal relationships on which the Soviet party, state and economic management are based. For Lipatov it is a self-evident maxim that the 'right man for the job' does not reach his rightful place without career ambition; he will not be appointed just by objective criteria. Then there are the scenes where Pronchatov is wrestling with the fossil patriarch Nechamov, whose family have their grip on half the political and technical functions in the timber station, and the town attached to it, to round off the picture of local society. In a curious way the hero had once had his war experiences exorcized by one of the surviving shamans. This is consistent, for if he had been compelled to reflect on them, he would not have shown the lack of consideration necessary for his role. Balzac also recognized a subjectivity calculating entirely on external success as a condition for advance in post-revolutionary France. It is evident that the industrial exploiter, even if he appears as a technocrat, must never think twice.

The Story of Director Pronchatov is a book with a certain life to it, but one would have to be truly forsaken by all the spirits of socialist theory to see even the most distant similarity between the character of Pronchatov, and his whole milieu, and socialist models of leadership.

But was I not maintaining how impulse is restricted in a society where all activity is forced into the form of bureaucratic rivalry, while we have now seen against the background of this same system a character of absolute initiative, as we might say? Is there a specific dialectic that fosters the creation of this type of hero? Lipatov even gives us an intimation of this. For him, the party is justified only in so far as it places the Pronchatovs in the positions that require them. It may also dictate to them certain external principles of behaviour. In this respect Lipatov indicates the great creative potential of the Soviet intelligentsia, who are

9

Party and Bureaucracy

The weakness of impulse that results from the interaction between the forced labour bequeathed by class society on the one hand, and the bureaucratic organization of the general social connection on the other, is the immediate and incontestable everyday experience of our population, the functionaries included. Our social order gives greater scope to 'natural' human inertia and negligence (which of course really have a completely historical determination) than does capitalism, and it does so not only to those 'at the bottom', but also to those 'at the top'. The indolence of the bureaucrat corresponds to the lack of interest of the worker, and the dissatisfaction of the specialist. (It is scarcely necessary to add that living individuals cannot be reduced to these tendential figures.) Almost everything that is undertaken is marked by a characteristic disproportion between cost and effect. Individual initiative is stymied by an experience like that of Sisyphus – if generally quite undramatically. It is no accident that the officials have the ironic motto: 'Everything works by itself'.

The principal job of an executive bureaucracy is precisely to follow through the decisions and instructions that have been given, to take care of all eventualities and to eliminate whatever deviates – as a danger to law and continuity. The bureaucratic body possesses, simply by virtue of its gigantic size, an inertia that can properly be called physical. The modern productive forces, which are based more than ever on people being creative, are effectively braked by our bureaucracy precisely in their most sensitive and sensory zone, this braking mechanism, moreover, keeping them almost invariably at a stage of development that has already been superseded, because when a change of course is inevitable, it takes place only with a characteristic delay (in as much as it is not a question of political survival). And the party, which alone can function under the conditions it has brought about as a motor of industrial and social progress, is deeply trapped in this omnipresent spider's web *by its own apparatus*, a web which lets no region of social life escape it, no matter how removed.

But if the bureaucratic sclerosis of the power apparatus was the sole prevailing tendency, if its undoubtedly burdensome effect was actually decisive, then we could never have had the still relatively high rate of economic growth that is precisely characteristic of those non-capitalist countries working under parties of the Marxist-Leninist tradition. I have shown how bureaucracy raised its conservative head already in the Lenin period of the Russian revolution, and immediately showed its unchangeable symptoms. Yet there followed the tremendous economic dynamism of the 1930s, and the apparatus that Stalin to a large extent personally renovated proved to be the terroristically tamed tool of political and industrial revolution. Even today, the bureaucratic form of our superstructure still reduces quantitative growth less than it does qualitative, though it reduces the latter in a manner that is incorrigible on the basis of the established premises. It is very important to understand, however, in the search for an alternative, how and why our power apparatus does not just get absolutely stuck in its vicious circle.

There are two reasons for this, which should be distinguished analytically even though it is difficult to disentangle them in political practice. One of these is the apparatus's interest in self-preservation, in the face of the unfading challenge of a world-historical partner and opponent who is superior in material technique. The original Bolshevik motivation for economic emulation, of course, never particularly stimulated the broad mass of bureaucrats, once the world revolutionary idea of October was proscribed in the mid-1920s. But Lenin's reminder that productivity of labour would ultimately prove decisive can still not be silently glossed over, because it still formulates today the condition for the survival of our system in a society that has largely become disillusioned with it. The hectic activity that time and again spreads convulsively from the top down through the whole society, is part and parcel of this situation. But as in the children's tale I already referred to above, the tortoise has already arrived. The Soviet situation of today still has a lot left of the old external challenge that stirred Peter the Great to swing his whip across Russia's back, and this meant first of all: across that of the Russian bureaucracy. The general run of party and state officials are not driven to have heart attacks by their restless consciences – their visible mentality fits all the models of traditional official conservatism – but rather by the desire for self-preservation of the highest functionaries, who are at no price prepared to give up the levers of power. In this connection, of course, the party leadership are less the creators of a new civilization than the interpreters of those impulses which 'over there', under late capitalism, keep technical economic progress in full swing. They make desperate attempts to crank up the economic motor, most recently even in honest cooperation with North America, Japan and the EEC. From the economic standpoint, the late-capitalist grouping can well renounce its former 'roll-back' policy, since our bloc is successively being reintegrated into the unitary world market which they dominate. If the Soviet leadership considers its country and itself, it can have no other choice. If we take things as they actually are, and not as they should be, then its relative industrial and agricultural success is still its most respectable legitimation.

Domestically, the major dilemma is that the masses judge their promises less and less by the small steps forward that successive annual plans are supposed to give them, and more and more by the absolute gap that separates the Soviet Union from the 'consumer paradise' of the late-capitalist industrial states. The upper stratum of the bureaucracy, together with its retinue, itself offers the people this orientation, in the Soviet Union still more strikir.gly so than in the GDR. There is no longer anything of the traditional Bolshevik modesty which counted it an honour to share the material deprivations of the poorest. If satellite technology does completely liquidate the anachronistic isolation of the Soviet masses from the 'world picture' of the present that is now appearing, then the apparatus in Moscow will find itself sitting on a volcano of unsatisfied material needs. This, and nothing else, is the root of the panic feeling that can be sensed for example in Gromyko's draft convention on 'Principles for the use of artificial earth satellites for direct TV transmissions', a document reminiscent of Tsar Nicolas I. What is at issue in the Soviet Union today is not defence against 'ideological subversion' in the traditional sense. The propaganda machine is completely powerless against the mere appearance of the 'affluent society'. It is an open secret that even the more westerly countries of its own bloc cannot be exposed to the general view of Soviet citizens. If a change comes about in the Soviet Union, then it could first of all be precisely economic policy, which will be faced with so gigantic a demand from the masses to catch up with the West, that poses the most severe test for a new leadership.

But there is also a second and as it were higher reason for the relative ability of our system to function, higher that is than the mere interest of self-preservation. In many developing countries we see parties and bureaucracies without a Marxist-Leninist origin struggling far less successfully for the economic legitimation of their rule. They do not even manage to master corruption – a different corruption from that systematic corruption of the state that Stalin organized *from above*, which in the last analysis never escaped control from the centre. Even the characteristic discipline of the genuine Stalinist bureaucrats ultimately rests neither on the hierarchy of privileges nor simply on the constant threat of violence in case of deviation. There has remained through to today a residue of moral loyalty based on a certain world view, decisive for which is the formal retention by the political leaders of a small catechism of the pure doctrine. What is involved here in the case of parties based on such a world view, just as in the case of churches, is observance of the preservation of an original inspiration, which counts as one of their conditions of existence. Despite its role as a state religion, despite orthodoxy and the Inquisition, the Christian church is still not dead today, because and in as much as it has managed to keep alive in the belief of at least some of its members the mission of Christ as a behavioural ideal described in the New Testament. (In their worst crises, churches are saved by their heretics.) In all our parties holding state power, there are still people, right up to the very top, who are tied to the Marxist idea at least by their bad conscience.

Even in the Soviet Union, where the revolution is already so far in the past that the leaders of today have scarcely learned anything from it but Stalinist bureaucracy, the communist tradition still bequeathes a certain uncomfortable inheritance. If they publicly renounced the idea, they would immediately be swept away. Pursued by an inescapable legitimacy complex, they need a distorted Marxism as their daily bread, and they must even believe in it themselves, at least in certain honest moments, for the sake of their own psychological survival. The Marxism which they have betrayed and spoiled is still the currency in which they conduct their usury. As Marx and Engels put it in *The German Ideology*: 'The more the normal form of intercourse of society, and with it the conditions of the ruling class, develop their contradiction to the advanced productive forces, and the greater the consequent discord within the ruling class itself as well as between it and the classes ruled by it, the more fictitious, of course, becomes the consciousness which originally corresponded to this form of intercourse . . . and the more do the old traditional ideas of these relations of intercourse, in which actual private interests, etc., etc., are expressed as universal interests, descend to the level of mere idealizing phrases, conscious illusion, deliberate hypocrisy. But the more their falsity is exposed by life, and the less meaning they have for consciousness itself, the more resolutely are they asserted, the more hypocritical, moral and holy becomes the language of this normal society'.[1]

The members of the apparatus are mentally trapped in a hopelessly defensive situation. Their immediate responsibility for the apparatus of administrative power permanently reflects on the principles on which the higher authority and justification of their power depends. In movements that appeal to a Messianic ideal, to some kind of 'world-historical mission', the contradiction between the emancipatory intention and the repressive practice of domination inevitably leads to heretical rebellions which aim at a reformation. The kernel of their argument is always the same,

---

[1] *Collected Works*, vol. 5, p. 293.

whether it is Luther speaking of 'that devil's sow, the Pope', or Trotsky of Stalin as the 'grave-digger of the revolution'. It is in no way decisive how far such epithets are genuinely apposite, if at all. What matters is the intention behind these reformation movements, the aim of freeing the idea once again from the power apparatus that has perverted it. From a higher point of view, this mechanism can be depended on even today.

Where does the weakness of the Stalinist bureaucracies have its roots? Why are they unable to conduct a *fuite en avant*, to take the initiative themselves in breaking out of the dilemma between their original revolutionary task and their practice of domination? Functionaries who see somewhat further ahead, such as Kadar for example, repeat Lenin's dictum that in conditions where the party holds sole power it must itself take on the simultaneous role of an opposition. But this is never successfully managed, since their own bureaucratization, their subjection to the gigantic apparatus and the needs of its reproduction, makes them quite incapable of taking a critical distance from the state machine, from étatism.

Finally, we should give up the last residues of the illusion that the mass of political and administrative bureaucrats are in any sense *communists*, who are simply superficially commissarized or bureaucratized, so that one might perhaps be able to address them at a deeper level of their encrusted consciousness. No, the bureaucracy has long since ceased to be merely a superficial and alien form. It has become as it were the natural political form of existence of a major group of people with pronounced special interests, who have crystallized around the trunk, boughs and branches of the power apparatus. The general interest of society now has to find a way through these special interests, if it is to be officially recognized as such – precisely as was the case under all previous historical relations of domination. This social group essentially embraces the *higher offices* of all political, state and 'social' managerial pyramids, including the military, police and ideological branches, i.e. precisely the extensive party, state and higher economic officials in the broadest sense. From a political-economic point of view, they tend to stand in an antagonistic relationship to the immediate producers (including the specialists, even if one section of these are absorbed by the staff functions of the power apparatus).

State property, as the domain of this politbureaucratic and administrative power of disposal, represents a relation of production *sui generis*. 'For the good of the people', as it cannot stress loudly enough, particularly after its fright at the Polish December events of 1970, the oligarchy at the top of the pyramid decides the goals for which the surplus product should be used, and subjects the *entire* reproduction process of economic, social and cultural life to its regulation. As in the case of all earlier systems of domination, the steady reproduction of its own monopoly, and when possible its expanded reproduction, goes into the overall calculation of social development and has to be paid for by the masses. Just as a worker under capitalism not only improves his own conditions of existence by good and responsible productive activity, as well as the general conditions, within the limits given by the system, but above all expands capital, so under actually existing socialism he increases the potential for the party and state machine's power of disposal, and thus increases his own impotence in relation to it.

In the face of a corporation closed against them, the working masses can influence the process of disposal, itself organized according to a division of labour, only spasmodically and accidentally; fundamentally, they have no access to the positions where the various threads run together, and so can control nothing essential. Vis-à-vis the concentrated property of the state they continue to stand in a 'proletarian' position, and since the trade unions are no longer *their own* associations, but rather associations *for them*, they are even more powerless, in institutional terms, than before. Under actually existing socialism, people are atomized even *within* the so-called social organizations, and so too, in a quite specific way, are the party members within the party, something that is precisely anchored in its statutes. Naïve people often marvel that the party can weaken itself by accepting so many 'unworthy' candidates; but in reality the power of the bureaucracy grows with the number of souls subject to its administration.

People and functionaries – this is the unavoidable dichotomy of every proto-socialist society. It is the most important 'contradiction among the people'. But the antagonistic consistency that it exhibits in all countries under Soviet inspiration is something quite specific. It results from the fact that the party leadership is working not to overcome this late class society of ours, but rather to consolidate and perpetuate it, and would like to confine social and economic progress to their necessary limits. Experiences in Yugoslavia and China have shown that it is possible not only in theory, but also in practical politics, to take account of the reality of the state in proto-socialist society, and to use the state apparatus for revolutionary transformation, *without* making a virtue out of a necessity (out of an evil, as Engels put it) and finding a pseudo-dialectic according to which the 'growing role' of the state from one party congress to the next will lead to its withering away – at the Greek Calends. But this is precisely the ideology of a party apparatus which celebrates in the permanence of the state machine the conditions of its own unending reproduction. In reality, it is precisely the given form of existence of the *party* (not so much so of the state) which makes necessary the idolization of the state. For the party apparatus is not only the motor of social development, but also its helmsman, while the state machine is simply the tool. It does not produce any ideology of its own (contrary to the Yugoslav case, for example), if we leave aside its economic-managerial branch linked directly with the economic process, which tempers the official ideology with a technocratic emphasis.

To explain the party apparatus, I must recall once again the genesis of our social conditions. Lenin's conception of the mechanism of proletarian dictatorship sought to subordinate the aspect of 'internal' suppression to the far more comprehensive educational role of the party towards the masses, a role basically oriented to a communist perspective. But the idea of the relationship party/trade union/masses as a transmission mechanism never functioned in the sense Lenin intended, not even in relation to the working class proper. The trade unions were to be both schools of socialism *and* instruments of struggle against the bureaucratic deformation of the state power. They became neither one thing nor the other. Their role suffered from such dystrophy that they are a millstone even round the neck of the state machine, as was shown in the Polish December events. In actual fact, transmission from the party to the masses cannot work basically in an educational way, it must be primarily administrative and repressive; and this transmission mechanism is precisely the state apparatus. The question then arose, in view of the absence of any corrective from below, as to *how* the party was to control the state machine so that it did not end up degenerating into the spontaneity of bureaucratic routine and corruption. The solution offered was *to construct an additional bureaucracy over and above the state apparatus in the form of the party apparatus.*

Every political party, of course, needs an organizational apparatus in the shape of offices, secretaries, or whatever one might like to call these *ancillary* departments. But the original significance of the concepts is turned on its head in the practice of our ruling parties. There was no previous system of domination whose leading figures called themselves mere 'bureau members' and 'secretaries'. From these very descriptions we can see the mastery of the living party body by its bureaucracy. It is hardly accidental that the party life of today no longer produces any leading political personalities, any genuine conceptual ideologists. We find rather that the various levels of the party right up to the Central Committee apparatus, which is really just the extended totality of the Politbureau functions, actually *double* the corresponding branches and levels of the state and 'social' bureaucracy, without exception, in a compressed form, just as all branches of social life are already doubled in the apparatus of the government and the official 'social' organizations. The elaboration, execution and control of party decisions must be apportioned to its own bureaucracy, since the party cannot appear as initiator through the self-organization of its members, giving them genuine representation, but only through its apparatus. In this way, what is erected over the administrative bureaucracy of the state is not the sphere of popular sovereignty as represented in bodies of popular assembly (in the Soviet system, Soviets do not play any role worthy of the name, but are chosen by bureaucratic selection under party supervision), but rather a special political bureaucracy, which in turn manipulates the inner-party elections. At the head, in the shape of the Politbureau, stands an institution which in fact elects itself. It is those already in this leading body who decide who is to be newly coopted onto it, and not even all of them. These 'communists' even go so far as to prescribe a special protocol for their internal seating arrangement, according to levels of rank.

The Politbureau dictatorship is a grotesque exaggeration of the bureaucratic principle, in as much as the party apparatus subordinate to it is at the same time both church hierarchy and superstate. The whole structure is quasi-theocratic. For the core of its political power (I do not mean here its hypertrophied executive and police organs) is power over minds, with the constant tendency towards inquisition, so that the party is already in itself the real political police. The party apparatus as core of the state power means a secularized religious state, something that the Christian church was fortunate enough never to succeed in establishing other than locally. Never since the decline of the original theocrats of the first civilizations were temporal and spiritual authority united in this way in a single hand. Since the apparatus is thus 'responsible for everything', it must suspect every departure from the details of bureaucratic practice as ideological heresy. It is precisely the *major* errors that generally escape any criticism at the time this is needed. With their pretence to know the laws of history and the true interests of the masses, any political decision, no matter for example how costly it might be in economic terms, can be justified. The 'primacy of politics', transformed into the Magna Carta of subjectivism, automatically means, given the monopoly of opinion formation by a Politbureau clique, that arguments of fact have no sway where the biggest issues are involved. Whenever what is at stake is not simply millions worth of the surplus product created by the immediate producers, but rather thousands of millions, those responsible can only be found at the very summit of the summit. They alone have to take charge of all risks, since they bear them 'for society' instead of with it. There is a whole undergrowth of apologetic sentimentalism for this 'burden of responsibility', which in the last analysis relates to the course of the world as a whole. It is borne like a cross, and must naturally be compensated for by certain conveniencies of life. It is the source of all justifications for the corruption of the bureaucracy itself from above, in which is manifested most visibly the appropriation of other people's labour by the tenants of the power apparatus.

Politbureaucratic centralism makes a lot of fuss about its scientific character; this is an indispensable act of faith for it. According to the half-baked understanding of history that it bases on Marx, if quite against his own meaning, there are historical laws that exist independent of the concrete needs and actions of men, which are known by the party and applied to the actual society, no matter how much society might struggle against them in its unenlightened view of its own interests. The will of the party is therefore necessarily perceived by society as a compulsion laid upon it, and must be forced on society all the more in practice. It *appears* as 'true' and 'scientific' precisely to the extent that the compulsion functions effectively.

It is quite nonsensical, moreover, to assume that a society still divided into groups with essentially different interests could bring its general interests onto a *scientific* common denominator, such as would prescribe impartially to social contradictions the direction of their development. Science, and social science in particular, primarily gives expression to those interests that most coincide with the ruling forces in society. If it is possible to arrive at rationality only via the state and the party, then science *serves* these institutions and becomes an instrument of struggle for the social stratum involved in them. It is 'scientifically proven' that the high-placed bureaucrat must receive for his services a special salary starting at 2000 marks per month, while a cleaning woman is paid only 400 marks. Our system does not possess any social organ for impartial knowledge, for an objective analysis of existing conditions. In any investigation, the premises of particular interests intervene from the start, premises which precisely falsify the basic structure of social facts before they are even cast a first glance. Nothing can come out of such an investigation that contradicts the prevailing interpretation. If this does exceptionally happen, then the intention that led to the undesirable conclusions must have been wrong. The researcher in question was lacking in party spirit. A science of this kind deserves no more than contempt, precisely from the Marxist standpoint.

In the best case, therefore, the party leadership experiments with society in a purely objective fashion – i.e. if we ignore the special interests of the top official stratum, which could only be repressed by shock therapy. The party apparatus is the organized refusal to make use of the subject-quality of the social object. Instead of understanding itself as a part of this general subjectivity, even if a prominent one, the party leadership confronts society with the claim to represent its entire relevant consciousness at every moment. As knowing subject, it constantly maintains itself to be already in advance of the social object, it lays claim to absolute divine knowledge on questions of fundamental social needs, by the very essence of things. Its general reason already always claims to include the 'definition of man'. But this theological adaptation is simply the reflex of the objective role that it plays as the sovereign subject of central planning. In the context of its mechanistic model of society, whose elements and structures are ascribed only linear 'further development', it is naturally 'all-knowing', as anyone less initiated, who wants to debate with it on the ground of its own premises, invariably finds out to his cost.

When all is said and done, the uncontrollability of the Polit-bureau and its apparatus presents the foremost political problem under actually existing socialism, the first object of the transformations that are necessary, this institutional identity of state authority, power of economic disposal and the claim to ideological exclusiveness. *The centralist monopolization of all economic, political and intellectual decision-making leads to an insuperable contradiction between the social task of the party and its political and organizational form of existence as a political organization.* The party dictatorship proves a failure at the most elementary level at which *any* system of domination has to maintain itself, if it wants to fulfil its social function.

The role of the party is often compared, and by no means falsely, with the role of the brain in the animal organism. Such a comparison naturally already presupposes that we are still deep in a state of polarization of social thought and directly productive labour. But taking this as given, the party must at least be the organ of knowledge, with the aid of which society adapts itself to the changes in itself and its environment in a regular way and at the right time. If an individual brain is no longer ready or able to grasp the environment as it actually is, and to adapt the organism to deal with it in a practical way, then we speak in psychology of neurosis, if not worse. In social institutions, the problem does not consist chiefly in the personal malaise of the representatives, even if reactionary institutions, for example, attract more than their share of compulsive characters and other active neurotics. What is involved is rather the structural analogy between the psycho-physical organization of the individual and the institutional structure of society in its capacity as an information-processing system.

What I maintain is that the party organization, as we are concretely faced with it, hangs on to an obsolete picture of the world and model of behaviour, that it functions sclerotically as a social organ of knowledge at the 'physiological' level, and neurotically at the 'psychological' level. Brains whose capacities and functions are disturbed and reduced in this way generally lead sooner or later to the demise of their organisms, since the decisions that they make lie too far from the optimum, and *must* do so, often being only suited to entangling the overall system still deeper in crisis. The party organization of today is a structure that *actively produces false consciousness on a massive scale*. At the summit, this false consciousness leads to decisions and resolutions that *cannot* represent an adequate interpretation of social needs, necessities and possibilities. It is conditioned like a Pavlovian dog which needs a long period of time to unlearn a habituated reaction to a signal once this signal's significance changes.

Its situation is even worse than with this dog. It does whatever is possible, and sometimes even attempts the impossible, in order to hold the accustomed signal as far as possible to its previous meaning. As far as lies in its power, it can see to it that the expectations according to which it makes its decisions are confirmed, and particularly the negative ones, which time and again justify the maintenance of the repressive mechanism. Incoming information is firstly distorted by a filter which sends good information on ahead and throws bad information out, and above all the resulting résumé is always coloured by the *a priori* evaluation that is given by the rigid programme. Unpleasant experiences undoubtedly conceal the class enemy, whether that of the past or the present. What does not fit into the schema, because it does not form part of the presupposed official self-portrait, is labelled a diversion, left out or played down in its significance (as an 'untypical phenomenon').

The apparatus is blind, to an extent far beyond the individual limitation of its agents, to all social reaction, blind also to its own burdensome and provocative existence. The individual bureaucrat may make mistakes, or at least may subsequently be found to have made mistakes, but the party, in other words the apparatus as a whole, is always right, as our free-thinking poet Louis Fürnberg put it. The official historical materialists are therefore regularly sent chasing for scapegoats so as to excuse the inadequate functioning of the social whole that they oversee.

If society tried to take the party at its word, it might sum everything else up in one single fundamental reproach. The party should be the social structure for the development of the social knowledge process, something like the cortex of the social nervous system, an organ in which all thinking elements of the people can participate (truly not a maximal demand). Instead of this, it shifts about like a tinted and distorting lens between social thought and reality, and moreover one with systematic blind spots. The working masses, who cannot be told how this lens is developed and constructed, how it is employed and adjusted, what it obscures, what systematic errors it gives rise to, can only abandon the attempt to use this instrument, and this is indeed what they do; they switch off before the official prayer wheel has rattled out its first sentence. But the real tragedy is that they are thereby forced to renounce all differentiated knowledge, since our society does not possess any alterative structure for this. Worse still, the only theory that is fit for penetrating the jungle of bureaucratic centralism and its politbureaucratic holy of holies, i.e. revolutionary Marxism, has been so effectively usurped by the party bureaucracy, by the apparatus's total power of disposal over the means of mass communication and education, that it meets with the general mistrust of the masses. Whatever the variants in which it appears, people are suspicious that it has been produced as a basis for the present rule of the party.

Given the high level of vacuum that has thus arisen, the ideological mass production of the West interposes itself wherever its communications technique allows. And the contradictions of our system have gone so far that the bourgeois propaganda apparatus plays at least in part a corrective role. Where its influence is lacking, as at the present time still in many parts of the Soviet Union, the mental and political situation of the working people vis-à-vis the politbureaucratic regime is still less favourable than it is in our own case, that of the peripheral countries of the Soviet bloc. How do communists in the East European countries get to know the real life of progressive movements in the rest of the world? How do we come to know something of the socialist experiences of Yugoslavia and China, or the 1968 Action Programme of the Czechoslovak party? Who is it that quotes, no matter how tendentiously, the Italian communists' *Rinascità*? The list could be continued endlessly. The anti-Promethean character of the dominant 'fraternal parties', above all the Soviet and our own German party, is a devastating fact. *Their inherent constitution and their form of rule as a super-state apparatus are the decisive developmental obstacles* on the way of further human emancipation in our countries. The party that once was Lenin's, and the party founded by Liebknecht and Luxemburg, are today functioning in reverse gear.

Communists in these parties are organized against themselves and against the people. Simply by its physical existence, without any special perfidy, the party apparatus of today is the gravedigger of the party idea and of individual party sentiment. It renders superfluous precisely those people who are communists from their own character and inner conviction. Further still, if it does not succeed in making them into bureaucrats, integrating them into the apparatus, they can in fact only 'make trouble', so that it is logical to put the machinery against them on a permanent alarm footing. The best thing still in the mechanical logic that governs the whole edifice is that the very style of the party itself calls oppositions into being, even where comrades with some feeling still do not manage to penetrate its law. The original emotional basis of all articulated oppositions is the protest of thinking members against the watchdog stupidity of a party apparatus no longer able to serve, but only to dominate.

In the hour of transformation it will become clear, as it did in 1968 in Czechoslovakia, that beneath the hard shell a different, new party – and *at least one*, we must say – is waiting to be released. We must try to anticipate what kind of party this will be, for it is readily understandable that its actual nature will only to a very limited extent follow our own fundamental desires. Marxism offers us only the possibility of extrapolation from the character of the given society and its contradictions. And it remains the historical right of the individual communist to make his own personal choice and exert his own influence on the direction of events – a possibility that he does not possess as of now. This alone would be a great step forward. It is meaningless to demand in advance guarantees that everything has to go the way clever people think it should. This should be borne in mind by all those, particularly among the old communists, who always meet new developments and theories first of all by pronouncing moral judgements based on the principles which they grew up with in a very different situation. Can we forget that these very principles have themselves made their contribution to the metamorphosis of the party into an apparatus of power, and that to swear by them today can only lead to leaving everything as it is? Was this not the reason why many old Czechoslovak communists, from subjective motives of this kind, helped to restore the discredited Novotny regime after the August invasion? We must set our course for a new beginning, instead of condemning ourselves to inactivity under the weight of our previous defeats.

1973–1975

Part Three

The Strategy of a Communist Alternative

10

The Present Conditions
and Perspectives for
General Emancipation

This last part inevitably presents the most difficult task, and will be the least secure and most inadequate portion of the text. The programmatic dimension, moreover, is something that should derive, not just on epistemological grounds, but also on sociological, from collective public practice, which for us in the countries of actually existing socialism is for the time being still notoriously forbidden. It must be attempted none the less, and I intend to express myself quite forcibly here, even at the risk of utopianism on individual aspects.

Marxists have a defensive attitude towards utopias. It was so laborious to escape from them in the past. But today utopian thought has a new necessity. For that historical spontaneity that Marx conceived as a process of natural history and which our Marxist-Leninists celebrate in the name of objective economic laws, *must* today be overcome. Today we must realize what the founders of Marxism anticipated when they wrote that the communist movement 'for the first time treats all naturally evolved premises as the creations of hitherto existing men, strips them of their natural character and subjugates them to the power of the united individuals'. It must make it 'impossible that anything should exist independently of individuals, insofar as reality is nevertheless only a product of the preceding intercourse of individuals'.[1] Natural processes normally end in a retrogression; the most probable path that arises from the interplay of accident and necessity is the parabola of rise, culmination and demise

[1] *The German Ideology*, in *Collected Works*, vol. 5, p. 81.

253

that governs all forms of individual life. It becomes a condition of survival, therefore, to put human existence 'on its head, i.e. on the Idea', as Hegel idealistically transfigured the moment of 1789. This is first of all a demand for the industrially most developed peoples, who possess the material-technical prerequisites for it and who, in giving themselves the social organization needed, can put an end to the destructive pressure that the civilization coming out of Europe has had on the life of all other peoples.

Today it is general emancipation that is the absolute necessity, since in the blind play of subaltern egoisms, lack of solidarity, the antagonism of atomized and alienated individuals, groups, peoples and conglomerates of all kinds, we are hastening ever more quickly towards a point of no return. This is something we must be aware of before we ask *how* it is possible. The general emancipation of man, or human emancipation pure and simple (as distinct for example from mere political emancipation), is nothing more than the subjective side of the communist movement. Communism is characterized by the 'genuine and free development of individuals' being founded on 'the universal character of the activity of individuals on the basis of the existing productive forces'.[2] There can be no doubt that Marxism originally anticipated such a *general* emancipation, the appropriation of the *totality* of socially produced productive forces by individuals as such (not simply by their association). They expressly write that in the communist association, 'a mass of instruments of production must be made subject to each individual', as well as 'property to all'. *Only* – this we must stress – 'with the appropriation of the total productive forces by the united individuals, private property comes to an end'.[3] Only then, and not before! Marx and Engels later expressly repeat once again that 'We have further shown that private property can be abolished only on condition of an all-round development of individuals, precisely because the existing form of intercourse and the existing productive forces are all-embracing and only individuals that are developing in an all-round fashion

[2] *Loc. cit.*, p. 439.
[3] *Ibid.*, p. 88.

can appropriate them, i.e., can turn them into free manifestations of their lives'.[4] And in summing up yet again the content of the communist movement, the movement of human emancipation, they maintain that 'the abolition of a state of affairs in which relations become independent of individuals, in which individuality is subservient to chance and the personal relations of individuals are subordinated to general class relations, etc. – that the abolition of this state of affairs is determined in the final analysis by the abolition of division of labour'.

The general emancipation is therefore the liberation of individuals from all socially determined limitations on their development, which necessarily had to have the outcome of their exclusion from participation in the determination of general affairs, from the conscious bringing about of social changes. I showed in the first part of this book how with the demise of primitive society the general social context began to constitute itself over and above the individuals involved, and how in this connection the subjective mediation of the individuals' particular modes of manifestation with the social whole was also lost. General emancipation will promote first and foremost the conditions for the *activity* of appropriation to become universal. It is accomplished to the extent that men are positively placed in a position to appropriate creatively the social totality – or to put it another way, to make subjectively their own the quintessence of the overall cultural achievement that mankind has so far produced or reproduced (i.e., handed down). It is a condition for this that social life in general, and in particular the process of production, including its informational superstructure, is organized in such a way that everyone can acquire all the individual abilities that correspond to the general level of the existing productive forces and the system of social regulation.

Here it already becomes evident that the conditions for general emancipation go far beyond the provision of material means in the narrower sense. The major 'means of development' becomes more and more the organization of the social whole as such. It is in this field above all that the objective basis for the 'development

[4] p. 439.

of individuals into complete individuals'[5] must be created. Instead of establishing in a pseudo-Marxist fashion the particular consciousness that necessarily arises from the existing conditions, with a view to satisfying the corresponding alienated needs, the question to be asked is what realities have to be created so as to break through the vicious circle of reification and change the content of needs. For the existing conditions are characterized less by a definite level of development of the material-technical basis than by two outmoded modes of production, two superfluous relations of production. Conservatives in both systems raise a hue and cry about voluntarism. But this only gives it away how they fear changes, or at the very least do not want to lead and take responsibility for them. We must bear in mind that it is a social body in its *subjective capacity* that has economic laws, and not the other way round. If a nomadic people break out of their steppes to exploit and subdue a civilized country, then with this collective act of subjectivity they overthrow their previous economic necessities and create a new system in contradictory cooperation with the people they have subjugated. Our problem might appear incomparable with such an archaic example, since today there is nowhere left to move to, and we can no longer demolish the past like a nomadic encampment, the tremendous weight of the world of things, on which we are more dependent than any civilization before us, lending economic compulsions an extraordinary inertia.

Yet 'where danger grows, so does the remedy'. Even mechanical materialists today have an inkling that the 'growing role of the subjective factor' involves something quite different from the mere conscious execution of historical laws. Marxism has always claimed that being can determine consciousness precisely to determine being *anew*. Human nature, itself a social creation from far back, goes into the laws of history *from within*, with its fundamental needs and strivings, and becomes the source of change if its contradiction with the objective circumstances that arise from material practice become too painful for it. Consciousness is ultimately its most prominent organ. Today we have for the first time in history a really massive 'surplus consciousness',

[5] p. 88.

i.e. an energetic mental capacity that is no longer absorbed by the *immediate* necessities and dangers of human existence and can thus orient itself to more distant problems. Previously, the scarceness of the means of satisfaction and development that are necessary for production and reproduction of the higher intellectual faculties always counterposed educated elites and uneducated masses. This component of the class struggle found expression time and again in a tendency to cultural regression on both sides of the social divide – exclusive arrogance on the one hand, the envious desire for destruction on the other, as major driving forces of economic and political action. Now this confrontation is losing its sharp edges, since technology demands educated masses and at the same time brings about the conditions for liquidating individual underdevelopment and subalternity. The problem is to drive forward the 'overproduction' of consciousness, so as to put the whole historical past 'on its head', and make the idea into *the decisive* material force, to guide things to a radical transformation that goes still deeper than the customary transition from one formation to another within one and the same civilization. What we are now facing, and what has in fact already begun, is a *cultural revolution* in the truest sense of the term: *a transformation of the entire subjective form of life of the masses*, something that can only be compared with that other transition which introduced humanity into class society, by way of patriarchy, the vertical division of labour and the state. In this second cultural revolution man will found his existence on his consciousness, on the 'highest mode of existence of matter', and concentrate on the social organization of this noosphere so as to regulate his natural relationship anew from this point of departure.

The perspective of this cultural revolution is bound up with certain problems that did not have priority, or even independent significance, for the old socialists and communists, particularly for scientific Marxists. In many respects Marxists are faced with a situation which is new from the standpoint of their previous self-conception. The general emancipation of man, according to their traditional understanding, had to be mediated by the emancipation of a class, the working class, but while the former conditions of existence of the working class have in fact still to be abolished in order to free society, the barriers in capitalist society which the proletarian struggle overthrows could not by a long way be the final ones. (The analogous point is of course still more true for the oppressed and exploited masses in what have been up till now predominantly agricultural countries.) As has been shown, in the complex industrial societies of both formations human beings come up against more general obstacles to self-realization which are not bound up with a specific class structure, against a layer of relations of domination that are very far from melting away with capital. Since under these circumstances the working-class movement in the capitalist countries is too narrow a base for transforming society (do not specifically working-class interests often even play a basically conservative role?), the West European and Japanese communists are already in the process of adapting themselves to the world-changing needs of *all* progressive elements, no matter what traditional class, stratum or section they may be ascribed to. It is evident enough that quite different fronts of interest arise from this, which already indicates a new order beyond the former economic one.

Precisely in the case of Italy, where this is most strikingly apparent, the phenomenon is not completely novel, from the standpoint of world history. Just as today, in the general crisis of the old order which affects *everyone* in that country, the communists have to make proselytes in all circles of the population, so in former times the Christians won over Romans at a level that transcended class contradictions and portended a new type of state and society, leading their movement from its plebeian origins to the position of a dominant church. Of course the analogy has its limits. But what is important to recognize is that *material* interests, which of course also lay at the root of the ideological conquests of the Christians in the latter days of Rome, are in no way reducible to such a simple *economic* antithesis – in the narrow sense of the concept, which is how the class struggle of the workers was undoubtedly originally organized. Rome, too, had its era of the Gracchi, when its social law of motion seemed as purely reducible to the problem of land ownership as that of European society in the 19th century did to the problem of capitalist exploitation. In both cases, the periods were ones of a social formation's youthful development. The antitheses that were once so strikingly dominant may well remain, but they lose their value to the point of relative insignificance when the question is raised in the later phases as to what is going to happen next. The entire structure of the traditional antithesis may then become irrelevant, and its mechanism a retarding element on the process of transition.

How should the revolutionary forces act if a whole society, as in Italy today, and tomorrow mankind as a whole, is overtaken by crisis? Marx and Engels recognized the historical possibility of the *common ruin of the contending classes*[6] in a particular society. We now have a similar danger in the overall human situation. Communism only remains possible if this danger can be banished. Under these conditions, the communist movement can no longer take up the standpoint of exclusive and particular class interests, which moreover transcend less than ever the limits of the various national and supernational economic complexes. Instead of the (today illusory) 'hegemony of the proletariat' over the bloc of revolutionary forces of different degrees,[7] we need *the creation of an overwhelming* – even if formally eclectic – *consensus for solving the general crisis, the constitution of the party with its mass following reaching into all social strata as the general representative of a new order, the continuity of the basic functions of reproduction, the isolation and expulsion of the obsolete fractions of the old regime from the living arteries of society, and not least from the levers of the state and administrative machinery!* Behind the formula of the historic compromise, which in practice has replaced the 'dictatorship of the proletariat' only in its superficial political aspect, stands the substantial idea (substantial not because it is new, but rather because it now has a practical perspective of success) of a comprehensive social regeneration which is to base itself on *all productive forces* in society. This is the conception of successively reducing the dominance of the capitalist structure in national life, by attaining control over a state apparatus that is ever more important for economic functioning, while at the same time the

---

[6] 'Manifesto of the Communist Party', in *The Revolutions of 1848, loc. cit.*, p. 68.
[7] As Lenin still could and indeed had to see the question: see, for example, *Collected Works*, vol. 6, pp. 37ff.

traditional class struggle is made less sharp by the accelerated integration of the under-developed classes and the productive employment of the non-parasitic elements from the privileged classes. It will in all probability emerge that the genuine democratization of national life under conditions of fairly pervasive state monopoly regulation can spell immediate actual progress in the *economic* emancipation of the masses, and can open the gateway to a path of increasing self-management from below in all society's institutions – something we could hardly expect from a sudden total expropriation that amounts to statification, from all the experience of actually existing socialism.

Here we have the connection with a further aspect from which the problem of emancipation goes beyond the context of class liberation. We know that for Marx, too, men did not belong to social classes in their capacity as individuals, however much they were affected by their class membership. Thus they were not automatically liberated as individuals when they were liberated in class terms. Marx and Engels easily overcame this problem, since for them the class struggle of the proletariat directly spelled general emancipation. As early as 1845–46 they wrote, 'In the present epoch, the domination of material relations over individuals, and the suppression of individuality by fortuitous circumstances, has assumed its sharpest and most universal form, thereby setting individuals . . . the task of replacing the domination of circumstances and of chance over individuals by the domination of individuals over chance and circumstances'.[8] Only today, however, through the modern superstructure, does the oppression of individuality so directly become a *universal* stumbling-block that opposing forces are formed and set in motion from this basis. Specifically human needs are inseparably connected right from the start with the fact of individuality, and they require for their satisfaction relations between people, personally significant communication with others, with a responsive and influenceable society. All objective culture would lose its sense (unless demands were pressed back to the mere preservation of the species) if the social context forfeited the character of concrete, humanly

---

[8] *The German Ideology, loc. cit.*, p. 438.

connecting communication to such an extent that all activity allowed nothing more than a comfortable private vegetation. The devaluation of the person before the objective spontaneity of an information process ultimately centred in a world government would exclude any harmony between individual and society. The negative utopias of Orwell and Huxley have essentially not yet disappeared from our horizon.

We must be clear about the psychological dimension of the problem of individuality in a supercomplex industrial society. The various spheres of life – work, education, domestic living, recreation – are separated to such an extent, and almost all activities so far depersonalized, even private relationships robbed of so many necessities, that alienation of man from man threatens to become the general fate. The misfortune of loneliness, of total loss of communication under the gigantic surface of abstract, spiritually indifferent functional activities, is encroaching ever deeper. We find lack of emotional connection even in the intimate contacts of the small family, this final residue of original communality. A mode of life that spells so much disharmony for the individuals involved may well be progressive according to some arbitrary criterion, but it does not offer any perspective of human emancipation.

But all these questions, that of the social subject of a revolutionary transformation, of the mastery of the bureaucratic challenge, of the reintegration of man into a communal life – are determined by a further level of problems that underlies even these, which are perhaps still less reducible than is the new orientation on the question of class to the original presuppositions of the Marxist tradition, and all the more persistently demands a new adaptation. Our customary idea of social transition is that of the dissolution and replacement of a social formation *within* the underlying conditions that European civilization, which has culminated in industralism (not in Europe alone), has created or brought forth. Even such a profound thinker as Gramsci accepted technique, industrialism, Americanism, Fordism *as a destiny*, and represented us communists as the proper executors of human adaptation to modern technology and machinery. Marxists do not often stop to think that humanity must not only transform its relations of production, but must also fundamentally transform the overall character of its mode of production, *i.e. the productive forces as well*, that it should consider its perspective as not bound to any one historically inherited *form* of development and satisfaction of needs, or to the world of products that is designed to serve these.

The whole nature of expanded reproduction that European civilization has brought about in its capitalist era, this very avalanche of expansion in all material and technical dimensions, is beginning to exhibit a runaway character. The success that we had with our means of dominating nature is threatening to destroy both ourselves and all other peoples, whom it relentlessly draws into its wake. The present mode of life in the industrially most advanced countries stands in a global antagonistic contradiction to the natural conditions of human existence. We are feeding off what other peoples and future generations need for their own life. At the very least, our wastage of all easily accessible resources increases their necessary labour and thus keeps their liberation under the old historical constraints. The present problems of resources and environment are the by-product of only two centuries of industrial activity by a small fraction of humanity. Based on the economic principle of profit maximization, still a powerful governing force under actually existing socialism, this is an essentially quantitative progress leading into a bad infinity. It must cease, because if the planet is to remain inhabitable the portion of the earth's crust that can be ground up in industrial metabolism with nature is limited, despite all possible extension and acceleration of this process.

Futurologists fascinated by science and technology like to forget that the opening up of the comparatively inexhaustible energy sources that they promise presupposes first of all the maximum deployment of an existing energy reserve which is already in process of exhaustion. If the development of the next few decades is going to lead to 10 or 15 thousand million individuals, as present extrapolations would suggest to be the likely limit, all aiming at the same maximum levels of consumption and waste products as the most developed countries, then the coming generations will have to produce oxygen for the atmosphere, water for the rivers, and cold for the poles. Under the heading of the 'basic distinction between the two world systems', Soviet theorists seriously and optimistically discuss the possibility of cannibalizing other planets or else smelting the earth's mountain ranges, which might be a little more modest in cost. The technocratic and scientistic belief that the progress of science and technique on existing lines will solve humanity's social problems is one of the most dangerous illusions of the present age. *The so-called scientific and technical revolution, which is presently being pursued predominantly in this dangerous perspective, must be reprogrammed by a new social revolution. The idea of progress in general must be interpreted in a radically different way from that to which we are accustomed.*

In a previous generation Tolstoy warned of the insatiable appetite that the capitalist epoch, then in its infancy, was stirring in the starving souls of the more enterprising Russian peasants, after their centuries of waiting for land. In his story 'Land Enough for a Man' the devil promises Pakhom as much land as he can walk round between sunrise and sunset. The peasant strikes out on so wide a circle that he finally falls down dead on the hill that he has to reach in order to close the circle. His farm-hand takes up a spade and digs him a grave 'just enough to reach from his feet to his head – six feet in all'. This allegory has an immediate universal significance today, as the old prophet was already aware. Per capita consumption of raw material and energy, per capita production of steel and cement, are the criteria *par excellence* of a totally alienated progress. The strategy of 'economic competition', which subjects itself to this inadequate standard of measurement, chains us to the most fundamental madness of our epoch: rather consider an exodus from our own solar system than set our minds on a bold new organization of human existence on this earth. For those who set targets for output in these terms, so as to keep pace with the demand of political and military power, conformity in the characteristic 'competition between systems' is so much more comfortable and devoid of personal risk than the attempt to move the masses against their old habits towards a change of course and a new direction. Here we cannot see the least affinity with Chekhov's answer to Tolstoy, that man needs not just six feet of land, nor even a little farm, he needs the whole earth, the whole of nature. This is called *belles lettres*. By contrast, economic planning in the GDR, for example, pursues the goal of a four-fold increase in commodity production in the years 1970–90, and with certain reservations almost as much in the consumption of raw materials. The innermost driving forces of this battle for production can never make it possible to overcome the balance of terror so sacred to all military leaders, nor to overcome the scarcity of means of existence and development. In a direction that Marx never intended, 'the realm of natural necessity expands with [man's] development, because so do his needs', an expansion with no visible limit, and we are pushing ineluctably ahead of us the 'stage at which compulsion and the monopolization of social development (with its material and intellectual advantages) by one section of society at the expense of another disappears'.[9] The rise in labour productivity, as an instrument to expand the time available for individual development, is alienated to become the vehicle of this doom-laden rat-race.

With the Comecon 'internationalism' of our ruling parties, not to mention the West-Europeanism of the PCI, PCF, etc., we find ourselves aligned by our immediate interests in the same boat as capitalist state monopoly and neo-colonialism, even if on the decks, in the holds and in the engine-rooms there is a struggle over which course to take and how the proceeds should be allocated. Our social life, just like that on the other side, is organized in such a way that a second car is closer for the working masses than a single meal for the slum dweller and peasant on the southern half of the earth, and closer too than a concern to expand their consciousness, to realize themselves as human beings. If our aim is to catch up with capitalist standards then we shall have our work cut out for a long time to come in dealing with our own problem of 'growth'. In so far as communists simply adapt themselves to these highly particular interests, they are precisely not what they give themselves out to be: champions of general emancipation. They are seeking with all their might to make their own the evil that they planned to do away with: the rule of reification, of alienation, and the anarchic competition of special interests. Not

[9] *Capital*, vol. 3, chap. 48, 3.

a growth in production, but cultural revolution – as the present form of *economic* emancipation – is the means finally to dissolve the capitalist structure.

Biologically, man has a bigger brain than any other form of life, but conscious regulation of the 'inorganic body' he has given himself is overwhelmed in the social totality. Man as a *species* 'knows' less about what is good for him than do primitive species, as a result of the inadequate organization of his noosphere. Apart from the need of developing countries to catch up (which, however, does not have to be measured in terms of our present per capita performance), it is not true that we need this economic growth for future generations. In this way humanity is only giving itself more problems than it can undertake to solve with the existing social structures, even with the aid of science, technique and organization. All too often we try to use Beelzebub to drive out the devil. And the policy of growth proves rather to be a stabilizing agency for the present relations of domination. *The communist association, as a social body that will be master of its problems without having to strangle its individual members, can only be a system of quantitatively simple reproduction, or at most very slow and well thought out expanded reproduction, of men, tools and material goods.* Only in this way can a relative surplus of the goods that are needed for life come into being on a world scale; given the continued dominance of the old economy with its permanent 'revolution of rising expectations', driven forward by the latest needs for luxury of the time, society must *always be too poor* for communism. On this basis, it will still be held against communists in a hundred years time that they want to make poverty universal.

Moreover, it is only in the context of a slow evolution of technology that a reliable self-regulation of the social process can gradually develop, something that would be the opposite of regulation by a bureaucratic mechanism, which, with its pretence to absolute knowledge, is constantly trying to cope in an underhand way with the disproportions and dysfunctions that it gives rise to because its knowledge actually always comes too late. Bureaucracy is the inescapable consequence of the spontaneity with which the laws of our fetishized world of things dominate us. As long as necessary labour does not cease to pursue men, as long as more and more objectified labour becomes 'necessary' to satisfy the needs of a single person, then the struggle for necessities cannot disappear, and neither can the equal right of unequal individuals, or the state.

In order to make itself master of nature, humanity had to reproduce itself and its tools on an expanded scale. But in order to remain in nature and to obtain control over itself, humanity now has to reach a stable relationship with nature. Taken on a world scale, the 'springs of cooperative wealth' must still for a short historical period flow more abundantly than before, but above all they must flow differently. The epochs of expanded reproduction were characterized by the priority that the production of things had over the development of man. The model of social inequality for the sake of cultural progress, which still marks the society of actually existing socialism right to its very foundations, has finally led to that terrifying lack of collective self-consciousness towards our world of things which is a problem for us today.

The extensive phase of human development is coming to an end one way or another, either in the good way or the bad. Our species can and will continue to improve its material base, but it must break with megalomania for the sake of its own survival and of the meaningfulness of life, it must learn collective respect for the natural order, which up till now it has managed to disturb rather than to improve. It must continue its ascent as a 'journey inwards'. The leap into the realm of freedom is conceivable only on the basis of a balance between the human species and its environment, with its dynamic decisively shifted towards the qualitative and subjective aspect. If we do not succeed in organizing society in such a way that it can embark on this new direction at the right time, then society will later be forced to it under the blows of catastrophic collapses of civilization, under the sign of barbaric struggle and dictatorship.

Through a misunderstanding that emphasizes the fetishism of the world of things characteristic of our cultural self-conception, the fear is often expressed that renunciation of economic growth would mean the loss of our species' dynamic impulse. This is based first of all on the easily made mistake that an order of simple reproduction need also renounce a rise in labour productivity – because greater output seems the evident purpose of such a rise. Common sense cannot give it a different meaning, since the protagonists of 'economic competition' are in full and public accord over the evil of unemployment. This is where actually existing socialism is so much superior to late capitalism, in as much as it offers people the secure perspective of full employment in alienated labour. But the deeper prejudice lies in the assumption that human creativity can only develop with an economy of expanded reproduction. Since however the qualitative development of the essential human powers, and thus also their objectification, never comes to a halt, the maintenance of the balance in its relationship with nature remains an 'eternal' problem. And for generations to come, the re-establishment of ecological stability will pose a creative demand of the first order, and of extreme diversity.

Over and above this, it has by no means been shown that man must generally and for all time obtain the *major* impulse to his activity from the sphere of metabolism with nature. At the centre of practical and theoretical activity we are undoubtedly faced more and more with the problems of *social* regulation, with the internal contradictions of the ensemble of social relations, and not least also with the problems of *individual* regulation, i.e. of human physiology and psychology. Seen from the individual standpoint, we are faced with the almost insoluble and yet decisive task, decisive for participation in intersubjective communication, of the appropriation of the social totality. For much as the 'journey inwards', the internalization of individual existence, involves a component of emotional abstraction from everything objective, its fundamental content naturally is and remains the same overcoming of alienation, the same metamorphosis of the civilization created by our species, that Hegel saw as the major work of the subjective spirit. Man can only obtain enjoyment from his existence in society and culture, from communication and competition with other individuals, through the effort of all his senses, powers and capacities. Most of all, we love to be known, as Christa Wolf once wrote.[10] But this is a tremendous factor driving

[10] Christa Wolf is a leading East German novelist, best known for her works *Der geteilte Himmel* and *Nachdenken über Christa T.*

a person to achieve something.

This all leads to the consideration that, from the experience of the 20th century, even the generally understood concept of the abolition of capitalist private property is still too narrow, is no longer sufficient, and from a certain point of view is even mistaken, when it comes to conceiving communism as the future of humanity. What comes closest to today's requirements in this respect is the goal projected by the young Marx, with its orientation, in the tradition of Rousseau, to the abolition of private property as a *reconciliation between culture and nature*, something which was later pushed to the periphery of Marx's thought. In the *Economic and Philosophical Manuscripts*, communist society is spoken of as the true resolution not only of the contest between man and man, but also of that between man and nature, including man's own nature. Marx conceives communism here as the mode of life appropriate to human nature, in which connection he lays stress on the social character of human nature. 'Only here', under communism, 'has his *natural* existence become his *human* existence and nature become man for him. . . . *Society* is therefore the perfected unity in essence of man with nature, the true resurrection of nature, the realized naturalism of man and the realized humanism of nature'.[11] But in Marx's time this goal did not come into any contradiction with the further expansion of the productive process. On the contrary, it required the unleashing of the modern productive forces for the most rapid increase in output. It is this perspective that now needs most urgent correction. Communists must modify their understanding of the so-called basic economic law of socialism – 'the object of ensuring full well-being', which is Lenin's starting-point[12] – i.e. of a surplus of material goods as the presupposition for communism. Far as the great teachers of socialism and communism were from reducing the task of socialist accumulation to the maximum production of material goods, their formulations still mirror an epoch in which the working masses were never sure of their minimal existence in food, clothing, housing and education. Today, when late capitalism even spares

[11] *Early Writings, loc. cit.*, pp. 349–50.
[12] 'Draft Programme of the Russian Social-Democratic Labour Party', *Collected Works*, vol. 6, p. 28.

its unemployed these insecurities, to a large extent, it is readily apparent that we do not need socialism simply to ensure well-being – as long as resources don't run out.

What socialism must begin with, however, are the profound *structural changes in production and consumption* that are necessary. A rich country such as the GDR, which is only now in the process of solving the question of housing, 5 to 10 years later than would have been possible, has for the past twenty years been spending labour on a growing scale for comparatively luxury products such as the inevitable private cars, various state palaces, second homes for all privileged strata in recreational areas, and much else besides. We can hear the director of a Berlin textile works, a factory moreover which predominantly employs female labour, say on the radio that 'the growing needs of the population dictate to us the three-shift system' – even if wardrobes are bursting! If you do not want to remain 'backward', you must throw out your furniture three times in the course of your life. We accelerate the 'moral depreciation' of technical consumer goods. We conjure up a new branch of industry in order to waste the complement of alienated labour, alienated leisure time. With overtime work for the fulfilment of the plan we secure with a good deal of trouble the growth of a range of goods, services, entertainments, etc. which, under the given circumstances, with their surplus over what is really necessary, do not so much promote the development of the personality as rather compensate for a personality develop-ment that has remained backward, the same as under capitalism. The question as to *why* we carry on driving this roundabout quicker and quicker is left to the secret desperation of isolated individuals, and the response can be seen among other things in the rising rate of suicide.

This is not the place to go into the full diversity of factors that make our state planning the executive organ of growing needs of this kind. I have explained the fundamental points in the second part of this book. There is also no doubt that even a revolutionary leadership could not proceed in an abrupt and predominantly restrictive way. But where and how are opposing positions to be constructed, positive facts created in the distribution of resources, investments, labour and education facilities, so as to press the structure of social need towards forms of life that promote the *purpose* of 'full well-being' as the *foundation* of general emancipation, i.e. of 'free, all-round development for all its [society's] members'?[13] Where is even the preliminary theoretical work for this carried out? The party leadership puts forward its social scientists – clever ones, too, who must know better, such as Nick[14] – to declare such questions bourgeois sabotage and cover up the 'global problems of humanity'[15] in a clever way with slogans of efficiency and intensification, which are suitable enough in a more limited connection. 'Let us beat capitalism in our production of goods, value against value! No rest until we can count at least 51 per cent of world industrial production! Don't you see that the present recession gives us the chance to catch up another few per cent?' This is the inner spirit of such propaganda, which places itself short-sightedly and stupidly in the service of historical spontaneity.

The development of the industrially developed countries in the last few decades has *proved* that the problem of general emancipation does not in any way consist in ensuring a sufficient material foundation in terms of means of subsistence. This certainly remains an indispensable precondition (though the necessary scope of this basis is probably more variable than we usually assume, when we fix our glance too narrowly on the actual present standard of our own society), and 'when you've covered your nakedness, you've got dignity' – *but not automatically*. The quantity and range of goods and enjoyments that intrude for consumption and distort the individual's deployment of his time, on the one hand by an increase in abstract labour, on the other hand by the passive reception of what has been 'bought for dear money', can even end up blocking the sources of emancipation and producing a parasitic mentality. The present economic policy in the Comecon countries will only improve conditions for the development of the personality where there are still genuine shortages to be eliminated. Yet it produces the growth in education that is indispensable for scientific and technical development in

[13] Lenin, *ibid.*
[14] *Einheit*, 1976, no. 5–6.
[15] These still show through! – *ibid.*, p. 539.

such forms that refuse a person any benefit for the development of the personality even in the educational process itself. We can no longer place our hopes in this direction.

What stubbornly proves to be the real problem of general emancipation is the *alienation* of individuals from the sources of the social power that they have themselves produced, their impotence and lack of influence on their overall destiny that is still actually increasing, and the poverty of their relations of real communication, no matter how much this is vainly juggled away by the self-interested agencies of officialdom. And yet the concept of alienation is too abstract, it laments and denounces more than it explains and mobilizes. My analysis in the preceding two parts of this book will allow us to give the demand for an abolition of alienation a more precise formulation as a present-day task, which particularly in the countries of actually existing socialism has acquired a pure form, i.e. is no longer concealed by the capitalist form. This is a long-run task, but it has a concrete socio-economic content, and can *directly* be taken in hand – as far as the material and technical conditions and developmental tendencies of our social structure are concerned. What is lacking is simply the reformation of the political power, a political power of the kind that would be ready and able to create the ideological consensus and the organizational framework for the cultural revolution.

The historical task which I have in mind is the *overcoming of subalternity*, the form of existence and mode of thought of 'little people'. At its core, this means the abolition of the traditional vertical division of labour, and the revolution of the entire orientation and structure of needs that is bound up with this. It proceeds by way of a radical change in all our customary institutions and modes of procedure in society and in the economy. *The overcoming of subalternity on a mass scale is the only possible alternative to the limitless expansion of material needs*. It can stem the forces that drive on the growth of needs in the former sense, its inertial mechanism anchored in the creation of surplus-value, and the reason for this is as follows. The surplus consciousness which I already referred to, that free mental capacity which is no longer absorbed by the struggle for means of existence, is divided complementarily into two diametrically opposed phenomenal

forms of social interest. These are both related to certain fundamental human social needs, which is why they generally compete
with one another also in each individual consciousness, so that
they divide individuals less than do earlier antithesis into firm
social groupings. Their struggle begins when 'one soul seeks to
sever from the other' in the individual consciousness.[16]

The *compensatory* interests, first of all, are the unavoidable
reaction to the way that society restricts and stunts the growth,
development, and confirmation of innumerable people at an early
age. The corresponding needs are met with substitute satisfactions.
People have to be indemnified, by possession and consumption
of as many things and services as possible, with the greatest
possible (exchange-) value, for the fact that they have an inadequate
share in the proper human needs. The striving for power can also
be classed with the compensatory interests, as a kind of higher
derivative.

The *emancipatory* interests, on the other hand, are oriented
to the growth, differentiation and self-realization of the personality in all dimensions of human activity. They demand above all
the potentially comprehensive *appropriation* of the essential
human powers objectified in other individuals, in objects, modes
of behaviour and relationships, their transformation into subjectivity, into a possession not of the juridical person, but rather
of the intellectual and ethical individuality, which presses in its
turn for more productive transformation.

This is a preliminary and very general definition. The emancipatory interests are as old as class society itself, as the exclusion
of the working masses from a growing number of historically given
activities, relations and enjoyments – even if these generally
could not be broadly developed and socially manifested. There
are recognizable barriers from which men have always sought to
emancipate themselves, in order to obtain access to something,
and appropriate something, that is conceived time and again in
the ideas of freedom, joy, happiness, etc., which no cynical irony
can expunge. The inexhaustible possibilities of human nature,

---

[16] 'Two souls, alas, dwell in my breast, Each seeks to sever from the other',
Goethe's *Faust*, Part One, lines 1112–3.

which themselves increase with cultural progress, are the inner-most material of all utopias, and moreover a very real, and in no way immaterial material at that. They inevitably lead to the desire to transform human life.

It follows from this complementarity of compensatory and emancipatory interests in surplus consciousness that the cultural revolution that overcomes subalternity is the *condition* for a break with the extensive economic dynamic, and for the rearrangement of man in his natural balance. But in order to discover the concrete directions in which to aim, the feasible lines of action and the necessary practical steps, for the circumstances of *today*, we must remember the positive preconditions for the appropriation of culture by all individuals, and investigate how they are to be brought about. These are at the same time the preconditions of genuine social equality, which as history has sufficiently shown in the meantime, are not to be found in the dimensions of distribution of income, social security, or any form of consumption.

All people must obtain the real possibility of *access* to all essential realms of *activity*, and moreover right up to the highest functional level. For cultural goods are appropriated only as far as it is possible to share in their creation – either oneself, or by the mediation of other individuals with whom one can *communicate on an equal basis*. In principle, everyone must be able to raise himself to the level of the scientific and technical means which our society uses in its relationship with nature, and especially to the level of social regulation and institutional functioning. Social equality also demands in emotional and aesthetic life certain mental structures which allow a graduated reaction both inwardly and outwardly, one which corresponds with the degree of abstraction of the more general connections represented by higher levels in the hierarchy of information processing. The question accordingly arises as to how individuals can acquire and learn effective behaviour, the corresponding dispositions of a motivational, cognitive and emotional kind, and how work, education and life, the organization of society, the system and the mode of function of its institutions, should accordingly be constructed.

Subalternity, which in varying degrees and characters affects the overwhelming majority of people today, is an effect of the

entire modern mode of production and can therefore only be overcome with its transformation. We saw how it stands in relation
to the concrete community to which individuals belong, or more
precisely, in relation to the highest level of active social organization that is erected over them as an autonomous entity. The degree
of possible subalternity grows with the number of steps in the
hierarchy. Here there is a profound contradiction in the historical
process. The greater and more complex the social association, the
more subaltern individuals become. In the gens and the tribe it
is impossible to be as subaltern, as impotent and as devoid of
influence as in the modern national state. We can see from this
how great the task of the cultural revolution is, in seeking to
restructure the objective conditions of development of human
subjectivity. The major directions of its intervention against the
causes of subalternity and for the realization of genuine equality,
directions which mutually presuppose one another, are as follows:

– a redivision of labour according to the principle that everyone should perform an equal share in activities at the various
functional levels, and the establishing of social equality between
those carrying out the tasks of necessary labour by making it
impossible for any person to be subsumed by a certain restricted
or subordinate activity;

– the opening of unrestricted access for all to a general education
embracing natural science and technique, society and art, at the
highest ('university') level, as the alternative to the differentiation
of social strata according to levels of education and to socially
incompetent bodies of specialists;

– concern for a childhood which fosters and promotes the
corresponding capacity of and readiness for development for the
overwhelming majority of the new generation, instead of inhibiting
and destroying this for most of them as does the style of education
of a patriarchal society geared to economic performance;

– the establishment of conditions for a new communal life
on the basis of autonomous group activities, around which fulfilling human relationships can be crystallized, so as to put a
limit to the isolation and loneliness of individuals in the isolated
compartments of the modern world, e.g. work, school, family
and leisure;

– the socialization (democratization) of the general process of knowledge and decision, its constitution outside of and above the hierarchical apparatus that secures the normal functioning of the reproduction in progress.

There is neither the hope nor the danger that these goals, of which none is prior to any other, none realizable without the others, can be achieved 'too quickly'. A society cannot be taken by surprise or with a coup d'état. There can be no expectation of weaning people overnight from the spontaneous quantitative increase in production, the traditional division of labour, the rationing of higher education, patriarchal family upbringing, distribution of income according to work, lack of community and bureaucracy. Any attempt of that kind would undoubtedly give rise to collapse, chaos, anarchy and despair, above all for those who suffered most under the old order – everything that the defenders of the existing situation might desire as a pretext for alarm. The question is rather to create first of all the political and mental conditions for treating the fundamental needs of our life no longer as definitive virtues, to be 'further developed' in the future by people who do not know what they are doing. I shall return in the final chapter to the problem of the political approach to the cultural revolution and its step-by-step realization. For the moment, I want simply to indicate the considerations which led me to formulate the five directions listed above.

Firstly, the redivision of labour. If it is the case in the rich countries in general that the centre of gravity of the class struggle has shifted from the appropriation of the material means of subsistence (though of course this is still not sufficiently ensured) to the appropriation of culture, this shift is particularly noticeable in the non-capitalist industrial countries. The appropriation of culture is in the first place a question of the social organization of labour, of the possibilities of human self-development that are programmed into it in advance. The social character of labour and its functional content are well known to determine the direction of education, and indeed of childhood socialization in general, however much this sphere reacts back in labour in its turn. In the *Grundrisse* Marx formulates the conditions to be introduced with the abolition of the traditional division of labour. He continues, after speaking of the 'really free working, e.g. composing' that obviously begins only outside the sphere of production: 'The work of material production can achieve this character only (1) when its social character is posited, (2) when it is of a scientific and at the same time general character, not merely human exertion as a specifically harnessed natural force, but exertion as subject . . . as an activity regulating all the forces of nature'.[17] The first condition concerns the de-bureaucratization and genuine socialization of the activity of management, the participation of all individuals in disposal over the reproduction process. The second condition bears on the elevation of the collective worker to the level of the given principles of science and technique of the time, which are at work in the production process.

Both these aspects indicate on the present-day horizon the real possibility that *all* people can share solidaristically in labour, and in particular can obtain a genuine influence on decisions at the highest level of consciousness. The major strategic problem of this cultural revolution does not of course consist in some kind of 'degradation' of the privileged, but rather in raising up those strata who have formerly been confined to the subaltern spheres. To put it in traditional terms, it consists in beginning the social evolution of the human essence into an ensemble of individuals *all* endowed with *philosophical self-consciousness*. We must take into account, however, that the complete liquidation of simply physical and schematic work – which is anyway an extremely questionable goal, and one which as I see it is not even desirable from the biological standpoint – lies in an unforseeable future. From the humanist standpoint, it is only labour that is too heavy for the body or monotonous (unskilled, one-sided) that must disappear; all other kinds can then serve as a rational balance. Whether we lament the 'primitive' character of Engels' example or not, it is still the case that *precisely* a society that seeks to set itself up as a free association *over* its reproductive performances must demand that architects too are prepared to do their share of

[17] *Loc. cit.*, pp. 611–2.

'portering', as long as this remains necessary for technical and economic reasons.

According to GDR statistics, for example, the early 1970s still see a degree of automation of only some 7 per cent, so that this is still not at all *qualitatively* significant for the relations of production in general, and embraces only more or less isolated acts of labour or industrial processes. The automation of manufacturing industry and the computerization of economic information-processing can in their preliminary phase even lead to an intensification of the old contradictions, i.e. objectively to a greater concentration of the power of disposal, and, for the subject, to a further increase in those phenomena that are characterized as alienation. But this is a question of social strategy. The connection between general emancipation and the transition from the age of mechanical machines to that of cybernetic machines is in no way so direct, even for the future, as is assumed by those who seek refuge from their disappointed hopes of socialism in the promise of the scientific and technical revolution. The idea that it would be necessary to wait for the *complete* withdrawal of human labour from all repetitive functions in the material and informational reproduction process is the most suitable way in which the technocrats can come to the aid of politbureaucratic conservatism.

Present-day practice finds its concentrated ideological expression in those conceptions of social cybernetics that like to see society after the model of an information processing system, a kind of idealization of the human brain, with its hierarchy of functions, understandings and competences (Georg Klaus for example).[18] The hope seems to be that it might still be possible to establish a natural caste organization, rather than the universality and capacity for transformation of the human species character. In reality, the turning-point for the *subjective* productive forces is already on the horizon. And it is only the shattered illusions about the principally *political* character of this 'leap' from the realm of necessity into the realm of freedom, that leave their expression of resignation and defeat in these perspectives. The

---

[18] Georg Klaus, author of *Kybernetik und Gesellschaft*, Berlin 1973; East German philosophy professor.

abolition and the overthrow of the traditional division of labour –
not of course as a violation of living generations who have already
internalized their confined character, but rather as a planned process to be executed in historical time – this will be the key theme of
a revolutionary maximum programme, which has to be converted
into a concrete political and socio-economic strategy, into a
succession of political struggles and socio-economic demands and
measures, not least in the sphere of educational policy.

The *redivision* of labour, then, in which I see the first decisive
step in this direction, is in no way completely identical with the
abolition of the traditional division of labour. It may seem at first
glance as if we were seeking with such a demand to anticipate
artificially and romantically a process that the scientific and technical revolution is bringing about almost automatically. The same
people who hold the abolition of the traditional division of labour
to be a Marxist illusion suddenly turn round and quote how 'In
all previous revolutions the mode of activity always remained
unchanged and it was only a question of a different distribution
of this activity, a new distribution of labour to other persons,
whilst the communist revolution is directed against the hitherto
existing *mode* of activity, does away with *labour* . . .'[19] To this we
must reply that Marx and Engels, in their own social perspective,
did not see themselves as waiting for the Greek Calends, when
all or almost all 'traditional' labour would be superseded. They
sought to intervene actively in the abolition of traditional labour,
with a process that I would today describe with deliberate political
intent as a cultural revolution, since they believed – *at that time*
somewhat too optimistically – that the general level of productivity
was already sufficient to set free sufficient 'disposable time' for
the development of the general abilities of all people, by the
participation *of all* in necessary labour. This is why their orientation to a change in labour was far more than a remedy against
monotony, as it is often envisaged today. Certainly, the trouble
that is taken to enrich and diversify the content of labour at a
particular functional level, for example in the assembly shop of a
factory making electrical appliances, deserves support and

[19] *The German Ideology, loc. cit.*, p. 52.

attention. But the result here can only be greater satisfaction in work at the given restricted level of activity, which therefore only improves the conditions for overcoming subalternity in so far as the general stupefaction of mental powers is thereby avoided.

And yet any modern industrial enterprise today, even one of average size, offers a whole range of tasks at all levels of function, from mediation between the special interests that characterize it as an economic unit and the goals and value of society as a whole, right down to cleaning the workshops. On the assumption that its personnel, as will be discussed under the next head, consisted of people of an essentially similar level of education, there would simply no longer be any possibility of tying anyone permanently to activities that make little demands on people and are inherently unpleasant. If we hear today that 'no one who has completed his studies could be allowed for a long time to come to work in a field decisively below his level of qualification', we do not generally consider the consequences of this, i.e. that there have to be other people whom these college-trained specialists with their monopoly of development-promoting activity condemn to spend their whole lives in precisely those mind-numbing activities that they indignantly reject for themselves. A demand such as this is incompatible with real social contact between the privileged and the disadvantaged strata of the collective worker. In the final analysis it comes down to the proposal to commit *more* people to the lower functional levels, i.e. to practise an even stricter *numerus clausus* for college entry. In this perspective, however, the logic of the demand for entry into labour at the level of qualification that is reached is reversed into one that can only be met if *no one* is withdrawn from activities of a lower level, for otherwise there would soon be college-trained cadres for whom there was no suitable activity.

It can only be a very great advantage as far as the overall effect is concerned, if, with respect to the qualitative change and intensification of the technique, technology and organization of production, we put an end to the fragmentation and social division of the collective worker, as this causes such great economic losses (e.g. by the systematic holding back of effort by the merely operative workers) and superfluous expenditures (e.g. for the

setting of norms which is required by the conflict of interest).
Let us imagine on the other hand a unitary type of producer,
alternately applying himself in a particular specialized branch, in a
deliberately established temporal rhythm, to activities at all the
given functional levels of the collective work process being carried
out. People who concern themselves with the new or further
development of machines, technologies or products will orient
themselves far more quickly and accurately to the requirements
of mass production if they are also active in the operative technological functions. The relatively short time, let us say a third
of their total work, that they spend in servicing the production
machines, will be useful for the creative improvement of the labour
process. The conditions of labour could be rapidly and continuously improved, if those who construct the machines also
worked at them for prolonged periods. The entire apparatus of
management and administration could be freed both from many
control functions and from the ignorance of detail that increases
with the number of levels, if its personnel again had a hand in
the whole range of material and problem-solving activities (the
continuity of management would be maintained by systematic
multiple occupancy of positions). We can just as well imagine the
everyday situation in a hospital, to take an example from a
different sphere, one still more strongly burdened with the
prejudices of the traditional division of labour, in which the
entire staff consisted of people with full medical training, or other
pertinent qualifications, who also took part in all nursing and
ancillary work, and in social and economic functions as well.

It will readily be understood that in indications such as these
we are concerned to define a principle, not to lay down a blueprint. A course set towards the redivision of labour is designed to
prevent the existing structure of work positions and levels from
being immediately transformed into an alienated if 'adequate'
structure of human labour-power. A reorganization of the division
of labour, such as would put an end to the exclusion of the many
from appropriation of the social and cultural totality, is, as we have
already said, the link in the chain on which the possibility of
transition from a quantatively to a qualitatively oriented type of
growth depends. This connection is so important that it deserves

repetition here once again: i.e. even if material need is overcome, so long as the masses still have to compensate for their subaltern situation by the appropriation of material comforts, they will continue to be forced to hang their self-consciousness on external props and to waste the leisure time they obtain; since they cannot take part in social communication as equals, we simply *have to* produce more and more. There can be no talk of justice, finally, as long as not only incomes are unjustly distributed, but also labour itself, since very different opportunities for self-realization are ascribed to individuals in a planned way by their subsumption under the law of economic proportionality. And all the less so if the 'performance principle' of reward according to work also impedes the material compensation of those disadvantaged in this way.

Many intellectuals secretly consider it their own moral merit if (in Teilhard de Chardin's formula) they prefer 'to know and to be, instead of to possess', whereas it is really the acme of their privilege to be able to live in such a way. (The quietist emphasis of Teilhard's expression, which aims more at satisfaction of existence than at the infinite development of essential human powers, may be left aside here.) The American Romantic Henry Thoreau wrote: 'Most of the luxuries, and many of the so called comforts of life, are not only not indispensable, but positive hinderances to the elevation of mankind. With respect to luxuries and comforts, the wisest have ever lived a more simple and meagre life than the poor . . . None can be an impartial or wise observer of human life but from the vantage ground of what *we* should call voluntary poverty.'[20]

There is a great deal of truth here, even if not an absolute truth. It would have been difficult for Thoreau to have reached this attitude if his father, instead of paying to send him to Harvard, had employed him in his pencil factory. The question is to create the objective conditions so that everyone *can* prefer 'to know and to be, instead of to possess'.

Secondly, a unitary course of education for fully socialized people.

[20] *Walden and Other Writings*, New York 1962, p. 115.

The road to the redivision of labour depends – in a pessimistic calculation, i.e. reckoning with a further phase of education being essentially unproductive economically – on whether 'society can afford' to give up an additional five or six working years for each of its members. In practice, however, this renunciation, particularly as it could be realized in stages, would only be temporary and relative, since a raising of the general level of culture would necessarily have its effect on the discipline and productivity of labour, and even in the execution of more simple tasks; the tendency that can be observed under *present* conditions for highly skilled people to lose their motivation when they are employed in work that is lacking in sufficient demand, is *no* basis for concluding the opposite. The blatant fact that practically all leading functions of society have recently been occupied by people with an academic education is sufficient proof that a relatively comprehensive scientific general education at the highest level is required in order to participate effectively and competently in the synthesis. Marx indicated the ascent of thought from the concrete to the abstract, and from there back to the concrete-in-thought, Lenin the active progress of knowledge from appearance to essence, from first-order to second-order essence, and so on. The dialectic of objectification and mediation needed subjectively to penetrate and master a highly complex social and scientific-technical development, is acquired by way of a degree of theoretical and practical familiarity with categories such as the educational system can in no way offer as a general rule by the age of sixteen, at least given the present set-up and organization of the socialization process.

Whether society has the means or not is a question that we are naturally not allowed to ask our economists in their capacity as advisers to the State Planning Commission and ideological representatives of the status quo in the structure of needs. The answers, moreover, would not be completely independent, to put it mildly, of whether they themselves believe it necessary to double and redouble the production of goods, or whether they would risk considering an alternative economic strategy. In the final chapter I shall go into the problem of an economic alternative in more detail. For the time being it must suffice to introduce here some ideas of the Soviet physicist Kapitza,[21] which, without having this as their specific intention, present the economic possibility of a cultural revolution that encroaches on the division of labour itself in a manner both readily apparent and convincing.

Kapitza starts out from the multiplication of labour productivity in the developed industrial countries compared with a century ago. 'If we count the number of cars produced in a large factory in relation to the number of those employed, it is clear that each worker produces more than one car a month', he writes, and continues: 'Economists are of the opinion that, given the present level of labour productivity, only a third or even a quarter of the labour-power in a country is needed in order to provide the population with sufficient means of subsistence of all kinds – food, clothing, housing, means of transport, etc. If more people than this are presently employed in industry, this is principally because of the needs of the defence industry, economic aid to the less developed countries' (would that this really deserved the name!), 'scientific progress, services for the population, tourism, radio, TV, film, sport, press, etc. The number of those employed in these fields today is by no means restricted; its level depends obviously enough on the amount of labour-power available'. We must add here that not only in the war industry, but also in almost all other spheres listed above, powerful repressive structures of need have become established, reducing the opportunities of freedom for the individual person. In all these activities relieved of elementary necessity, what is secondarily necessary and fruitful is structurally clogged up with aspects that pertain to our civilization's mechanism of self-destruction, and inextricably so failing a revolutionary dissolution and reintegration.

Kapitza believes that with this high productivity of labour, the 'decline in the burden on the working population', i.e. the very foundation of surplus consciousness, 'now gives us the possibility to prolong considerably the education of youth . . . Today there are no economic reasons (*sic*) to prevent an economically developed country from giving its entire youth not only a complete high school education up to age sixteen or eighteen, but also a univer-

---

[21] *Wissenschaftliche Welt*, vol. 15, 1971, no. 1.

sity-level education up to age twenty-one or twenty-three'. *'The state will probably have to offer the entire population the opportunity to pursue higher education, quite irrespective of whether this is necessary for the practice of their profession or not.'* This is certainly true. Under these circumstances, of course, there could certainly be no question of a higher education that turned out restricted specialists, cheated of their cultural entitlements, as is the present programmed standard, but rather the creative acquisition of an all-round philosophical (sociological, psychological and economic), artistic and scientific-technical education which opens access to any kind of activity.

If Kapitza is even approximately correct, then the quantitative economic feasibility of the cultural revolution is established beyond any doubt, particularly since it is clear that the additional expenditure on education would flow back in the longer run, and the extra loss of labour-time be made up for. We can thus put forward the task of *revolutionizing the system of education.* This expression is necessary, since under the name of educational *reform* we see the state monopoly attempt to rationalize the education of specialists tied down to each level of function and specialism for the existing matrix of the traditional division of labour. The new conception of education will not proceed from the basic structures of the existing division of labour, christened 'demands of society' and 'prognostically' extrapolated into the future, even though it must of course pay heed to these structures, which it is a question of transforming step by step. Via the system of education, we must realize what Marx had in mind when he demanded the abolition of philosophy and similarly of course of art in the proletariat, as well as polytechnical education as a basis for the humanization of the remaining necessary labour.

At present it is decided through the plan how many people are to be excluded at each step from the higher functional levels of labour. The existing division of labour is programmed into the educational system more rigidly in our society than under capitalism. Teaching syllabuses for the transmission of knowledge according to clearly differentiated functional levels are derived from the existing social structure of the work positions to be filled. In postgraduate training and higher education in general it is almost exclusively the narrow interests of the branch, the enterprise and even the department that dictate. Someone who is a specialist in chemistry can as a rule only become a chemical engineer and nothing else. But in the most developed industrial countries an 'oversupply' of academic training becomes unavoidable, once the least concession is made to the flood of young people into the tertiary sector and the 'national economic need' for specialists is gauged on the basis of the present functional structure. Symptoms such as college education for already more than half of the age group in North America, the success of the Open University in Britain, the discussions about the abolition of the *numerus clausus* in West Germany, indicate unmistakeably that the educational striving of young people is bursting the barriers of the established functional division of labour, and of so-called economic requirements in general. The attempt can of course be made to meet this developmental tendency with reactionary restrictions, and this is precisely the quintessence of the educational policy pursued by such parties as the SED. Its Politbureau has shelved a plan for admission quotas in individual specialisms up till 1990. There is scarcely any better way for a political party to indicate its attitude towards the problems of its society's development today than by the general tendency of its education policy.

The present system of general education up to the 10th grade prepares people in the best of cases for activities which fall in the third of the five functional levels outlined in Chapter 6. Their instruction is anti-aesthetic, and so superficially rationalist and scientist that the subjects of German, History, Civics, etc. give hardly an inkling of the human condition. It goes without saying that just as at all other times, there are teachers whose personal quality enables them to break through this restriction. But they are cutting against the grain. Knowledge of human affairs that is taught and accepted without aesthetic emotion must be basically untrue, and particularly so for the individuals involved. Aesthetics, as a method of education, means simply the attempt to present all knowledge that man requires in such a way that it appeals to his own self, and receives a subjective meaning for him. There are many things in our own tradition which we could seek to link up with in the interest of a new synthesis. Let us take simply the

Soviet experiments of the 1920s, the inheritance of Makarenko, which well deserves reviving, or the practice of the Soviet Ukranian educational romantic Suchomlinsky. All these of course came out of the pre-industrial era. Yet in the present scientific and technical revolution we shall again be able to do something with these stimulating initiatives, once we cease to equate its significance with that of the first industrial revolution.

For the whole of early and middle childhood, up to the onset of puberty, the powers of rational abstraction are not yet so developed that the abstract concept can be the guiding means for organizing one's own experience and establishing its connection with the overall whole. Where our rationalistic concept of education has led to the stunting of emotional motivation and fantasy, where therefore the immediate aesthetic reflection has been abandoned before rational reflection even begins, a gulf is already created which separates one section of children from the creative life, for creativity does not exist without contact at the level of synthesis. The entire educational process must be organized in such a way that the youthful development of all people leads up to the summit of art and philosophy, the emotional and the rational bridges from the subjective microcosm to the totality. If this is a utopia, it is Marx's utopia too.

The solution of this problem is in theory extremely simple: *young people must have both an artistic and a political-philosophical practice.* To put it another way, they must be able to appropriate directly, as *tools for some use,* the means of patterning and the concepts that allow them to differentiate and synthesize both the small world and the wide world. Young people who are given a political and ideological catechism, yet who are prevented in a repressive manner from changing the social relations on which the political and philosophical categories depend, cannot raise themselves up. They sit in the hall below and are allowed to ask questions. The rostrum is occupied by people who already know the truth. And things are at least as bad with the appropriation of art. Ruling classes, particularly those of earlier civilizations, have almost always introduced their children to at least an amateur practice of some kind of artistic activity. In our case, however, just to take one example, even in those music lessons that the syllabus does tolerate, children do not learn to read music, even though the standard of the teachers is now very advanced. Someone who does not himself learn the discipline and enjoyment of an instrument, who does not even join a choir, can generally not share the joy contained in even the simplest theme from Haydn. The emancipating and humanizing power of all art – as a human intervention in the object-world, as a means of civilized displacement of emotions outward instead of their repression within, as a medium of self-purification 'by awe and compassion' – all this remains the privilege of a very few. The cultural revolution and its educational policy must draw the lesson from the uncontestable experience that people who grow up without the possibility of political-philosophical and artistic practice are condemned to subalternity, even if they become specialized scientists.

Subalternity, as we saw, is simply another word for that alienation from the overall community which set in for the masses with the exit from primitive society. The previous small communities could be grasped in their totality by every one of their members, since all took part in their vital functions. The abolition of this alienation from the community is unthinkable, given the large societies of today, if individuals are not placed in a position where they can represent to themselves, by way of art and political philosophy, their complex subjective and objective relationships to one another, and on this basis participate practically in determining these. By philosophy here we mean of course simply the general concept for what is contained in the overall range of social sciences from the standpoint of the subject, in as much as this is oriented to the question of meaning and links truth to humanity's subjective practice. In ontogenesis and socialization the entire differentiation of the self-consciousness of the species must be produced anew. Our present educational system wants the specialist whom official species self-consciousness, itself specialized, can address to a suitable pigeon-hole. It says to him in Mephistopheles' words: 'Believe the likes of me: the single whole/ Was fashioned for a god alone'.[22]

But this era is coming to an end, since the special functions

---

[22] *Faust*, Part One, lines 1780–1.

that individuals will still have to fulfil in the reproduction of their material basis have already divided individual life up among them through the educational syllabus, before the human being as such could stake his universal claim. Here we are dealing with something other than the priority of a basic training for the *instrumental* sciences, which is already at least acknowledged as necessary. What is involved is rather the 'basic training' of modern social man, who should be able to say without the devil's pact of privilege: 'Whatever is the lot of humankind/I want to taste within my deepest self'.[23]

Free individuals will share in the special functions 'from above', descending from this summit to the various levels of coordination of consciousness.

The essentially aesthetic motivation, oriented to the totality and to the return of activities to the self, will enable man (who had an excellent early childhood) to appropriate for himself in a meaningful way the fundamental *instruments* of spirit and feeling: language (more than one) for mastery of the qualitative aspect of the world, mathematics for mastery of the quantitative, cybernetics for mastery of the structural aspect, and the technical capacities for the artistic expression of the self. These four pillars alone require a strict syllabus that insists on a controlled appropriation. This instrumental structuring of consciousness will always need a certain culturally sanctioned compulsion, since it is hard at first to find the motivation to persevere in mastering the abstract material. It is only the adolescent, for example, who starts complaining that his parents did not have him learn a musical instrument. The economy of human lifetime makes it necessary even for the child to perform steps of labour which as yet appear to him to have no concrete meaningful connection.

There is also the question of equipping individuals to participate in the production process, in the metabolism with nature. This is the problem of polytechnical education which Marx placed in the closest connection with the abolition of the traditional division of labour. J. D. Bernal maintained at the end of his life that within two years he could become sufficiently at home *in any*

[23] *Ibid*, lines 1770–1.

scientific discipline he chose that he would contribute to its progress. Marx expressly called for the 'absolute disposability of man for changing demands of labour . . . modes of manifestation that successively replace one another'. Polytechnical education today means that all young people should become acquainted both with tools, machines, apparatus and equipment (including computers), and with the fundamentals of the natural, technical and economic sciences, up to the level of practice in experiment, construction and the calculation of costs and expenditure of time. By the age of 20–25 people could be in a position to specialize in whatever creative branch of work they chose, and to choose in connection with this the shares in work at the simpler functional levels most suitable for them, acquiring the corresponding skills. Since it will be far more possible in the future than before to complete the overall general polytechnical training in a special branch of the technical division of labour, there will be no real break between a 'delayed matriculation', as it were, and specialization. Education time will also generally neither be a deduction from ordinary production time, nor will young people be exempted from simple labour – something which is the greatest educational nonsense. Certain exceptions from the polytechnical universality sketched out here, moreover, would have far less social significance than any limitations that related to the basic instrumental training. There is a great difference between someone who *among other things* has also specialized narrowly in some kind of complex performance, and the specialist stratum as a form of social existence.

Finally, for that general education which provides a more concrete foundation for aesthetic-artistic motivation and political-philosophical practice, and concerns itself with objective material, no compulsory syllabus is required, no control on performance, but rather an organized supply of information, necessarily supplemented by *personalized, competent teaching*. In our schools, and often even in universities, literature for example is treated in such a manner that any writer or work that is studied is reliably protected from future use by the student. In history, a formal survey of the teaching material is transmitted, which enables young people to answer questions without having the slightest understanding of a single historical event in its human substance. This is even the case with the history of music and art. In these aesthetic and historical disciplines, everything depends on making the human whole shine through in the intensive cross-section, and arousing the passion for greater knowledge. It is still true today that anyone who has understood just the history of the ancient Greeks in its full interconnection could understand any historical period as soon as he felt the need to do so. It is simply necessary for the systematic character, the overview, to be made comprehensible. This whole field must be pervaded by the freedom of self-education and ruled by aesthetic form, enjoyment of self-knowledge via knowledge. Only in such a way can we link up with the human essence of all other peoples and times, without which solidarity must remain an empty word.

Thirdly, securing the capacity for education and the motivation to learn. It is clear that the possible tension between individual capacity and species culture becomes ever greater with the progress of civilization, and in particular with entry into a historical stage at which the mode of production and social life in general is founded upon science. It is extremely difficult, for all that, to separate methodologically the biological causes of differentiation from the social. It seems quite obvious to me that we have every reason to emphasize the social causes of individual underdevelopment, since these affect a far greater number of individuals. I proceed on the assumption that the overwhelming majority of people have all the faculties needed to acquire the necessary scientific and artistic general education at an academic level. Genetic and other pre-natal injuries can in part be foreseen early enough to avoid births of this kind with minimal complications; their occurrence can in part be prevented altogether, or at least we can stem the present growth in their number, which is the product of a particular stage in medical and hygenic progress. At the present time, the boundary between this biological problem and the psychological problem of post-natal injuries is often shifted towards the pre-natal, by knowledge about the decisive importance of the first year of life (*cf.* the work of René Spitz, E. H. Erikson, J. L. Conel and others) for later capacity for education and motivation being insufficiently recognized. Very much of what we call talent or special gifts is only decided as the outcome of the early childhood situation. If we are faced with a fourteen-year-old who *can* only become a 'skilled worker' (not all can even become skilled workers), then this is seldom a natural restriction, but it is almost always the existing social structure that has been successful in reproducing itself.

The question naturally arises here as to how society can intervene in childhood without violating the life of the adults involved. In their behaviour towards their children, parents are guided far more than they are generally directly aware by their own early emotional fixations, which can only be later corrected if they are recognized, if the genesis of these reactions is understood so that a critical distance can be taken from them. This makes necessary an organized political-educational effort in the area of individual biography, i.e. it is necessary to provide the individuals involved with the impulse and the scientific preconditions for self-awareness. They must be enabled to understand rationally the unconscious errors of their parents, so that they do not pass these on in turn to their own children. Parental love for their children must in this sphere advance to meet political and cultural enlightenment. Public opinion must discriminate against all those customary practices of socialization that produce anxiety in the child, disturb a trusting orientation to the social and the natural environment, poison initiative with feelings of guilt, devalue achievements, break the child's will and turn its energies back on itself, where they form the basic model for mistrust, spitefulness, aggression and substitute behaviour of all kinds. The result will be a remarkable growth in the consciousness and capacity for responsibility of the next generation of children. We shall then see how great is the potential to educate people right up to the highest level.

The humanization of childhood is most closely connected with the regulation of sexual life, so that it is necessary to go into this briefly too. Society must finally provide young people with the framework for a comprehensive collective and individual understanding of themselves, at the right time, and of the great task that they face in bringing eroticism, education and marriage as far as possible into harmony with one another. Since we have sufficiently come to know how damaging sexual repression is in the phase of youth, this must go together with an improvement in the conditions for erotic communication, which will become more civilized if it can develop in an atmosphere of security and sympathy. It is most probable that the less proscription there is on the needs of sexual love, the more happy intimacy in youth, the more humane will be the general educational climate for the next generation. Since there will be, in contrast to former practice, a critical public awareness of the basic contradictions that exist between the natural need for the manifold erotic communication of the sexes and the institution of marriage and family, most people will understand better how irreplaceable the roots of marriage and family are at the present stage of development. The present problem in this field must be whether we cannot unburden and improve the family situation, which is still completely indispensable for the socialization of children, in such a way that the absolute identification of marital union and exclusive erotic partnership is demolished in public morality. For the elaboration of new perspectives, it is also necessary to give room and support to responsible social experiments, such as young people are pursuing with the establishment of communes, for example.

The countries of actually existing socialism, and, by and large, communists in general, have nervously ignored and passed over, for many reasons, the revolutionary discoveries proceeding from the work of Sigmund Freud. I am deliberately speaking of Freud himself, even though he has long since passed into history and has been overtaken by the development that he set in motion (not only in so far as the theoretical superstructure which he gave his discovery was bourgeois, idealist and pessimistic). For Freud was the first to have uncovered the *dialectic of the psyche*, the existence of a law of the formation of individuality, a phenomenon equivalent to Marx and Einstein in significance. We cannot afford to overlook this and pass straight on to the present scientific situation, because we have all too great a need to catch up with the foundations. We had a criticism of Freud before we had even read a single one of his works. The KPD expelled the communist Wilhelm Reich, Freud's most significant pupil, in 1933, a man who sought to make fruitful use of the potential of psychoanalysis for the workers' movement, and developed it further into a sexual economy. At the present time there is the feeling in our country that we are forced by the rediscovery of Reich in the West into the childish game of refuting him on his weaker points, so that no one tries to get to the root of what he was saying. What is decisive of course is his contention that industrial despotism cannot do without patriarchal labour compulsion and the psychic terror pertaining to this, sexual repression, etc. We must therefore begin from the beginning. Integrated into Marxism, a matured psychoanalysis freed from its bourgeois-individualist shell and its various onesidednesses, and particularly in the form further developed by Reich and others, is an essential pillar for the specific theory and practice of the cultural revolution. The destruction of prejudices against it will be one of our most important and stubborn battles.

There would be so infinitely much to say on this theme that it would burst the bounds of the present discussion. I shall therefore just refute one single error current at the present time. The polemic against the performance pressure that characterizes alienated labour, and also the practice of anti-authoritarian education, can very easily lead to propagating and creating an insufficiency of achievement. Work, family, school – all these must be superseded and raised to a higher level from inside, not simply destroyed. It is pure subjectivism to try and begin for example with the 'abolition' of the family and marriage, instead of adapting its internal and external conditions of existence to the new possibilities.

Why are there some children who master the demands of school as if in play – however irrational these may be? Because in their development from the earliest years on, everything that promotes pleasure in life, confidence in the environment, involvement in communication, has decisively outweighed the experiences of unhappiness. Because they were cared for by psychically intact parents and were not deprived of any joys. Because they were not annoying, and were not pushed around. Because they did not experience any brutal or mocking devaluation, and did not have to practise defiance, deceit, bribery or theft. Someone who grows up in such a way, does so with the desire for knowledge, for work, for friendship and love, and education can only lead them to discipline and achievement, to the effort of all essential powers. The will needs a resistance on which it can sharpen itself. Sublimation is not a compulsory commandment, but rather the individual realization of culture. It is untrue that this could not be the same for everyone.

Society could do very much to increase the probability of a happy childhood, an excellent socialization in every sense, within a few generations. The cultural revolution will investigate all conditions, in all spheres (school, work, public life, etc.), no matter how indirectly they operate, to see whether they disturb or promote human development. But if it does not set foot in the family, then as long as this is where primary socialization takes place, it will always come too late. Only when it penetrates there, can it gradually reshape the overall process of learning and labour, and on this basis unburden both public and intimate relationships of the external controls that poison and cripple them.

Fourthly, personal communication in the context of autonomous groups. For personal communication, without which people can neither experience nor develop their individuality, what is needed, according to all psychological knowledge and social experience, is a context of *small groups.* But this is only established when several people unite for such common purposes as require the ego-participating collaboration of one with another, where therefore people are not used as replaceable average individuals, but take part as specific persons. This condition was once so prevalent that the law of exogamy and the incest taboo were needed to balance what would otherwise have been an overwhelming internal contact within the primary human groups, who performed their entire life process communally. Since the Renaissance, however, or since the dissolution of the social order of the high middle ages, our civilization has got ever closer to the opposite pole, since the process of social life is consuming the substantial purposes for which *groups*, i.e. networks of personal relationships of communication, *can and must be formed.* By the vertical division of labour, ever more socially necessary functions are taken care of at a level above the primary group connections. By the horizontal division of labour, the various functions of reproduction are divided up, from the standpoint of the original primary group (for example the extended peasant family). In both cases, new, but more or less artificial groups arise for more specialized purposes, unstable on account of their connection being conditioned by a single function, and of limited continuity. And this is moreover a phenomenon which, as I see it, does not appear just with the subsumption of individuals to the division of labour, but already with the division of labour itself, i.e. with functional specialization *per se*. Personal communication in such specialized groups then depends all the more strongly on individual accidents, the less objective substance, temporal extension and subjective interest is given or can be aroused by the object of activity. But whenever we come across a production collective that genuinely deserves this name, we will always find that it has come together in the course of solving a problem or a task of a non-routine character, or even through meaningful free-time contact. The present argument can be summarized by saying that a group life connected *on the basis of socio-economically and functionally abstract labour* cannot arise to the extent, or with the intensity and reliability, that is required for the satisfaction of social needs.

This conclusion, which at first sight may seem pessimistic, must be clearly stated, in order to make clear the illusory character of such substitute solutions dictated from above as 'socialist labour brigades', impressive merely in the statistics of the apparatus. We must turn our attention in a different direction, and investigate the possibilities of a group formation around economically and psychologically concrete and fairly complex activities, in order to look for a solution. If there is such an answer, it is connected with Marx's perspective of the *abolition of labour* and of a *realm of freedom*, i.e. of free (psychologically productive) activities and enjoyments. The denial of individuality and the repression of personal relationships that we experience in our production apparatus is simply the negative expression of a process which, once transformed, bears the promise of far richer and more intensive human relations than have ever before been offered the working masses. At present the tension is great, and still growing, because we have not yet reached the turning-point from which to develop a meaningful perspective.

The tendency towards automation, which has such great potential not only in production itself, but also in its informational superstructure, has the initial effect of a further reduction in the degree of freedom for individual action in what are already the objectivized subordinate functions of the collective worker. These subordinate functions lose their significance for the positive self-confirmation of individuals, as long as they perform them under the pressure of standardization. The content of these tasks is often no longer sufficient to crystallize personal communication around it, or to form any kind of on-going groups. The technical division of labour in many cases either leads towards the complete disappearance of cooperation from the primary collectives of immediate production (if for example people are working at machines with the same function harnessed in parallel), or else this becomes compulsory. The centre of gravity is shifted towards materially mediated relations between collectives, which can no longer be borne by the individual, particularly as they ever more frequently overstep the limits of the enterprise. In this realm of necessity, where what matters is simply a functioning as devoid of friction as possible, the character of labour is inescapably one of social and economic abstraction, technologically schematic and uncreative. Here freedom can only consist, as Marx already saw, in the rational regulation of the overall process and its details. 'But this always remains a realm of necessity. The true realm of freedom, the development of human powers as an end in itself, begins beyond it, though it can only flourish with this realm of necessity as its basis.' Hence Marx's conclusion oriented towards a *new* economy of time, 'The reduction of the working day is the basic prerequisite'.[24]

I do not intend to go into any detail here on the rightly much discussed question as to whether this sharp opposition between the two 'realms' must necessarily be maintained. In any case, it only appears as acute as this in the final volume of *Capital*. What is clear, though, is that the formula of labour as a 'vital need' is

[24] *Capital*, vol. 3, chap 48, 3.

quite incompatible with the Marxian perspective of abolishing labour; it is at least based on a confusion between the concepts of labour and activity. What strikes me in this connection is rather that the sphere Marx denotes as the 'realm of necessity' today justifies less than ever the hope of a reinstatement of individuality, a re-establishment of personal communication between individuals. In the Marxian framework, the 'humanization of labour', strictly speaking, remains in every respect an inherent contradiction. The development that is possible here will consist in the elaboration of a discipline that is no longer external and repressively enforced, and the redivision of labour is the precondition for this. The present social inequality of conditions of appropriation, which legitimizes all lack of discipline as a protest against the injustice of the division of labour, obstructs the elevation of economic requirements to the rank of effective moral demands, internal obligations that would render superfluous external compulsions of either an economic or an extra-economic nature.

But if freedom cannot develop *within* the realm of necessity, and with it the general and personal communication that are inseparable from freedom, these will still have to be even more *dependent on it* than on what is still their most important object. In other words, the border between the two realms naturally runs *within* the factory, between creative activities, those oriented towards development and change in the reproduction process, and on the other hand that routine work in production and administration that is to a large extent useless as far as personal development goes. A better way of putting it might be that this boundary *could* and *should* run within the factory, and that it *must* run there in the future, and moreover right through the time-schedules of all individuals involved, who must do their share on both sides. Yet present conditions still tend to subject the overall activity that is spent on the reproduction process to laws that govern its routinized and impersonal functioning. This is precisely the reason why we have to describe the machine that realizes the requirements of administration as a bureaucracy from this point of view as well, i.e. why we have to stress its character as a mechanism of domination. What has happened is that such intrinsically creative activities as the development of new products, reconstruction, new building, etc. are undertaken by a host of unhappy, discontented people, each of whom would desperately like a different job. This need in no way remain the position.

Furthermore, the objectivized routine functions are performed in a system which, on account of its size, complexity and structure of command, is impenetrable to communication. The apparatus tends as if by law towards that Weberian ideal type of bureaucracy that seeks to eliminate genuine individuality and collectivity. Administration is supposed to be a well-functioning machine, whose ancillary functions still require human labour only on account of their lack of technical perfection; they require this of course in a standardized form. Here there is neither room nor object for individuals and collectives *as such*. But the small group, on the other hand, is the absolutely adequate form of social organization for creative scientific work in the broadest sense, i.e. for the comprehension, analysis and solution, both theoretical and practical, of every kind of problem that man faces in his natural condition and in his social and individual relationships. The cultural revolution can create the preconditions for the great majority of people to be effectively associated in problem-solving collectives, above all by the redivision of labour. The share of necessary routine work that falls to each person must thus be inserted in his overall time-schedule, so that continuous concentration on psychologically productive activity becomes possible, and there is increasing room for the free choice of objects, i.e. for committment to this or that creative group.

The transition from this creative activity related to production to 'really free working, e.g. composing', would then be a smooth one, within an already given flexible social organization that would favour the shifting of individual activity. Given the greater scope for deployment of people with an all-round education, we can assume that the dissociated spheres of activity such as labour, hobbies (a wretched word, which defines free activity in terms of that lack of social ties that presently characterizes it), domestic living, recreation, friendship and love, would be more closely and more frequently linked together in groups such as these. The fragmentation of human activity into thousands of subordinate functions which are each of little significance in themselves, leads

to the atomization of individuals. Creative group work on unsolved problems can also be the point of departure from which
the identity of cooperation and communication is re-established.
(It goes without saying that there are also other purposes for
creative groups than the scientific-productive ones that have been
emphasized here.)

For this perspective to be realized, society needs first of all
a surplus of labour-power, a genuine reserve of this, rather than
one of goods and services. It does not have to produce more than
it needs, but it must *be able* to produce more. If it is to give
individuals and collectives 'disposable time', time for development and self-realization, time for increased feedback into the
economy, then the first condition is that there is sufficient labour-
time available in general. The reproduction process must be
organized in such a way that the plan does not lay claim, right
from the start, to the entire available labour-power, for the
satisfaction of social needs, since it is impossible without a reserve
of labour-power, without a buffer of this kind, to uncouple a
sphere of free and mentally productive activity from the realm of
necessity. This is not a mere technical economic question, but a
genuine question of political economy. Available labour-time will
be expanded by raising productivity without raising output, and
by making superfluous, through the equalizing of material and
cultural conditions of existence, the greater part of the gigantic
apparatus of control over all individual and particular interests.
In the next chapter I shall briefly speak more specifically about a
policy that would make disarmament a necessity, instead of simply
a topic for discussion between the competitors in the arms race.
In any case, disposable time is the condition for the re-establishment of a communal social life, for it is only the 'realm of
freedom' – naturally still in relation to the 'realm of necessity' –
that offers the objects and space for fulfilling human relations,
such as are not least sufficiently complex and many-sided.

Fifthly, we come to general communication about social alternatives.
The 'cultural-educational mission' of the state (and the super-
state) makes the masses into the *object* of a bureaucratic salvation
which lacks even what was best in the analogous attempt of the

church, i.e. transcendence. For according to everything we are told, we have already reached our final destination, aside from those little accidental inadequacies that 'are already being eliminated'. Now, society only has to execute the finished blueprint of an ideal political reason. Just as our educational science has revived the traditional conspiracy of authorities against the autonomy and fantasy of the child, in the form of the 'unitary educational collective', so our political instructors, right down to the lowest gate-keeper, speak to the people with a single voice: 'People, we are going to teach you, so that you will remain ignorant' (Reiner Kunze). The consciousness of the masses 'grows' with the degree of their demonstrative conformity. This is the formal intellectual life of 'socialist society'; the true, informal life, which fortunately is ever more difficult to suppress, remains private.

The cultural revolution would contradict itself if it led to a new vanguard establishing itself in the old administrative monopoly of education and opinion forming. The human architect, Marx said, is distinguished from the bee by anticipating the plan of his building in his mind. The building of a society free from domination can only be brought about if it is not drawn up in an exclusivist political spirit, but arises rather in open communication with the masses. It is in *social* consciousness that it must be anticipated. A programme that involves the restructuring of the entire objective and internal human world, the ensemble of all our social conditions, can only function if it is the work of all those mental powers that have something to gain from the liberation of society from the abuses of political bureaucracy. The ostensibly difficult task of ensuring the permanence of the cultural revolution without an interruption in reproduction is a task requiring the active consensus of the great majority. Even those strata who remain most backward, since they were previously most heavily disadvantaged, must be involved right from the start, at least to the extent that they are won over at each step, with this principle being ensured by the institutional guarantee of their right to veto, i.e. by political representation of their particular interests.

I have stressed that the essence of bureaucratic domination

consists in its power of disposal over the social nervous system, the hierarchy of information processing. It is in this way that the corporation of functionaries appropriates the wealth of society. Socialization of the process of social knowledge, therefore, this specific and positive expropriation of the bureaucrats, is both the means and the end of the cultural revolution. It is firstly the formation of the general will that must be made independent of the bureaucratic apparatus, which has to be transformed step by step into the ancillary organ that it gives itself to be even today in its official ideology. Now that the problem of a general assembly of the people is solved from the quantitative and technical aspect by modern computers and means of mass communication, it would be possible at least in principle for all individuals to participate regularly in deciding on the distribution of new value, in establishing future perspectives for society, and fixing prognoses. Yet computers and the mass media are precisely the most perfect organ for excluding the masses from this, precisely because 'the universal spirit of bureaucracy is *secrecy* . . . appearing to the outside world as a self-contained corporation', because 'openly avowed political spirit, even patriotic sentiment, appears to the bureaucracy as a *betrayal* of its mystery'.[25] In our present system all genuine information about problems that demand *new* solutions remains private and confidential. The Politbureau may already have taken a necessary decision, but anyone who demands it a day before it is announced commits a major offence against political propriety. The bureaucratic principle is incapable of any genuine mediation between general, particular and individual interests, it is inevitably a direct interference in their dialectical adjustment. The solution consists in institutionalizing the to and fro flow of all information that bears on qualitative changes in the existing state of affairs outside the hierarchy of management and administration. This hierarchy would remain in place only for the regulation and guidance of the reproductive aspect of the overall process.

This separation would obviously not be an absolute one, and in

[25] Marx, 'Critique of Hegel's Doctrine of the State', *Early Writings, loc. cit.*, p. 108.

particular it would not affect the state and economic employees *as people, as citizens.* On the contrary, their civil liberties, which they too now forfeit under the bureaucratic regime, would in this very way be established. As citizens, they too would both make use of the general information and give vent alongside others to the particular interests tied up with their own work. It is simply a question of *immediately* making the work of state and administration into an activity just like all others. This will require that the information that is integrated at any given time at the various levels of elaboration is prepared and published by the appropriate specialists for the needs of public decision-making, and not simply transferred within the pyramid. In as much as the human and civil rights of the specialists in question are fully guaranteed, and among other things, in as much as they are not obstructed in their publication work by bureaucratic secrecy and dependence, the control by society of the apparatus hardly presents a special problem. Any manipulation of data that bore on something essential would come to light. In a bureaucratized society, however, the circuit of information is disturbed by feedback having to be conducted in narrow channels through a whole hierarchy of filters, while the downward flow of command and instructions rolls ahead with exceptional force down the pyramid's cascades. The number of levels may be the same in each direction, but the conductivity of information is certainly not so. In addition, the various levels and lines are carefully separated from one another. At the bottom, the various particular interests find themselves systematically isolated, so that they have no prospect of being directly taken into account in the synthesis. This can only come about by the decision-making process being subjected to qualitative changes that place it decisively at the centre of public attention, so that the individuals involved are externally constrained neither from right nor left, from above or from below, and can participate as fully as possible according to their inherent competence.

As a general rule, the 'decisive instances' have no greater knowledge in their decision-making than any ordinary citizen could have *if he was fully informed of the alternatives,* over which those 'up there' have often had more than one serious battle behind their closed doors. It would only need public access to more generalized information, with the entire society having an elementary right to this, and the use of the mass media to discuss the various possible solutions. This need in no way mean that every individual must expressly pronounce his opinion before the whole society, which would in any case not be possible. Those interest groups that objectively exist in a differentiated society will have their formally elected spokesmen, and not least also those selected informally. The mechanism for deciding between various interests, which only in exceptional cases need take the form of a plebescite, is ready to hand in the inheritance of that political democracy that stems from the great bourgeois revolutions. The precise form of the institutions will be readily found. What is decisive is that democracy beyond capitalism is divested of its merely formal and abstract character, its bourgeois class content, and that individual participation in the formation of the general will can regain, by way of an appropriate organization of mass communications, something of the directness that it had in simple communities which were immediately susceptible to general comprehension.

The Potential for a New Transformation of Society

If I see the cultural revolution as not only necessary but also possible, as far as its most essential objective conditions are concerned, this implies a clear idea also of its active subject. Without this, the proposal would be no more than a personal illusion. Only if what is necessary and possible shows itself to be a field of needs, demands, and compulsions requiring action by concrete social forces, are we faced with a genuine perspective. I therefore now intend to try and explain the subjective basis for a communist alternative in the countries of actually existing socialism, not least in the Soviet Union itself, and this moreover on the basis not of certain political, military, or even secret-police conjunctures, but rather of the *political-economic* conditions that I have so far sketched out. The potential for an alternative that already exists is generally totally underestimated, indeed even overlooked altogether, not simply because it can scarcely be publicly articulated, given our present political set-up, but above all because its socio-economic dimension remains unrecognized This also leads to its indirect expressions not being understood either. Everyone, for example, can notice an accumulation of bad feeling and discontent in their everyday work. But the symptomatic significance of these things only becomes clear when they are seen in their connection with the dysfunctions of the bureaucratic-centralist state and economic management that are also systematically apparent.

Under our existing conditions, the progressive potential must be regularly abreacted in the displaced form of unproductive emotions, which makes it more or less unknowable. Only *once* in the sixty years since the Russian October revolution have the forces pressing for a new organization of non-capitalist industrial society fully appeared in the light of history. Certainly, the moment was a short one, but they were at least able to develop positively to the extent that their real features, their real possibilities and perspectives, could be approximately assessed. This was those first eight months of 1968 in Czechoslovakia, which are so unforgettable for all those in the East European countries who are committed to socialist progress. It became evident then, if not before, that actually existing socialism generally *does* contain a latent bloc of interests directed against the existing political regime, i.e. against the dictatorship of the politbureaucracy, and one that is progressive as far as its essential lines of force are concerned. In addition, it became evident that the majority of active party members are waiting to break out towards new shores. Finally, in Prague and Bratislava, what was demonstrated was nothing less than the survival capacity of our social order without the politbureaucratic dictatorship.

It is and remains the greatest political crime of the Soviet leadership since the Second World War to have deprived the peoples of Eastern Europe, including its own country, and the whole of progressive humanity as well, of the irreplaceable experiences that would have been gained from the success of the Czechoslovak experiment. Right up to the time when this was forcibly brought to an end, nothing indicated an impending failure, or any kind of serious danger to the non-capitalist foundations. It was not accidental that the fraternal helpers from Moscow and Berlin publicly prayed for a few anti-communist pogroms, to make their *ultima ratio* somewhat more plausible. Yet they were reduced to planting quite amateur 'evidence' of planned counter-revolutionary attempts. The leadership of the SED bears a particularly serious responsibility, next to the Soviets themselves, for deciding that the National People's Army of the GDR would take part in aggression against the strivings of a Slav neighbour, which had ceased only twenty-three years before to be a protectorate of Hitler's Germany. German communists are still faced with the task of demonstrating to the Czechoslovak people their total rejection of this act of international politbureaucratic reaction.

It is only on the premise that the reform policy of the Czechoslovak Communist Party under Alexander Dubcek was the common cause of all those who want to see a renovated communist movement in harmony with the needs and hopes of their peoples, that there is any sense, and consequently therefore a necessity, to make a careful and critical account of the successes, problems, dangers and weaknesses of the post-January policy in Czechoslovakia (an analysis which I cannot attempt to undertake here in any comprehensive way). The well-known motto of Wolf's *Sailors of Cattaro* is very pertinent here: 'Comrades, we'll do it better next time!' If this premise is forgotten and discussions of supposed intended or actual counter-revolutionary tendencies are allowed to creep in, then that is to place oneself already on the ground of the politbureaucracy and its manipulation of public opinion, in which the justification for the intervention becomes the measure of how great the danger was. The intervening powers are most profoundly interested in presenting any threat to their form of domination as an attack on the socio-economic foundation of non-capitalist industrial society. On this point, a stand has to be clearly taken. A danger for what and for whom? What was endangered was the kind of 'socialism' that can only exist under the control of an all-powerful party apparatus, and with the poorly concealed omnipresence of secret police and censorship. Those people who take for granted the suppression where their writ holds sway of every deviating opinion by the political police and inner-party inquisition, could only bewail the fact that the masses were now threatening these ultimate 'solid' champions of the old principles and methods with reprisals – reprisals which on closer investigation consisted only in curtailing their political rights for a certain period. What was endangered, and from a political standpoint indeed already lost, was the power position of the old politbureaucracy. The impending 14th Congress of the CPC, which then had to take place 'illegally' in Vysocany, was elected to lay out its corpse, which is why its date determined the time of the intervention. Using the pretext of counter-revolution, the politbureaucratic reaction aimed above all to attack the policy of consistent reform itself.

The real content of the supposed counter-revolutionary

tendencies in Czechoslovak social life in 1968 consisted of those nationalist feelings that aimed to restore the institutional *forms* from the time of the bourgeois republic. It is only natural, in a phase when various social forces are politically unleashed, that elements who would like to turn back the wheel of history also appear and express themselves. We can ask what weight these have. Twenty years after the Czechoslovak revolution of 1948, they were from a socio-economic point of view completely fragmented and obsolete. The sentiment behind them was based on the accumulated resentment of those who had suffered in the previous stage, in part inevitably, in part unnecessarily, and if these included some people in practically. all strata, they were principally to be found among the former petty bourgeoisie. They had no real political chance, particularly as the international bourgeoisie, well understanding its own interests, had no aspiration to recapitalize the Czechoslovak economy (viz. the analogous case of Yugoslavia).

The real problem was posed by the differentiation within the progressive block, that standing positively on the basis of actually existing socialism, among which at least two different orientations could be distinguished, without these already being definitively crystallized. Besides the policy laid down in the Action Programme of the CPC, there formed spontaneously that tendency which put forward the special interests of the intellectuals, economists and technicians. Its hallmark was the superficial and impatient political radicalism that was expressed in various documents and many commentaries, and which ultimately served the purpose of securing the uninhibited and uncontrolled development of these privileged forces on the TV screen, in culture, in the state apparatus and in the leading positions of economic management. This was the tendency of the 'glorious revolution', of the appropriation of political power on the basis of 'competence', i.e. of the effective socio-economic status that its representatives had acquired in the two decades since 1948. It needed no special programme apart from that of 'pressing forward'. It was in no way formed into a party, not even into a clearly demarcated wing within the CPC. At most, the bourgeois and restorationist tendencies could use it as a screen. It should be borne in mind, incidentally, that the political character of this tendency cannot be judged simply by its slogans, many of which read today as more or less expressly 'Eurocommunist'. It lay rather in the use of these in a particular situation, in which what was at stake was the alternative between this 'glorious revolution' and the consolidation of a new kind of ideological hegemony with a communist, i.e. cultural-revolutionary, perspective.

Those ideologists who free themselves from the apparatus, and the masses who place themselves behind them in this movement – if the apparatus does not itself first move against them – represent, right from the start, and for all the differences of motive among them, a *universal* interest that points in the *direction* of a comprehensive cultural revolution: the intention to dissolve the politbureaucratic dictatorship as the *sine qua non* of any further perspective. This does not indicate by itself how far such a development would proceed beyond the immediate political impulse, which at first is predominantly a negative one of overthrowing the old regime. An oppositional potential is easily perceived in our countries as far as the sphere of political institutions is concerned – this was sufficiently confirmed by Czechoslovakia in 1968; but hardly the potential for a struggle to overcome subalternity in the more far-reaching sense discussed above. This superficial political opposition – *not* a political-economic, socio-economic and cultural opposition – is a reactive response to the anachronistic forms of appearance of the politbureaucratic dictatorship. Its common slogans are democratization, often with the by-word 'socialist', and human or civil rights. The longer the present state of affairs continues, the more the apparatus brings the thinking elements of society to despair, the more consistently it obstructs them from understanding for themselves the possible changes, then the more do all energies focus simply on destroying this apparatus, and the greater accordingly must be the initial chaos of conceptions, the greater the danger of mere disorganization.

It is even to a certain extent probable, unfortunately, that the minimal programme of a democratic revolution against the politbureaucracy becomes autonomous, and demands a stage of its own. In Czechoslovakia, the continuity of the communist idea *after* August 21st was all too evidently so seriously damaged that the people will probably initially embark, at the first opportunity, on a prolonged detour of political restoration (despite everything, even then not a socio-economic restoration). It would obviously be desirable if this forecast proved mistaken. Democratic demands, despite the bourgeois-restorationist form that they can easily assume, since the inheritance of bourgeois democracy is not yet raised to a higher level, are necessary elements of the changes occurring, but they do not reach deep enough and do not touch the heart of the matter. In actual fact, they mean precisely the self-restriction of the movement to the specific interests of the intellectuals.

Actually existing socialism does not need to catch up with bourgeois democracy as a particular phase, one-sidedly fixed on its 'guarantees' and thus precisely restorationist in form. Democratization is all too ambiguous a term, and not seldom does it lead to error. As I see it, it is above all in connection with the fifth of the major directions of the cultural revolution as above defined (socialization of the process of knowledge and decision-making to make this a general public affair) that it has its actual and practical significance for us. So-called liberalization is advancing anyway; it is simply a natural by-product of the decay of the old superstructure. The increasing contact between our higher strata of functionaries and their western counterparts in cooperation between the two blocs is speedily removing the final subjective content from the present orthodoxy. If this liberalization attains its goal, then our intellectuals will rejoice in a similar repressive tolerance to that which their Western colleagues already to a large extent enjoy. To aim at this is to aim too short, to desire too little. It would be to mistake the really potent historical subject for an only seemingly active and by nature fragmented potential for short-run results, perhaps not even to perceive this subject at all (hence, among other things, the defeatism of so many intellectuals after military intervention put an end to the 1968 experiment). The communist minority (for it is initially only a minority who recognize the problem and make it their concern) will naturally struggle against the democratic revolution acquiring this autonomy, and for the permanence of the movement, for its transition into the cultural revolution.

In assessing the balance of forces in Czechoslovakia during the final months before 21st August, it should not be forgotten that the Soviet leadership, closely seconded by the leadership of the GDR, did everything it could think of to poison the process of ideological reorientation. With provocative military manoeuvres, the customary tactic of concerted non-information and mis-information, with ultimata and with the threat of direct inter-vention ever more strongly detectable in the atmosphere, it continuously fanned the flames of 'correct' feelings, and procured its political spokesmen the appropriate nationalist sounding-board. In this way the alternative, communist tendency in the party was placed under pressure. The intervening powers also helped the tarnished conservatives make their way onto the Presidium and Central Committee. In this way the party of the Action Programme – for this is what the CPC was – did not obtain sufficient space for the full development of the social reform it had in mind, and remained stuck in its practice to the basic out-lines of its policy, which were not yet precisely enough formulated. On many points its perspective was thus weak and centrist, simply because it was not sufficiently in command. It was of course correct not to seek refuge anew in the 'tested' methods of police-state repression. Without the pressure from outside, and this means above all from the other Warsaw Pact states, there would have been no 'counter-revolutionary danger' worth the name, if indeed this ever existed at all. It had to be created, to make the intervention possible.

The Action Programme of the CPC was in no way refuted by the intervention. For the first time since the Yugoslav example, a ruling communist party definitively took up many necessary proposals that had long been the demands of Marxist oppositions to the politbureaucracy. The position of the new communist party was rooted firmly in the masses – quite differently to the case in all other countries of the Warsaw Pact. All that was lacking was the final stroke, the ejection of the vacillating elements from the Presidium and the Central Committee, so as to give the party a leadership set on its direction of struggle, a task already too long delayed, as was proved on 21st August. Here the group around Alexander Dubcek lacked the final decisiveness, which was particularly bound up with illusions about the Soviet Union, and the social nature and interests of the Moscow leadership. Few people saw things as clearly as did Josef Smrkovsky. Otherwise it would have been possible to save the experiment and obstruct the intervention by following the example given several times by Tito, mobilizing the country and temporarily imprisoning those potential collaborators still in key positions.

The lack of resolve shown by Dubcek and his comrades, and in particular their wrong assessment of Soviet behaviour, can certainly be attributed to the defects of their theoretical analysis. Since 1953, the progressive communist forces – even ignoring their objective weakness while the Cold War was still in progress – have time and again proved insufficiently prepared. At bottom, they still stood on the same political and theoretical basis as their opponents, and could be ideologically blackmailed by them via their common interest in the autonomy of the non-capitalist road. Above all, they had a poor understanding of the ground on which they were fighting. Their various action programmes were based more on temporary negations than on socio-economic analysis. And we can discern here the lack of theoretical discussion and synthesis attributable to the politbureaucratic suppression. In the Action Programme of the CPC, too, there was still a lack of clarity about the 'contradictions among the people', the social structure of non-capitalist industrial society, and accordingly also about the objective conditions and requirements of the progress forward to socialism. This was largely responsible for the tactical uncertainty of the reform policy both vis-à-vis the 'right wing' and also vis-à-vis the 'conservatives'.

Today it is both possible and necessary to study the Czechoslovak development, to see how the reforming potential presented itself on the political surface, in order to go back from this starting-point to the basis of interest in which this was deeply rooted. For the *course of political mobilization* both before and after the January decision to change the party leadership allows us to draw conclusions as to both the nature and structure of the forces in play, as well as to the nature of their conflict with the power apparatus. It justifies the analysis of the social structure I have given in the second part of this book, but also points beyond this to a perspective for the future. It is worthwhile recapitulating this process.

The movement started not at the base, but rather in the personnel of the superstructure, or more precisely, among the ideologists in the strict sense of the term. At the beginning we had the discontent among leading writers, artists, social scientists, etc. with the conditions of intellectual life and with a censorship that blocked the critical uncovering of contradictions. Parallel with these ideologists, more and more leading scientists, technicians and economists came to the conclusion that the introduction of economic reform without social reform, i.e. as a mere 'structural change' within the governing apparatus and its planning mechanism, would not unleash sufficient initiative to escape from the mediocre level of efficiency and the old routine. The pressure of these two groupings made the more volatile elements within the central party and the state apparatus unsure, and made inroads among them. It was sufficient to bring down Novotny and above all Hendrych, whom the First Secretary had hoped would be sufficient sacrifice.

When Novotny was dismissed, the majority of the Central Committee originally pursued only the goal of calming the storm and reestablishing the conditions for a beneficial collaboration with the intelligentsia. There were only a few loosely conspiring minorities, whose leaders had already been promoted into the leadership, who wanted to start the ball rolling in the way that actually happened. But after the January Plenum the reorientation took an accelerated pace, in fact in the form of a snowballing rebellion, first taking hold of the ideological section of the intelligentsia (the broad mass of artists, social scientists, journalists), then without a break the whole of the rest of the intelligentsia (with the exception of the most comfortably positioned bureaucrats) and not least the young people, with the students in the lead. And this powerful social force, which today has its roots firmly in the process of material reproduction, acted as a transmission belt to the workers in the factories and the other strata of society. We can see therefore that the turn began among the ideologists, and that *mobilization for the reform ran like a chain reaction through the structure of education, from top to bottom.*

Since this mobilization gripped all the key strata and groups of the collective worker, and did not even leave the personnel of the apparatus unscathed, there must be an interest that has a unifying effect far beyond the immediate aspirations of the intellectuals. This common interest showed itself first of all as directed to getting rid of the privileged power of opinion formation and decision-making on social affairs, i.e. in essentials getting rid of the statified, bureaucratic form of disposal over the productive forces and over the entire process of social life. Politically and psychologically, it expressed itself in the demand for an end to the permanent tutelage of society by the state, the permanent treatment of people (individuals and collectives) as infantile objects of education. In a positive sense, what was involved was the promotion of social self-management at all levels and in all realms, identical to a large extent with the demand put forward in the previous chapter for a socialization of the social knowledge process so that people can reach their own understanding of things via the values, goals and paths of their common life. This demand touched on a secondary aspect of the cultural revolution, in as much as it was not directly aimed at a change in the base. Yet all experience shows that it acquired the role of *a key and a lever for the introduction* of the process of transformation. This for the simple reason that it was directed against the decisive *barrier* that blocks the way to the progress of general emancipation in the countries of actually existing socialism: against the monopolizing of public affairs by a special apparatus which confronts society as an external and foreign power.

The substance of the common interest is surplus consciousness; it is this that engenders the mobilization against the polit-bureaucratic dictatorship. Before the question of general emancipation is raised again in its full complexity and profundity, the emancipatory interest is focussed on the *political conditions* for this. The politbureaucracy must be disarmed, the *domination* of the apparatus over society removed, the relationship between society and state newly arranged, and the communist movement newly constituted so as to open to society from within the perspective of a cultural revolution. It was precisely this process, which unlocks the *access* to a comprehensive cultural revolution, that began in Czechoslovakia in 1968, a process generally if somewhat inexactly described as democratization. The potential that found expression there is naturally still in existence and unreduced. Certainly its *immediate* political orientation, which was ambivalent for reasons which we have suggested, shifted markedly to the right as a result of the military action of 21st August. But nothing has changed in its progressive *social* quality and long-term perspective. We have seen how various strata of the collective worker in Czechoslovakia committed themselves according to the degree of the accumulated surplus consciousness they had accumulated, and moreover on a scale that underlines the mass character of this phenomenon. They thus brought the proof that an end is coming to the succession of ages in which the functions of direction and development of society have to be monopolized by a privileged corporation.

In this view, a revolutionary strategy must be *based on a completely specific balance of forces within social consciousness, more precisely, within the overall mass of accumulated expertise, or subjective productive force, on the balance of forces between this surplus consciousness and the absorbed consciousness.* The concept last mentioned can serve to characterize the mental expenditure that is tied up on the one hand in the hierarchy of bureaucratic knowledge, on the other hand in the routine functions of daily production and reproduction. As far as the surplus consciousness is concerned, I have already distinguished in the previous chapter the emancipatory and compensatory needs or interests within it. I proceed therefore from the following diagram (Table 3).

What is politically decisive is the relationship between the emancipatory interests and the consciousness tied up in the apparatus. These are the two poles, and the forces that crystallize there struggle for their influence to be dominant on the mass of conscious potential that lies between, tied up in necessary labour and in compensatory satisfactions. They must strive to isolate their antipodes ideologically. As long as the apparatus is dominant, the emancipatory interests are confronted by the overwhelmingly subaltern behavioural tendency of the remaining three fractions of social consciousness. Subaltern behaviour is then 'normal' behaviour. Individuals subject themselves to alienated authority

TABLE 3

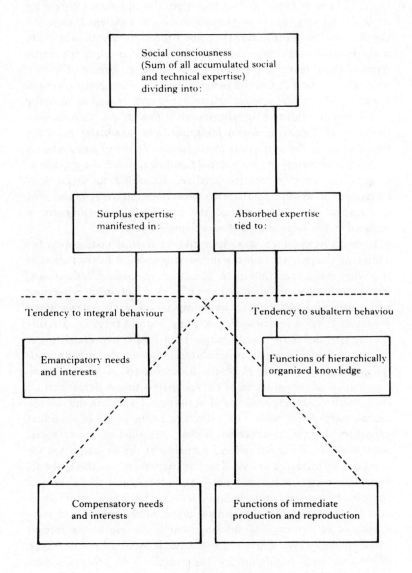

and seize on the rewards for good behaviour that are held out to them. There is logic in the fact that the apparatus threatens isolated representatives of emancipation with the madhouse. In the cultural revolution, however, the preconditions for which are maturing, the problem is conversely to isolate the ruling apparatus from all the remaining fractions of social consciousness. This is a process of construction: the penetration of the integrally oriented behavioural tendency, that oriented towards insertion into the whole and the positive appropriation of this by individuals, into the field of forces of social consciousness, gradually robs the domination of the apparatus of all raison d'être. In particular, it makes the necessary organizational functions, which the apparatus originally existed to institutionalize, accessible to social self-management, in other words it prepares the subjective dispositions for this, so that their bureaucratic and étatist imprisonment is reduced to the simple goal of exercizing power.

I must discuss once again here the theoretical justification for analyzing the potential for the impending social transformation in this way, as a question of a structure of social *consciousness*. Consciousness is involved here not in its function of reflection, but rather as a factor of social being, whose growing role itself possesses a 'consciousness-determining' significance, i.e. a significance that alters its *content*, something that is expressed in the spread of the emancipatory needs or interests. As already said, the traditional division of labour differentiates people precisely by the level of coordination of consciousness that is demanded by their work functions and social activities. I showed this in the second part of this book with reference to the realm of absorbed expertise. In the connection under investigation now, social consciousness is considered in its quality as the precondition for any kind of human activity, 'free' or 'necessary', as the embodiment of society's subjective productive force, and therefore as a completely material and economic reality, on which attention is now focussed because the appropriation of the means and conditions of enjoyment and development is coming to the fore in social struggles. We might say that what is involved is a new type of informational regulation for the overall social process, a new social organization of the work of *knowledge* and its institutional equipment. The apparatus, the state itself, is known to be an 'ideological superstructure', a consciousness that by its very substance is alienated, functioning to dominate, a hierarchically organized 'knowledge-power' (*Wissenskraft*), to use an expression of Marx's. Since the apparatus is the most prominent object of transformation, it is only natural that the potential bloc of its antagonists should appear first of all with the head. The intellectual life of society in general, with its centre of gravity in the process of information and decision over reproduction and its goals, is the battlefield of the cultural revolution. Progress in world history is expressed in the fact that the struggle in the industrially developed countries has already shifted into the sphere of the specific and essential human powers, and is no longer principally a question of body and stomach, clothing and housing.

The balance of forces between surplus and absorbed consciousness, and in particular between emancipatory interests and the interests of the apparatus, appears far more uneven in political terms than it does from a socio-economic standpoint. The reason for this is that the absorbed consciousness is by its very nature thoroughly *institutionalized*, precisely in the pyramid of society's organization and direction of labour, which I analyzed in Part Two, whereas the surplus consciousness is kept carefully *atomized*, as well as being obstructed by the police in every political expression and organization. The possibility of political organization is of decisive socio-psychological importance. The apparatus offers individuals monopolistically a powerful complex of reciprocally confirming and supporting modes of behaviour, from which they can only distance themselves *as* individuals in the subjective exception, and even then as a rule only by the technique of *reservatio mentalis*, a risky procedure from the standpoint of mental health. The influence of these behavioural models stretches far into the surplus consciousness, in the area of compensatory interests, where it is generally confronted more by its Western counterpart than by the emancipatory forces of the two systems. For the mass of individuals, nothing remains but to enlist at least formally in subalternity, as long as there is no socio-psychologically effective base of operations for the emancipatory interests. This is the very reason why the lesson of the

Czechoslovak experience, that the most developed elements from *all* social strata and groups are *individually for* change, is not refuted by the superficial phenomenon of its political defeat. 'On the bed of the Moldau, stones are rolling. . . .'[1]

Who exactly is the apparatus? Is it a further social stratum or group alongside the others? This is true at most for the personnel of its actual command structure, and above all (of course with individual exceptions) for the ranking functionaries in the party, state and economy. These are indeed the representatives of hierarchical, bureaucratic knowledge against the surplus consciousness of society. Psychologically they represent first of all, since obedience is the precondition of their trade, a typological selection of particularly adaptable and authoritarian people, making few intellectual or moral demands. Secondly, they are forced to stand in daily opposition to the recalcitrant masses. The experiences that they have in this connection are food for the officer mentality and the desire for stronger means of discipline. It is only this particular minority, more or less predisposed to their role, who are absorbed by the apparatus in their entire life process, at least in essentials. These people, and these alone, are also subjectively so bureaucratized through and through that there could be no other productive form of existence for them, they are the enemies of change of any kind, because they would unavoidably suffer from it. And they are so ideologically isolated that they stand constantly in need of military intervention in their support, as the guarantee of their own safety. All that society obeys is the brute force they are able to unleash.

Of course, even this element is not homogeneous, and the more recently established the new order, the less so, since in its early phases some people at least are drawn into it by genuine feelings rather than inspired by a career, people who now occupy the middle and even the highest positions – not seldom with a concealed division in their conscience – to the extent that they have not been driven out. I have already stressed that it would be quite mistaken to condemn the apparent bureaucrats simply by their official physiognomy and the ritual actions and techniques of

---

[1] The first line of a poem by Brecht on the theme of Czechoslovak history.

behaviour that are bound up with their functions. The more the bureaucracy is subsequently recruited from the intelligentsia, the more frequently this further reason also gives rise to an ambivalent and distanced relationship to the prescribed roles, so that a capacity for critical reflection is set free. In the long run, therefore, even this core element of the bureaucracy remains 'unreliable' in terms of its personal substance. The essence of the whole situation is precisely the way that a surplus of *human* consciousness, not reduced to an abstract functioning for limited purposes, is set free at the most diverse levels of the collective worker and presses beyond the existing division of labour.

The great mass of people employed in the apparatus are certainly in danger of becoming absorbed in the toils of their functions, deprived of the development of surplus consciousness and particularly of emancipatory interests. This absorption involves a very real process of expenditure and erosion of psycho-physical energy. As long as society produces only a small amount of expertize, only a small elite, then the apparatus absorbs the greater part of the mental energies and capacities set free from immediate production, and can to a large extent corrupt the remainder by preparing the conditions for productive leisure or parasitic consumption. Today, however, society produces such a mass of general ability (even though the apparatus brings down the rate of expansion) that this cannot be directly employed by the apparatus. Under present conditions society simply does not have sufficient use for its subjective productive forces. Hence the incessant effort of the politbureaucracy to annex the unspent surplus consciousness to compensatory interests. This is the innermost content of the 'unity of economic and social policy' (not a genuine policy for society), as far as its power-political function is concerned. Yet even if compensatory needs predominate in the mental structure for most of those involved, so that they end up taking refuge in the most varied private satisfactions, they still make an inward withdrawal from official authority. And reduction to the existence of a mere number causes individuality incessant suffering.

Seen as a whole, therefore, the personnel of the apparatus can in no way be equated with the apparatus itself (on the other hand there are of course also people with the bureaucratic mentality even outside of the apparatus). Only to a very limited extent can a classification be made according to employment position. For most of those involved, the front goes right through their own head. We can assume therefore that all individuals participate more or less in all four fractions of social consciousness. The only question is which of these fractions now *dominates* a person's motivational structure. It is this that is the present battleground, and not – as one might unreflectingly believe – actual behaviour in the manipulated public roles of working life, which does no more than mirror the prevailing power relations, and not the ideological process that expresses the development of the subjective productive forces.

I referred to the tendency towards a bureaucratization of the intelligentsia, in other words to the enlistment in the apparatus of the very forces from which the reforming potential has particularly to be recruited. In principle, in fact, the apparatus embraces all the managerial personnel of society, since every managerial function, no matter how small, even that of the trade-union shop steward, appears in the first instance not as a component of the collective process of the base, for which it is necessary, but rather as a derivative of the overall management, the government authority. Further still, as I already showed, not only the administrative functions, but also the mere requirements of administration, and even technological requirements, affect those carrying them out in the same way. Virtually all knowledge that is directly relevant for the reproduction process is counterposed to the immediate process of work and life in the form of management, administration and the preparation of production. And yet the *individuals* who perform these increasingly standardized subordinate functions are subjectively for the most part no longer identified with the corresponding activities and positions. In other words, the apparatus can only integrate them as far as it lays claim to their abstract labour-power, while their subjectivity more and more escapes its grasp. This tendency certainly does not rule out that the experiences that those in charge of various managerial functions might have from the confrontation between apparatus and society may not give rise to a certain degree of solidarity between all those who have some such function to perform. But this spontaneous corporate solidarity can easily be undermined by critical reflection on the overall situation, and it is particularly no longer viable once social contradictions come to a political head. Many functionaries then rapidly abandon the position of hierarchical knowledge and are guided by the developmental needs of their surplus consciousness. This is precisely what could be seen in Czechoslovakia.

In the Soviet Union the contradiction between the apparatus and the surplus consciousness is particularly deep, since the polit-bureaucracy there is less cultivated and adaptable, as a result of the backward semi-Asiatic mentality it inherited, and less susceptible to assimilating the new social forces in compromises of various kinds and degrees. Soviet statistics claim that three-fifths of those working in industry now have either college or full secondary education. But the skilled elements are politically kept under tutelage in the same paternalist manner as the meanest kolkhoz peasant, who might still be living under the Tsars. Even those most qualified are treated in this respect as subordinate specialists, as cogs in the gigantic clockwork of the state economy, kept wound up by the anonymous activity of the bureaucracy. Undoubtedly there have been genuine changes since Stalin's death in the atmosphere of factories and other institutions, and these are extremely important; but the perpetuation of the old *principle* is thereby all the more reactionary. This is the major reason why the productivity of Soviet economy and science stands in such striking disproportion to the number of skilled people. Many millions of people have acquired, if only in a specialized field, the powers of abstraction and differentiation that enable them to take part in decisions over the destiny of their country, and its perspectives of social development. But they are not allowed to use their heads for this purpose. The greater part of this potential energy is still tied to compensatory interests by the persistence of shortages and by exclusion from public affairs, if indeed it is not reduced to the traditional stupidity that always marked all levels of Russian society, the manor house as well as the peasant cottage. A few years ago the writer Yuri Kasakov created a new symbol for this energy evaporating into thin air in his story *Larifari*. But the surplus is far too great to be expelled through some kind of vent, and it is concentrating in the country's industrial and administrative nodal points with the further promise of gathering the scientific and artistic forces together.

I must stress yet again how the character of the present contradiction between the Soviet superstructure and the new productive forces is historically determined. The Soviet Union began, just as China did later, with a minority of cadres who confronted a majority of manual workers (particularly on the land). The form of the old Oriental despotism was also decisively linked with the size, or rather lack of size, of the available elite, its level of expertise and laws of reproduction. But at that time this expertise, characterized by the duality of ideological (priestly) and administrative (official) authority, was produced merely on the scale required for the simple reproduction of the existing relations of domination. In material production, in fact, there was scarcely any need for intellectual work. The economic revolution that the Lenin-Stalin apparatus initiated in the Soviet Union, on the other hand, itself created the new subjective productive forces that have now outgrown it and are protesting against its control.

First of all it has created a new working class, at least a 'class in itself'. Since industry was completely new to the masses, even to the young specialists of the 1930s, who in the precipitate haste of the time could appropriate only the most absolutely necessary knowledge (and yet in an almost romantic spirit), their skill was largely absorbed by their activity. Today these are the older strata of the collective worker, biologically as well as historically. As things stand, they now require the mediation of more developed forces for their emancipation. Objectively their social position is the very worst (after the majority of kolkhoz peasants), except in so far as the individuals involved have risen up the hierarchy, and the contradiction between them and the apparatus the greatest. Subjectively they are passive and resigned. These two poles correspond to one another, they are flesh of the same body, precisely the Soviet social body of the 1930s.

In the other East European countries the *tendency* to subordinate the equivalent strata to the apparatus is similarly present, but it does not have the same relative success, since the apparatus has not grown up together with these strata, as their commanding superstructure, but has simply taken up the positions left behind by the previous bosses. In the GDR this Soviet stratum has its counterpart at most in that generation that emerged from the War in 1945 young enough for a relatively new beginning. Yet we did not experience that patriarchal structure that can still be observed in the Soviet Union, after being further strengthened in the Anti-Fascist War.

In any case, the future lies with groups that are historically more recent and more developed. In the Soviet Union the industrial revolution of the 19th century passed directly over into the scientific and technical revolution of the 20th. Those strata and groups of the collective worker who were socially and intellectually in a better position could also struggle better, particularly since, if we leave aside here the particularly outmoded managerial pyramid of the Soviet Union, they also have going for them the energy and hopes of youth. They are linked with the most modern forms of production and its preparation, and are themselves the very embodiment of the new productive forces. It is naturally in the younger generation that are reflected most strongly those social changes that the whole society has undergone, in relation to which the apparatus has remained behind as an essentially stationary structure. In the Soviet Union, too, it will be these elements who are the first to rise, elements who, even though they too are subject to the traditional division of labour (if in part artificially so), still cannot be completely absorbed by its realm of domination, so that they are least subject to its economic compulsions, and feel all the more violently the political compulsion, the political restriction.

To this extent, we can see as symptomatic a certain development that can be traced in all the countries of actually existing socialism, through which the apparatus is forced to take directly to its bosom that very element which is most dangerous to its rule. I mean the grouping of its own ideologists, whom it degrades into executive specialists in agitation and propaganda. It is a social law that the intellectual leaders of the anti-bureaucratic bloc come from this grouping. It is the ideologists who are first in a position to reflect on their frustration by the system of bureaucratic roles, which distorts the development of their personality and obstructs every individual expression, and who by reflection are able to trace it back to its social causes. Through the party they have become acquainted with at least the basic tenets of Marxism, which for the reasons we have already gone into, the party cannot abandon. The more that they succeed in a genuine reading of Marx and Lenin, through their official work and its contradictions, the more persistently will they be stirred by the spirit and temperament of these revolutionary teachers, which is so expressly subversive of our existing conditions. The unspent potential of a universal intelligentsia, i.e. an intelligentsia oriented to the universal, has always been a rebellious one, and a revolutionary one against the background of new productive forces. 'Philosophers' or ideologists cannot come to terms with restriction to the status of obedient specialists for the manipulation of social consciousness according to pontifical recipes.

Those ideologists of all kinds who are pressed into the roles of party and state officials, from social scientists through to journalists, from artists to their censors, from the strategists of natural science to teachers of history – these are all continuously demeaned, both directly and indirectly, by proscriptions, by the reprimands and the praises of the arrogant politbureaucrats (the petty ones still more than the great ones). In order to follow the norms and rituals of official 'intellectual life', they must mostly learn to present the public image of pathetic cretins. Their task, in full view of the whole society, who all more or less see through the ideological shadow play, is assiduously to weave the emperor's new clothes. While the only social justification for their life and work lies in discovering and spreading the truth about social conditions, they must in fact conceal their insights, lie to the people without this even having the desired effect, and put up with the people's growing contempt for this. Their productivity is consumed and devalued in the eternal petty compulsions of adaptation, in cynical self-censorship, in the pains taken to conceal a cautious new idea under a sufficiently large heap of the customary verbiage. People do not often even charge these ideological functionaries with parasitism, though the charge would be pertinent enough. They simply say, 'They have to talk like this'. And are they not daily corrupted?

In this unhappy consciousness, which is an ever growing burden in all Soviet-influenced countries, and lurks not only outside the gates of the Central Committee buildings, but even outside the doors of the Politbureaus themselves, we have the summit of the reforming potential. The Czechoslovak experience shows quite clearly, as Hungary already did in 1956, that the closer any sphere of society is to the Politbureau, i.e. the closer it stands either intellectually or functionally to the power of disposal over the mechanisms of regulation of information, *without actually being admitted to this realm*, the more the rule of the apparatus finds there its dangerous enemies. At the decisive moment a leader will always appear in the Politbureau itself, placing himself for whatever motives in the service of a shift in power, even if initially this affects only the personnel. It is only a question of the historical opportunity; for the dissolution of the politbureaucratic dictatorship is already socially and economically overdue. Society, Soviet society included, will then liberate itself from this residue of an earlier epoch.

Was it not a similar degradation of the intelligentsia from which generations of Russian revolutionaries sprang in the 19th century, right down to the founders of Bolshevism? But what a difference! At that time, the intellectual stratum was socially isolated, and always in search of a powerful sounding-board. First of all it adapted itself to the real or imagined needs of the Russian peasantry, then finally it found its army in the young working class. But in any case it had to enter into an alliance with forces of a completely different kind. Today those ideologists who are excluded from setting goals and giving meaning to the social process simply find themselves in a situation that is also experienced by ever greater portions of society in general. Surplus consciousness is precisely a continuum, even if of varying strength. Eventually the immediate producers, too, express profound discontent with their role as subaltern compartmentalized workers, a role that corresponds ever less with their level of education, at least through their passive resistance to the entire intellectual staff of management, administration and often also engineers as well, for all of whom they generally use the summary term 'bureaucrats'. And the reform potential is particularly strong among specialists in the social policy element of the staff, who stand outside the bureaucratic lines of command. The work they perform is both analytic and synthetic, often guided in detail by certain ideal representations, or at least by the need for technical economic rationality. But these specialists are still generally deprived of any possibility of initiative, and this particularly annoys them because their actual activity is itself relatively satisfying. Their product is thus as much alienated as is that of the immediate producers. They are divorced from the conditions of realization of their creative power. Still closer to the discontented ideologists are the massed ranks of future specialists; the student youth has not yet lost faith in the universal ideals that provide the foundation of the official world view, and demands their realization. They have an obscure suspicion that their training will lead them back to the confinement and subalternity of the traditional division of labour, to which they seem for the moment to be hardly subject. It is particularly among these young people, who generally receive a passable if limited specialist training, that there is scarcely a stratum that does not dispose of at least a minimum capacity for free consciousness.

Against this background I must repeat once again that the confrontation in our society cannot be understood in the categories of traditional class contradictions. The subject of the emancipatory movement is to be found in the energetic and creative elements of all strata and spheres of society. The problem, however, is that these strata and spheres, already conditioned by the mechanism of social differentiation in the development and education of individuals that is characteristic of our social system, do not exhibit an equal share of these active elements. Lenin once remarked, 'I do not yet know whether we shall emancipate "all" oppressed "humanity": as, for instance, the oppression of people of weak character by those of very strong character'.[2] In our system, selection makes far more immediate use than in other formations of mental mechanisms which act to give unambiguous preference to the more educated strata. We know today that even

[2] 'Notes on Plekhanov's Second Draft Programme', *Collected Works*, vol. 6, p. 54.

this differentiation of character is conditioned by social inequalities. In particular, a motivational atmosphere in the family of origin, which is becoming ever more decisive for later development, corresponds more or less with the 'objective demands' of the educational institutions and the style of education that these approve of – and of course this in turn depends on the education and activity that the adults were themselves apportioned.

This has its consequences for the distribution of the emancipatory potential, this being biassed against the immediate producers, and these consequences are all the greater, the stronger the performance principle is pushed through in our schools. It is certainly correct that 'Their underprivileged position in production organized according to the division of labour, and their place in the pyramid of "democratic centralism", are the factors that will press for change and produce the consciousness of its necessity', as Volker Braun already noted in 1968.[3] But we may still ask who will show this effect, or at least who will show it first. Braun continues, 'The workers as a *class* have the strongest interest in changes, and *this is bound to lead to something*'. But up till now there have been no signs, not even in Poland, that 'the workers' under our conditions could be a 'class for itself', and that their 'objective interests' could effect the first step towards general emancipation. The great hope that is placed on social change and motivates a commitment in this direction, is dependent – at least unless quite extreme pressures provoke an uprising – on the pent up energies that seek room to develop. This essentially mental mechanism of differentiation of activity has always played an important role in situations of radical change. As long as classes still confront one another, it can of course only explain the distribution of initiative *within* these various classes. But it is different in the transition periods at the beginning and end of class society, in which social differentiation according to the functional level of social labour is far more immediately bound up with the natural and quasi-natural mental distinctions. Less than ever shall the last be first. That entire way of thinking is no longer

---

[3] Volker Braun is a well-known East German writer, particularly for his work *Die Kipper*. Bahro lost his post as deputy editor of *Forum* magazine after printing Braun's *Kipper Bauch*.

viable. The perspective must be a different one: changes will still proceed from the objective *contradictions*, from the burdens that are placed *on society as a whole and its process of reproduction by the existence of strata with a subaltern position.* But the *initiative for these changes* can only proceed from those elements who are most bound up with the *developmental* functions and tendencies of the forces and relations of production. That is not a demand, but a reality. What one can and must demand is that these elements do not merely act in their own special interests, but gather and organize around them all forces with the desire for change.

The question may be raised at this point as to whether anything can come out of a process of this kind other than simply a new distribution of power in favour of the intellectuals, scientists and economic managers. This is a far broader stratum than the polit-bureaucracy, which at present still manages to keep its appetite within bounds. The politbureaucracy needs the good behaviour of the working masses and is therefore prepared for compromises in social policy; here, too, it is tied to an ideological residue from the past of the workers' movement. What will happen if the technocrats are freed from all control and work only for technical-economic results? This is the voice of those unofficial apologists for the politbureaucracy who present the existing state of affairs as a lesser evil for 'the workers'. It was in a completely similar way that the patriarchal exploiters of two hundred years ago warned against the capitalists. Apart from the fact that it is precisely the still restrained but self-glorifying technocrats who are now the breeding-ground for the politbureaucracy, so that they are simply threatening us with a cudgel they have already carved (I would recall once again here Lipatov's *Story of Director Pronchatov*), the emancipation of society from the present political tutelage would already in itself be a step forward, according to all historical logic, even if the worst croakings of Novotny should at first prove true. We would at least have the uninhibited develop-ment of social contradictions. The working masses would learn very quickly that the rule of the directors is not the only possible alternative to the politbureaucracy.

In reality, however, the examples presented by the politbureaucracy of 'irresponsible journalists', 'egoistic scientists', 'unsocial technocrats', etc. naturally give a tendentious caricature of the future perspectives of a society in which the intellectualized strata of the collective worker will for the time being inevitably set the tone. The apologists for the existing state of affairs cannot of course take into account in their preventive criticism the emancipatory interests and their future political organization. The propaganda against the intellectuals, in the broadest sense, which is in part overt and in part subliminal, comes from a narrow corporation which *is itself made up of intellectuals who have become reactionary and bureaucratized*, who have usurped all social power for themselves. The power apparatus is seeking, while taking its personnel from the intelligentsia and declaring itself the vanguard of the working class, to use the traditional strata of workers against the agents of predominantly intellectual work, and it therefore makes a special appeal to the popular hatred against that corruption of intellectuals, scientists, doctors, artists, etc. which it has itself organized.

In this connection, it can also use the enforced bureaucratic integration of opposition elements. Before Novotny's overthrow, these elements, (whose core typically grows up within the party and evidently includes functionaries of the apparatus itself), could only express themselves in private, i.e. they could not publicly distance themselves from the rule of the apparatus. We saw in Czechoslovakia how there was scarcely a functionary in the younger to middle generation who could not have been classed as reliable without personal acquaintance, before political forces were revealed. The most well-known cadres must wear a particularly impenetrable disguise, if they have opposition views, and they often play the role of devil's advocate. Most oppositionists necessarily act in some way or other as servants of the apparatus. Since the apparatus maintains the appearance of unity and pursues as best it can the integration of all intellectual work into the directing hierarchy, it keeps in reserve the option vital to its survival of playing off the two wings of the collective worker against one another under its aegis.

But this possibility exists only as long as it is backed up by the police and military force. The Czechoslovak experience showed how our social structure, at least in the westerly countries of the Soviet bloc, including Hungary and Poland, is ripe for recrystallization. As soon as the politbureaucracy is 'off its guard' (as it sees it), as soon as it has a weak moment, then the *de facto* hegemony of the intellectual elements immediately comes into play over the entire social bloc that feels itself spoken for by them in its surplus consciousness. The working masses then very quickly accept the new and decisive lines of demarcation between 'progressives' and 'conservatives', a division according to negative or positive attitude towards the former ruling apparatus, which then stands suddenly revealed in the complete isolation that has always been its invisible stigma. The grouping around the apparatus is rightly afraid of losing control completely if it gives as much as an inch in confrontation with the expectations of society. This is a quite correct assessment of its own political-ideological strength and that of the potential being prepared against it just under the surface. As soon as it starts to slide, it must consider its special political and hence also economic position as already lost. This was precisely made clear by the Czechoslovak example. And that is why any serious opposition on the part of the intellectuals, when it attains any real scope, so quickly touches the nerves of the power apparatus.

Now the presence of a revolutionary potential does not in itself mean a revolutionary situation, but simply the possibility of one. Its appearance presupposes a specific intensification of the internal aspects of crisis and its exploitation also requires a favourable international conjuncture. There is one question here on which the official apologists still have a certain effect on the masses. From the experiences of two world wars, the members of the older generation in particular react with spontaneous anxiety to *any* disturbance of the balance of power between the two blocs, real or apparent, or even the mere possibility of such a disturbance. Undoubtedly there is increasing bitterness at the blackmailing manner in which those who monopolize disposal over all resources that actually existing socialism can counterpose to NATO use this internally to secure their domination. But many completely disaffected people, and party members not least among them, find their daily compromises made easier by the fear that a weakening of the power structure that controls both our economy and our war machine could create a momentary vacuum into which NATO would penetrate. Pursued to its logical conclusion, this idea prohibits *any* activity, *any* initiative that might in any way weaken the politbureaucratic dictatorship. The first thing to say on this point is that the developments in Czechoslovakia failed to give it any support. The lessons of 1968 are that the immediate task of the reforming forces vis-à-vis the military consists simply in winning the army leadership for an attitude towards the changes that is at least neutral and tolerant, thereby ensuring that the fighting forces remain unaffected in their capabilities during the change in power. This was precisely what took place in Czechoslovakia.

A more detailed analysis of the military situation is beyond the compass of this book. Yet we have to be clear that while there is not the slightest sign of a pause in the arms race, the existing political constitution of the Warsaw Pact states makes it impossible for them to take the offensive on the question of disarmament. The apparatuses could not pursue such developments as a reduction and withdrawal of forces simply because of the specific risk this would mean at home. A genuine initiative towards disarmament presupposes the creation of a united front of progressive forces in both blocs, in order to put coordinated pressure on the politico-military complexes. Otherwise no fundamental progress is to be expected from the negotiations between them. Social changes in both the capitalist and non-capitalist countries of Europe are thus the *precondition* for breaking through the vicious circle of the arms planners and diplomats of disarmament, and setting a process of escalating disarmament under way on both sides. A certain risk must be run, bound up with the unevenness of internal political development on either side which can scarcely be prevented, in order to escape from the total danger that lies in the incessant perpetuation of the arms race. The singer Wolf Biermann found a formula that precisely expresses the dialectic of this situation from the standpoint of the revolutionary forces: 'If you flinch from danger, then you'll succumb to it'.

In addition, the discouragement of the progressive elements that followed the forcible interruption of the 1968 upsurge, and which is still not overcome, goes back to the fact that many have not yet managed to raise their vision beyond the impressive realities of power politics, and military realities in particular, that stand in the foreground. The opposition forces are divided on the question of the *possibility* and the *meaning* of a communist opposition, particularly in the East European countries outside of the Soviet Union. The considerations of reflecting people all tend in the direction of my analysis as far as the *description* of our conditions goes. But many people shy away from following their ideas through to a conclusion, since they are afraid of the consequences. Genuine concern about the political and military balance in Europe here supports the individual need for social security. And quite apart from many contentious specific arguments, it is most comfortable simply to dismiss the idea of a consistent opposition as illusory or even provocative. 'Can we really make a move? And should we? Isn't it better to wait on developments? How else could the movement end, even in the unlikely case of initial success, if not with the omnipresent Soviet tanks? Look at Czechoslovakia today, and see what comes of attempts of this kind!' As Lenin was told in 1905, it would be better not to have taken up arms. . . .

This historical reference is justified first and foremost because the present attitude of resignation shows as little understanding of the strategic balance of forces as the Russian Mensheviks and liquidators showed in their time. The Soviet leadership would find a repetition of its 1968 decision considerably more difficult, and it might be ready this time to pay a fundamentally higher price not to be confronted with such an alternative. Even though the trauma of 1968 still has its psychological effects, the other countries under Soviet domination today have a greater room for manoeuvre in domestic policy. The possibilities of opposition have considerably increased in the most recent period (Helsinki, Berlin Conference of European Communist Parties).

The ability to take military action against popular movements in other countries can only be assessed to a very limited extent in technological terms. As always with military questions, experience shows that it must be seen as a variable dependent on many other factors. It would be a renunciation of historical materialism to forget that troops cannot in the long run hold back new and higher productive forces, on which moreover their own equipment depends. And the international situation does not make it probable, even in shorter periods, that the Soviet leadership can maintain its role as regional gendarme after the USA has already come to grief as world policeman. A renewed intervention on the lines of 1968 would destroy its entire foreign policy, including its compromise with the West European communist parties. Not least, internal bureaucratic stability would be more deeply shattered by any further political police action of a major kind than it was by the last one. The misuse of young Soviet soldiers will leave its traces on the morale of the army, and particularly on its officer corps. It is well known how the victory over Novotny would not have been possible without the collaboration of such officers as General Prchlík. There is no doubt that Soviet generals do not consist simply of blatant reactionaries either. In Moscow, too, a Soviet Prchlík will be found as well as a Soviet Dubcek.

Where precisely is the nerve centre (to leave psychology aside) at which the reaction of discouragement arises, i.e. this error in political evaluation? Does it not lie in the national confinement of opposition ideas? The national phenomenon is a very important fact. Its roots lie in the historical and present uneven development of peoples, giving rise to the opposition between national interests. The Soviet leadership is provoking a nationalism directed against it both inside and outside its own borders, by the same recipes that Lenin so decisively rejected in 1922 when he commented on the conflict in Georgia.[4] It can evidently not do otherwise; in fact this is the least it can do. Nationalism has an objectively necessary role to play in the destruction of the holy alliance of party apparatuses, in as much as it shows that these have not settled the national question in any productive way; they are simply in the way here, as with so many things. But the constant pin-pointing of Soviet tanks as the enemy, which allows the apparatuses to present themselves to the world as 'internationalist', represents a standpoint that is simply the reverse side of the

---

[4] 'The Question of Nationalities or "Autonomization"', *Collected Works*, vol. 36, pp. 665ff.

great-power-politics component in Soviet foreign policy. The opposition will learn to take not just its own national conditions but the entire East European stage as its battleground, and to steer clear of any kind of nationalist prejudices and stereotypes. Not least, it will take up an attitude of active solidarity with the progressive forces in the Soviet Union itself, which are held back or helped forward according to the political development in Eastern Europe. The Soviet opposition needs the support and encouragement of our examples. What are decisive here are not the national differences and animosities, but rather the fundamental contradiction between the social interests of *all* peoples of Eastern Europe and the interests of their political bureaucracies. The peoples of the Soviet Union need a new order of political life as much as the peoples of Czechoslovakia, Poland, Hungary, etc.

Certainly, no one can say today how soon the hour will come in Moscow, Leningrad or Kiev. Given the character of our superstructure, it is a general rule that long accumulated inflammatory material catches light 'suddenly', because the contradictions that are steadily coming to a head have no organs through which they can express themselves at the time needed. Even in Czechoslovakia, where much might have been anticipated in 1966–67, the speed, breadth and depth of the transformation were surprising. But the situation has worsened for intervention, for the doctrine of limited sovereignty both in foreign and in domestic policy, and the apparatus must try to find new ways, and even take new risks, in order to prevent a crisis developing. More than before, it can be influenced within the existing conditions by popular feelings, pushed forward or even pressed back, as once again recently happened in Poland. Experience shows that it would like to get away from merely negative and restrictive measures. It should not be ruled out that at least partial regenerations may occur, somewhat along the lines of the strategy of reconciliation that the Hungarian party leadership attempted after 1956, not without some success. There is more than one possible course for historical events, and a *politique du pire* is never in the interest of the masses. The only question is whether the traditional forces can still use delaying tactics. Bureaucracies that have passed their peak have seldom undertaken reform in any way other than too little and too late. But the Soviet bureaucracy in particular stands today under the pressure of ever more threatening contradictions, both internal and external, for which there are no longer any solutions in the sense of the former models of response. The Politbureau, the Central Committee, the entire ramified apparatus, can in the long run not remain united on the old basis, which is proving increasingly ineffective, and failing both in practical life and in ideological struggle. The more enlightened part of the polit-bureaucratic personnel will necessarily strive to rid themselves of the dead weight of the most rigid and reactionary elements.

In any case, the decision that is ultimately the sole alternative for the Soviet leadership, the extension of industrial and scientific cooperation with North America, Western Europe and Japan, will strengthen precisely those forces in their own country that played the major role in the struggle against the Novotny regime in Czechoslovakia. The Soviet scientists, technicians and econo-mists will come up more obstinately than ever, and ever more frequently, too, against the fundamental incompatibility between the old superstructure and the new productive forces. The progressive artists, social scientists and journalists, for their part, have long been in a position to destroy the official apologetic image of Soviet society, and to give voice to the reality of Soviet life which departs so fundamentally from this. This process, too, can only be accelerated by comparison with the world outside. The climate of peaceful coexistence, the evident retreat of the problem of immediate survival, will have an unavoidable effect in promoting the internal contradictions of the new society. For a time, this 'large-scale cooperation' might bring some relief to the ruling groupings of both systems; in the Soviet Union, in parti-cular, it can pacify some surplus energies by giving them relatively meaningful employment. In the long run, however, the evolution that this introduces will call into being the grand alliance of cultural-revolutionary forces against both forms of state mono-poly. The unavoidable oscillation of the leaders between relaxing and tightening the screws which keep the intellectual and cultural life of non-capitalist industrial society under pressure, will add its own weight to forming the critical mass of discontent and anger that is needed. The apparatus can no longer 'put things right' again, its very nature and condition make this impossible.

Taking all these factors into account, the Czechoslovak experience is a hopeful one precisely when it is judged from outside the immediate national context. Not only does it show the opposition the way, it encourages it in striving for political hegemony in the context of the Soviet bloc as a whole. The genuine and great opportunity of our non-capitalist base can only come into its own on this larger terrain. The least that would be achieved would be a solidarity across national frontiers when the next confrontation comes, a solidarity not only noticeable at the level of public opinion, but one which materially restricts the freedom of action of the repressive forces. The revolutionary movement has time and again had bitter experience of the depth of the capitalist system of defence, most recently again in 1968 in France and latterly in Portugal. Our politbureaucracy on the other hand has only a single life to lose, as we could clearly see again in the case of Czechoslovakia. If it is deprived of its political and military force, this apparatus of repression will be neutralized, and the way made clear for the socialist transformation of our social system. This already showed itself in the popular joke, in the form of a 'listener's question' to 'Radio Erevan', after August 21st, as to where the troops would come from to combat a Soviet Dubcek.

We can only hope for the Soviet people that a leadership does take over at the right time in Moscow capable of introducing a guided and gradual process of reform, in order to spare them a spontaneous and destructive rebellion, and this not least for reasons of the international situation. The Berlin Conference of European Communist Parties gave the Soviet Union and its allies a challenge that requires a positive and constructive response, in the interest of all, a response that the progressive forces in the Warsaw Pact countries could only find together.

As everyone knows, the *form* of the political superstructure with which the anti-capitalist transformations in Eastern Europe were carried through after 1945 was foisted on the peoples of the region from above. Neither in substance, form, or time was it the outcome of their own national developments, but rather the result of the overwhelming Soviet share in the victory of the Anti-

Hitler coalition and the subordination of the other communist parties to Soviet state interest that had previously been effected by the Comintern. The export of the Soviet 'model' originally had a revolutionary and progressive significance. Even in its inadequate form, this superstructure at first played principally the role of an instrument of social and industrial progress in Eastern Europe, relatively least so, understandably, in the most economically developed countries. In the case of the GDR, the level of economic functioning was moreover concealed by the fact that German imperialism had lost a third of its sphere of influence. But be that as it may, the historical situation did not offer Eastern Europe any better solution. Here the Soviet Union gave what it could give, by the logic of its own internal conditions, and moreover right to the limit of its possibilities. If it had renounced this initiative, then the industrial breakthrough of Eastern Europe would have been delayed, the semi-colonial status of most of these countries prolonged, and the bourgeois structure reestablished. And yet none of the new states that were created in this way, Yugoslavia naturally excepted, escaped the situation of an external power confronting the immanent strivings of the national society. In the Soviet Union the despotic internal form and customary constitution of the state was not installed artificially, but was organically determined in the framework of a quite specific balance of 'revolution-restoration' (Gramsci) by the semi-Asiatic economic and political tradition. The despotic apparatus of power is as oppressive there as it has ever been, and has meanwhile become an obstacle to development; but it is in no way foreign. And the task of the progressive forces is thereby made much harder.

In Eastern Europe things are different, at least in Czechoslovakia, Poland and Hungary. Different too in the GDR – for all the Prussian tradition of military bureaucracy, which somewhat reduces the discrepancies. These countries belong either completely or in the main to West European civilization. Their economic, social and cultural relations demand an institutional superstructure for the full breakthrough of socialism in which this tradition, one very different from the Russian, will be raised to a higher level. They now need not only, like the Soviet Union, a new adaptation of the superstructure to the far more developed productive forces, but also a 'national restoration', in other words the re-establishment of national continuity with respect to the character of their social institutions. It is ultimately a question of fitting the institutions to the general *form of individuality* that is stamped by a particular historical development, and which is in fact the specific substance of the so-called national character. In this sense, the Czechoslovak masses were completely correct to conceive and affirm the national constitution which they sought as 'socialism with a human face'; the concept of humanity, in other words, has here a quite specific West-European national content, of course also with its corresponding limitations and prejudices.

The socio-political role of the post-Stalin rule of the apparatus in the Soviet Union, as against Eastern Europe, consists today, as has become historically notorious after August 1968, in obstructing the peoples of this region in their progress towards socialism in the form appropriate to them, and therefore driving them as a further consequence into the arms of a *political* restoration. It is counter-revolutionary in this double respect. The increasing nationalism in the East European countries – and its concrete label is 'anti-Sovietism' – has a progressive function in as much as it is *directed against the chains that the hegemony of the Soviet apparatus lays on their internal social development*. The essence of the problem of sovereignty, its salient point, consists for the East European peoples in the necessity of completely separating their own socialist progress from the quite different social situation in the Soviet Union, which is being far too slowly transformed for their needs. This is precisely what was at stake in 1968 in Czechoslovakia. And it is precisely this which the Moscow leadership, just like Tsarism in analogous cases in its 19th century sphere of influence, responded to with a military police action. It is characteristic, too, that the most active communist parties in Western Europe did not accept this, for reasons related to their own basic interests.

The following consideration is suggested by the Berlin Conference. As soon as there is a *practical* West European road to socialism, the political process in the East European countries will not only lead more forcibly to a more independent foreign policy, but above all to the institutional reform that has up till now been suppressed. A reaction against the existing state of affairs is unavoidable. The continuity of the revolution and the stability of European peace require that communists are prepared at the right time to give this a constructive and gradual form. The East European peoples want not only security, but also a political constitution of the type that Berlinguer, Marchais and Carrillo outlined at the Berlin Conference. If by that time neither side in the 1968 (inter-communist) conflict has drawn the real lessons, then things must come to an open break between the two tendencies over the unavoidable movement of separation in Eastern Europe and the corresponding pressure from Moscow, a break which could only exert an unfavourable influence on the European situation in general and on the internal Soviet situation in particular.

The East European communists have urgently to consider whether they are going to concede the necessity of domestic political change from a strategically defensive position, or are going to meet it offensively. Defensively would mean looking forward in the long run to a separation from the Soviet system of alliance, to a time of Soviet weakness to which a national liberation movement would then react – with unforeseeable dangers for European peace. Offensively would mean working for a reversal of the flow of influence, i.e. actively presenting the Soviet ruling stratum, from the more developed and progressive periphery that lies both outside and within its own borders, with such problems as would compel it to undertake urgent and fundamental domestic policy transformations in its own country. To me the second strategy seems not only more productive, for Soviet development as well, but also more hopeful in its prospects, particularly in the light of the new socialist offensive in the Latin countries of Western Europe. Once the non-capitalist countries of Eastern Europe are supported in their strivings for an adequate superstructure for their further socialist progress by actual and democratic processes of transition in France, Italy and Spain, the Soviet superstructure will no longer be able to avoid a new adaptation. The Soviet intelligentsia will play a striking role in this process, because it has to take on at a qualitatively new level the function of an active, 'westernizing' adaptation to the more progressive West European conditions.

In the other case, the Soviet Union would most probably lose its western periphery *completely*, for there is no way in which this will remain in its present status of limited sovereignty. From the point of view of a well-understood Soviet future interest, which the opposition there will make its own, the question is precisely to unburden the East European countries preventively at the right time, so as to strengthen them in their role as reliable partners in economic cooperation and voluntary integration. The Soviet leadership should not be too late in understanding that a 'proletarian internationalism' of the kind to be seen on the platform at the last SED Congress endangers it much more in the long run, on account of the anti-Soviet feeling it provokes, than does a temporarily somewhat over-compensatory 'national communism' as in Romania. The Soviet Union could give the East European *peoples* the opportunity of seeing the genuine advantages of the alliance, especially its extremely far-reaching economic perspectives, which are at present too little perceived on account of short-sighted Soviet decisions (e.g. on oil prices). A planned evolution in Eastern Europe would be the surest means of averting a later European conflict over this zone. Otherwise it cannot be ruled out.

One of the most essential aspects of a meaningful evolution is the active struggle for the open and public presence of an alternative communist position and discussion in our countries. As a result of the Berlin Conference, which can be seen as a real milestone, this orientation will gain ground. After the reaction of the Italian party leadership to the latest conflict in Poland and to the request of comrade Jacek Kuron for political support, a more effective solidarity of the West European communists towards a serious and responsible opposition in the countries of actually existing socialism is evidently a force to be reckoned with. If larger groups of comrades with an opposition orientation, and other sympathizers, were now to meet *without a lot of conspiracy*, but rather with the knowledge of a certain interested public opinion, to discuss for example the materials of the Berlin Conference, and to distribute its conclusions in various forms, the ruling apparatus would be faced with a difficult problem. The most important speeches at the Berlin Conference are *de facto* illegal in the GDR, for example, even though they were published in the central party organ – not that this should be surprising. The apparatuses would prefer not to have to show their hand on this. After they have recognized that there can be different standpoints on quite key problems *between* the various parties, they will see themselves faced with the demand to acknowledge the same for *inner-party* life, and for society in general. The representatives of the new positions in the European communist movement have an interest in the conclusions of the Berlin Conference not being interpreted as a kind of Augsburg peace: *cujus regio, ejus religio*. The apparatuses are clearly taking pains to present their own position in opposition to the progressive West European communist parties, the cleverest variant being the argument that 'quite different conditions' obtain. In the long run this demarcation cannot succeed.

It is absolutely necessary to conduct a discussion in the international communist press that is not governed by the mentality of non-intervention in ideological matters. The attempt might be made to transform the periodical *World Marxist Review* from an organ of cautious monologue after the Augsburg model into a platform in which, besides the official standpoints of the parties involved, the views of individual comrades and communist groups could also be put forward for discussion. Otherwise a new international communist review must be set up, whose columns would obviously be open also for dialogue with other progressive tendencies. An interesting development in this connection is the initiative of three Yugoslav theoretical periodicals to found an 'international world platform for socialism'. According to the Yugoslav magazine *International Politics*,[5] this brings together Marxist and other socialist theorists, fighters for socialism from various countries, movements and tendencies, with the aim of common theoretical discussion, individual persons, i.e. not just official representatives of movements, parties or countries, being also invited. The contributions and discussions of its annual

[5] No. 628, 5 June 1976.

meetings will be published.

In the last few years, the internal subjective conditions for a more effective organization of opposition elements have also improved. It is still more of a socio-psychological reality than a political one, more the expression of a political demand, when we speak of a communist opposition. No one should have any illusions on this score. And yet ideological development is moving towards a qualitative turning-point. Until the end of the 1960s, what was typical was the appearance of individual personalities isolated from each other, though even these could already not simply be placed completely outside the legal pale, however much harrassment they faced and still do face. More recently, as far as one can tell, in Hungary and Poland larger groups of sympathizers are already in semi-overt contact with one another, and in particular are in no way ideologically isolated, winning influence on critical individuals in essential branches of the apparatus. In Czechoslovakia the energizing core of the movement for socialist renewal has still not capitulated; it is symptomatic of this that Alexander Dubcek has surrendered nothing of his post-January position – the moral authority of the reform policy remains unbroken. In the Soviet Union, too, we can no longer speak simply of lone figures. Roy Medvedev's well-known book, for example, cites and discusses various points of view. (As far as Bulgaria and Romania are concerned, I have to keep silent for lack of information.)

In the GDR, so far, least has happened – though recently the Biermann case has cast a different light on the scene – and this for a whole series of reasons which I shall confine myself here simply to listing: its exposed position vis-à-vis West Germany, its relatively successful economic performance, the Prusso-German tradition of obedience to the state, the density, vigilance and relative efficiency of the whole system of social control. But here, too, the number of committed people is perceptibly growing, people who can no longer see any rewarding perspective in the overall situation of existing conditions, in their merely gradual extention to cure simply the symptoms. The need for separation from the apparatus, for a personal distancing from bureaucratic roles, is taking hold, a subjective pressure to publicly show one's real face, at least to those close at hand. This phenomenon, which at first glance is simply psychological, has a completely comprehensible sociological basis. In the GDR today, the generation standing at the crossroads is the first to have had the fortune to remain largely unscathed by fascism and the trenches, and could therefore – at least that portion of it that was psycho-socially available for this – make an unbroken 'idealistic' decision of youth in favour of the communist idea. We might recall here the kind of subjectivity that is expressed in the writing of Volker Braun.

The activists of this generation, after fifteen to twenty years of service to and within the apparatus, which acts to inhibit, channel and standardize their initiative, suffer from an inward ebb of their energy. Given the degree to which they are tied to the cause of the party, which was characteristic of these people, the process of dissolution could not depend on insights suddenly acquired, but rather on a gradual deepening of their experience. It took time, therefore. Someone for whom the cause of communism, in other words genuine equality and general emancipation, was once seriously meant, who therefore has always mistrusted the refuges of *Realpolitik* that are needed to hold things still, can in no way avoid freshly posing himself the question of meaning. Why function a further twenty or thirty years without inspiration in a system that no longer provides any food for one's hopes and ideals?

There is therefore a group latently prepared to 'bail out', as we say, indeed morally compelled to do so, and this is more important then mere numbers; a group prepared to break out and make a fresh start. What is still lacking is the initiative to meet together with a view to a deliberate dialogue in search of results. Certainly, what this will mean first of all is basically a theoretical-ideological and propaganda circle, not yet a mass movement. The first task is to get the majority of people politically committed to socialism, both within and outside of the party, to have faith in the possibility of an alternative. The presence of such groups would itself be significant proof of this possibility. The time is ripe to bring those people together, and not of course from this one generation alone, who best represent, with the highest level of consciousness, the new subjective productive forces, tackling with patience and courage the problems which a profound transformation of non-capitalist industrial society will bring with it. Taken to its logical conclusion, what is required, and has already begun to stir, is a new and different communist party. I shall speak of this as a League of Communists, to make clear the distinction already present even in the ways in which ruling parties call themselves communist. *How* this Communist League is to proceed from such beginnings must be left to the development of the movement itself, and all the more so in that various courses are conceivable – not simply on account of national differences. In particular, the opposition grouping *in statu nascendi* will in no way immediately face the task of becoming an autonomous party organization in the strict sense of the term, something that could only bring the danger of sectarian encapsulation and dogmatic dispute. The ruling parties are ideologically so empty that the possibility of a conquest of power 'from within' must be ruled out from the start. They have already for a long time been 'infected' and 'undermined' by the burgeoning emancipatory interests which move the great majority of their thinking members, including many functionaries. It is only due to the apparent lack of a practical alternative that these can express themselves merely in private indignation. If today there are more and more people in all the East European countries who, despite the certain prospect of years of unpleasantness, make applications to leave the country, it is then time for the communist minority to demand openly that life should change *here*. (This could moreover lead to a qualitatively key portion of those presently resolved to emigrate opting instead for a different and more fruitful path of self-realization.)

The perspective of a shift in power within the party, which is indicated by the Yugoslav, Hungarian and Czechoslovak experiences, even the Polish, should no longer be understood in the opportunist sense of a long march, furtive and silent, through the institutions, with those petty everyday tricks of adaptation required so as not to be noticed, not to be thrown out – until the central organ publishes an obituary for faithful service. The beginnings of the new association can only lie outside of the existing party structure – formally, since open oppositionists are immediately expelled from the parties, and in some cases also for a certain period from society, and essentially, since the focal points of a new and different consciousness do not fall within the jurisdiction of official party 'knowledge'.

It is the presently prevailing conditions that directly prescribe the path. The party statutes proscribe with sanctions any 'fractional activity', and therefore in practice any expression of tendencies, even any kind of group with a discussion purpose. Every thinking communist who meets with two other thinking communists to exchange ideas must consider himself as already expelled by party rules. The text of the constitution, on the other hand, still guarantees citizens the freedom of assembly. Since public premises will not be made available, people's homes must serve as the first meeting places. The politbureaucracy will undoubtedly try more than one method of suppression. But circumstances will not allow it to make use of the most extreme means. Once it meets with the decision of even a small group of people rather to renounce family, well-being and popularity than a higher reason for living, the entire machinery of political defence is bound to fail miserably. Against this Hercules, the opposition will prove an unconquerable Hydra, with three heads growing where one is put in prison or expelled from the country. At the very moment I am writing this, hundreds of people in the GDR, if not thousands, cannot sleep peacefully in their beds because of the example of just one singer. A suspicion is going round that the train of history is moving on towards the next station, and that it is time to get on board.

The apparatus still has a certain success with its tested tactic of making it impossible publicly to express any fundamental criticism within its own society, while at the same time branding distribution of such criticism outside its ideological jurisdiction as proof of its external character. The opposition is to be faced with the choice between keeping silent (and this means political non-existence) or 'serving the enemy'. As can easily be seen, what is involved here is an effect produced by the dictatorship itself, since it is most profoundly interested in making internal contradictions into external ones. Here we are dealing with the *final* means of ideologically shoring up the politbureaucratic tutelage of society. In this respect it is time to draw a clear line of separation between loyalty to the non-capitalist base and loyalty to its outmoded superstructure. It is extraordinarily important to make use of all possibilities of communication within one's own country, and construct as effective a network for this as possible. But we should also not flinch from using the resources of the other power bloc in the political struggle. Who owned the sealed railway carriage in which Lenin travelled from Switzerland to Russia, and who gave the go-ahead for this trip? What was decisive was what the 'German spy' took out of his pocket in Petrograd. On that occasion, it was the celebrated April Theses.

Their very autonomy will allow the first consistent nuclei of the new League to fulfil their task of drawing all individual communist elements intellectually and emotionally towards themselves and away from the official structure. The party apparatus will not be able to keep them down, for by its very nature as a rigid pyramid it stands still, while the thinking elements, driven by the contradictions of life, tend always to take up 'ex-centric' positions. This means in the first instance a scattering, but only so long as there is no point of assembly towards which they could orient themselves. It is not a question of artificially forcing this process of dissolution, insisting on a break, putting comrades who come into this circle under the pressure of political-moral decision. The situation itself will take care of this, once the time is ripe. The function of catalyst can be fulfilled to sufficient effect for the time being by a resolute minority. Besides, a form of pressure and influence of this kind, unorganized, as the apparatus sees it, and using ideological means, anticipates much of the later and developed mode of functioning of the Communist League itself. Whether this League will be formed as a new party alongside the old, or whether it will take the shape of a renovated old party, we cannot prescribe to history.

It could be asked, however, how far the continuity of the party idea can be taken for granted. Does it follow from the existence and the defeat of the old party that a new or renovated one is needed in order to synthesize the progressive potential? As I have shown, the existing order is formed almost like a church, so that the idea comes to mind of applying to the party the model of a *reformation*. Time and again, this word rears its head. Reformations do not perhaps always achieve their aim of reconstruction, re-establishment and regeneration, indeed rebirth, but this is at least their intent; they are thus essentially 'positive', if not seldom with ultimately conservative consequences, as in the case of Luther. It is a constant for any kind of church organization that its reformation has to come from its most fervent heretics: the temple must be destroyed in order to build it anew, the money-changers driven out, so that the faithful can again make their appearance. There is no doubt that this psychostructural model plays a role in the present situation, where we are facing the rapid ideological decay of the power of the 'catholic' party. As reformations of the church presuppose the Christian sentiment, so party reformations presuppose the communist. It is therefore all the more important for their activists to have a *critical* attitude towards this 'imprisonment of faith' which is completely necessary, both historically and pragmatically, so that the product is not simply a new orthodoxy of internalized protestantism.

There is no metaphysical necessity about the party. The renovation of its existence is bound up with a certain historical situation – even if a relatively long-term one – and in changing and overcoming this it is still an indispensable *tool*, which itself perishes with the situation and must always be reassessed for suitability as regards the next step towards general emancipation. The unevenness of conditions for human development at the various functional levels of labour makes some kind of social authority still indispensable for the time being, one that stands relatively sovereign over all special and particular interests. Without the *organized* ideological hegemony of the emancipatory interests, there can be no transforming a society which is still characterized by the unequal distribution of labour and knowledge that is yet to be overcome. If the interests of privileged strata should too far prevail, many people would even hanker after the old despotism, on the basis of their subaltern behavioural tendencies. Both for reasons of principle and for political considerations, it cannot be allowed that those groups who already have preference should anarchistically prepare to divide the state up among themselves. The 'protection of the weak', moreover, would not have become one of the first and most stubborn justifications of the early despotic state without an originally rational core to it,

12

Communist Organization

In proto-socialist industrial society the party is the centre of the political structure. The problem of the party, however, can only be concretely and correctly posed after making clear the structure of social interests that it has to synthesize politically and to articulate.

For parties of specific classes or similar groupings, with a particular interest vis-à-vis the social whole, it is relatively simple, as a rule, to recognize their function, since the interests involved here are relatively circumscribed. It becomes more complicated, and in societies with unconcealed class contradictions as well, to reconstruct theoretically the party or parties of the ruling class(es), since these always represent more than simply their own immediate interests, in fact a compromise between all interests that are decisive for an orderly social functioning – however imperfect the form of this compromise may be. As Engels put it, 'political supremacy has existed for any length of time only when it discharged the social functions that formed its original grounds of existence'.[1] The case is analogous with parties of those classes that first claim a hegemonic role and subsequently prepare to appear as general representatives of a majority bloc, at least at the moment of revolutionary change. It becomes still more difficult to recognize the function of a party – perhaps principally for reasons of the unfamiliar perspective – in those transition periods beyond a fully developed class society, where as a rule there are not *parties*, but rather simply *the party*. At least in some

[1] *Anti-Dühring*, Part Two, Chapter IV.

of its basic features, the party represents something completely different from the customary parties of bourgeois society, and moreover, as a result of the historical 'return' to classless society which I have referred to several times, something that is both modern and also archaic.

I would like to begin by saying that the tendency to a single party that can be observed in all variants of the non-capitalist road can scarcely be seen as allowing any choice; the conception of party pluralism seems to me an anachronistic piece of thoughtlessness, which completely misconstrues the concrete historical material in our countries. A plurality of political parties rests on a class structure consisting of clearly different and even contrary social elements. Parties that have their roots simply in *fractions* of a class already do not have the same fundamental status. The spectrum of workers' parties, for example, presupposes more than just a differentiation within the working class, i.e. the bearing of these internal differences on the possibilities of realizing the class interests that derive from the prevailing situation. To put it more exactly, it is only then that the internal differentiation is fixed, and becomes a political one. If this connection is lacking, then the various strata or fractions within classes do not form themselves into different parties; the distinctions then remain psychological, motivational and differences of feeling. A sharp political fragmentation of the workers' movement is in any case rather a phenomenon of groups of intellectuals, with their claims to power and their rivalries.

In the economically developed capitalist countries, the transformation can certainly be introduced by a bloc of different parties, who represent the existing differentiation within the revolutionary camp. But this complex of parties liquidates, after its victory, the social structure that brought it about, just because it leads the transformation forward and creates a new social structure. We could say that it recasts the social structure. The political structure then becomes obsolete. In the countries of the non-capitalist road, which are for the most part backward countries, the modern class structure was altogether too weak to bequeathe a relatively durable spectrum of parties. Once the post- or non-capitalist structure has become economically dominant, and the overall social organization is thoroughly realized as a single state monopoly system, there simply no longer remains any foothold for a multiplication of parties (still presupposing the traditional type of political party), except the too narrow and confined one of the particular interests in their difference and antithesis to the general interest. Even the ruling party is for the most part a survival of the original party spectrum, in a formal historical sense.

To aim at a revived social-democratic party in our present conditions would be a pure anachronism. The existence of this party is bound up with the critical loyalty of certain strata of workers, employees and intelligentsia towards the bourgeoisie. What could its specific task be after the liquidation of the bourgeoisie as a class? Its state monopoly option has been only too well raised to a higher level in the formerly communist party now in power. It is unquestionably unfitted to defend the ground won from the bourgeoisie. Its support for democratic forms of political life – in so far as it does not simply plump in crisis situations for a counter-revolutionary compromise in the interest of the bourgeoisie, one way or another – has certainly a certain historical justification, in as much as the communists have so far nowhere shown their ability to transcend democracy in a positive sense. But as soon as it could in any way be relevant in real political terms to speak of the new formation of social-democratic parties in our countries, they would in this respect already be superfluous. For then we would already have that socialist democracy that the social-democrat Rosa Luxemburg originally bequeathed to the newly formed West European communist parties.

We can lay down as a general rule that in our society the various interests that are bound up with the social structures analyzed in the second part of this book do not reach the sufficient degree of autonomy and independence from one another that is required for party formation. The polarizing tendency that is still visible in the overall social body leads more to a statistical than a real grouping. The strata and groups that are defined by the character of their activities and levels of education pass relatively continuously over into one another, with major overlaps between one mode of behaviour and the next. It is only the hierarchical rank order more or less directly correlated with political influence that gives rise to sharper demarcations according to the degree of disposal power over people and resources. But this is precisely not a social-structural effect in the strict sense, but already bears on a different problem.

The non-antagonistic character of these distinctions also gives society the possibility of ensuring in a different way from the administrative balancing of interests that has formerly been practised, that the many and varied competing interests, competing still over much that is absolute rather than just relative, do not give rise to friction. Analysis of our social structure shows, however, that those strata anchored in the higher functional levels of labour, with a higher degree of education, will have greater opportunities in the context of a democratization of the decision-making process for bringing their particular demands to public attention and carrying them into practice. Thus for example the natural scientists and engineers can easily present their particular interests in more comprehensive ultra-modern and thus expensive technical equipment as having absolute social necessity, not only subjectively (as a result of their highly developed powers of expression), but also objectively. The existing division of labour makes many scientists inclined to let their human interests encroach far too much on their scientific interests, and on their competition for recognition in their own specialist world. This is the same kind of particularism as is shown by other interest groups too, but in the particular ambitions of groups privileged by the division of labour we are inevitably dealing with the most blatant residue of the old class domination.

I have already said that it necessarily falls to the party also to block the imposition of these claims as far as possible, and all appropriation of influence, resources and consumer goods that is disproportionate. If the real social structure was expressed in the superstructure without let or hindrance, then the special interests would simply advance according to the degree of their relative social power. But it is still quite unproductive to draw political dividing lines between these different strata and status groups, given that the ruling apparatus as a whole is not in too bad a state of dysfunction and is continuing to damage the general reproduction processes. This competition for the share of activities, skills and enjoyments, for the optimization of the existing situation of appropriation and realization, is rather normal life, leading to nothing more significant for actually existing socialism than does the competition between capitalists in bourgeois society. This is the field of representation of the various corporate interests, by professional group, sex, age group, level of education, leisure pursuits, etc., which can bring their claims into non-antagonistic comparison all the more easily, the more openly these can be recognized and expressed, and are weighed against one another by public opinion in general. Here, plurality and diversity must fully prevail, precisely so that these interests are not anachronistically driven to set themselves up as universal interests and form into political parties. The trade unions will continue to have the greatest importance in this connection.

The position is quite different at the level where the rules of this normal life are themselves at issue, i.e. where what is at stake is a change in the relations of production and the superstructures. The institutional system reflects first of all the demands of the specific revolutionary moment at which the power of the old ruling classes was broken. To this extent, the revolutionary party is first of all quite regularly identified with the new state, and with the new institutions that are created under its leadership and with the aid of which it then protects itself against the blows of the enemy. The trouble begins when it seeks to make the needs of the first days, months and years into virtues of decades, and forgets that the position which it occupies is that of the superstructure of a society that is for the moment not yet changed, or scarcely so, a superstructure which must necessarily be conceived as a provisional and masked form of the new order. To the extent that the basis of society actually does change and develop, at the level of its productive forces, as its new quality assumes material shape, and in particular the shape of a higher subjective potential, then this mask quite naturally becomes an obstacle to further development.

This problem was the subject of an extraordinarily instructive comment by Gramsci:

'It is difficult to deny that all political parties (those of subordinate as well as ruling groups) also carry out a policing function – that is to say, the function of safeguarding a certain political and legal order. If this were conclusively demonstrated, the problem would have to be posed in other terms; it would have to bear, in other words, on the means and the procedures by which such a function is carried out. Is its purpose one of repression or of dissemination; in other words, does it have a reactionary or a progressive character? Does the given party carry out its policing function in order to conserve an outward, extrinsic order which is a fetter on the vital forces of history; or does it carry it out in the sense of tending to raise the people to a new level of civilization expressed programmatically in its political and legal order? In fact, a law finds a lawbreaker: 1. among the reactionary social elements whom it has dispossessed; 2. among the progressive elements whom it holds back; 3. among those elements which have not yet reached the level of civilization which it can be seen as representing. The policing function of a party can hence be either progressive or regressive. It is progressive when it tends to keep the dispossessed reactionary forces within the bounds of legality, and to raise the backward masses to the level of the new legality. It is regressive when it tends to hold back the vital forces of history and to maintain a legality which has been superseded, which is anti-historical, which has become extrinsic. Besides, the way in which the party functions provides discriminating criteria. When the party is progressive it functions 'democratically' (democratic centralism); when the party is regressive it functions 'bureaucratically' (bureaucratic centralism). The party in this second case is a simple, unthinking executor. It is then technically a policing organism, and its name of 'political party' is simply a metaphor of a mythological character.'[2]

The critical moment thus approaches at which the decision must be made; either the party must take the initiative in the task of liberating society from its institutional mask, or else it will cling to this in a conservative and apologetic way, continuing to identify itself with the mask. If it persists in wearing the corsets

[2] *Selections from the Prison Notebooks*, London 1971, p. 155.

of last year's policies, then it *cannot* remain unified, it *must* split. This split will proceed vertically down through all strata and groups of its membership, including the apparatus, through the entire society, therefore, that it represents. As long as it remains latent, it will be only a question of tendencies formed according to psychological preferences, differences of individual character. People will make their choice according to their mental balance between hope and fear, demands and resignation, self-confidence and timidity, and this will determine the moment of change for them. The social structure will certainly influence the proportions of such a division, which may differ from one stratum to another, from group to group, but it does not determine the substance of the division itself. The manner and form of the split, its overall social and vertical character, indicates the major contradiction described in the previous chapter between the emancipatory interests and those of the apparatus, which both have a profound economic content, since they are ultimately based on alternative principles of social organization and management of labour, on a difference between social formations.

The contradiction between the emancipatory interests and the apparatus interests is intrinsic and inescapable, as long as the old division of labour is not overcome, so that the society still produces the state as a special apparatus of repression. The historical necessity of a communist party in proto-socialist industrial society, and non-capitalist society in general, is based on nothing more than the existence of this contradiction. The party has no more fundamental purpose than that of relating society and state, the perspective of bringing the state back into society. Bureaucracy as a form of political domination is the key phenomenon of any non-capitalist or post-capitalist society that has left its birthpangs behind it and disposes of the most necessary economic foundations.

The tendential, 'ideal-typical' unity of the party that is prescribed by the actual conditions themselves thus depends in practice on how it masters this challenge. If it succeeds in organizing itself in such a way that institutions are adapted at the right moment and successively anew, with the necessary radical consequences, if it is able to lead this process, then the dialectic of unity-division-unity remains latent, and the continuity of the single party is maintained, even if never the complete continuity of its leading personnel. But it must be made clear here that what is involved really is the replacement of one political constitution by another as the lever of further economic transformation, not simply petty reforms and 'structural changes' in some institution or other. Society cannot wait too long for this decision. It is precisely because from the standpoint of progressive general emancipation under the conditions of overall social organization there has to be *one* party, that the existing party must be broken and split as soon as it abandons its major task of pursuing social homogeneity in this direction, thus above all demolishing the traditional division of labour and with it the preconditions for the state and the étatist-bureaucratic syndrome. To persist in étatism or press forward to general emancipation, forward to the cultural revolution – that is the alternative.

If our non-capitalist society is forming politically against the prevailing type of party, then as things stand it is gathering against the oldest, most characteristic and sharpest expression of the traditional division of labour, against the autonomy and monopolization of general affairs in the hands of an authoritarian oligarchy which has entrenched itself behind the state machine and has no thought of working with the people for its liquidation. The opposition grouping that necessarily emerges already spontaneously in these conditions, does not strive accordingly to become a second party alongside the old, or, more exactly, does not strive to remain so. Rather, its intention can only be, both subjectively and objectively, to re-establish unity by overcoming the contradiction, negating the negation, and thus giving the party the kind of internal constitution for the next step which will ensure it as far as possible against a new loss of its revolutionary potential. The split is a transient moment of the historical process. It is directed not against the idea of the party, but rather against its apparatus, against its decay into the state that is embodied in the party apparatus. Society is again to have a leadership that is not located in the apparatus, not a leadership composed of Politbureau members who are principally the directors of specific branches of the party and state machine, and remain tied to their specific interests and inertia. The leaders must live in society and share in its everyday life, so that they cannot avoid taking direct notice of the real needs and requirements of the masses.

Right from the start, the opposition contends that the ruling party oligarchy has abandoned the position of the emancipatory interests, so that these no longer possess any political representation. The position is vacant! To the extent that the party loses out to the state and apparatus, it is no longer in a position to integrate organically the various particular and corporate interests that there are in society, and to maintain the natural authority that can flow from discharging necessary functions of leadership. For this integration presupposes a revolutionary perspective. Its policy now no longer functions in an integrating sense, but rather – and this is a decisive difference – simply a universalistic one: it must force a consensus on society from outside and from above, which is then nothing but the old particular spirit of state and church, seeking to keep itself in a position of power and grace. In this way the party finds itself precisely in that condition where its edifice must be torn down and erected anew. The communist movement only exists when and where it transcends something of the existing state of affairs in its everyday practice, and brings general emancipation and real equality and freedom perceptibly nearer. Those who simply reproduce the existing conditions and defend themselves terroristically against all progressive criticism, are communists neither objectively nor subjectively, whatever doctrine they might profess to express. The ruling party apparatuses have as little in common with communism as the Grand Inquisitor with Jesus Christ.

Now, as this stands it is still an abstract argument of principle, which could be dismissed as dogmatic and voluntarist, so as to disqualify it as a demand for action. There are churches, after all, to continue this analogy, which have passed the greater part of their existence in such a situation, or at least with the same danger, and yet still survive. But the situation of the party in the non-capitalist industrial society of today is quite different in two decisive points, which I have already gone into in some detail. Firstly, the factual existence of surplus consciousness – the potential for a League of Communists to replace the former party, and for its social sounding-board, is no longer a mere hypothesis, and since 1968 we can see the practical possibility of establishing it. Secondly, the *necessity* of the cultural revolution – the insoluble contradictions of material life in the context of the existing mode of production, and particularly of its technical base, i.e. the material productive forces themselves, demand ever more pressingly a radical economic alternative and thus the organ of its intellectual preparation. The cultural revolution can in no way be conceived of as the action of a party and state bureaucracy, even one three times as 'enlightened' as the present. The apparatus does not think, it repeats what its founders programmed into it and what circumstances have since required of it in the way of superficial adaptive reactions. The idea and strategy of a social transformation cannot even be meaningfully discussed, let alone carried through, with people who have chiefly to consider what their superiors and colleagues will say about them.

At their summit, the governing parties have sunk completely into their role as super-state apparatuses, while at the rank-and-file level they are reduced to an ancillary role in the stagnant execution of managerial functions and the ceremonies of an artificial public life, and take care of the disciplinary subjection of the most active and conscious elements to the abstract requirements of the hierarchy. The party has been killed off by its bureaucracy and hyper-bureaucracy. The 'cadres', those individuals who represent the party, are almost completely absorbed by the bureaucratic functions of the party, state, economy, science, culture, etc. If, for example, the Central Committee of the SED has a meeting, then this is a meeting of the highest party, state, economic and social-organizational officials. Scarcely a minister will be absent, apart from those of the 'bloc parties'. Today they are the Central Committee, and supposedly determine party policy. But tomorrow the General Secretary can summon more or less any of them, almost without exception, for 'instructions' or to report, since they are all his subordinates or the subordinates of his subordinates. This entire apparatus – even if we leave their police-sheltered lifestyle out of consideration – is a machine totally isolated from the people, from the masses, and cannot possibly generate any enthusiasm. Either instruction and orders for the officials, or else inspiration for the people and the youth. These are the alternatives. And if anyone should object that it is wrong to make this choice into something absolute, we can reply that it is not the declarations of critical ideologists that have brought this alternative to its present truly metaphysical exclusiveness.

No new paths can be broken with this party machine. This does not lie simply in its existence as such, it lies in the fact that the machine is *everything*, that the party is *nothing apart from the machine*. Party members are in no way communists with a base of their own, they are not considered to have any competence as such. If they are addressed as communists, this means invariably that the apparatus is appealing to their military discipline. There is also no communist *leadership*. Appearances here are deceptive. The General Secretary is the highest ranking subaltern in the whole society, the most polished product of the bureaucratic hierarchy – as long as its continuity is not interrupted by internal crises, as those of 1956 in Hungary and 1968 in Czechoslovakia, or by spontaneous mass actions as that of 1970 in Poland. There is nothing to be hoped for from the machine. The whole system of political institutions, monolithic in its construction and mechanical in its mode of operation, is incapable of actively changing itself. In general, even the most modest proposals for change are blocked by that instructive concept of 'viability' which in no way bears on objective social and economic conditions in general, but rather on the objectivity of bureaucratic functioning. What is 'viable' is what the Politbureau will presumably concede. It is evident that many things will be simply 'impossible' when considered from the standpoint of a governing party hopelessly stuck in its opposition to the masses, a party that cannot demand anything from them. The cultural revolution is only possible at all as a *movement*, which knows how to attack the administrative institutions, and the political secretariats in particular, in their very midst, in many respects in a real pincer movement.

In order to exert political influence on the historical process, the emancipatory interests must be organized in a connected and serious way at an overall social level. The forces in power will defend their positions with the systematic oppression of all oppositional activity, and deploy their entire ponderous mechanism so as to destroy it and isolate its protagonists. Without a certain concentration of forces it is impossible even in the present phase of ideological preparation to struggle effectively against the apparatus, which has monopolized the means of mass communications and whose police keeps them sealed against all emancipatory purposes. It is necessary to take concerted action and foster connections in the apparatus itself. We can see in the developed capitalist countries how the experimental initiatives of very many small groups get lost in isolation, even though they at least have the space provided by bourgeois political freedoms. In our case, individual thought, feeling and action are already subject to the irresistible suction of subalternity and alienation. In the subordinate functions, irrespective of what labour is absorbed and occupied with the satisfaction of their natural and compensatory needs, people only find support and affirmation for their public behaviour in an officially approved system of roles. Anyone who gives voice to his emancipatory needs is 'crazy', 'deviating from the agenda', 'stopping work', 'has not yet understood' – and is therefore either simply discouraged or pushed to the sidelines. If he consequently attempts deviant behaviour, then he comes up against a programmed escalation of sanctions. Absorbed consciousness is organized as a seamless web under the aegis of the apparatus. Against it the revolutionary potential needs a powerful base of operations of its own, offering people a solidaristic back-up in their emancipatory needs and containing a higher moral-political authority than the apparatus, by making possible and protecting the advance of integral modes of behaviour that foreshadow a new whole. For the future, too, this base must remain unconditionally independent of the relations of subordination in the realm of hierarchical functioning and necessary labour that would otherwise be unavoidably dominant. If not, then revolutionary action will remain isolated and dependent on individual accident. People need a firm point outside the existing relations of domination, if they are to overcome these by that practical-critical activity, constantly reoriented to the goal, which is indispensable.

To provide this base for revolutionary and transcending action and behaviour is the task of a genuine communist party, a League of Communists united around the idea of general emancipation. It must inspire the system of social forces and organizations in the name of a constructive but substantially transforming counterforce, which puts the state hierarchy in its proper place. In principle, this means a division of social power, the installation of a progressive dialectic between state and social forces, and not just temporarily as within the party process itself, but rather for the whole duration of the transition. The result will be a situation of dual supremacy, in which the étatist side gradually becomes less dominant. The precondition that communists are no longer a governing party in the traditional sense is the prerequisite for them to be able to participate again at all *as* communists in the work of government, which is in the highest degree necessary. For naturally it is no good the emancipatory interests confronting the state apparatus merely externally, as an abstract negation of existing conditions and immediate necessities. What is required is rather that they subordinate to themselves the activities of the reproduction process, including the functions of hierarchical information processing, which can only gradually be reduced to pure administration.

It is only in this way that the League of Communists will show that it can effectively lead society onto its new path and guarantee its normal functioning. In so far as they cannot be transcended, the state functions will thus be lent a higher degree of authority, by being ensured of the voluntary respect of public opinion and thus making sanctions against anti-social behaviour gradually reducible to mere moral pressures.

This perspective may well sound illusory from the standpoint of a party that is completely hidden in and behind the state machine, and therefore cannot possibly attain the ideological hegemony which is the precondition for a cultural-revolutionary practice. People mistrust it and are not prepared for the discussion in which alone a common conviction could be formed, with truth having so long been a question of power position and tactical decision. To achieve ideological hegemony means to establish the predominance of an integral behavioural tendency in the perspective of general emancipation, among all groups and strata of society. What is needed for this is that the party, instead of being organized as a super-state apparatus, must be organized as the *collective intellectual*, which mediates the reflection of the whole society and its consciousness of all problems of social development, and which anticipates in itself something of the human progress for which it is working.

The concept of the collective intellectual is the quintessence of all ideas about the political leading function and internal constitution of the communist party that were elaborated from Marx and Engels, via the young Lenin, Rosa Luxemburg and Gramsci, down to the new approaches to Marxist thought of today. In the countries of actually existing socialism, the party has to fulfil this role of the collective intellectual in relation to the emancipatory interests no longer simply of a single class, but rather of all strata and groups of the entire society. It is of the greatest present significance to conceive *how* it can function in this sense. All questions of party building, of the party statues, the position of the party in the state constitution, which I can only indicate here, will then appear in a new light. The many repressive sanctions that have presently to compensate for the visible absence of ideological authority must be abandoned, and moreover even before they become positively superfluous. The party must be prepared to wager its old institutional existence for the sake of its spiritual renewal.

The party's ideological authority is directly dependent on the quality of its intellectual production, on the power of the model in which it reflects social reality so as to grasp social relations and indicates the direction of change to mobilize the people. If in the different dimension of the historical process, its achievement is subject to precisely the same criteria and has also the same general conditions as the work of a group of scientists working with a model of certain natural relationships. For the work is an activity of knowledge – naturally in the complex Marxian sense, in which knowledge as an overall process involves an object that is above all else a subject, and takes the understanding thereby won to fuel its own will and activity.

The specific problem of the party consists in how the emancipatory interests, which determine the standpoint of its analysis and synthesis, can be reconciled in a practical way with the diversity of existing conditions, and thus with the immediate interests based on these. The party is the instance for bringing together the various interests of different strata and groups, where these diverge, by always making the standpoint of the higher synthesis prevail. All immediate activity on the basis of particular interest simply reproduces the status quo, and particularly creates at the base the luxuriant economism of the hunt for productivity and efficiency, the spirit of economic spontaneity. At the same time, however, all progress towards freedom must go through the existing structures, must be wrung from the realm of necessity in the face of the institutional expression which this had yesterday. The prerequisite of cultural revolutionary practice is therefore constant criticism and self-criticism, while for this practice the majority of individuals must also have understood the limits of their previous form of existence, even in their objectivity and former rationality. Without the effort of reflection, without the application of dialectical structures of thought which mirror the contradictory process of history, no further progress is likely. The overall social organization requires more than any other a collective process of knowledge at the high level of abstraction that corresponds to the complexity of the actual conditions. (This obviously requires also a struggle for a comprehensible language. I am convinced that it will be possible to formulate much of the content of this book in a more accessible way than I have so far managed to do.)

The concept of a collective intellectual is in no way aimed at representing the special interests of the intelligentsia. Since all people have emancipatory interests, which cannot be sufficiently realized under the conditions of the traditional division of labour, the attempt to reflect the problems of realizing these interests must in principle be a universal one. The League of Communists must therefore be open to all those who have the need to go beyond the pursuit of their immediate interests, having recognized that the barriers to their self-realization bear a social character. By this action they act as intellectuals. This is of course a use of the concept that goes beyond the traditional social structural sense. It assumes that all thinking people are at least potential intellectuals, and can acquire the ability to think dialectically beyond the hier-

archy of social connections and intervene in these as active experi-
menters and constructors. As Gramsci wrote: 'That all members
of a political party should be regarded as intellectuals is an
affirmation that can easily lend itself to mockery and caricature.
But if one thinks about it nothing could be more exact.' 'The
problem of creating a new stratum of intellectuals consists therefore in the critical elaboration of the intellectual activity that
exists in everyone at a certain degree of development. . . .'[3] In
as much as the intellectuals still form a traditional stratum or
group, they must become conscious of their special interests
with the aim of restraining these as far as possible. This asceticism
in relation to the satisfaction of their own immediate needs is
precisely the condition for belonging to the party of general
emancipation, the proof of the ability to think as a communist.
The social situation in non-capitalist industrial society is characterized not least by the fact that the surplus mobilizable here for
emancipatory action is greatest where the potential for egoistic
appropriation is so too. Here we have the very pivot of the
intellectual and political debate on and within the intelligentsia.
Anyone who seeks in the League of Communists simply the most
favourable conditions for producing his own individuality will
today remain socially unproductive. In traditional China, under
the Tang dynasty, Buddhism culminated in a character who can
be seen as sister to Prometheus. In the very process of attaining
Buddahood, Kuan Yin, 'hearing the cries of the world', turns
back and vows to renounce her own divinity until, with her aid,
all the suffering of the world is extinguished, and all beings have
attained the same highest level of spiritual existence. This metaphor may well be appropriate for that type of solidarity which needs
to prevail in society when the focus of social inequality is shifted
to the division of labour and education.

The conditions for it to do so are favourable. Precisely because
the nature of inequality in our society no longer hangs on the
private appropriation of material goods (although there still is
this), but rather on the privileged appropriation of culture as
determined by the division of labour, a culture whose sources

[3] *Loc. cit.*, pp. 16 and 9.

today are no longer inherently scarce, the cultural revolution need not on the whole take away from some people what it gives to others. And it can present itself to surplus consciousness as the tremendous creative task of both satisfying its emancipatory needs and pacifying its compensatory ones. Even in eras of fully developed class rule, the intellect developing towards freedom, though tied by its conditions of existence to the interests of the exploiters, time and again saw beyond all immediate interests, with its objectively in-dwelling emancipatory tendency. How else could we explain the movement of so many intellectuals onto the side of the oppressed? And the Marxist revolutionaries from the intelligentsia were not moved simply by 'comprehending theoretically the historical movement as a whole',[4] for all their excellence in this regard. What lay at the root was rather always an elementary feeling of solidarity between man and man, which was ever the same right from the earliest doctrines of justice. Now that there are millions upon millions of intellectualized people, who are moreover not held back from solidarity by any constraining barriers of interest, and finally are themselves hungry for a more comprehensive social communication, it must already be possible to *work out through discussion* the necessary compromise of interests and carry it through primarily with the 'gentle power of reason'. In other words, the League of Communists will and must be in a position, as the collective intellectual, to resolve already within itself the particular problem of the intelligentsia. And this naturally all the sooner, the more it succeeds in uniting in itself the *entire* emancipatory potential from all groups and strata of society.

In order to be this collective intellectual uniting all energies directed towards general emancipation, and to be able to mediate their confluence in a programme of action that is steadily actualized, the League of Communists must be organized differently from the old kind of party. The organizational structure must be governed by the character of the principal activity that it has to perform. A successful work of knowledge requires the access of all participants to the totality of significant information, the

---

[4] 'Communist Manifesto', *The Revolutions of 1848*, p. 77.

'horizontal' and non-hierarchical coordination of investigations on the basis of the self-activity of those involved, the admission of hypotheses that break through the customary frame of ideas, unreserved discussion of different interpretations without any kind of official evaluation by an agency empowered to 'confirm' or otherwise, etc. The point of departure must be that the research of the most diverse individuals and groups, presupposing the basically agreed orientation of those involved, leads from the logic of the actual relationships themselves, on which it is focussed, to a common understanding, to approximation to the truth, i.e. to the adequate expression of the emancipatory interests in view of the conditions that are given and to be changed. Distortions arise far less from the prejudices and reservations of individuals than from those of institutions. Convergence of proposals is produced, and there is no need here for any special and additional conformity, when the social facts are unreservedly taken into account and thought through, with differences of view being aired before public opinion at regular discussion conferences or the like, where what counts are the better arguments. This is the royal road of social science, however much professional social scientists have also to concern themselves with methodology and with individual cases. This free and convergent dialogue between communists, from which their general will can take shape in the form of an ever more concrete model of social change, is the road on which the party programme will be established and corrected, from its far-off goals to the measures of the present day.

It goes without saying that positions which remain in a minority at congresses and thus do not go into the decisions reached, can still be pursued further at the theoretical level. The League of Communists will have different tendencies and wings in this respect, and at times even its fractions – in particular if the mediation does not succeed, i.e. as signs of crisis, which should not then be blocked from having phenomenal expression, but rather overcome in their causes, by the common elaboration and championing of a better and more integral political model. This naturally presupposes that the state and administration are not directly dependent on the League and its internal debates. The general social institutions must be subject to the control of *society*, so that it is society in its majority that must be convinced before a new party opinion, which yesterday may still have been the particular standpoint of a wing or fraction, can be transformed into state policy. Certainly, the leadership of the revolutionary process will devolve now on this group of individuals, now on that, according to the power of conviction that these develop by the keenness and farsightedness of their ideas. If there is free political communication, then nothing can prevent society from gearing its practice to a new conception whenever the previous impulse has been expanded. Whenever society is faced with a choice, the alternatives under discussion will be so much simplified down to their ultimate human significance, to their position in the perspective of emancipation, that a general vote will be possible that has nothing in common with the paternalistic plebiscites which any despotism is always proud to hold.

If the League of Communists is to be in this way the organ for the socialization of political unity and power of decision, then the first condition for this is a party constitution that is *open* towards all genuine social forces, which makes it possible to invite for collaboration and attract to it without any kind of exclusive sectarianism, any power-secrecy behind padded doors, all the living and productive elements of labour and culture. The party could insist exclusively and intolerantly on its purity so long as it had to maintain its principles and the interests of those it represented in a predominantly hostile environment, in which the ideas of the ruling class incessantly threatened the political autonomy of the movement. In the developed social structure of actually existing socialism, there are no longer any strata or groups worth the name (problems such as that of the peasantry in Poland I shall not discuss here) who would have to be excluded from the original formation of political opinion on account of their influence. The effect of external pressure, which at the present appears so immoderately great and in many respects is so, would rapidly decline if our society had a superstructure appropriate to its requirements. The danger of distorted reflection of social interests proceeds first and foremost in our case, as we have already seen, from forces that stand from the start very close to the centre of social power, and urgently require control by being confronted with autonomous partners not dependent on them. As soon as party membership is no longer a means of attaining a particularly favourable place in the social division of labour, a process of almost spontaneous self-purification will set in. What will rightly again appear as the criterion of membership, and can then also be wielded jointly by public opinion, in a suitable form, will be the political and moral character of the party members. It is generally very well known in any immediate milieu not only who behaves as a communist in practice, but also who does so from conviction, and who is 'the man for the job'.

The consistent setting-up of the party as a collective intellectual will also be the means of its self-liberation from imprisonment to its own excessive apparatus, from its superior existence 'in a house with telephones'.[5] Already in the old social-democratic type of party, and not only in the Bolshevik party of a new type, the bureaucratization of the party structure was programmed into the very foundations of its organization. We might consider how far the form of organization was in its turn the unavoidable expression of the sociological relations at the base of the party. In any case, this form was to a large extent the counterpart to the subalternity of the base, which it not only reflected, but also helped to reproduce. It is an organization which sees below it its 'infantry', providing for these a suitable military structure and discipline – a discipline of the Prussian kind, as Bakunin already saw. In 1914–15 Rosa Luxemburg surveyed the results in rage. 'Without discipline', she wrote with respect to the official party criticism of Liebknecht's opposition in the Reichstag debate of December 2nd, 'there could be no factory, school, army or state. But is this the same discipline on which the Social-Democratic Party is based? In no way! There is a fundamental and radical opposition between our social-democratic discipline and the discipline of army and factory'. Luxemburg meant that there *should* be such an opposition, for what she actually had to record was as follows: 'It is precisely the powerful organization and much praised discipline of German Social Democracy that has enabled a handful of parliamentary deputies to order a body four million strong to make an about-

[5] A reference to Brecht's poem *Wer aber ist die Partei?*

turn at twenty-four hours notice and harness them to a different carriage . . . Marx, Engels and Lassalle, Liebknecht, Bebel and Singer schooled the German proletariat so that Hindenburg can lead it.'[6]

If the task of liquidating subalternity and blocking the sources of its reproduction is correctly posed, then within the party we must necessarily get rid of that glorification of proletarian discipline which Lenin took over from Kautsky, since it was fitted for Russian conditions. What Lenin emphasized in his time was the capacity for military organization, the readiness of the mass of workers to follow a strong leadership, to subordinate themselves to the superior intellectual power and vision of a political general staff. If the troops are on the battlefield, they naturally need orders, and it would be wrong to waste time with too lengthy discussions. The assessment of the intellectuals that Kautsky and Lenin gave in this connection was strongly dictated by staff requirements such as this. It had its place in history. But in the present conditions of actually existing socialism, the intellectual elements of various social strata and groups have every reason not to let themselves be placed under such pressure of time.

It is evident enough that today effective organization still requires an apparatus and a discipline, not only in administration, etc., but in the party too. Communists, however, must reverse in their own organization the balance of power between, on the one hand, the levels of discussion and decision over values and goals, and the ways and means of their policy, and on the other the apparatus for putting these into practice. Discipline must consist above all in allegiance to the party programme, which arises from the comprehensive and unconfirmed discussion of the entire base – and not just from the overbearing commands of a party bureaucracy which, besides prescribing the programme, can turn it upside down as much as it likes in the practice of carrying it out. The overall social process in which the state machine is transformed into a subordinate and administrative tool, and its domination thereby broken, can only be set under way at all if this *begins to be done within the party itself*, if the domination of the

[6] *Gesammelte Werke*, vol. 4, Berlin 1974, pp. 15 and 23ff.

secretaries and secretariats over the party is abolished.

In its present position and role, the party apparatus is the centre of the rule by apparatus, the apparatus state. This is where the power of the state derives from, and where it returns again from all its emanations in the various directing functions. The redefinition of its role and function, the rigorous reduction of its scope, its subordination to the political and ideological life of the Communist League, will thus be one of the first objectives in the struggle to set under way the process of cultural revolution. Among other requirements is that of an absolute personal separation between the elected political directorates and the organ in charge of the technical conditions of their work. Without abolishing the domination of the apparatus within the party, there will never be the inner-party democracy that is indispensable for the knowledge process of the collective intellectual, whatever its statutes may say.

The apparatus embodies a mistrust of the entire quantity of intelligence that society sets free in all its various strata and groups. The structure of a papal church, and the spirit of the party hierarchy which is from top to bottom that of a curia, must be relentlessly rooted out. Communists must free their policy from any kind of determining influence by a party apparatus, and re-establish their collective sovereignty over it. Those people who are active in the apparatus – right down to the politically uncommitted and unimprovable bureaucrats among them – must themselves be given a maximum interest in such a solution, since only in this way can they re-establish their own sovereign existence as communists, and thus also bring their own personal opinion into the political arena. Every communist must have the possibility of withdrawing if need be from his role as a disciplined member and making a decision of conscience.

If the League of Communists, while freeing itself from its internal chains, also stands outside the continuity of the state apparatus, then it obtains the possibility of also bringing contradiction into the government apparatus, renovating this in a fundamental way, socially instead of just bureaucratically. If the party revolutionized society in the first phase of actually existing socialism with the aid of the state, the apparatus (and up to a certain point successfully so), then the question now is to re-organize the state and the apparatus with the aid of society, basing this on the surplus consciousness assembled in it. This is in no way a mere administrative task. The apparatus is the sphere of work of a large number of people, whose professional complex of interests develops laws of its own. This complex must be dissolved, to prevent the formation of a political bloc around the special interests of these personnel.

The subjugation of the state apparatus to society is the quintessence of the long proclaimed transition from domination over people to the administration of things. If a bureaucracy uncontrolled from below was the original cause of the party having previously had to play the role of a controlling bureaucracy, a super-state apparatus, then there is only one single solution: the party itself must place control of the bureaucracy and state machine by social forces at the centre of its policy. It must spur people to this task, and inspire them to it by communists having dealings with everyone and uniting everyone with them who 'thinks a bit' about their work and their life. They must organize the social forces in such a way that these confront the apparatus on a massive scale as autonomous powers, and can force it into progressive compromises. This means organizing communism as a mass movement. Only proceeding from a communist mass movement of this kind will the League of Communists no longer be compelled to erode itself, as the old party had to, in its control as an apparatus of the state machine. The political situation would then develop beyond the connotations of the concepts 'above' and 'below', which apply to the hierarchical relationships between the functionaries themselves and between their corporation as a whole and the people. It will become possible to broach the measures anticipated by Marx and Engels in their writings on the Paris Commune of a democratic selection of the state personnel. Instead of appointment or nomination from above, the occupation of positions will be decided on the basis of the proven ability of the candidates, in a dialogue of cultural-revolutionary practice with the masses, working with the autonomous social forces from whose midst the League of Communists itself operates.

The political structure of the cultural-revolutionary practice is not in itself something novel, what is new is rather the necessity of keeping it going permanently. At all historical moments when communism is the real *movement* abolishing the existing state of affairs that Marx intended it to be, it does not tend to become a relationship between three distinct instances: party/state machine/ people. The communists and the people rather form together a comprehensive bloc whose internal structure cannot be described in terms of relations of subordination. There have been historical moments which have something to tell us as to the possible *form* of the transition. We can see those moments in many books of the Old Testament, in the New Testament, in the chorales of the Reformation and the songs and hymns of the infant workers' movement. There have always been times in which people pressed beyond existing arrangements without being subordinated to the rule of a priestly caste, times of movement, times of a people led by *prophecy*. Only in such movements did masses and classes who were otherwise inevitably subaltern manage to reach the level of a historical consciousness, of immediate communication with the universal. In movements of this kind, fishermen from Galilee and Paris workers suddenly rose to the highest possible human dignity attainable. The essence of the coordination of consciousness that prevailed in such movements consists precisely in the convergence of the ideal substance. It is hope that leads the people, and its prophets are nothing more than interpreters who give their deepest emancipatory needs a concrete, articulated and historical expression, in which the totality of what is promised is not lost.

We may recall the vision of the old workers' song: 'See how the train of millions/Springs endless from the gloom/Until your deepest yearnings/The dark skies overcome'. In the state, the consciousness of individuals is dimmed, and it cannot be otherwise. In the communist movement, it is illuminated. Light has always been the symbol of self-awareness and freedom. Light is ahead, it is never reached by all at the same time, and does not penetrate all ranks with the same intensity. But it is for everyone the same light, there are simply gradations of the same universal consciousness. And history is not a narrow tunnel; the masses can flood through, those in front need not block the light from reaching the others. Ahead prevails the spirit of that Promethean solidarity which has always filled authentic revolutionaries. Communists will only deserve their place at the head of a society in movement to communism if they are the first to recognize each new opportunity that arises for bringing closer the equality of all people, and if they actually live by the principles for which they stand.

Whether there is any real opportunity of organizing communism as this kind of movement in the industrialized non-capitalist countries will depend simply on whether the reformation of the party is successful. We must realize how intensely our society, purged of capitalism, is waiting for a renovated communist party. This holds even for the greater part of those elements who, in the face of the existing conditions, are trapped in anti-communist prejudices. How much hope the Communist Party of Czechoslovakia united around itself in 1968, even at the very beginning of its renovation process, when its goals had not yet appeared with their full clarity. What ties people to a movement (differently from to a firm that 'gives work') is the promise of connecting the details of their lives with a meaningful whole, of opening up to them a space for self-realization in trans-personal and historical dimensions. Individuals are already organized around their particular interests (and membership in the ruling parties has in fact become one of the preferred vehicles for this). In a compensatory sense they ultimately get satisfaction of a kind, in some degree or other. But where can we find that union in which they can commit their emancipatory hopes? Where can their consciousness grow in collective communication, instead of just their special expertise for various limited purposes – however important these might be?

The traditional parties were formed, as we all are aware, in an epoch that is now long in the past, and for quite different tasks. Their membership is as split today, beneath the cloak of official unity, as it was in Czechoslovakia in the 1960s. Ideologically and morally it is as heterogeneous as is only possible in parties having a monopoly of state power. Even their leaders are sometimes enraged by this. And yet the greater part of the energetic elements predestined for the beginning of a social renovation are still enrolled in the existing parties. In order to win them for a breakthrough, we have to revive the traditional communist promises.

These are as necessary as they have ever been. They are the signs of recognition for gathering together the true communists among the party members, and uniting them in struggle for the cultural revolution on a new basis, naturally also drawing in many fresh forces from the youth and from all strata of society who can never be won by the communist parties in their existing constitution. The new League of Communists will reflect in its composition, in its organization, and in its style, the present structures and demands of proto-socialist society, and anticipate its future perspectives. Above all, it will be based on the intellectual participation and practical intervention of communists on all fronts of work and life. It will lead society through the influence of its plans for the processes of social transformation. It will stand for the fraternity of working people in international as well as domestic life.

This gathering must be prepared by a patient propaganda of cultural revolutionary positions, tasks and goals, spelling out their urgency and significance for individuals as something important to their lives and altering their existence. This propaganda can start at the level of those informal small groups which are even today to a large extent left undisturbed, which have come together for the most varied of purposes and are no longer susceptible to ideological control. It is precisely in discussion with the many people who, though profoundly interested in these perspectives, are still sceptical and pessimistic, or else see other priorities, that the concrete mode of procedure, the future Action Programme, can be made more precise. If communists themselves raise the problems of alienation, of subalternity, of the inequality of opportunities for development, and of the irrefutable claims to happiness of all members of society, then they can unreservedly allow themselves a dialogue of partnership with other tendencies. This holds not least also for the traditional strivings of Christianity, which converge on precisely the same problems. In our struggle against the rule of reification, the tradition that appeals to Christ's Sermon on the Mount is an indispensable ally, in so far as it does not enclose itself within the church. A genuine competition for spiritual influence on society, not spoiled by power-political aims, can only arouse Marxism as a living force, and help it to rise above its primitive catechisms. All indoctrination based on force must naturally be abandoned.

If the individual measures of a political-economic alternative, the basic direction of which is our final subject for discussion, are to achieve anything fundamental, if we are to avoid the force of everyday habit leading yet again into the reproduction of subaltern modes of behaviour, then we must set in train a mental upswing which particularly inspires the majority of young people directly at the level of the political and philosophical ideal. The collective movement itself must give rise to so irresistible a promise of emancipation for all that millions of young people manage to break through to overall social, in fact overall human consciousness. Without the component of emotional uplift, which is the shortest route from the particular to the general, or from the individual to the community, there can be no revolutionary mass movement. The wisdom of resignation is of no use to anyone. It is precisely the consciousness kept down in subalternity, which cannot immediately recognize its strivings in the abstractions of the theoretical idea, that needs a vision of total human possibilities which is evident directly to the emotions. Only in this way can it put the necessary transforming pressure on the ponderous material and informational structures that are so impressive in their detailed rationality. Emotional conviction is right when it sees existing conditions as irrational in their overall constitution. What is decisive here is that the process of cultural revolution not only *flows* at a distant horizon into the dialectical abolition of all government, of the traditional division of labour and the state, but that it can be palpably felt already in itself as the *road* to the greatest possible emancipation of the greatest number of people.

Before I go on to the question of the Action Programme, I would like to summarize in a few antitheses what the League of Communists, on the far side of capitalism, must be:

Not a workers' party in the old sense, which has long since become too narrow, but rather the organization of those emancipatory interests that are characteristic of all people in all strata of society;

Not a mass party of the kind in which a self-appointed leading elite manipulate the numbered members according to statistical laws, but rather the union of like-minded individuals, i.e. individuals of equal competence who are committed to solving the same problems in the same direction;

Not a corporation of those who know better, shut off in sectarian fashion from society, but rather a revolutionary community with an open periphery that lets society in;

Not a super-state that guides and controls the state and administrative apparatus proper from outside and above, but instead the ideological inspirer of an integral behaviour for all groups at the base, enabling the majority of members of society to take control of all processes of decision-making from within;

Not an obedient army that carries out the politbureaucratic consensus on the extension and preservation of the status quo, but instead the collective intellectual that creates and practises a consensus on changes in democratic communication.

Its major function, which it performs in all these capacities, will be the unification, coordination and direction of intellectual and moral efforts for elaborating a strategy and tactics of cultural revolution.

13

The Economics of the Cultural Revolution – I

There is no need to repeat here what has already been elaborated in Chapter 10 as to the foundation of the cultural revolution, a movement

– against the traditional division of labour,

– against the exclusion of the many from an education giving them the ability to participate in determining the social synthesis,

– against the patriarchal model of childhood that restricts development,

– against lack of community, and

– against bureaucracy.

We have rather to investigate now where the cultural revolutionary, communist movement can apply the lever, at what points in the existing mode of production and life its idea can first become a transforming material force. This is the problem of bringing the masses into the cultural revolution, of the realization of a majority consensus in a growing action which presses ever more deeply into the contradictions of the modern human situation. In the two previous chapters we have dealt with its social potential and its political preconditions (the renovation of the party, the achievement of democracy), as well as with its introduction by way of an anti-bureaucratic and anti-étatist breakthrough. On this assumption, the entire complex of cultural-revolutionary practice, positively formulated as the struggle

– for a redivision of labour,

– for a unitary form of education for fully socialized individuals,

– for children to be rendered capable of education and motivated for learning,

– for the conditions of a new communal life, and

– for the socialization (democratization) of the general process of knowledge and decision-making, can be conceived as the problem of the economics of the cultural revolution, the *radical political-economic alternative* that it counterposes to the existing economic system. This alternative must be drafted in the form of a programme by stages, directed towards the dynamization of social relations in the reproduction process, which constructively breaks through a status quo in which the social factors are presently in a stalemate situation vis-à-vis one another in the economic process, and brings the *political* debate over the new economics into the workplace.

I cannot undertake in these final chapters to put forward a global 'Political Economy of the Transition Period', apart from the fact that this formulation would already assume the simplification that we are dealing here with a process along the line *capitalism*-communism. I shall confine myself rather to a survey of the possible practical measures, or at least their general directions. And yet some summary remarks are necessary in advance, so as to indicate the place of such steps in the general framework of economic theory.

Since subalternity and alienation have their roots in economic relations, they must ultimately be attacked there too, whatever the tactics of this process might be. This much is generally agreed among Marxists. But it is of extraordinary importance that this core economic problem, the essence of the economic barriers, should be grasped correctly. In my view – which emerges of course from the whole of the preceding analysis – this core problem is located in the vertical division of labour which takes the general form of a hierarchy of labour functions (and of the levels of coordination of consciousness that correspond to these), and particularly a pyramid of managerial functions. This means that I see all theoretical approaches that seek to explain the political-economic problematic of actually existing socialism from the perspective of the particular categories of the capitalist economy as basically inadequate. On the basis of my concepts, such problems as the relationship of plan and market, or the more important question of the dominance of use-value or exchange-value in economic regulation, and even the far more fundamental dialectic of centralization and decentralization of disposal, only bear on three superficial layers of the non-capitalist economy.

It is quite untrue, for example, that the dominance of the plan as against that of the market guarantees that social interests are being carried through, let alone 'proletarian' ones, or even that it heavily implies this; rather the contrary. And it is similarly untrue, on the other hand, that the role played in our economy by the law of value and commodity production means that the plan is materially only a fiction, really being a vehicle of the market, because it still presupposes the market by *determining* (at least beyond simple reproduction) what society will demand (or will not demand, in which case the plan also presupposes the black market). It goes without saying that one reason why demand does not directly appear in the plan as far as its material (use-value) quality goes is because exports must be made to a world market that is essentially independent of it; but here exchange-values also mediate the concrete object of imports. One should not confuse the major *instrument* of bureaucratic control over the economy, the indicator of commodity production that is rightly the object of so much dispute, with the real content of the process of state planning. As I see it, there is no doubt that this is one of material accounting.

As far as the dilemma between centralization and decentralization goes, as a theme of 'economic reform' (and we must nowadays say dilemma rather than dialectic), it will remain an unproductive model of *inter*-bureaucratic activity, a tug-of-war between the *leadership* and the *middle* ranks of the *managerial* pyramid, as long as there is no autonomy for the social forces at the base that are outside the administration. Up till now, in any case, the centre still always enjoys a preponderant position. In case of conflict, *it* represents the overall social interest, no matter how alienated. The functionaries in the middle and at the base represent the unbridgeable gulf between the apparatus as a whole and the masses, or more exactly, the so far unorganized sum of emancipatory and compensatory interests.

The picture would of course change at one stroke if 'economic reform' were to be supplemented by 'social reform', i.e. if it really were undertaken by the unleashing of social forces. What would then exert pressure on the pyramid would no longer be the pale and weak particular interests of the managers, who would like to improve their conditions of work, life and survival. No, then it would be the *general* human interests (at first, of course, with a large compensatory component) that would leap over the dividing and protecting ditches; they would confront the corporate armour, bureaucratic solidarity would break down, and the human potential in the apparatus itself would begin to flow in the opposite direction. This is the storming of the power pyramid by the forces of society. We need only remember this, and think how economic problems would then stand, in order to recognize already at the intuitive level that it is not a question of plan or market, use-value or exchange-value, or even centralization or decentralization. Which is in no way to say that these problems would disappear; simply that their secondary significance would then be apparent. Given an overall social organization of labour, *political* democracy becomes the decisive constituting moment which determines whether the goals of the economic process, the qualitative contents of the plan, are decided by authentic social interests or rather by the restricted power relations and structures of knowledge within the bureaucracy. This idea, moreover, at least in intent, has already been inserted into the most recent Yugoslav constitution in the form of the so-called system of delegates.

And yet political democracy, for its part, does not come into being by the abstract good will of a leadership. It is not in the last instance a question of constitutional law. When I set out to write this final section, I was able to read some recent political-economic writings on the critique of actually existing socialism: Mandel, Bettelheim (only in quotation), and particularly the works of Renate Damus of the last few years, which present a theoretical conception very close to my own. But what struck me in these was a certain gulf between political analysis and analysis of political economy, which I would like to note here in passing. Ernest Mandel, it seems to me, is guided in his *political-economic* writings by the insufficiently restrained prejudices of the *political* assessment that Trotsky offered in his time on the premise that an immediate socialist perspective was possible for the Russian revolution. I cannot understand how, for example, it is still possible in the 1970s to insist that our bureaucracy is 'simply a parasitic excrescence of the proletariat', disposing 'of no political, social or economic mechanism with which to link its particular material interests' (and these certainly do not pertain just to the sphere of consumption) 'with the development of the mode of production from which it draws its privileges'.[1] With Renate Damus, on the other hand, his far more moderate political-economic approach remains somewhat abstract and unintentionally functionalist, even 'economist', in that he persists in his political conclusions in indirectly appealing to the better understanding of more or less 'high-placed' readers in the GDR. The economy of actually existing socialism has a different relationship to politics than does that of capitalism. It must be derived from 'politics', i.e. from the source of politics in the relations of power and domination in the labour process. This conclusion, in fact, already emerges from Renate Damus' own analyses.

The first problem for the practical economic policy of a Communist League is that of the initial kindling required to set society in fundamental motion from the base up, and to destroy the psychology of political inequality according to which those below have to ask modestly, and those above answer with authority. We know that the Czechoslovak economy in 1968 was functioning at least no worse than before. Output and productivity were rising, even though the reform movement showed itself extremely undecided about intervening in the economic process. By all appearances, there was, despite certain more coherent projects in individual heads, a fairly eclectic confusion of strivings that were in part trade-unionist, in part managerial and 'economic reformist', and in part in the direction of a democracy based on workers' councils. No guiding synthesis elaborated by the party was as yet evident, at least not one that was even approximately systematic (I do not see the report *Political Economy of the 20th Century* published by Richta and his group in Prague in 1968 as a suitable programmatic foundation, since it reflected too much the special

---

[1] *Internationale*, Special Number 3, p. 96.

interests of the privileged strata of the collective worker).[2] As a consequence, mobilization in the factories was on the whole far too slow, and above all far too superficial, being principally stuck in general political questions. In the last analysis, this is the root of the undeniable imbalance in the achievements of the reform movement, an imbalance in favour of the interests of intellectuals and managers, and which endangered the cultural-revolutionary perspective that was a possibility inherent in the situation. Slow as the process of civilizing transformation will be to penetrate down through the social formation, it is still necessary for some facts to be rapidly created in the first few moments, in order to set its dynamic in motion. In particular, the apparent inescapability of 'material compulsions' in industry, the hierarchical social structure of the labour process, and the absolute barriers of the division of labour within the factory, should not remain unchallenged in the phase of the first political upswing. To delay repeatedly all the necessary interventions to a later period of consolidation would mean confirming the existing industrial situation yet again, and with new emphasis, in its apparently self-evident and unimpugnable character.

There are an initial series of immediate measures to be taken, particular 'abolitions' which, however, also bear with them a constructive and positive tendency by their political and moral effect. I want to anticipate these here, so as to show in brief their revolutionizing function, before I go into them in somewhat more detail. The most important initial measures are:

– the liquidation of bureaucratic corruption from above, in all its open and hidden, sanctioned and unsanctioned forms;

– the abolition of piecework and work norms;

– the planned periodic participation of the entire managerial and intellectual staff of society in simple operative labour;

– a systematic revision of wage-scales according to simple and perceptible criteria, undertaken by way of a protracted consultative discussion at the base, with the aim of taking a decisive step toward just wage relations within the collective worker.

[2] This is available in German translation: Radovan Richta, *Politische Ökonomie des 20ten Jahrhunderts*, Frankfurt 1971.

Once these measures are seriously undertaken, even in a preliminary way, they will have the effect of cleansing the social atmosphere, bridging for once the gulf of silence between the political superstructure and the masses, and the clash of interests between the scientific, technical and economic intelligentsia and the workers on the shop floor, at least by making the lines of division more fluid. In particular, they will remove without expense some superfluous provocations that drive a large number of people, whose life chances are cut short already in childhood, to unproductive protest actions, providing a partial justification for undisciplined, destructive and unsocial behaviour. But they will not only lend the very pressing demand for solidarity in industrial cooperation the unchallengeable moral authority that it urgently needs. They have a positive mobilizing significance too, by showing society in a convincing way the *honesty of the revolutionary leadership, its desire for justice and its determination to restrain itself from any kind of enrichment and additional appropriation of privilege.*

Rudolf Herrnstadt[3] used the historical example of the upsurge of popular initiative at the beginning of the Jacobin dictatorship to emphasize the tremendous significance this had for the functional capacity of the new social relations, for their character as a new social *order.* He emphasized above all how the Jacobins managed to get everyone *working*, and moreover with a 'devotion never previously seen . . . even by people who had never been inclined to work'. (Subbotniks are in no way specifically socialist or communist, except in a very broad sense.) 'Some may have joined in from fear, others from curiosity, but the great majority worked enthusiastically because they finally felt at one with the course of world history.' Herrnstadt notes the sudden surplus of talent in all fields – and also that the Jacobin dictatorship had no problem with the youth: 'It had the young people on its side. The problem of the positive hero was unknown to it; it was generally seen as contemptible not to be a hero'. The form of national life was determined by a genuine dialectic between revolutionary government and popular organizations, above all

[3] *Die Entdeckung der Klassen*, Berlin 1965, pp. 183ff.

the communes. The Paris sections had a *de facto* veto; if they were
not in agreement with the Committee of Public Safety, then they
did not go along with its decisions. In between, as a mediating
link, there were the revolutionary clubs, quasi-fractions of the
revolutionary party, which did not yet have a formal existence.
But it was not this mechanism itself that was decisive. Rather,
'there were two reasons that enabled the entire ramified and often
contradictory organism of the revolutionary democratic dictatorship to function: 1) because it undertook far-reaching economic
changes' – at that time particularly land for the peasants and
maximum prices for means of subsistence and raw materials –
'which were long overdue and were beneficial to the masses;
2) because these changes were pursued under the stimulus of a
high moral principle'. Without the second of these conditions,
no regime can win over the people, no matter how much it tries
with social measures to do so. There was a standard of civic
virtue: 'honourable, self-sacrificing action in the interest of the
revolution: What have you done to be hanged if the counter-
revolution comes?' 'What was your wealth before 1793? how
much wealth do you possess today? If your wealth has increased,
then how?' And since the Jacobins were relentless in prosecuting
the profiteers of revolution, even in their own ranks, they won the
confidence of the people and unfettered their initiative. It is not
true that the greater part of individuals *never* act 'selflessly', or
that they only ever have contempt for a leader if he shows himself
a brother to them instead of a master. The Jacobins, and after
them the Bolsheviks, proved the contrary, for a lengthy period:
'They gave the distrustful masses, exploited for millenia, irrefutable proof of their honesty'. As far as immediate measures are concerned, it is not least in importance to achieve an atmosphere
inconducive to the demoralized and lumpen element. Historical
example should be instructive here.

In a broader perspective, the more comprehensive problem of
the right attitude towards the compensatory interests in cultural-
revolutionary practice has already been touched. I shall return to
it after some remarks on the immediate plan of economic action.

Firstly, the liquidation of bureaucratic corruption from above.

Anyone who holds political power automatically possesses power of disposal over relatively large portions of the surplus product. Nothing is more suited to arouse the distrust of the people, and nothing confirms to them more palpably that 'everything is just the same', than abuse of power by political activists and their retinue for the preferential satisfaction of their own compensatory needs, not to mention the corruption of a broader stratum in their wake. The corrupt elements who display such behaviour quickly see to it that the spirit of corruption becomes general and obligatory. In a very short while they create a climate in which the honest functionary who consciously tries to renounce these advantages is despised, not only as stupid, but as lacking *esprit de corps* and striving from unclear motives for positions which the hyenas have already occupied.

There is no harmless dose of this bureaucratic corruption from above. It is essential to combat its very beginnings, and to get right to its roots. In particular, it is completely impermissible to compare it, for example, with certain additional incomes which accrue spontaneously from the economic process to traditional social strata such as artisans. The chauffeur who fetches the bureaucrat from his front door, even though there is a perfectly good tram service, is incomparably worse (as a privilege) than the luxurious week-end allotment of the car repairer who has bought it with his work on the black market. Nor should the advantages that the intelligentsia draw from their connections in the system of higher education be compared with the systematic training of specialists for the most repressive branches of the bureaucracy with the aid of special salaries. When things have come to such a pass that the central party and state agencies accept official residences, luxury limousines, holiday villas and special clinics, then the only remedy is their wholesale ejection from power. The political revolution will undoubtedly have the support of the majority of the population if it decrees and carries through the following measures in the immediate course of the movement:

– Reduction of all salaries presently above the upper limit of the normal wage-scale. As all communists are aware, Lenin, and not he alone, held that 'the corrupting influence of high salaries – both upon the Soviet authorities . . . and upon the mass of the workers –

is indisputable'.[4] The conditions that led him to drop the principle of skilled workers' wages for managerial activity have long since ceased to obtain. What then hinders those who so firmly appeal to Lenin from putting this principle into practice? The differentiation of income among the mass of those involved in the reproduction process in its present form ranges in the GDR between say 500 and 1500 marks. Anything above this goes to people who are already privileged in other ways, and thus simply receive an additional reward for their bureaucratic obedience or for special services to the ruling power. Salaries or incomes of 3000 marks and upward can only be based on the exploitation of other people's labour, given our present average income. (This cut in salaries will of course also affect other people, for example certain monopolists in the artistic field, who may well work hard themselves, but create around them a semi-parasitic milieu.)

– Abolition of all special material, social, medical, cultural and other private support establishments of the apparatus, in as much as these do not serve demonstrable public purposes and are not kept within the bounds of the ordinary social establishments of factories, etc. Reduction of prestige expenditure in the broadest sense (buildings, cars, receptions, and much else); abolition of the government ghettos; reduction of personal security staff of government officials; an end to the special bureaucratic influence on admission to higher education, which tends among other things to turn over the occupancy of certain branches of the apparatus, such as the departments of internal and foreign affairs, to family tradition and other personal connections.

– An end to the petty-bourgeois pomp of honours and decorations, in particular the cancellation of all emoluments connected with these, with immediate effect. The whole hotch-potch of prizes and bonuses, which is for the most part a constant farce, is also urgently in need of control and at least a rigorous thinning out. It is necessary among other things to confine pensions and other compensation for resistance fighters and victims of fascism to the actual persons involved. The 'recognition' of acts of heroism in

---

[4] 'The Immediate Tasks of the Soviet Government', *Collected Works*, vol. 27, p. 250.

the revolutionary past in the form of material privileges of the most varied kind in the present, and for their heirs as well, can only be a source of shame for all honest fighters for socialism: it equates them with rebels of the type who dream of the villas and fleshpots of the old ruling classes. Moreover, the best of the old communists and socialists are compensated in this way only for what they must necessarily experience as the post-revolutionary society's betrayal of their former ideals. 'What did we struggle for, then?'

The leaders, activists and functionaries must share in the average material living conditions of the people. Where scarcity is not overcome, they must stand in line. They must live their private lives in the midst of the population and document by their everyday habits that they know themselves to be replaceable (which has nothing to do with the value of the person) and will shortly be ordinary workers again according to the constitution of the state and the social institutions. An organized public opinion must make sure that the government cannot again be denatured into the self-presentation of a corporation elevated over society. At least, the liquidation of bureaucratic corruption from above will make service in the apparatuses unattractive for the ordinary run of careerists and bureaucrats.

Secondly, the abolition of piecework and work norms. Nothing reminds the immediate producers under actually existing socialism so unmistakeably of the specifically capitalist past as the piecework 'deal'. What is it that piecework and norms ultimately reflect? Under what conditions is it necessary to fix in an obligatory way the output of the *individual* (beyond rough calculations of capacity)? The fixing of norms and financial incentives for individual performance only makes sense if 'society' thereby receives a higher surplus product, i.e. if individuals would save their energies and abilities without such inducements. This system presupposes, even if it does not try and drive the worker beyond the physiologically justifiable limit of intensity, that holding back on output is a normal reaction to the given character of work. In other words, it presupposes alienated labour in the dual sense that this takes place under relations of domination, and that the time spent on it is concretely lost, in the main, for the development and enjoyment of the individual involved. In a community based on solidarity, everyone would feel required by common morality to give of his best, so that comparisons and additional stimuli could have at most a moral significance in emulation between those individuals who were most successful at the activity in question. The real injustice would be seen as seeking to subject unequally gifted and developed individuals to the same demands.

No one could challenge the fact that piecework breaks down the solidarity of production workers both among themselves and with respect to their place in the industrial collective worker as a whole. It necessarily represents and ensures, both for those it affects and those who impose and operate it, an undignified and unjust social relation, and reproduces the conditions that underlie this. The very act of time-study as such represents an immoral and vicious relationship, a denial of solidarity and interdependence between equal partners at work.

The worker becomes the *object* of a procedure that he can only control in appearance, in its superficial immediacy, while in its systematic connection, which cannot be fully perceived without specialist knowledge, it is rather the procedure that controls him. The time-study process designates him as an 'applied force of nature', and this presumption is all the greater, the harder, more monotonous and more elementary is the effort to be rated. In addition, the norm makes an unjust distinction among the workers themselves, particularly at the limit separating production workers from staff, the technical and economic specialists as well as the actual management, a distinction between those who are subject to this procedure and those who are not. While everyone knows that more labour-time is wasted in the office than on the shop floor, it is precisely in those workplaces where the technology already most degrades people, by demanding for example endless repetition of simple operations, that the rate-fixer is busiest with his stop-watch.

It is evident enough that this opposite number of the worker also has his own role distorted. His performance is evaluated by the saving of time that he can measure and reckon. No other employee, neither foreman nor engineer, represents more clearly to the worker the rule of objectified labour, in which appears the rule of one man over others. The completely superfluous function in the hierarchy that he occupies symbolizes precisely the rift that divides the technical-economic intelligentsia and the rest of the management personnel from the production workers. The rate-fixer, more than anyone else, is continuously faced with the simple question, justified as much as in the past in terms of the classic distinction between labour and non-labour: 'Why don't you work?'

And in fact, why doesn't he work? Does the cost of rate-fixing in any way justify its results? For the chemical industry in the GDR, for example, an employment norm prescribes that one rate-fixer is to be employed in 1980 for between 30 and 60 production workers (depending on the character of the process). In order to have a positive effect, this rate-fixer must first of all save the approximately 1750 hours of effective labour-time that he could himself spend each year in production. A large portion of the saving in labour-time is purely nominal, since it bears on norm times that are in practice undercut. If for example a norm which prescribes an output of 100 items in eight hours is undercut by 20 per cent, and this improved performance is included in the future norm, then in the first place there is still the same 120 items, though a saving of 80 minutes' labour-time is counted. This means that the real growth in capacity is generally far lower than would be supposed from the saving of norm time that is calculated. The output may actually rise to 125 items. . . . On top of this, the foreman, concerned for the complement of his shift, in view of the shortage of labour-power, still has the option of compensating for the increased norm by allocating a greater portion of time to be paid at the average rate.

In the long run, modern technology is itself increasingly restricting the application of piecework and the assessment of performance with the stopwatch, in two ways: firstly, because the technical cycle more and more frequently determines output during the effective running time of the machinery; and secondly, because the labour spent in more complex production processes is a variable dependent on many kinds of disturbance, and would take far too long for the rate-fixer to assess. Where the worker can simultaneously influence a large number of variables, e.g. the quality of the product, the consumption of raw material, the functioning of the technology, the cycle time and the running time of the machines, it is impossible even to speak of 'technically based work norms'. The attempt to apply these then only acts as a further disturbing factor, generally a fairly considerable one, on the optimizing of the process, i.e. on the uninhibited use of mental productivity. In many cases, indeed, the average output even falls, as the worker will keep back in the norm a general reserve for eventualities, which he cannot therefore disclose in times of less disturbance.

All things considered, then, the rate-fixer can generally not even save the labour-time that he himself costs.

What remains therefore besides the general disciplinary effect of maintaining the intensity of labour that has been attained? Are work norms really necessary for this? Recently, their effectiveness is coming to be doubted even in the highly developed capitalist countries – and even though this effect is greater there than in our case. The capitalists are beginning to take to heart the fact already recorded by Marx that production on the basis of scientific technology gradually ceases to depend on the physical or psychophysical intensity of living labour. In 1970 striking miners forced Swedish state capital to experiment with abolishing work norms; wages were subsequently paid simply by time. It is instructive here that productivity did not decline, while the relaxation of the relationship with the workers improved the climate for technical and organizational rationalization. It seems that the countries of actually existing socialism plan to hold on to piecework longer than the capitalist countries, where its ambiguous influence on economic performance is gradually being recognized.

The situation of the pieceworker gives rise to protest and defensive behaviour, sabotaging the normal functioning of machinery and technology, costing quality and material, producing a solidarity against colleagues who produce more, increasing sickness, etc. The overall sum of mental energy that is spent or deducted for this is lost from the development of the productive forces, in fact it works against this both actively and passively. In the longer run and on an overall economic scale, the damage that piecework and norms cause are greater than the superficial benefit, even on a purely economic consideration.

Of course, the abolition of work norms should not be confused with an abandonment of indicative figures for the average expenditure of labour per unit of output, either within the factory or within society as a whole. Such figures, which have the character of guiding values for the calculation of costs and the proportioning of capacity, and also express a certain expectation of the individual worker's performance, are evidently necessary. What disappears is simply the linkage between these expected values and the level of wages, which is then fixed by a time-rate, one that may also be related to quality in as much as this is relevant. Work performance then depends on the socially influenceable situation in the work collective, on the creation of a certain attitude of readiness in its ranks as well as on the moral authority of the manager. Some workers may grow up to exhibit undisciplined or parasitic inclinations. Workers who despite correct and comradely advice do not deploy their skills, for whatever reasons, can either be given other activities more satisfying to them, or be deliberately withdrawn from the collective, without further discrimination. The general level of productivity has long been sufficient to give the human solidarity that was known in the most primitive communities a space in production; it is simply the egoistic customs nourished by the old economic system that for the time being still frequently prevent this.

The establishment of production figures will itself become far more simple and exact if the primary data do not have to be determined in the distorting conditions of a social contradiction of interest in the workplace, and if records, calculations, etc. do not have to be manipulated, with an eye to possible cases of conflict, as potential pieces of evidence in legal proceedings. 'Technically based work norms' exist as an economic reality only where they are in actual fact superfluous. Everywhere that 'labour-power' has an influence on the quantity produced, norms can only represent social compromises; their numerical precision is almost always fictitious. In a non-capitalist society, moreover, which both offers by and large a good deal of social security and programmes into its economy a constant shortage of labour-power, these compromises probably lead to a fairly moderate level of intensity in comparison with capitalism. The whole pseudo-scientific fuss and bother can thus simply be dispensed with. Once the effective labour-time or machine-running time per shift is known (and under present conditions observation of this naturally has the moral status of espionage against the workers), then production statistics assessed over a protracted period provide sufficient information as to the average output per unit of time or the average expenditure of time per work process or stage of manufacture, right through to the finished product. In this way information is also obtained as to real capacity, in as much as this depends on the quantity of labour-time available, and more-over at a far lesser expense than calculations on the basis of norm times, which then have to be corrected by a special statistic for the average norm fulfilment.

Thirdly, general participation is simple operative work. This measure is certainly not a panacea for the rift that divides the collective worker; it can only anticipate in an external way some-thing of what the redivision of labour is designed to achieve, and in particular it has no direct emancipatory function for the immediate producers. Yet it has more than the mere symbolic significance of expressing the solidarity of the privileged elements with the less skilled and developed strata. It will rather be an impulse that could scarcely be otherwise attained for all those who on the basis of the traditional division of labour practise principally managerial or creative activities, such as are favour-able to self-development, to concern themselves unremittingly and without a self-righteous idealization of their own position in society, with the causes and results of social inequality under actually existing socialism.

Functionaries at all levels, and intellectuals of every degree, need the enriching experience of direct participation in the condition of the majority who are largely disadvantaged in the present division of labour and education, and in the distribution of income as well. They should all for example experience what shift-work means. A form of regular and relatively protracted connection with certain work collectives must be created for them, naturally with maximum rationality in the allocation of personnel. The concept of 'involvement in production' would certainly be too narrow. I am deliberately speaking not simply of physical work in immediate production, even though discrimination against manual labour, and especially against factory work as such, is always the salient ideological point. There are forms of manual work that enhance creativity, and there is today a tremendous amount of strenuous and often mentally deadening routine work outside of material production, for instance in the service sector, in administration, and in data processing. Limitation to manual work would mean all too many exceptions for genuine or alleged reasons of health, and thus knock holes through a principle that should bear no exceptions, in particular no exceptions for those at the top.

If functionaries and intellectuals work long enough in certain particular collectives, for example some four to six weeks per year at a stretch, then a trusting communication would arise that could not be obtained in any other way. This could make a major contribution to bridging the considerable gaps of information and difficulties of understanding between the social strata, and in particular would eliminate the official disinformation process about political feeling at the base.

Systematic longer-term involvement of industrial engineers and other specialists in the production departments of their own factories or in related production processes could have a specific benefit of its own. At present, rationalization in the factories suffers from the inadequate knowledge of detail and personal interest of the specialists with regard to the various work processes and operations.

In the last analysis, the massive confrontation of functionaries and highly skilled people with everyday work in production and distribution, in the service sector and in administration, can only have fruitful results on all sides for the more rapid critical examination by the whole society of its apparatus of production and administration, and of its mode of production and life in general.

Fourthly, the rectification of the wage scale. The existing wage-scale in the East European countries is scarcely different from the capitalist (apart from the extremes being somewhat eroded), which it has taken over without any fundamental modification. Additional distortions have arisen both from the initial need, at the start of the anti-capitalist transformations, to bribe certain specialist groups, and from the subsequent need to give preferential satis-faction to workers employed in those branches most essential for reconstruction. On top of this came the consequences of invest-ment and structural policy in conditions of a permanent shortage of labour-power (in the more developed countries without a large reserve of agricultural workers an absolute deficit, but the lack of skilled labour-power can produce the same effect even in other cases). The leadership frequently sought to meet inherited or newly emergent disproportions in capacity with ad hoc modifi-cations of wage policy. Moreover, the interest of the apparatus in the political quiescence of the production workers, in their function as ballast for the ship of state against movements in the intelligent-sia, persistently drove them to distort the principle of reward according to work that was theoretically espoused in the relations of net wages or salaries to the disadvantage of the broad mass of college-trained specialists.

The most evident defect in the wage-scale consists in the way the same activities are rewarded at different rates as a result of these historical circumstances. This becomes particularly striking where functionally identical positions are involved. A technologist in a textile firm does essentially the same type of work as his colleague in engineering, but 'earns' on average far less. Attempts to rectify this have been periodically prepared by the central government and trade-union organs, but then abandoned in favour of further ad hoc efforts at the bottlenecks of the time, since the party is afraid to create too big a stir in society by a general solution. On top of this, it is really not worth the trouble – and this is the real problem – thirty or sixty years after the inauguration of non-capitalist relations, unless the undertaking is governed by a new socio-economic perspective.

Changes in the wage system have a more profound effect on economic relations than the three measures previously sketched out, at least if the establishment of a standard of equity in wages is conceived as a deliberate step towards the equalization of incomes, as the preparation of the cultural revolution requires. For the great majority of workers, this tendency towards equalization is already in progress even now, 'semi-spontaneously' via various government decisions, but in a manner that has no consequences for emancipation, since the objective intention under the existing relations of production is simply that of pasting over the more fundamental social contradictions and inequalities. Since moreover the principle of reward according to work is still maintained, the actual process fuels reactions of conservative discouragement from the more highly qualified elements, in particular the technical-economic intelligentsia in the factories, who on this question can easily take a position counter to the real perspective of historical progress. Interventions of this kind only function in a cultural-revolutionary sense if they *openly put in question the validity of the performance principle for the distribution of income and the use of so-called material incentives as the most important regulator of performance behaviour.*

It goes without saying that such interventions can only have the desired effect in a context which gives those social strata with the fullest demands suitable sublimated goals for their motivational energy. And the transformation also needs a certain time, both for the formation of public opinion – which is of course accelerated in a revolutionary situation – and above all for the accumulation of the resources for this adjustment to take an upward direction for the great majority of workers.

A strategic decision against continuing the policy of economic growth so far pursued – and this merely in parentheses here – can of course not be put into practice immediately. Growth is needed at first in order to pursue the structural change in the reproduction process without too much disturbing friction, among other things precisely on the question of incomes.

Seen from the theoretical standpoint, the equalization of incomes is the most immediate step possible and necessary towards overcoming wage-labour in the strict sense of the term. As long as sharply differentiated wages are paid, their connection to the reproduction costs of labour-power remains evident to the great majority of working people, despite all the ideological hair-splitting; allocation from the general consumption fund does not actually become the dominant relation. If we consider the problem from the standpoint of the *allocation* of income, then the first question is to establish the quantity that accrues to the individual, i.e. the amount of objectified labour per capita that is available for consumption. (In complex societies with a highly developed technical division of labour, this aspect remains generally relevant even though the problems of proportionality cannot be directly grasped; and in no way does it necessarily imply that the reproduction process is regulated by the law of value, not even if we take the position that money will remain indispensable as a unit of account and that the idea of a successive release of means of subsistence from monetary distribution is impractical.)

After those deductions from the total product whose necessity is in principle clear to all (i.e. leaving aside their level, concrete use, degree of centralization, etc.), then the product of a certain number of hours of abstract labour is planned to be available for distribution for the purpose of individual consumption. From this it is easy to reckon the average share that accrues to individuals or families, households, etc., and this is indeed how statistics are calculated. It is simply that this average arises at present via a differentiation that is impenetrable in practice even more than it is in theory, and has long lost all semblance of internal logic, a differentiation, moreover, which ties up an immoderate amount of direct and indirect labour, and scarcely still plays any role as an incentive to greater effort.

I have already said that equalization is advancing anyway; it is only a relatively thin upper stratum who break the normal limits of distribution, and for the most part they are not motivated principally by the financial stimulus, no matter how happy they may be with it. Social differentiation proceeds on the whole by different mechanisms. We could make the whole system very much more simple and cheap if we based it on the assumption that all individuals were to receive this average amount in their capacity as members of society. What is the purpose, for example, of the millions of calculations and book jugglings of income tax and social insurance payments? Actually existing socialism literally gives evidence of its poverty by acting as if it could still maintain the observance of the obligation to work and an intensity of work corresponding to the level of needs only by way of the primitive 'material lever' of class society. What is really reflected here quite uncritically is simply the fact, which is anyway undeniable, of the subalternity and alienation of individuals in their reproduction process, together with the consequences arising from this. Given the existing economic system, society in fact gets ever more deeply stuck in that system of incentives in which it is only the bonus that ensures a more or less adequate intensity and quality of labour. Individuals must look to recovering their costs outside of the work sphere, in private life, and hence try to get as much money as possible.

It goes without saying that the *principle* of equal consumption for all would lead to absurd results if we tried to apply it mechanically. The present differentiation, which in so far as it is still enforced, is according to quality and the functional level of work, and thus follows the rule 'To him that has shall be given' (i.e. to him that has work that promotes personal development and hence also needs), is no compensation, but rather an additional reinforcement, for the inequitable division of development opportunities, education and work. The new differentiation will act in the opposite sense. No addition for creative and development-promoting work. If society pays the costs of education and lets each have his share in consumption during the education period too (certainly not necessarily from the beginning in full), then there is no longer any reason for this, particularly since the acquisition of education is already a reward in itself, and develops the spirit and sensibility for higher and more differentiated enjoyment. Restrictions are needed only on individuals who culpably shirk for a long period from making their contribution to reproducing the conditions of life. Compensation, however, is due for heavy work, monotonous work, unpleasant work, night-work, in short for all work that acts against the possibilities of development (as long as this is not shared more or less equally among all). This solution has long been already pressing itself into practice in an unplanned way. (And here, moreover, we see the price-regulating component that wages contain, as long as there is no direct distribution of labour-power. Society must bring into the correct proportions the supply and demand for labour-power in the various more or less attractive branches and activities. If no one can be found for important activities, on account of their unpleasantness for the individual, it is not unfair to allocate additional income for these jobs until the places are taken.)

Two things alone still remain to be settled. Firstly, the duration of labour-time, to which the same principles are to be applied in as much as this is differentiated, as well as also bringing stronger hygienic and educational principles to bear. And secondly, an adjustment for the number of family members not taken care of by a job or other social institution, in particular children. It goes without saying that pensions have to be taken into account in this equalization, and also brought into approximate agreement with the average share.

All members of society would accordingly have more or less the same claim over abstract labour. Given the considerable degree of free play above the existence minimum, this would not impair the qualitative diversity of their structure of needs. On the contrary, from this aspect too, barriers specific to each stratum and its capacity for enjoyment and experience could more quickly be broken down. Individuals could choose between means of satisfaction and development that are very different in their concrete use-value and purpose, as to which of these they wanted to spend their individual share of the surplus product on. Assuming a supply in approximate proportion to these needs (however much they might change), I can consume my share according to my inclination primarily on a comfortable home or on travel abroad, on *haute cuisine* or an extensive library (as has long been the case in the developed countries, irrespective of the unequal shares, with economic compulsion ever more seldom involving an absolute renunciation of certain standard enjoyments in favour of others). Every individual in the GDR, for example, could already 'afford everything' they might need for a rich development of their personality.

On this whole question of relations of distribution, a passage from the early French communist Jean-Jacques Pillot, written in 1840, is more applicable than ever: 'Everyone owes it to society, in return for what he receives, to exercize all his abilities for the better well-being of all. The law of equality dictates the basic rule: Whoever does what he can do, does what he should do'. 'The capacities of the body such as health and strength, and the capacities of the mind such as power of thought and acumen, do not posit any distinction between one person who possesses particularly much, and another who possesses particularly little, other than that one has a greater task to fulfil than the other. The various functions that the administration of the republic or commune require are all simply duties which every citizen fulfils for the better good of the society; they cannot be for those who exercize them either a reason or a pretext for distinctions in the satisfaction of physical or intellectual needs.'[5]

The common denominator of all these initial measures is their function as a connecting link between the achievement of political democracy and a fundamental change in the structure of social needs. They are certainly only possible – this we took for granted – after politbureaucratic absolutism is overthrown, i.e. after the balance of forces between the *emancipatory* interests and the interests of the *apparatus*, which last has so far been decisive, has been shifted significantly in favour of the former. Then, however, a *further* balance of forces immediately becomes the focal point of the movement and is decisive for its future destiny, for ensuring it both against a direct étatist counter-revolution and against gradual bureaucratic restoration: the balance of forces between the *emancipatory* interests and the *compensatory* interests. And these immediate measures have a strategic bearing precisely on this balance.

It is a question of the highest importance how the cultural revolution is to conduct itself with respect to the compensatory needs of the masses. Taken in themselves, the compensatory interests are for the most part a reservoir of political conservatism. In order to subordinate or neutralize them, we need not simply direct political action, but also a further struggle between the tendencies of politbureaucratic reaction and the cultural-revolutionary movement. In dealing with the compensatory interests, a

[5] From Höppner and Seidel-Höppner, *Von Babeuf bis Blanqui*, Vol. 2, Leipzig, 1975, pp. 462ff.

completely different position is required than against the interests of the apparatus, and not just because what is at issue here is a contradiction within the surplus consciousness. The compensatory interests are anchored much deeper in the life process of individuals. The problem raised by their predominance in the surplus consciousness can in no way be solved by a political blitzkrieg carried out at a favourable moment. Spontaneously, i.e. left to themselves, the compensatory interests become demands for short-run compensation for the degradation and constriction of the personality that is suffered, with a tendency to become prophylactic anxiety reactions to any proposed change in social possession of privileges, goods, prestige positions, conveniences, etc.

Marxism, by starting to unravel the tangle from its material end, by giving first place to the question of the conditions of development of the under-privileged masses, has the greatest opportunity of solving the problem in a practical movement. If Marxist analysis suggests a special role for the intellectual strata in the present situation, it does this in no way to flatter the traditional pride of the intelligentsia, but rather to determine its tasks in the overall process of general emancipation. It is decisively against any misinterpretation of the concept of freedom in the sense of political liberalism. The working people have gained very little, at least immediately, by the intellectuals winning the freedom to shine unrestrained and eloquent in the mass media. The doctrine of the leading role of the working class is highly problematic, as I have discussed at some length, but the *political and moral intention behind it,* where it expressed the duty of progressive intellectuals to the cause of general emancipation, will only become obsolete when the categorical imperative of the young Marx is fulfilled.[6] Its original significance is active solidarity with the most oppressed, without whose liberation all emancipation must remain half-unfinished and thus false. It is necessary to shake the intelligentsia out of their spontaneous class feeling against those less developed, to make them conscious of the reality and extent of their privilege (which involves understanding the mechanisms

[6] See above, p. 24.

of motivation and character formation and their social mediation), and the extent to which their frustrations are precisely bound up with the way that others are also frustrated and seek with similar spontaneity to escape from the unfair conditions of competition in school and factory, for example by lack of pleasure in learning in childhood, later by holding back on productive effort, lack of care for materials and machinery, etc.

Above all, it must be recalled yet again that society does not break down into classes or even strata of individuals with compensatory needs on the one hand, and with emancipatory needs on the other. It is precisely the intellectualized strata who react by seeking refuge in a private lifestyle for which very many consumer goods are 'absolutely necessary', to a frustration that is occasioned by the political state of affairs. In our society it is a general rule that *arrivistes* and the privileged can satisfy their compensatory needs very well, while the masses can do so only relatively poorly. Those who are disadvantaged in this way do not enjoy any kind of advantage of innocence, but are bought off with the less valuable products of material and intellectual culture. In these compensatory needs, too, there is naturally a dialectic of progress. In the means of consumption the two types of need that are different in the abstract are united in the concrete individual. What it boils down to is their arrangement in the individual life process, what enjoyment actually means here and now. There exists a social structure of their use and consumption. We cannot and should not seek to break through the reproductive circle of the production and consumption of needs by a policy of reducing consumption, which would be borne by those strata who are already disadvantaged and would lead to the intensification of social contradictions along the wrong lines. On the contrary, in order to lead society out of the vicious circle, we must bring about a genuine equalization in the distribution of those consumer goods that determine the standard of living. Up till now, an advance for those at the bottom has always been measured against the *consumption* of those at the top, in other words against their appropriation of material goods, sensual and cultural enjoyments, and not by disposal over the social process, let alone a cultural revolutionary sublimation that can dispense with material wealth.

In my opinion, we can conclude that *a levelling of society with respect to the quantity of consumption would be the condition for rising above the principle of quantity, above compensatory consumption.* A policy of this kind would also have the tendency to limit the development of new luxury needs and in the long run put a brake on the growth of material needs in general, which is primarily driven forward by the social inequality of powers of appropriation.

The concept of the cultural revolution thus pursues the goal of draining as great as possible a quantity of motivational energy from the compensatory complex. On top of the positive attraction of surplus consciousness by political activation, something must happen to *neutralize certain pressing and massively present compensatory needs, at best, moreover, by their relative satiation.* First of all, this would involve the adjustment of the most elementary social injustices in income distribution, and a first approach also to those in powers of decision-making. This equalization would aim above all at unburdening the cultural-revolutionary movement to tackle the profound transformation of the structure of needs, shifting the focus of the struggle of social interests away from the appropriation of material means of subsistence and enjoyment that is characterized principally by consumption, and towards the appropriation of culture (which of course also means a different structure of material consumption). The danger of an 'explosion' of material needs is particularly threatening for the transition situation, while equalization of incomes is the most important initial measure, and one which equally offers scope for the relatively undisturbed practice of new habits.

If in the socialist motto 'From each according to his abilities, to each according to his work', it is the second part of the formula that most merits attention, in the communist motto 'From each according to his abilities, to each according to his needs', it is rather the first part. Taken to its logical conclusion, the demand is that of *abolishing the principle of reward according to work* (with respect to the distribution of incomes) *in order to realize it* (with respect to the exercize of abilities). The two slogans from the *Critique of the Gotha Programme* are far less commensurable than they might literally appear. The problem as to the possibility or impossibility of an unlimited satisfaction of needs will prove devoid of any object, merely a reaction to the present conditions, once we break out of the reproduction cycle of compensatory interests. For then the expansion of material consumption beyond a certain threshold will be of disservice to those who pursue it. It will be recognized as an obstacle to the self-realization of individuals. As Sève has well shown in his book on Marxism and personality (see above, p. 180), the proportions of time spent on various activities, which is what constitutes the personality, are shifting in the direction of an undue prevalence of psychologically unproductive consumption (as distinct from psychologically productive consumption). The individuals set in this direction are impeded in that 'accumulation activity', the accumulation of abilities and knowledge, which is decisive for their social worth and their relations with others. Such people are then viewed with the same mixture of sympathy and mild disdain with which we are already accustomed to consider people in sufficiently prosperous countries who 'live for food'.

The far-reaching elimination of material incentive provides the basis for clearly establishing for the first time in mass social practice the new driving force of intersubjective emulation, the unequal division of abilities and activities which is to be the central theme of the cultural revolution, and presenting this to the general consciousness as a problem. For important as equality in the sphere of consumption is, it still pertains to the periphery of the cultural revolution, which bears on the *content* of needs, and inherently remains more of a means than an end. Yet this periphery must first be secured, in order to organize the forces for the transformation of civilization, and lead these ideologically so far beyond the old structures that they can be reorganized in a new way. In other words, the question here is to produce freedom of movement for the emancipatory interests, to conquer a terrain on which they can stretch out and expand. The communist strategy therefore consists in bringing about a situation in which people can place their immediate interests in relation to the general possibilities and requirements of the epoch, and can rise above all those appropriations that restrict their cultural development. At the same time, communists will avoid acting in any merely restrictive manner towards these compensations, being well aware that the decisive equalization of material conditions of existence for all members of society is the precondition for gradually overcoming the compensatory orientation of interests and hence the complete dissolution of the former relations of distribution.

In this way, the starting-point will be won for a breakthrough into the cultural-revolutionary process proper: for doing away with the traditional division of labour, the source of all sub-alternity and alienation, by way of far-reaching interventions in the distribution of labour, in the conditions of socialization and education of individuals, and in the forms of regulation of the reproduction process. This process should not be conceived simply as a mechanical succession. The very project of sub-ordinating or neutralizing the compensatory interests can only get off the ground if the elimination of financial stimuli for the masses is linked with much more far-reaching hopes and per-spectives, so as simultaneously to build up the new motivations and avoid the disorganizing effects that otherwise would be temporarily inevitable.

14

The Economics of the Cultural Revolution – II

The positive economic task of the cultural revolution can be summarized in a single concept: *to create that new organization of labour and social life on which it will at last be possible to base a community that deserves the old name of a free association of individuals in solidarity.* This is a society in which there is no longer any domination of man by man, since the ground is removed for those social inequalities based on subordination to subaltern work functions. The organization of labour on an overall social scale is the heart of the ultimate problem of economic emancipation, and with its solution we already have the beginning of emancipation *from* economics, i.e. from its dominance over the social whole. Transformation of the organization of labour naturally has the result of reprogramming the *entire* economic system, the overall relationship between production and needs, as well as the informational regulation of the reproduction process. What is involved here is man's self-liberation from the rule of reification, from the fetishization, directed against individuality, of the produced material world. Both the growth of production and the growth of labour productivity, which in the past were very seldom critically questioned, will lose *in practice* their halo of indispensable economic requirements, which does not mean making a new law of 'zero growth', but rather *displacing the criterion of quantity from its dominant position.*

If a society is so far industrialized that it can fairly reliably satisfy the elementary needs of its members at the level of culture that has been attained, then the planning of the overall process of reproduction must be gradually but decisively transformed to give *priority* to the all-round development of human beings, to the increase in their positive capacities for happiness. Non-capitalist industrial society is on the whole rich enough for this, or at least at the threshold where it becomes possible, although, as we have already argued, if the supremacy of the former economic system continues it will *always* appear too poor. Those economists who are so quick to produce calculations of what 'we cannot afford', always take the existing structure of material needs as a tacit assumption. Material insatiability costs us our freedom for higher development, subjects us to mental regulations which rest on compulsion, and produces a miserly social attitude. And yet the discontent of individuals with the existing civilization, which is ever more widespread, has long since signalled a contradiction that would make the former mode of life untenable even if the reduction or deterioration of resources set no limits to material expansion. Historical examples show, moreover, that the same or similar results of human development and human happiness are compatible with fairly great differences in the quantity of disposable products. In no case can the conditions for freedom be measured in dollars or rubles per head. What people in the developed countries need is not the extension of their present needs, but rather the opportunity for self-enjoyment in their own individualized activity: enjoyment in doing, enjoyment in personal relations, concrete life in the broadest sense. The remoulding of the process of socialization in this direction will be characterized first of all at the economic base by a systematic reapportioning and restructuring of living labour and accumulation in favour of the conditions of development for human subjectivity.

This is the maximum programme of the cultural revolution, which has now to be investigated in greater detail in a series of derivative aspects:

– The goal of production as rich individuality, i.e. a remoulding of planning and organization in all areas of the national economy and science, revision of their criteria of efficacy with a view to realizing the unity of the labour and education process (unity of production and appropriation of culture), opening up of a general space for freedom for self-realization and growth in personality in the realm of necessity itself;

– A new determination of the need for material goods and the availability of living labour from the standpoint of the optimization of conditions of development for fully socialized individuals (priority of expenditures for education), instead of from the standpoint of the traditional demand for material values, in such forms of political democracy as make possible a social process of education and research with the broadest participation of the masses;

– A more harmonious form of reproduction, i.e. a shift of priorities away from the exploitation of nature by material production towards the adaptation of production to the natural cycle, from expanded reproduction to simple reproduction, from the raising of labour productivity to care for the conditions and culture of labour; development of a technique and technology that accords with nature and man, the re-establishment of proportionality between large-scale (industrial) and small-scale (handicraft) production;

– Accounting for a new economy of time, i.e. the displacement of preference in planning, statistics and the measurement of production away from the basis of price towards that of labour-time – labour-time accounting as an instrument for working towards an economic structure on the human scale;

– Individual initiative and genuine communality, i.e. construction of a form of economic regulation that gives the basic units of combined labour and social life a broad scope for the preconditions of plan realization and ensures them the proportional development of their own structure; society as an association of communes.

These demands, too, must finally be translated into measures that can be directly undertaken. A certain institutional ability, above all a political organization that is really manageable, even given controversial discussion over the next steps to be taken, was already presupposed even for the immediate measures. It must be ensured all the more, and re-ensured time and again, when the process enters its more mature stage. The question for the leadership will be at what point to begin, where first to concentrate the forces for the breakthrough. Here I intend to anticipate the basic ideas, since it will then be easier to define the operative functions of the partial aspects mentioned. For the systematic connection does not imply any temporal sequence, and still does not give any indication as to which link in the overall network is decisive for action.

This key link is given by the analysis of the balance of forces in social consciousness. *The production of surplus consciousness that is already in train spontaneously must be vigorously pursued in an active way, so as to produce quite intentionally a surplus of education* which is so great, both quantitatively and qualitatively, that it cannot possibly be trapped in the existing structures of work and leisure time, so that the contradictions of these structures come to a head and their revolutionary transformation becomes indispensable. The emancipatory potential that is gathered in this way, and finds itself under too great a pressure in the confines of the existing conditions, has no other way out than by attacking the traditional division of labour in the reproduction process. Already, the economic leaders of both systems are complaining of a surplus of over-qualified people, for whom there is 'no work', i.e. no place in the plan and its compartments. If these compartments are already occupied, then society can adapt itself accordingly, and not spread any more knowledge than can be turned to profit by the scientific and technical factory system in its present social constitution. It would be dangerous, however, to try and chain people who are motivated to creative work by the character of their education, year in and year out to those stultifying activities that are continuously allocated to unskilled people and trainees (with particular preference to women), and quite often even to skilled workers. If the existing division of labour is to remain, then the rate of education should rather be reduced than raised.

The cultural revolution demands the opposite policy, in which the main point is naturally not simply a numerical increase in specialized skills. It has to break with the principle of regulating education according to the requirements of isolated compart-mentalized job positions, and direct itself towards all those conditions of development that favour the massive creation of fully socialized and free people. The organization of industry and science will then be adapted to the needs of the most comprehensive polytechnical and polyscientific education, and of the growth of the personality in general. All those genuinely developed individuals that society already possesses will become non-professional teachers to young people, irrespective of their other functions. There is no reason to believe that this kind of humanistic turn would necessarily reduce the total product and the overall level of productivity, even in the short run. Marx, as we well know, assumed the direct opposite in the longer term. At least in those spheres in which specialized intellectual labour is now performed, there are indications that the traditional principles of rationalization are killing off the motivation for creative effort. In any case, the cultural revolution will lead society out of that situation in which the output of industry in a certain unit of time is treated as the decisive criterion of progress. If society organizes both education and production in such a way that all individuals can acquire a general scientific and artistic education at the highest level in corresponding theoretical and practical activity, making it possible for them to get a differentiated appropriation of the social whole, then this potential makes the redivision of labour and the self-management of all social affairs a practical necessity.

This attack on the core substance of the relations of domination, however, cannot be pursued without a plan. The complex economy of highly industrialized societies cannot bear the shock of disorganization. The economic revolution, for all the radicalism of its aim, must have the form of an orderly transformation, and must therefore pay heed from the start to the systematic connection between the aspects of action outlined in the above list – without this making any claim to completeness – also maintaining due proportionality between the labour-power available. This makes it urgently necessary to think the entire complex of consequences through in advance. We would require collective simulations using the most realistic models possible. It would be quite justifiable to object that battle-plans are seldom or never as realizable in practice as they seem on the strategic drawing-board. And yet they are still indispensable, so as to make at least the activists familiar with the terrain of operations and with the various aspects of the situation that they have to expect.

Firstly, rich individuality as the goal of production. In non-capitalist production people are still organized as if for a war of survival, with new final reserves being sent each day to the front. In this realm of necessity there can be no secure scope for the free self-realization and growth of the personality. The emancipatory interests are largely excluded from it. It was in this sense that I treated production in Chapter 11 purely as a sphere of absorbed consciousness. It could well be said that this was a simplifying abstraction. This is certainly true, and it was also elaborated simply from the standpoint of the *political* analysis that we were concerned with there, and thus without any broader relation. Undoubtedly, even in its present form, based more than ever on *a priori* abstract labour, production gives rise not only indirectly but also directly to developmental impulses for particular individuals and groups. Yet these are accidental effects; they only fill minimal portions of these individuals' time, and seldom have any bearing on the central driving forces of personality development. Yet it is precisely towards the latter that production has to be reoriented. The strict boundary between the realms of freedom and necessity must be crossed by freedom.

In positing this goal, we cannot avoid standards that, as a result of the ideological defeat of alienation in official science since the beginning of the industrial age, have been ever more stubbornly underestimated, and only in the last few decades have again begun to come fully to consciousness, standards deriving from certain anthropological constants. Present-day Marxism-Leninism, as a result of its tie to the non-capitalist short cut to industrialization, has a profound distrust of anthropology; there is scarcely any point on which it must misconstrue Marx more fundamentally than here. Where Marx establishes that under conditions of alienation in general, and capitalist relations in particular, human nature is squashed by an economic process that becomes autonomous from the overall human connection, and can therefore not offer any firm point for the transformation of these conditions, Marxism-Leninism makes the *salto mortale* of declaring the whole anthropologically established basis as pre-historical, i.e. historically irrelevant, and excluding it from the materialist conception of history. Since it has ideologically to justify a system in which alienation flourishes, it precisely surrounds the phenomenal forms of appearance of alienation that are characteristic of this system with the illusion of perpetuity. Where it encounters the demand for freedom, it is quick to stigmatize this as an extra-historical illusion of absolute lack of restriction, so as to occlude and obscure the present barriers that stand in the way of human emancipation. (It is no accident that precisely the 'most liberal' party leadership, i.e. the Hungarian, saw itself compelled to practise this last conjuring trick in a particularly exemplary way.)

Original Marxism, I would like to recall once again, sees communism as a perfected naturalism, and in this connection it considers individuality not simply in a historical and relative sense, but also as the point of intersection of these fundamental needs of the human species:

– for a security of existence based on membership of society;

– for the developmental stimulus of social (or socially mediated) communication;

– for social confirmation and recognition of individuality as the highest self-related value;

– for the use of all developed individual powers in the sense of self-realization through autonomous action in the context of a community.

Precisely what is concretely meant by rich individuality at any particular time is completely determined by the actual historical situation, by the given level and diversity of culture. But it is quite untrue that, as Ranke put it, 'each epoch is equally close to God'. Firstly, because ever since the demise of primitive communism objective wealth could only be unequally appropriated, for reasons of class, and secondly, because different epochs were structured either *more* or *less* antagonistically in relation to the anthropogenetically formed basic social requirements. Capitalism, for example, is *the* epoch *par excellence* that is 'distant from God'. Still more than the material structure of cultural goods, it is often the manner and form of their actual appropriation that contradicts the natural measure of man. (Consider for example, as an extreme case, the abstract appetite of the money-lender as described by Balzac). There is a kind of psychology whose laboratory experiments nourish the conformist prejudice that this is simply a question of 'conditioning', and that people can become adjusted to any kind of situation. But it should not be forgotten that what this psychology manipulates as 'man' is simply an isolated and artificially prepared 'construct' of attributes, and that it refuses, for good and inherent reasons, to say anything about human subjectivity as an individual character, or about the conditions of human happiness. *One* of the essential preconditions for a cultural-revolutionary economic policy is a theory of development of human individuality, dominated neither by a fetishism of 'objective requirements', nor by the impressive adaptability of the psyche, and daring to make normative assertions.

The communist demand, in short, is that the overall production and reproduction of material life should be reshaped in such a way that man covers his expenses as an individual – to use an expression that reflects the prevailing alienation. This naturally assumes a quite different mode of social accounting from that customary today, one which, while always leaving a remainder, has nevertheless to be pursued all the more patiently and obstinately. No one can speak of failure on this score, since the attempt has never yet been made. The experiences of small groups naturally prove very little, even positively, if the practice of certain primitive communist communities was not already proof enough. We are dealing now with societies which are no longer even remotely covered and held together by a network of primary communal relations, and whose practice cannot directly be made sensibly perceptible. The question is how and by what criteria proportionate development of a major national economy has to be planned, if the goal of rich individuality is to have practical effect. For this is certainly not produced in the normal course of economic growth, as the official economic doctrine would have us believe.

'Real economy – saving – consists of the saving of labour-time', says Marx.[1] But Marx sees the purpose of this as being 'to reduce labour-time for the whole society to a diminishing minimum, and thus to free everyone's time for their own development', because 'the *surplus labour of the mass* has ceased to be the condition for the development of general wealth'. Capital on the other hand

---

[1] *Grundrisse, loc. cit.*, p. 711.

always strives 'on the one side, *to create disposable time, on the other, to convert it into surplus labour'*, so that it always 'posits wealth itself as founded on poverty, and disposable time as existing *in and because of the antithesis to surplus labour-time'*.[2] The party and state bureaucracy behave analogously to capital in as much as they are guided by the attempt to appropriate abstract labour, surplus labour-time, the substance of value, and use its congealed weight as a means of domination. The aim in this case is of course not profit as such, but rather the legitimation of power, still against the same background as in the Biblical story of Joseph. The granary has to be full if Pharaoh is to maintain his power over the people in the seven lean years.

But from this basis the antithesis between labour-time and free time, social production and private consumption, pervades the whole form of life of actually existing socialism, and the boundary between the realms of freedom and necessity is inevitably crossed by necessity: live, learn, consume, relax, enjoy, so as to reproduce labour-power for the next production cycle. From top to bottom, this is the vicious circle of the old economic system. To break through it is the genuine major task that justifies the existence and leading role of a communist party, and which the new League of Communists will have as the major field of its activity. For it is on this that depends the scope that the overall context of social life offers to the free development of individuals, the development of rich individuality.

The main condition is the shortening of the working day, as Marx laconically sums it up. This was at a time when there were still six working days in the week of some ten to twelve hours each. Today in the developed countries we are not far from having halved this. In the USA, Western Europe and Japan productivity is so high that capital, under state-monopoly direction, must itself take the initiative, for the first time in its history, in shortening working hours, so as to master unemployment in the recession phase of the trade cycle. A working week of five six-hour days, for example, would no longer place a quantitative barrier on individuals. The 'non-labour of the few' (including its more concealed

[2] pp. 705, 708.

forms) would have *decisively* ceased to be the condition 'for the development of the general powers of the human head'.[3] And yet experience since Marx's day has shown that the growth of free time is expressed only to a very limited extent in emancipatory effects, since the modes of activity conjured up by society presuppose both in working time *and* free time the subaltern character of the mass of individuals, which moreover even dominates the education sector. The shortening of the working day is thus not sufficient.

It seems to me that Marx's perspective on this point is somewhat unclear, in that, as has often been noted, he ultimately leaves the question of the *relationship* between the realm of necessity and the realm of freedom somewhat vague. The heart of the problem seems to be that he did not manage to elaborate explicitly at the level of *Capital* (the celebrated passage in Volume 3, Chapter 48, section 3) that dialectic between ability and activity that he had set down so clearly in the *Economic and Philosophical Manuscripts.* In the *Grundrisse,* the perspective is formulated as follows: 'The free development of individualities, and hence not the reduction of necessary labour-time so as to posit surplus labour, but rather the general reduction of the necessary labour of society to a minimum, which then corresponds to the artistic, scientific etc. development of the individuals in the time set free, and with the means created, for all of them'.[4] The intention in the second half of this sentence is clear enough, but it can still be asked whether the unmediated dichotomy between 'artistic, scientific etc. development' and 'necessary labour', which is inherently antagonistic, does not somewhat efface the real problem. The reduction of necessary labour to a minimum – indeed, in so far as necessary labour is alienated labour, or, more comprehensively, activity that is psychologically unproductive and rapidly also becomes redundant for physical adjustment. But the real question is whether the sharp division between necessary labour (in the more general sense) and free activity, even if it cannot be demolished (which would surely be too much to hope), cannot at least be made

[3] *Grundrisse, loc. cit.*, p. 705.
[4] p. 706.

somewhat permeable. Participation in all functionally characteristic varieties of necessary labour is becoming more strongly than ever before one of the most essential means for the appropriation of culture. The sense of reality in most intellectuals suffers greatly from their lack of a closer conception of what is still the central sphere of the overall social totality, and from an all too vague idea, or belief, about what economics is really concerned with, particularly in conditions of highly developed technology.

I propose to add to the demand for a reduction of necessary labour-time, so as to make this more precise with respect to the present situation: *priority for the shortening of psychologically unproductive labour-time within necessary labour-time.* This would have a series of important concrete implications for the planning and organization of the reproduction process, which would eventually bring about a gradual redistribution of labour, while being primarily aimed at expanding the scope for appropriating higher-level relationships by psychologically productive activities within the sphere of labour. Socialist economic planning must always *proceed from living labour,* i.e. *directly* from the balancing of social labour-time and its connection with the structure of needs, and not first of all from the balancing of the material stock, i.e. from objectified labour. Besides, from the standpoint of the production goal of rich individuality, we must even take a step further, a step back behind the *balancing of labour-time,* and begin with the social *balancing of time in general, with the time budgets of individuals as such,* taking this as the starting-point for anchoring the equality of development opportunities, at first quantitatively, in the contextual conditions of individual time schedules. It is particularly necessary to ensure that educational activities in *youth* reserve for *all* individuals the time needed for the goal of education sketched in Chapter 10 (which does not mean that the *way forward* lies necessarily – let alone exclusively – in the form of an expansion of the present system of higher education).

What would then take pride of place in planning is a *new economy of time.* This is *the* economy of time which Marx had in mind for the realm of freedom: the deliberate allotment of time for all-round development and satisfaction on a social as well as an individual scale.[5] This new economy of time will also save costs (*abstract labour-time*), but in the first place it will secure *concrete living time*. Its 'goal function' comes to be the maximization of 'time for development', 'time for the productive appropriation of culture'. Living time as a space for development – this is precisely what rich individuality is, seen as a process in a specific culture. As already indicated, economic planning provides the contextual conditions, as far as lies in its power, i.e. the markers for the individual's time schedule, and in this way it indirectly has a striking influence on the qualitative possibilities contained in it, the existing dispositions for individual activity far beyond necessary labour-time, in certain circumstances negatively so, down to an inurement to absolute inability of concentration.

The first problem that demands a completely new response, as a sign of the primacy of living labour in planning, concerns the economic *reserves in relation to the plan,* which cannot be restricted to the problem of a centralized state reserve. For all the official discussion there is on this point, it is not sufficiently understood either practically or theoretically, i.e. in its overall *social* significance. From the practical standpoint, planning should no longer begin with laying down the rate of growth, whereupon the question of the reserve emerges only in the distorted form as to at what point disturbances would become *unbearable.* The most far-reaching theoretical approaches have been made from the aspect of economic cybernetics. It would be more consistent to proceed from the bio-cybernetic analogy. As is well known, the stability of the organism's life process is ensured by its elements being multiply represented at the most fundamental cellular level, so that the more complex levels, up to the specialized organs, have reserves to draw on. (Reserves that for the economy would consist of 'organizational' and 'technological' capacities.) Social theory seems to have remained to a large extent unaware of how persistently the economy of permanent shortage poisons the entire work and life of proto-socialist industrial society, as a phenomenon not of poverty but rather of economic regulation. If the state of public health in the highly industrialized non-capitalist countries

[5] *Grundrisse*, pp. 171–3.

of Europe is not qualitatively superior to that in the capitalist countries, then one of the most fundamental reasons is that in our case the stress of the hunt for profit and income has found an 'equivalent' pathological substitute.

In official economic theory, the problem of reserves is generally introduced in the context of discussion over more intensive development, at least by the more profound writers, who see more in this term than the ultimate percentage capacity that could still be put to service in the current or forthcoming annual plan. But not even in theory has the attempt been made to determine measures which would give genuine precedence to what is known as intensification at the base. What is the point of promising priority to scientific and technical progress if, as is symptomatic of the pragmatic orientation that our system of economic management gives rise to, at the end of the year, quarter and even month it is necessary time and again, in countless factories, to 'put into production' the capacities that are set aside for this scientific and technical progress. Reserves of raw material and capacity, and also those reserves in the sector of industrial research and development, planning and accounting that are saved from bureaucratic gobbling, and indispensable conditions for a breakthrough towards an economy that really does work efficiently. To this extent, the criticism is simply immanent to the present system. What is decisive in this context – if undoubtedly seen as utopian in the experience of our present economic planning – is the demand for a *reserve of labour-power,* for a certain *planned surplus capacity of living labour* in relation to the existing machinery, and also in machinery and the production of raw material and energy in relation to output. A certain freedom of movement in the factory's fund of labour-time is the most basic condition for lending a minimum of reality to the expressions 'putting man at the centre' and 'man the master of production'.

But this is also important in a more distant perspective. The mass of individuals can only experience free self-development in a society able to produce more than it has to produce and actually does produce. A communist surplus, in any case a question more of the social structure of production and needs than of the absolute amount of goods and services, is first and foremost a surplus of production capacity, a surplus of potential living labour-time, 'disposable time' in the broadest sense. Only this surplus can guarantee the individual, *every* individual and *within* the universal labour obligation, the space needed to build up a personal economy of time related to his individual life schedule. As people become increasingly mobile between jobs, temporary departures of their time schedules from the average expenditure of necessary labour can be balanced out with a small amount of central guidance, in so far as the adjustment is not automatic.

At present, factories must plan their labour-power in such a way that its capacity, reckoned via the norm times of the items to be produced and the average norm fulfilment, and taking into account the effects of rationalization that are still to be realized, completely covers the plan for commodity production. Mothers, for example, are included in the plan as full-time workers, even though their drop-out rate is far above the average. Even if this is taken into account statistically, it still affects a special section of production, as well as reinforcing the psychological devaluation of women as labour-power. Of course the primary data are somewhat manipulated, so as to 'build in safeguards'. It would be irresponsible for any factory management not to do so. Besides this, the factories also have a certain hypothetical reserve of labour-power in as much as they could for example reduce a level of sickness that is higher than necessary, and various losses of time that arise from deficiencies in internal organization. But these reserves can only be mobilized to a very limited extent, for the sociological and socio-psychological reasons we have discussed. The climate of improvization and disorganization is rather itself the result of the dysfunctions occasioned by the system of planning and management, the lack of labour-power being not the least of these, which foster the demoralization of those people who are least socially conscious.

If disturbances then appear at some point or other in the execution of the plan, due to lack of supplies or technical problems, if new construction is delayed, if the management cannot fulfil the plan for reason of the general shortage of labour-power, etc., then the entire factory collective must experience an increase in the mental and physical intensity of labour, and moreover in circumstances which are not its own fault, if the plan is still to be fulfilled (and non-fulfillment, in so far as it affects the categories of goods, and not just production by value, is of course disruptive for the national economy). Worries pile up for the managerial staff at all levels, 'operative activity' increases because the normal rhythm is disrupted, and superior organs appear in order to see things put right; an additional portion of capacity, moreover, is claimed for production. The production workers find themselves forced to work extra shifts, which are both harmful in terms of social policy and as ineffective as they could be for the factory economy. Technological discipline falls, fidelity to the categories of goods planned is abandoned wherever possible, with the number of the most expensive (most intensive in material terms) products being taken as the sole measure, so as at least to make sure of the end-of-the-year bonus. The situation that arises from this is undignified and is felt as such by all workers, engineers and economists conscious of their responsibility, and it is all the more frustrating in its effect in as much as there is no longer even any discussion, since after decades of repetition of the same 'people's own trade cycle' (as it is popularly called), further discussion necessarily appears pointless. The effect is serious, but nothing can be done to change it. 'Nothing is so disheartening as not to be able to get an overall view of a game on which life depends', declared Auguste Blanqui.[6]

The burden can only be eased if the factory collective is able to produce with a genuine reserve of labour-power that can actually be drawn on, i.e. if the overall social plan is drawn up in such a way that it demands no more labour-power than is actually available – taking disturbances and eventualities into account. This means putting an end to the unhappy combination of growth rate and investment and structural policy that the centre presently dictates, and giving clear priority to the optimal use of existing capacities. The chase after quantity, after an increase in commodity production, leads in many individual cases to a *loss* of capacity, and most probably, when the small print is read, also for society

---

[6] Höppner and Seidel-Höppner, *Von Babeuf bis Blanqui*, Vol. II, Leipzig 1975, p. 529.

as a whole. New investments, in particular, tie up a constantly growing amount of labour-power for their production and operation. The deduction from existing capacities these occasion can only be planned in a very rough way, since the area affected is generally too complex in structure, and it generally proves to have been underestimated when the fundamental decisions were made. It is characteristic, for example, that only the main production stage, that with the most expensive equipment, has its need for labour-power correctly estimated. In certain circumstances the fiction is even allowed in the preparatory documents that almost four workers are required to fill a job on a three-shift basis, instead of simply three (holidays, sickness, instruction courses, other losses of time). In other words, new investment generally ties up a higher absolute number of workers, rather than releasing them, no matter how high the *relative* rise in productivity. The result is precisely disturbances of proportionality that cause losses to factories already in operation, the relative deprivation and neglect of all ancillary processes, in particular the maintenance sector, and a high rate of machine breakdowns which is due both to lack of production workers and to lack of repair staff. This again leads to more machinery being demanded, and thus further investments, additional expenditure on machine building, etc. It is a never-ending spiral.

For the production workers, at least, it is necessary to make more concrete this demand for a reserve of labour-power in relation to the plan, so as to give them the possibility of active appropriation *within* their working time, first of all at least of the overall context of their department and factory, by genuine collaboration in the planning and control of production, by palpable improvement in the conditions and cultural level of their work, by training in the maintenance and care of the machinery in service, by rationalization of technology and work organization. Why shouldn't the worker who repairs his own car himself not also repair his production machine? If necessary, he must be given systematic instruction for this. And can we accept relations of production that function in such a way that engineers are superficially confirmed in their opinion that switch-boxes must be kept locked up from the workers wherever possible?

Why should a worker spend his supposed free time if he wants to make experimental innovations, when for other people this activity fills their regular working day? Without a reserve of labour-power in relation to the plan, democracy within the factory is well-nigh impossible for the production workers. The employees, and above all the specialists among them, find relatively sufficient opportunity, not only from the character of their activity, but also from the flexibility of their daily time schedules, to acquaint themselves with factory information and problems, and at least to participate in the unofficial forming of opinion on these. A part of the time 'wasted' in the offices is completely necessary for collective self-understanding. The workers in immediate production generally do not have this opportunity. The relatively rare meetings at change of shift are always pressed for time. One shift wants to get home, the other has to get down to work. As a rule, therefore, it is possible to monitor only the most immediate symptoms of the factors which are disturbing production and the work environment. When workers bellyache, they either ignore the norm, at their own expense, or else, in the case of a 'good' norm, the managerial staff responsible for plan fulfilment have the headache of coping with the production shortfall. The plan may well set aside a certain time for such purposes, but this is generally already overdrawn for the adjustment of the various other eventualities of the working year. Although their own labour process often has the effect of making them disinterested, unskilled and unmotivated, the workers are expected to spend their free time on this kind of discussion. Since they are not even drawn into the process of planning and management, they can in no way intervene in it as sovereign partners, but only give expression to their most immediate interests. (It is highly significant in the Soviet film *The Bonuses* that workers could only obtain information for disclosing bureaucratic special interests and machinations that were destroying the plan from 'traitors' among the ranks of the technical economic intelligentsia, who also ran a genuine risk in this.)

In order to make a significant change here, it would be rational to keep the five-day week of approximately forty hours but plan for only $5 \times 6 = 30$ hours of better prepared and hence optimally effective production. This would mean covering the 24 hours of the day where necessary with four production shifts. The lost quarter of the existing capacity could be balanced out, at the overall level, by a number of non-manual employees twice as great as the number of workers employed in immediate production spending six weeks of the year on the shop floor. A glance at the GDR Statistical Yearbook (1976 edition) shows that this is in no way inconceivable in quantitative terms. Unfortunately, the number of production workers engaged in manufacturing industry at the basic shop-floor level can only be approximately deduced from this; the real social structure is literally concealed in our statistics behind the composite category 'workers and employees', which includes nearly everyone.

The number of production workers in all manufacturing industries is given for 1975 as around 2 million, on top of which are almost 0.3 million in the construction industry and a good 0.4 million in transport, post and communications, the last-mentioned category including many *de facto* employees, just as there is a general tendency even at the base to exaggerate the number of production workers. An indirect calculation from data about innovations leads to approximately 2.9 million production workers in total. Since a total of some 8 million economically active persons is indicated altogether, of whom around 7 million are workers and employees, the 3 million or so actual workers are backed up by some 5 million other economically active persons, including 4 million employees (the difference of a million here contains all those working in agriculture, which I am intentionally ignoring in this survey). Among these 5 million, moreover, there are no less than 1 million specialists with higher education. In manufacturing industry alone, some 1 million employees are listed against 2 million workers (naturally including a share of those with higher education), a number which is certainly not on the low side. Since these figures happen to come to more or less full millions, the proportions are very easy to see, right down to the fact that out of the GDR's average 8-hour working day, 3 hours are not work in production. It remains to be seen what the number of *basic* production workers is. From the 2 million industrial workers, for example, we have to deduct 22.2 per cent for the almost 450,000 workers in repair and transport, which still does not include all so-called ancillary workers in production. In the last analysis, we are dealing here with the number of those workers among whom actual production capacity is lost (many workers not directly employed in manufacturing already spend no more than 6 hours productively, without the remaining 2 hours necessarily being won for any kind of productive purpose). Taking all things into account, the figure of 1.5 million workers would not be an underestimate, even if a section of the quality control staff have also to be included, and we take into consideration that a four-shift system would demand somewhat greater repair capacity. Thus 3 of the 5 million remaining economically active persons, or of the 4 million employees, would have to perform 6 weeks' work per year in production. The gaps in the employee sector could be filled by reducing bureaucracy (in particular, the expenditure occasioned by the control functions in accounting), as well as by partial intensification.

What would still remain to be settled would then be the serious employment of these employees on the basis of a connection to definite jobs that was as far as possible self-selected, but also as stable as could be achieved. Even if they only worked at an average of 80 per cent efficiency, the basic production workers they relieve would be amply made up for, since we can assume that in practice only a half of that quarter of their labour-time nominally lost would be spent in actual operation. The solution put forward here would even notably raise the effective running time of the machines, so that if output need not grow to the same extent, then machinery could also be saved. Moreover, this survey entirely ignores the factor of rising productivity, and thus hypothetically makes this still completely available for quantitative growth, instead of supposing a reduction in the overall production mechanism, which is what would really be desirable.

What demands the most complex economic solution is the institution of a unitary education for all. This is more difficult than the steps so far considered, in as much as the rise in productivity that successively makes it possible is only in appearance the major part of its realization. Let us assume that the pure expenditure on training, i.e. time for learning that falls outside necessary labour, is extended by 5 years in the average individual's youth, and that on top of this every adult is to spend a further 5 years teaching and studying. Here again, then, the cost would be something like a quarter of the total present labour-time, on the basis of a current working life of 40 years. In order to make up the time for this, each generation would thus have to increase its productivity by just a third. According to the customary method of accounting in terms of gross industrial production in constant values, however questionable this is, productivity in the GDR is doubling every 10 years; e.g. its index rose by precisely one-third between 1970 and 1975. It goes without saying that the entire growth in productivity cannot suddenly be claimed for a single measure such as this. But we can see from the figures that the order of magnitude does not exceed the capacity of a single generation. This would also include the surplus expenditure on teaching staff which would be needed to reduce the size of classes in the school system to 15 pupils, the upper limit of the optimal range for collective processes.

Great difficulties, however, lie in the social organization of both the labour process and the system of education, in their isolation from one another, which has been scarcely more than superficially touched, and in their equally bureaucratic super-structure. (It is hard to conceive of a more pervasive bureaucracy than the educational one, since here the hierarchy also knows everything better in the specifically moralistic mode of the traditional teacher.) The calculation made here may well give a wrong orientation simply because it tacitly takes the present structures in the educational system and processes as invariant, and conceives of change simply in terms of a shift in quantities. Yet it cannot be the best solution even economically, leaving everything else out of account, to have the entire educational system simply extended in scope, but still in terms of the same kind of separated sphere, only pursued by specialists, and vertically managed from a single centre, as is the case today, where the unity of the educational system means above all the all-pervading character of its regulation. And it would be simply impossible to continue the reproduction process in the former way, which subsumes individuals to it, if people were available as labour-power only as men and women also having universal claims to life, being equally capable of finding themselves in special activities at all functional levels of work.

How exactly the organization of work within the factory would be shaped under conditions of such disposability and mobility of individuals, we can confidently leave to later practice, and in the meantime to utopian predictions. The realization of equality in the division of labour will bring about so natural a solidarity and discipline of individuals in the best possible execution of the necessary labour that repressive controls will become completely superfluous and the effectiveness of the collective, governed in the first place by quality and the saving of raw materials, will reach an optimum simply from the collective's own internal regulation. We can already see the necessity for a flexible and multiple connection between individuals and jobs – several individuals for each job, several jobs for each individual. Higher education, moreover, without being newly oppressed or provincialized by specialization, will draw closer to the workplace than to the home. Since it will become as common as the 10-grade school is today, it can also become communal. This may well be more than a mere play on words. The idea of the commune might well receive a practical significance in our perspective, in so far as this is seen as involving the unification of the population in comprehensible communities, which function with relative autonomy with respect to the basic reproductive functions of work, education and life, while they take part in the general social connection with a series of specialized activities, this in turn taking care of a number of special inputs that they need. (More on this under heading five.)

Secondly, a new definition of need. If rich individuality is to become the goal of production, then there must be a change in the material structure, the matrix of use-values in goods, services, outputs, etc. which the planned proportional development of the national economy is to aim at. The character and rhythm of this change, however, are not something to be laid down by pre-conceived ideological values, including those in the present book, and society is not to be dictated to on such a basis. The new preferences can rather be democratically elaborated only in a comprehensive political practice, the basic elements of which were discussed in Chapters 11 and 12. It is precisely on this point that the self-determination of society as the free association of individuals finds its decisive criterion. If this is not automatically generated, then it is in the political sphere that the impulse is lacking, or at least insufficient, as long as the cultural revolution is still in its early stage. I would like to emphasize once again that for me the growth of society into this genuine freedom and conscious self-determination of its fate seems inconceivable without the association of the most commited elements, those most conscious of the problems and of their own responsibilities, in a League of Communists with an open window towards society. Without an effectively organized and constant influence on the acquired mental and behavioural structures, the transformation of civilization is impossible, while the particular transformation that is necessary today demands by its own inherent purpose that this pressure functions in an emancipatory way, broadening and encouraging subjectivity, propelling it forward, giving it power and freedom. This is the political dialectic of the cultural revolution, and it is this that gives the Communist League the form and means of its influence.

As far as needs go, every society has what can be called a basic economic law governing its goal of production, whether this is explicitly formulated or not. This means nothing more than that any given society always strives towards an optimum specific to it between the production of means of subsistence, enjoyment and development, and the needs of the social ensemble, in which connection of course the interest of the ruling classes or strata in the reproduction of their own form of individuality is dominant in determining these needs, according to the relative degree of its influence. There is no need here explicitly to define the basic economic law of actually existing socialism; the elements of its definition are contained in Part Two of this book. The basic economic law of the socialist-communist formation will differ from that of all class society by the subject of the definition of need knowing no further differentiation except the natural differences of age, sex and ability, perhaps also the quasi-natural distinctions of character, so that the interest or needs of all individuals are taken equally into account. And it will differ from that of the primitive community by the *priority* that the level of productivity and wealth makes it possible to establish, a priority placed on the production of means of *development* in establishing the overall structure of need, i.e. of use-value, and accordingly of the expenditure of labour-time.

If we take this as the starting-point, then *the economy of individual time schedules* proves in fact to be *the decisive transition-point in planning.* If society is seriously to be guided by what proportions of time, and in what sequence, are optimally disposable for the various forms of individual manifestation (disposable, and *not* prescribed), so that its time budget no longer arises merely *ex post facto* as an average value, but is rather planned according to the individuals' general development requirements, then the overcoming of alienation really will have an economic basis, and the realm of necessity will be subsumed by the realm of freedom. This is the point of departure for the communist economy, which will only appear as an object of planning as long as it is not yet firmly established in the basic structure of the whole reproduction process. The consumption of means of subsistence will then automatically lose its compensatory prestige orientation, and the consumption of means of enjoyment will also lose this to a large extent, as well as being brought back to a natural normal level by the striving to win time for psychologically productive activity and communication. This department of production will become relatively unimportant in the plan, since it will be practically invariant. In general, the scope of the plan will be able to retreat a great deal, once an economy that is no longer oriented primarily towards growth, but rather to quality, has established a balance between production and consumption.

One economic problem that will increase very much in importance is that of a *sufficient object* for psychologically productive activity for all individuals. Here need will be restricted only by the production of genuine communality in all probability being given a far greater share in individual time schedules, with partnership-communication fulfilled by means of enjoyment and development in the most varied forms and for the most diverse purposes. The rest, even if for far-seeing economists it is a big remainder, is then a *question of the material nature of the means of development, i.e. a question above all of expenditure of raw materials.* We might consider, to bring this question somewhat unhistorically into sharp perspective, whether rich individuality *à la* Goethe would not presuppose a significantly greater expenditure of raw material than the average individuality of today, complete with car and basement garage. Expenditure of *time* is regulated by the limit up to which it is available without the production of means of development blocking development itself. Here the optimal disposition of the economic process is partly calculated in advance (see heading four below), and partly struggled for in the confrontation of the interests affected. The expenditure of *raw materials,* on the other hand, while it is *ultimately* regulated in the same way, is so only over too long a time. Here the present generation can in fact live on credits which it does not have to pay back. It can win time by squandering raw materials, which later generations will have to make up for by a hundredfold expenditure of time. This evidently bears on the whole environmental problem, which is not by a long way reducible to the finite character of the material resources that can be processed at justifiable expense (justifiable in terms of the goal of production). In the course of its striving to establish step by step the primacy of means of development in the planning of needs and expenditure (which of course affects more than just material goods), the cultural revolution must therefore seek to renounce those means of development that are intensive in their use of raw materials. But this already leads to the more comprehensive connection of the next aspect.

Thirdly, giving the reproduction process a harmonious character. If we are to put a stop to man's disturbance of the natural balance and bring this again into equilibrium, if we intend therefore to harmonize man's existence in nature wherever this is possible, particularly in its material foundations, then this *must lead to a consistent change in the habits of production.* The average type of large-scale industry on which the present civilization of the developed countries is based and which is spreading to all other regions, is naturally far removed from being simply a technical phenomenon compatible with all forms of society whatsoever.

It has arisen and been constructed on a basis of domination and the valorization of abstract labour. It is now being put in question by the ecological crisis on the one hand, and by the psychological crisis on the other, in particular the paralysis of work motivation. The customary and 'normal' investment policy, geared towards achieving reduced minimum costs for the production intended, is coming to have ominous implications. The necessary change in production habits requires that society accepts something like the following guidelines.

– Primacy of simple reproduction with the employment of existing energies and resources. Hence full repair of existing plant and equipment capable of further use must have priority over reconstruction, full reconstruction of existing and still serviceable plant over new building, new building on land already used for industry – and its regeneration in case of need – over 'green field' investment; corresponding maintenance of a machine-building industry that also permits the re-equipment of older and smaller factories.

– Care for machinery instead of innovatory competition at any price. ('Science and technology' in the sense of new equipment is not the primary factor in intensification, even if it is important.) Reduction of technical depreciation by way of adequate capacity and production of replacement parts for preventive maintenance, most cautious use of the category of moral depreciation in relation to functionable plant with respectable conditions of labour.

– Rationalization always to proceed from man, from the criterion of the conditions most worthy of his nature, and to be linked with effective expenditures for easing and enriching work as well as for a work environment and culture in which order, cleanliness and maintenance of value (presupposing the reserve of production workers' labour-time which we have already discussed) will become self-evident necessities; abandonment of productivity that is bought at the cost of vital human energies.

– Furthest possible reduction of damaging influences on man and environment from existing plant and processes, and the absolute avoidance of these in new ones.

– Strengthened macro- and micro-economic measures to reduce the use of raw materials and energy. Hence control of the rate of growth with the aim of decisively reducing the present increase in consumption; increased saving on material and improvement in quality as against the mere number of finished products.

– Orientation towards functionality, solidity (maximum durability) and aesthetic quality of mass consumer goods; suspension, replacement or substitution of any kind of throwaway product, synchronization of changes in fashion with the rate of natural wear and tear, an end to any kind of 'market-creating' advertizing.

– Complete recycling and regeneration of reusable raw materials from waste. (Equality in the division of labour will make handicraft work once again possible and expected where it has not yet been abolished or at present requires too great an expenditure.)

– Establishment of a sufficient handicraft repair and servicing capacity for communal and individual need, as well as procuring the raw materials required for care and maintenance work; an end to the absorption of structurally irreplaceable small-scale production by centrally directed large-scale production.

– With guidelines of this kind, we are back at the question as to whether the countries of actually existing socialism can afford this economic strategy, which involves renunciation of 'technological leadership' in the sense of capitalist efficiency, from a military point of view – whether it is otherwise seen as reasonable or not. Weapons production and the armed forces are the very paradigm of all squandering of raw materials and human labour-power, all lack of consideration for nature and man, even in the absence of actual explosions, burnings, defoliations and shootings. But the two blocs are in full agreement that armaments count as the most important means of subsistence. I shall not repeat here the remarks on an escalation of disarmament made in Chapter 11. What was discussed there was a synchronization of political and socio-economic transformations in both late capitalism and actually existing socialism, to be attained by the international alliance of 'Left', cultural-revolutionary forces against both power blocs. The resistance to the cultural revolution which is in any case to be expected will therefore be focussed particularly systematically on this point, precisely because it represents the most hopeful strategy for winning space to break out of the supermilitarist witches' cauldron in which humanity's strivings for liberation are presently killed off. Could it have been undertaken successfully in the context of the entire Soviet bloc, then an experiment such as that in Czechoslovakia would have already exercized a transforming pressure on the structure of Western Europe which would have had to be taken extremely seriously; clever reactionaries of the Strauss variety were quick to recognize this.

It is certainly true, in view of the probable temporal discrepancies between movements in the two blocs, that a consistent antimilitarist position cannot be pursued by way of uncompromising and absolute demands. The problem of security through the balance of terror is one of the realities of this distorted world. But the degree of 'overkill' on both sides is certainly great enough to allow decisive demonstrations of disarmament that are visible on a world-wide scale, and whose effects can be actively anticipated politically via the popular movement in the other bloc. In any case, we should oppose most decisively all irrational stereotyping of the enemy, in particular such as is politically deliberate. For those members of the older generation who have irrationally internalized all too much of the anxieties and fears of the two World Wars, we have to reduce this influence not by claiming that there is no danger, but rather by explaining the shift in the basis of danger in a changed historical situation. To view the entire capitalist world of today in terms of the experience of Hitlerite fascism, for example, it itself directly to endanger security. To those other people who have an interest in the military and security machine through their professional and status position, we must guarantee no reduction in their income, and full productive employment in the civilian community. And against the third group who use this machine and the feeling of a besieged fortress as a means of domination, we must wage an unflinching political struggle, precisely on this specific question too, to expose the special interests that are concealed behind their systematic demagogy.

A reproduction process that is altered in the direction sketched here is highly necessary also from a further international aspect, which is most closely connected with world peace on the North-South axis. One of the most important tasks of the cultural revolution in the economically advanced countries of both power blocs will consist in *doing away with the law of value in trade with the less developed countries.* Through the law of value, the naked exchange of equivalents, these countries are condemned to a pauperism which is perpetuated into the distant future by the drain of raw materials. It is not a question of procuring them a parasitic existence, which would only degrade them still further. *The solution must consist rather in exchange according to equal national expenditure of labour-time.* In the presently capitalist countries, there is evidently even surplus capacity available for such use, which however has presently to adapt to the economic development of their trading partners instead of breaking through the barriers this imposes. Technical solutions must thus be inspired and accepted from this starting-point. Economists will certainly find it hard to grasp, and will still continue for a while to mock the idea in their banal way, yet it would most probably be of advantage to more than these peoples alone if they could manage, as it were, to discover the bicycle a second time round, i.e. an autonomous technique produced by a non-capitalist economy. The developed countries can offer them people who want neither to play the foreign god in privileged European reserves, nor to accumulate moral credit for their later spiritual health, but rather to work, live and struggle with them fraternally, since in this way lies a profound common need and a profound individual meaning. Our civilization, moreover, has already produced individual models of such truly solidaristic and anti-colonial mission, people such as Las Casas and Multatuli, Albert Schweitzer and Norman Bethune, Che Guevara and Camilo Torres. And it must also be said that the Soviet Union has by and large practised towards its least developed peoples a policy that stands in clear contrast to the bourgeoisie's extermination of the North American Indians, and even recently those of Brazil, though now even this needs to be re-examined in the case of Soviet Asia. The Soviet bloc supported Cuba and Vietnam not simply within the limits of the law of value. But the cultural revolution must create the broad social basis, beyond the laws of national and bloc interest, on which a massive and economically effective development aid can be established on a scale appropriate to the magnitude of the North-South antithesis.

Fourthly, accounting for a new economy of time. The orientation contained in the guidelines of the previous section will be seen *to give use-value, the qualitative material and natural factors, greater importance* than does a system oriented to the maximal valorization of abstract labour-power. This is precisely what constitutes the desired change in production habits, when viewed from the standpoint of economic theory. This change, as can be observed time and again with people who still do love their work, is in full agreement with the needs of *concrete* labour-power, which likes to identify in a creative way with the object produced, even if this has not been produced simply by one individual. Such people, for example, always have the ultimately justified doubt as to whether the economistic calculation according to which it is in many cases cheaper to throw something away than to repair it, is really valid, even though immediate appearance often does confirm this. In fact, however, even if this is sometimes true in the individual case, it is still laden with ominous consequences when we consider the overall connection of our culture, which scorns to take care of the pence.

Many of these economistic arguments, however, are false even on the basis of their own assumptions, something that is only difficult to prove because, despite all appearance to the contrary, there is no reliable economic cost accounting of their premises and internal linkages. We need only think of the rise in productivity due to the industrialization of building techniques, which at first sight looks so significant, but on closer inspection proves to be largely self-deception. Even today, in Thuringia for example, traditional stone building can still be cheaper, even for a fairly large construction, than the same building in the hallowed style of prefabrication, and this is instructive, as the tricks of financial cost accounting are far more distorting on the macro scale than on the micro. What is needed to regulate the new economy, the rule of living labour over objectified, is a transition at the primary level of economic accounting from measurement in terms of value, or rather price, to direct measurement in terms of time equivalents. This is a major but sadly neglected task for the economists, though even Marx himself saw it as 'not so easy'.[7] To establish labour-

[7] *Grundrisse*, p. 153.

time accounting at all levels of production right through to the finished product, to gain experience of it by its consistent application, i.e. to carry it through on an overall social scale, is an indispensable precondition for finally divesting products also of their commodity *form*. We must strongly emphasize here that previous attempts in this direction (the time-sum method suggested by Behrens in the GDR) were never applied with sufficient thoroughness and patience for conclusions to be drawn from these results for or against the viability and efficiency of labour-time calculation.

Labour-time accounting has two socio-economic advantages over financial accounting that are of paramount importance. First, it alone can make the portions of individual, collective and overall social time schedules *commensurable across the boundary of 'necessary' and 'free' activity*. Up till now, alienation has insinuated itself even in the arbitrary character of the planning procedure, which has to posit absolutely certain 'social requirements', 'social needs', etc. without really being *able* to ask what this will lead to in terms of the development of the individuals affected, and the declared goal of production. Living labour *can* only subordinate objectified labour if it represents in the economy the *overall interests,* and thus the overall time schedule, of social individuals. Applied merely as an isolated cost factor of a particular production effort, it must necessarily disappear more and more against the mass of objectified labour employed. To establish the qualitative proportionality of time expenditure from the standpoint of the goal of production is simply the major task of the general plan. This can only be drawn up democratically if the mass of individuals are able to form judgements on the consequences of their own needs, if for example they know that private motoring and its infrastructural consequences claim, let us say, half an hour out of every individual's working day, or three working years out of each person's lifetime.

At this point the second advantage of labour-time accounting is already visible. As distinct from financial accounting, it makes economic proportions and problems far more comprehensible and penetrable, by involving far fewer distortions of actual expenditures (economists will certainly discover ways of taking into account such things as imports, for example, in a more or less adequate way), and making readily apparent the connection to the individual life process. Financial accounting based on prices is fundamentally unable to achieve this overall comprehensible character, since prices (in one function at least that will still be necessary for a while) must deliberately take into account the movements of supply and demand, in particular the scarcity of certain resources on the world market or in the national economy. They are of no use at all, therefore, for cost accounting, and should in no way directly come into it (i.e. in their deviation from actual expenditure). It is precisely the measurement of cost effectiveness that comes to grief, at least for comparison of performance *between* economic units, when expenditures of objectified labour are not accounted for in averagely necessary labour-time, and expenditures of living labour not in effective labour-time. Cost accounting on the basis of labour-time would permit what already purports to be cost-analysis in terms of use-value, but is only sporadic and applied to a limited horizon, to develop into the most decisive instrument for calculating economic efficiency.

Fifthly, structural conditions of individual initiative and genuine communality : society as an association of communes. On the question of the form of regulation, the anarchist tendency, in particular its syndicalist wing, has up till now been the only one that has expressly stressed the interest of *individuality* and the autonomous group as small enough to be controllable by such individuality. And even if it has not succeeded in sufficiently linking this completely essential aspect with the ensemble of social relations, i.e. with the predominantly systemic character of society as a whole, yet it cannot be simply dismissed as long as all other revolutionary tendencies remain stuck for this synthetic aspect in the perspective of the state. It is however necessary to rise above the dichotomy of 'cooperative-egalitarian' versus 'hierarchial-elitist' structures, since this falsely assumes that the flow of information and decision *could* flow primarily or even wholly from bottom to top. Does syndicalism not itself remain trapped in the trauma of the immediate producer, who dares not even hope to escape from his subalternity, and for whom equality instinctively means that all have to be equally subaltern? We have to relate ourselves here to the structural laws of information-processing in complex, 'organismic' systems. Through the various levels of development of biological organisms, the processing of information proceeds on what is constitutionally an ever more pronounced 'hierarchical-elitist' course, in as much as the cells and groups of cells at various levels have completely different functional levels and decision capacities. All the more complex living systems form brains that watch over their overall functioning. Technically and from the perspective of information theory, the functions of social labour are also necessarily in an order of subordination. Unless one is prepared to accept that the structure of regulation in interconnected production is objectively hierarchical, then the whole problem of socialist democracy can only be raised in an agitational way. Refuge is then taken in the regressive proposal that the historically arisen metastructures of a regulation that was based originally simply on horizontal linkage should be dissolved, so that a new 'centralization from below' can be constructed. Is the question not rather to give both centralization from below and from above a *social* character? The 'cooperative-egalitarian' concept takes a firm theoretical stand against subalternity. But in practice, as can be seen in more than a few attempts with the system of councils, it comes up against an intrinsic barrier as soon as there is any real question of 'organizing the nation'.

In my view, now that man has reached the threshold of socialism-communism, the question is to free the functional hierarchy that is required for regulating the process of social life and labour (with a balanced flow of information and decision-making in both directions) from being transformed into a *social* structure. If humanity consists of individuals who have all attained universality, then the material basis for this that has already been achieved also enables the social framework to cease from being that of the information-processing system which it makes use of for regulation and will continue to need. This is precisely why the abolition of the traditional division of labour is the central concept of my book. The final 'class struggle' revolves precisely around the organization of the process of information, knowledge and decision, so as to subsume this to the associated individuals, i.e. *to their overall ensemble*. The task consists in freeing people from being reduced to their functions within pyramidical systems, and objectifying the system of planning and direction itself to constitute it as a realm of necessity *over* which the associated individuals are elevated, while they share between them in an equitable way the subordinate functions that are required at the various levels. 'Cooperative', no matter how far the content of this principle is extended upwards, is never quite the same as 'social'. Historical experience rather suggests that the alternative between cooperative or hierarchical organization may simply bear in actual practice on the decision whether the social connection on the far side of capitalism is to devolve initially onto the competition of collective capitalists or onto the dictate of a single general capitalist. We should rather realize that 'cooperative socialism' can in the best case be a historically embryonic form of socialism, which arises in the ideal case when the workers appropriate the production units isolated from one another by capitalism in its phase of free competition in the immediate context of this isolation. It seems very questionable to me whether the idea of general association requires nothing more than the coordination of such producers' cooperatives. *How is an 'assembly' of the whole society possible, so that all individuals can decide over their reproduction process? This is the cardinal question for socialist democracy.* We have to realize that the question of self-management in a highly complex society demands a response not simply from the perspective of particular communal units, let alone factory units, but always also at the level of the *overall* process of reproduction.

Once this intention is established, then the *ability to appropriate* the general context, and this moreover understood as a *socio-psychological and socio-educational process* on a mass scale, naturally becomes the decisive measure for choosing the *form* of economic regulation, while the *guarantee* that the social synthesis, the general plan, *can be genuinely influenced from the bottom up,* becomes the most important question, which can only now be answered in a practical way. This choice cannot be made, nor the answer given, independent of the concrete historical and cultural level of development of the producers and of production. The real difference is precisely whether it is simply factories that have to be initially expropriated, or alternatively nation-wide trusts or even supra-national corporations. History has obstinately shown, and this should in any case have been recognized, that individuals cannot raise themselves in a single leap across all the intermediate stages of concentration of interests from the level of their subaltern partial functions to that of the overall social or economic connection. Immediate centralization of power of disposal is not only not identical with socialization, but unmistakeably erects a barrier against it. And total centralization without organic gradation will always remain a theoretical conception of compulsive characters devoid of imagination. What is ultimately central in the sense of the overall social level is simply decision over the (ethical) value concept by which the association is to govern its development.

Yugoslav communism certainly did not discover the 'only possible' way of promoting socialization (for there is no such thing); but the basic idea of first letting quasi-cooperative factory collectives operate with relative autonomy is certainly more rich in prospects from the standpoint of learning how to dispose of economic resources than is direction by a 'papacy of production';[8] Marx is referring to the Saint-Simonian bank which was supposed to be a unity of both state planning commission and central statistical office. The Trotskyist tendency has not managed to give this point sufficient importance, as is shown by the dogmatic character of its criticism of Yugoslav conditions. Even in countries with a higher initial level of economic organization and culture, decentralization remains for a long time the condition for self-management to develop. The question of its precise content and the instruments of its regulation derives its importance from this. Particularly in relation to the role of value categories, whose persistence or disappearance is determined by the economy, not by politics, this question can be posed in a way that is 'unprincipled' from the standpoint of the optimal functioning of a political-economic strategy oriented to a development towards complete socialization.

[8] *Grundrisse*, p. 156.

It would naturally be quite inappropriate to try and take the *present* economies of the GDR or Czechoslovakia, which have always been directed from the centre, back to the point at which Yugoslavia set out with its undeveloped economy in 1950, and repeat its mistakes instead of learning from them. Yet a certain type of decentralization is highly necessary in our case, too, if under our present conditions this is far more in the interest of unleashing skilled individual initiative and the formation of collectives around planned tasks requiring relatively autonomous realization, rather than that of building up economic resources in the abstract. What is needed is evidently a certain *combination* between systemic regulation from above (which in terms of information theory is unavoidably hierarchical), and the economic initiative of relatively autonomous basic units of combined labour and social life (which by no means function in all circumstances in an emancipatory sense). The mediation of the *overall social* connection can only become the common work of free individuals if this is not a separate activity that confronts all other necessities of mediation in an abstract and commanding way. Individuals would otherwise be faced with the contradiction between abstract freedom at the societal level and concrete unfreedom in all details, a situation in which the latter would always come to prevail. *For this reason the general connection must be articulated into autonomous collective subjects at various levels which themselves mediate their insertion into the whole.*

I would like to bring in here an analogy which may seem somewhat singular, and yet which I nevertheless find quite suggestive: relations *within* the ruling class during the rise of European feudalism. The order of dependence was hierarchical, and yet subjects at all levels had their own inherent importance, at least in the ideal type. These subjects must now take the form of collectives of associated individuals instead of patriarchal feudal powers. These collectives would of course introduce, by virtue of their egalitarian structure, a quite different objective authority from 'below' in the overall mediating process, so that as distinct from the pyramid of dependence, where it was always delegation from top to bottom that determined the legal order (though not always the real order), legality would in fact proceed predominantly from the base, so that delegation was from bottom to top. In a developed communist society, individuals are equally and simultaneously present at all levels of subjective interest. There is a 'top' and a 'bottom', but in a system that no longer defines *people* in these terms. In this way any jealousy on the part of the 'bottom' would become meaningless.

Here we can see the profound content of the word *association*, as chosen by Marx, which is suited like no other word to express the active self-unification of autonomous subjects, the coordinative, federal principle of their social organization, which alone can maintain the freedom of the individuals in their necessary connection. Association of individuals into unions in which they pursue the various specific purposes that make up the process of their social life; association of these unions with subordinate functions into communes as complex territorial units that embrace the process of social life in its all-round character; finally association of the communes into the society – naturally specialized at certain points in the framework of planned division of labour: this is communism from the angle of the *organization* of the social connection. The principle of association replaces the centralist superorganization which is constitutionally hostile to individuality and initiative, and is in fact a legacy of class domination from the Asiatic formation through to the capitalist. The future constitution of humanity can only be conceived in terms of association – the diametrical opposite of the nightmare of a bureaucratic world government. The modern superorganization may well be the necessary form of *genesis* which has governed the construction of the noosphere in the world-historical process, and this alienated totality may have been its shell. The realm of man as a conscious being, as a self-conscious being, once the foundations of his existence are assured, will be characterized by that associative communication that is just as appropriate to the free exchange of individualities as to the free exchange of ideas.

What will a communist society have 'centrally' to decide on, i.e. at the overall social level? In the first place, it has to ratify the scope and content of its needs, precisely from the standpoint of the concept of value that has been mentioned and which will certainly always be to a certain extent controversial. This is how the use-value structure of the plan will be established, which will then appear in the magnitudes of demand for particular goods and services, and appropriate capacities to meet them. To this extent, central controls, i.e. controls proceeding from the overall interest, will probably always be needed. The assortment of goods supplied, as opposed to the *conditions* of production, cannot and must not be freely chosen by the individual branch and factory, by any internal criterion of utility. The establishment and modification of the production structure is not an act of the production collective, but an act of *society*. This point is generally the least understood by proponents of the councils idea. The associated individuals do *not* determine the plan in their (still limited) capacity as *producers* with a specific interest, but rather as social individuals who, with a high level of understanding of the general interest, the many kinds of particular interest, and their own individual interests, strive for the optimal mediation of these in the goals of the plan. *The interests of the producers are particular interests among other particular interests,* and as long as they have their pivot in *producer* cooperatives, they are therefore fundamentally incapable of producing any plan that can satisfy the overall social requirement, no matter how democratically they are synthesized from the bottom upwards. If the 'cooperative-egalitarian' concept does not escape the subalternity of the oppressed proletarian existence, then the idea of council democracy on the basis of the self-management of the producers remains theoretically restricted by a basic condition of specifically capitalist *alienation,* the autonomization of the economic process and its abstract dominance over the overall social process.[9]

This is where the *idea of the commune* has its great and specific superiority. 'The Communal constitution would have restored to the social body all the forces hitherto absorbed by the state parasite feeding upon, and clogging the free movement of, society', as Marx puts it in *The Civil War in France.*[10] I must myself confess that four years ago, when I read through this great text for the first chapter of my book, I was not yet convinced, as I

[9] Lucien Goldmann, 'La réification', in *Recherches dialectiques*, Paris 1959.

[10] *The First International and After, loc. cit.*, p. 211.

am today, of its unqualified pertinence to the question of the economic-political constitution of cultural-revolutionary practice. In the organizational form of the commune, *all* aspects of the reproduction process can be integrated towards the goal of rich individuality, and the corresponding interests can be mediated and carried through both internally and externally. We can see how a population, basing itself on the organs it has set up, can share in the various activities from planning and statistics through to street cleaning and garbage disposal, from applied research to the dispatch of products, from teaching of various kinds and levels to the repair of machinery, from the construction of new buildings to the distribution of objects of use and the performance of services, while the general arts and sciences become as much the general occupation of all as the exchange between sexes, between generations, and individual or group enjoyment of the most varied forms of partnership, which will more than ever before become a source of pleasure.

A communal organization of this kind could also be the framework for breaking down the isolated dissociation of the spheres of work, domestic living and education, without in this way reinstating the traditional limitation, seclusion and compulsion that is typical of such one-sided and introverted social milieus as for example the communes of the middle ages. Socialist communes could reproduce at a higher level the human scale in building that was attained in the architecture of the ancient polis and the medieval city, instead of simply placing layers of isolated cells on top of one another to give aesthetically formless aggregates, against which the human form shrivels to the size of an ant. The housing construction that is carried out today, in conjunction with a bureaucratic allotment of housing which treats the individual essentially as a statistical quantity, would already make it materially impossible to try and develop communal forms of living, even if the political power ceased to distrust and prosecute such experiments, or rather to nip them already in the bud.

Viewed from the formal aspect, the communal (territorial) organization which presently balances the centrally directed industrial branch organization and the other pervasive bureaucracies only in an artificial constitutional sense, would have to be *the* medium-sized planning and directing instance, via which in particular all central controls would have to pass on their way down to the basic units of the various primary activities of the reproduction process. This principle cannot be distilled from the Paris experience of 1871, simply because this was just a *Paris* experience. By decree, the producer cooperatives of workers were obliged to unite on a national scale – a concentration of power which inevitably disregards the territorial communes and centralizes power over *society,* even if the single halter were to be democratically controlled. Connections on a territorial basis have throughout history always proved far more comprehensible and closer to the human scale than nation-wide branch networks. The commune would have the properties of a social microcosm, particularly if we imagine in the distant future the dissolution of the present urban agglomerations, which already lead to absurd results in many places. It goes without saying that there would be patterns of energy economy, of traffic and communications which would cross through the communes. The same would certainly apply also to certain (though not many) institutions of the superstructure. In general, what would remain would be the branch-oriented specialist flow of information, which could be looked after by relatively independent scientific branch institutes that could also be consulted by the communes.

The communes would have set for them the output of their industry for society, according to assortment and quality, in due relation to their input in resources (the above-mentioned reserves taken into account). In this way the communes would also be the economic units for the full complexity of accounting. Their councils of elected delegates would have to take the same decisions, with some restrictions, as the government of the nation as a whole, which would similarly be based on the delegate system. The communes could thus generate a very far-reaching interest in their activities, while they are presently objects of the most complete disinterest, and in particular completely insignificant politically (so that when communal elections take place it is impossible to discuss anything beyond roof repairs and shop opening hours). Above all, the communes would be able to study and influence not simply the question of taxes for general social purposes (for the state budget can be financed almost entirely via the communes), but also the whole economy of the community. And at the same time, the communal delegates in the national assembly would have from the start, as a result of the microcosmic character of the communities that they represented, the social power and competence also to decide the general plan for the associated communes.

Besides the unions for work and educational purposes, the articulation of the population in living communities would be one of the most important concerns of cultural-revolutionary practice. For everything indicates that the transition from the present small family towards larger units, though in no case units to be organized by the state, is the key to the immediate progress essential in two closely connected fields, whose backwardness would inevitably be a severe hindrance to the overall process of a transformation of civilization: the liberation of women and also the liberation of children, or more precisely the securing of the psycho-social conditions for an educational process that does not impose barriers on development. (On top of this, the communes would probably put an end also to the exclusion of old people from social communication.) The small family was the result of the contraction of the family function to the mere reproduction of labour-power (with the far-reaching exclusion of education). In this unit, which is now decisively no longer a genuine microcosm, since it has so restricted a horizon, the function of *management,* the *major responsibility* for its functioning, falls with high probability to the woman.

This probability is only partly determined by traditional custom. In a society oriented to material output, which operates with material incentives into the bargain, the man is more important in social production (even if more women are employed than men), and more important for the standard of family reproduction (to this extent, equalization of incomes is also an important condition for women's emancipation). And in the family it is the woman who, from the point at which the reproductive function *begins,* in the pre-natal and early childhood section of human development, naturally has a head start in coping with these tasks; she *is* the natural centre of the small family (as she once was the natural centre of the overall process of social life in the primitive community). This gives rise to a degree of *absorption by necessary labour* (from which housework is only omitted from the still ever-present 'capitalist' standpoint), and a *constant concern* which would be far greater still if all family members worked absolutely equal times in the public sphere: 'Women's work is never done'. She lives the role of manager and planner of the family economy in somewhat the same way as a fitter, say, who studies engineering and takes on the job of technical manager, finds out that he invariably 'takes the factory home with him' in the evening, no matter how small it might be, in complete contrast from how things were before. Since the entire system of services and welfare under actually existing socialism, by its underdevelopment and its indirectly pre-programmed lagging behind requirements, objectively makes family reproduction more difficult, the present economic system is more burdensome on women than on anyone else, their job opportunities, as well as all other social opportunities that are still to a great extent identical with these, being radically curtailed. Only in the exceptional case does it permit mothers with several children to concentrate their essential human energies on something other than the family functions.

In so much as the official social consciousness takes account of the *quantitative* burdening of women and the consequences of this for their health and their children, it inclines only too typically towards compensatory stipulations. Social measures such as the paid educational places that are given to mothers with many children solve the problem in a way that is of immediate advantage to women, but reactionary from the point of view of social policy, since it reinforces the unchangeable character of women's subaltern social role and stands completely in the way of their emancipation. Given the two or three children that are 'socially expected' of the healthy woman, this 'solution' means an average five-year loss of development precisely at the decisive point of the beginning of professional activity, often already at the completion of education. In this way, too, a decision is already made as to the general character of the subsequent ten to fifteen years until the children leave school. For the woman of forty to forty-five, external conditions of emancipation come too late.

This is precisely the place in the social connection at which the process of women's emancipation has fundamentally stagnated since the establishment of formal political and juridical equality, and where the subaltern role of half of society is laid down. It can only be overcome if the process of relieving the family of its functions is deliberately carried through to completion, the small family being abandoned as the reproduction unit of the 'human factor'. The millionfold isolated struggle over the division of tasks in the existing form of family can only give women partial victory, even with political union and the support of the Communist League; it can never be completely won. The commune organization of the population at the level of housing, on the other hand, offers three decisive advantages: firstly, the socialization (we should rightly say 'cooperativization', similarly for the second point) of housework and in particular of its planning and managerial function (care for this being temporarily more specialized); secondly, the socialization of child care and education, of the whole portion of primary socialization that is presently the concern of the small family (without the children having thereby to be withdrawn from the particular influence of the natural parents); thirdly, the possibility of a direct and united representation of interests against the patriarchal tradition, which transforms the claim of women for emancipation from a confined ideological rebellion devoid of prospects into a practical economic opportunity.

In the second of the advantages mentioned we have at the same time the most essential precondition for a profound and far-reaching guarantee of the full educability and motivation of children, the psychological problem which I touched on in Chapter 10. The small family has been recognized for fifty years as the 'psychological structure works' of society, the place where the relations of domination are mentally reproduced. By confining the network of personal relations, and with the parents moreover often in overt or latent conflict with one another and communicating this to the children, this produces in addition that primary neurosis that the individual can escape only by accident, and which is responsible for individualization in modern societies leading much more frequently to bizarre characters than to harmonious ones. I do not intend to go into this point in any more detail here, since it seems to me that the pertinent advantages of large families in whatever particular form are sufficiently demonstrated by ethnographic and historical material.

Having developed the background of the commune idea, I must now return once again to stress that this entire structure of association, which achieves its agreement on goals on the basis of all-round and understood solidarity, comes into being in an evolutionary sense not by bypassing the hierarchical organization, but rather by passing through it and coming out the other side. Just as the commune is itself a special kind of superstructure, special alongside the other special functions and representing their synthesizing comprehensive element, so too is society more than just a network of horizontally linked communes. This is already inconceivable purely from the standpoint of information theory; we can imagine the confusion of channels linking each commune with all others, and the constant to and fro flow of information that the diversity of the reproduction process involves. The association necessarily develops an obligatory vertical dimension. The communes of a modern society will certainly never be so 'self-sustaining', as Marx called the pre-colonial Indian village, that even their production of means of subsistence, for example, could be exactly balanced in structure and in time with their own needs. The connection between the communal organs or work organizations in their function as consumers, and the producers, will be regulated in its concrete modalities in the form of a direct contract. But the overall supply must be ensured in advance at the overall social level. This requires, firstly, central material balances which are met by tasks set by the plan for the various communes, according to their average productivity, and secondly, the maintenance of an insurance fund which is only at the economic disposal of the centre. Large-scale investments, furthermore, in so far as they have effects on the goal and conditions of production at a trans-communal scale, are to be disposed of by the society as a whole and allocated to the communes, providing these with all the resources they require. (Society would certainly be able to protect itself against hypothetical blackmail by particular local interests, which might for example try to exploit a production of key items that was allocated to them, as it would be based on the almost universal reciprocal dependence of all its members, always the real economic foundation of solidarity.)

This is simply to indicate the extent to which the association necessarily gives rise to central functions which require for their management that the delegates of the individual communes *have* to rise above their role as representatives of these particular interests. The communal (local) interests can never simply coincide with those of the association as a whole, or else there would no longer be any autonomous subjects affected by the law of uneven development, subjects who to this extent compete also for the quality of their life process and for the material prerequisites of this. The same holds for the basic units of combined labour and for the other interest groups with subordinate functions within the communes, who will naturally compare their conditions both with one another and also with analogous units in other communes. In a certain sense, the interest of any social unit that is not the overall society is more confined vis-à-vis the society as a whole than are the interests of single individuals. This has to do with the organizational structure of any such union, oriented abstractly to certain specific functions and purposes. Only the League of Communists can and must rise above all these particular limitations, and not least above the particularity of time – i.e. above the merely present interests of the association. The League of Communists is precisely the organization that corresponds with the universal tendency of individual interests.

Control over the national assembly, over the council of the general association, will then become a question of the actual general competence of all individuals, finding its medium in a public opinion that is absolutely free and unhindered both with respect to its content and also to the availability of technical means. The mode of election and recall of the delegates will accordingly be a secondary question, however important it is for a transition period that cannot yet be sure of its rules. *Control over the apparatus, over the administration,* will become the common business of the delegates and their generally competent electors, in such a way that even specially competent experts will collaborate in this in their general capacity as social individuals. They can do this all the more in as much as their life process can no longer be one-sidedly determined by the fact that they have charge at a given point in time, among other things, also of administrative functions up to the national and international level.

The most difficult thing remains *control over the local and particular special interests, i.e. over those of the communes and of the unions within the communes, associated for the various subordinate functions* – if this control is to have a social character, and be effective enough not to break down and conjure up the rebirth of repressive state agencies with their whole sorry retinue of bureaucratic planning, accounting and reporting expenditures. The principle of solidarity requires quite decisively that every commune, indeed every organized interest, should demonstrate a normal degree of effort, and this not just in possible critical situations. Otherwise it could not be ruled out that the *road* to communism, in particular, could tend to collapse into a process of cultural decline.

Besides the control of production according to need and quality that proceeds from the overall plan and is then mediated via the communes, there must be an overall socially required system of communication statistics, accessible to everyone, so as to measure the relationship between expenditure and output, and particularly on the basis of labour-time accounting. This system will have two focal points. The first pertains to a group's own performance, i.e. the living labour that is expended. The national economic calculation of productivity that is customary at the present time is well known to double-count all resaleable material and semi-finished goods. In this way, it is even possible to raise the commodity production displayed by one and the same enterprise. Every extension of the division of labour along the chain that leads through to the finished product can appear in the statistics as a rise in productivity. The second point bears on the handling of resources, i.e. the past labour that is expended, in which connection the financial aspect has also to be brought in. These figures cannot and should not bear the character of plan injunctions, but rather that of measuring instruments for each unit's assessments of its own economic activity and for evaluating the overall economic development of society as a whole. The results are not designed only for communal and central statistics, but must be generally published, with a depiction of trends over an appropriate period and a basis of comparison in the shape of best and average values.

A major transgression of certain limits of tolerance – should things come to this – will certainly give occasion for investigation and analysis of the causes, as well as for appropriate aid. But this will remain the exception. Closely defined plan indicators are already predominantly negative in their effect, because they tempt people to manipulate primary data, and frequently even compel them to do so. Together with the present mode of planning right down to the final reserves of capacity, they bear responsibility for the considerable grey zone in factory statistics in the countries of actual socialism. Since factories cannot 'withstand' double-entry bookkeeping, neither in relation to expenditure nor vis-à-vis their superiors, no one really has a clear idea of the factory economy besides those people directly party to the manipulation, and even these few easily lose this perspective. The problem for them is to keep the false figures consistent. This extremely damaging state of affairs can only be brought to an end if the system of planning and management no longer generates the motivation for it. The association has a maximal interest in basing its planning on valid data. The communes and factories need these valid data just as much, so as to be able to operate rationally and compare their performances (a sufficient substitute for much artificial emulation). At the present time any optimal performance is immediately suspect. Was it achieved in specially advantageous conditions, or by using hidden reserves, or 'with the pencil'? This is one of the worst and most costly dysfunctions of bureaucratic control, which must be unconditionally eliminated on the road towards the communist association, also on political-moral grounds, since it plays in all cases a desolidarizing role.

If we sum up these considerations about economic regulation with respect to the industrial enterprise, we can draw the following conclusions. The economic subjects have production tasks set by the association as a whole or by the commune, which indicate the planned expenditure in labour-time for a particular assortment of use-values. They themselves specify this expenditure, in contract with those they supply to. Conversely, the factories in turn receive specified quantities of the labour-power, machines and other inputs needed, also by a contractual agreement. It might be said that this is precisely the present system in the GDR. Up to this point, indeed, it is, apart from the role of the communes, and the basis of planning being labour-time instead of commodity production in marks. It would be an optical illusion to assume that the regulation presently complained of is rooted in *this*, and particularly in the material balancing. In its technical aspect, the system is in no way bad. If the balancing did not continuously lead to rationing, because the party and state apparatus programme the economy in such a way as to transform every increase in productivity into a growth in production, it could even be socially satisfactory, in as much as social satisfaction can be decided in this sphere. It is precisely the central production plan that must cease to disturb the normal reproduction and maintenance of plant, the quality of production and the rhythm of work, the improvement of material and psychological conditions in the workplace, as well as the entire sector of small-scale production and services. If the growth rate was no longer taken as the *planning priority,* and the state abandoned its present comic jealousy of the cooperative and private initiative which seeks to establish itself in the pores of centralized large-scale production – everywhere that there are 'gaps' in the market – then the GDR would have the conditions for harmonious prosperity as far as the aspect of economic regulation was concerned. (The provocative 'excess profits' of petty traders, etc. will disappear of themselves when the demand for their services is met.)

The greater part of regulative controls against the factories (their managements) can be done away with once resources are sufficiently ensured that it is possible to begin to use them in a rational way. The particular criterion that then governs the unavoidable remainder of controls is in no way decisive for economic impetus; the main emphasis may be put on economizing as easily as on profit, as long as there is a real room to manoeuvre, to shape the factory, to make improvements, to better conditions, and to claim aid from social reserves in case unfavourable conditions develop. Then a collective really can be welded together – as long as the basic unit is not so great, and scattered over such an area, that people no longer know one another personally. In no case may controls 'run ahead', and in this way make it unknowable whom the factory functionaries are really supposed to serve, the factory collective or the various anonymous higher agencies and legal restrictions that can curtail all genuine freedom of action. The economic system *must* be given a shape in which the obtaining of information for control purposes remains confined to the inputs and outputs of the factory system. Otherwise functional autonomy is lost, and with it collective and individual interest. Large factories should be split up into partly autonomous collective subjects, which can relate to one another in association rather than subordination.

The economic and social quality of functioning *within the factory* must be ensured by society not through any kind of external agency, but rather by the associated individuals there themselves. Besides the cells of the Communist League, the trade union, as organ of the staff as a whole vis-à-vis the system of management, will have a far more autonomous role to play than previously. Womens', youth and veteran workers' committees can also be active in this context. The right to strike, although re-established in the transition period, will necessarily lose significance in the course of the cultural revolution. It presupposes in fact that management organs *can* set themselves up autonomously against the collective that commissions them and has deliberately delegated individual functionaries by election. The power of organized public opinion, which in case of need can be reinforced by secret ballot, will then be enough to bring conflicts to a satisfactory conclusion.

It is basically unnecessary to go into too many details about individual aspects of the communist economy, even though I think this is not simply building castles in the air. For once its *principles* prevail, a brief period of practice will bring more wisdom than the most extensive speculation. Perhaps I have already gone too far, even if in the conviction that communist propaganda today must demonstrate more than ever with *concrete possibilities*. The principal thing has been to give a sketch of the systematic economic connection which the cultural revolution has to set up, and moreover on the assumption that the conditions for this are already maturing.

It is in this sense that I investigated the goal of communist production, which since Marx has uncontestably been that of rich individuality, in its consequences for the structure of material needs, i.e. for the planned needs of society, as well as for the type of proportionality that the plan must give to the overall reproduction process. As the common denominator that embraces the basic economic law of the communist formation and its law of proportionality, we have a new economy of time, which has its standard in the development requirements for particular individuals to acquire social universality, in their 'time schedules' for the all-round appropriation of culture, and its instrument in an economic accounting based on units of time. Finally, I have investigated how the communist individuals can rationally regulate their overall social process so as to both raise themselves above the realm of necessity and find in their community their freedom, an unrestricted field for self-realization in action, in thought, and in enjoyment of their personal relations.

The answer lies in the discovery of the *federative* principle which is inscribed in the idea of free association: subordination of the hierarchically ordered informational connection; association instead of subordination of individuals to their various subjective and objective purposes; association of their unions (not least of course of the basic units of the labour process) essentially into territorially grouped communes, as the decisive mediating links of the totality; association of communes into a national society; association of nations in a contentedly cooperating world; mediation to each higher unity by delegates elected from the base.

This is how we can conceive the order in which the conditions of genuine freedom coincide with those of genuine equality and fraternity. Communism is not only necessary, it is also possible. Whether it becomes a reality or not must be decided in the struggle for its conditions of existence.

1973-1976

Index